Thomas Kuhn

Thomas Kuhn (1922–1996), the author of *The Structure of Scientific Revolutions*, is the best-known and most influential historian and philosopher of science of the past 50 years and has become something of a cultural icon. His concepts of paradigm, paradigm change, and incommensurability have changed the way we think about science. This volume offers an introduction to Kuhn's life and work and then considers the implications of Kuhn's work for philosophy, cognitive psychology, social studies of science, and feminism. The volume is more than a retrospective on Kuhn, exploring future developments of cognitive and information sciences along Kuhnian lines.

Outside of philosophy, the volume will be of particular interest to professionals and students in cognitive science, history of science, science studies, and cultural studies.

Thomas Nickles is Foundation Professor of Philosophy and Chair at the University of Nevada, Reno.

Contemporary Philosophy in Focus

Contemporary Philosophy in Focus will offer a series of introductory volumes to many of the dominant philosophical thinkers of the current age. Each volume will consist of newly commissioned essays that cover major contributions of a preeminent philosopher in a systematic and accessible manner. Comparable in scope and rationale to the highly successful series **Cambridge Companions to Philosophy,** the volumes will not presuppose that readers are already intimately familiar with the details of each philosopher's work. They will thus combine exposition and critical analysis in a manner that will appeal both to students of philosophy as well as to professionals and students across the humanities and social sciences.

PUBLISHED VOLUMES:

Robert Nozick edited by David Schmidtz
Daniel Dennett edited by Andrew Brook and Don Ross

FORTHCOMING VOLUMES:

Stanley Cavell edited by Richard Eldridge
Paul Churchland edited by Brian Keeley
Donald Davidson edited by Kirk Ludwig
Ronald Dworkin edited by Arthur Ripstein
Jerry Fodor edited by Tim Crane
David Lewis edited by Theodore Sider and Dean Zimmermann
Alasdair MacIntyre edited by Mark C. Murphy
Hilary Putnam edited by Yemima Ben-Menahem
Richard Rorty edited by Charles Guignon and David Hiley
John Searle edited by Barry Smith
Charles Taylor edited by Ruth Abbey
Bernard Williams edited by Alan Thomas

Thomas Kuhn

Edited by

THOMAS NICKLES
University of Nevada, Reno

PUBLISHED BY THE PRESS SYNDICATE OF THE UNIVERSITY OF CAMBRIDGE
The Pitt Building, Trumpington Street, Cambridge, United Kingdom

CAMBRIDGE UNIVERSITY PRESS
The Edinburgh Building, Cambridge CB2 2RU, UK
40 West 20th Street, New York, NY 10011-4211, USA
477 Williamstown Road, Port Melbourne, VIC 3207, Australia
Ruiz de Alarcón 13, 28014 Madrid, Spain
Dock House, The Waterfront, Cape Town 8001, South Africa

http://www.cambridge.org

© Cambridge University Press 2003

First published 2003

Printed in the United States of America

Typefaces Janson Text Roman 10/13 pt. and ITC Officina Sans   *System* LATEX 2$_\varepsilon$ [TB]

A catalog record for this book is available from the British Library.

Library of Congress Cataloging in Publication Data

Thomas Kuhn / edited by Thomas Nickles.
p.   cm. – (Contemporary philosophy in focus)
Includes bibliographical references and index.
ISBN 0-521-79206-1 (hb.) – ISBN 0-521-79648-2 (pbk.)
1. Science – Philosophy.   2. Kuhn, Thomas S.   I. Nickles, Thomas, 1943–   II. Series.
Q175 .T4965   2002
501–dc21   2002022278

ISBN 0 521 79206 1 hardback
ISBN 0 521 79648 2 paperback

Contents

Contributors

HANNE ANDERSEN is assistant professor in the Department of Medical Philosophy and Clinical Theory, University of Copenhagen. She previously worked as curator at the Danish National Museum for the History of Science and Medicine. Among her recent publications are several articles on Kuhn and categorization and her book *On Kuhn* (Wadsworth, 2001). Shortly before his death, she extensively interviewed Thomas Kuhn about his work, early and late.

PETER BARKER is professor of history of science at the University of Oklahoma. His wide interests range from the history and historiography of the Scientific Revolution through nineteenth- and twentieth-century physics, psychology, and philosophy of science. He is the editor-translator (with Roger Ariew) of *Pierre Duhem: Essays in the History and Philosophy of Science* (Hackett, 1995) and author of numerous articles in the areas noted.

BARRY BARNES was a member of the Edinburgh group of sociologists who developed the Strong Programme in Sociology of Science in the 1970s and has continued to be one of the leading shapers of science studies. He is now professor of sociology at the University of Exeter. His many authored and edited books include *T. S. Kuhn and Social Science* (Columbia University Press, 1982), *About Science* (Blackwell, 1985), *The Nature of Power* (University of Illinois Press, 1988), *Scientific Knowledge: A Sociological Analysis* (University of Chicago Press, 1996), and *Understanding Agency: Social Theory and Responsible Action* (Sage, 2000).

XIANG CHEN is an associate professor at California Lutheran University. He is the author of *Instrumental Traditions and Theories of Light: The Uses of Instruments in the Optical Revolution* (Kluwer, 2000) and a series of articles on Kuhn, including "Thomas Kuhn's Latest Notion of Incommensurability" (*Journal for General Philosophy of Science*, 1997).

MICHAEL FRIEDMAN is Ruth N. Halls Professor of Arts and Humanities at Indiana University and Frederick P. Rehmus Family Professor of

Humanities at Stanford University. His publications include *Foundations of Space-Time Theories* (Princeton University Press, 1983), which won both the Matchette Prize and the Lakatos Award in Philosophy of Science, *Kant and the Exact Sciences* (Harvard University Press, 1992), *Reconsidering Logical Positivism* (Cambridge University Press, 1999), *A Parting of the Ways* (Open Court, 2000), and *Dynamics of Reason* (Stanford University, CSLI, 2001). He has served as president of the Philosophy of Science Association and as Central Division president of the American Philosophical Association. He is a member of the American Academy of Arts and Sciences.

RICHARD E. GRANDY is Carolyn and Fred McManis Professor of Philosophy and Cognitive Science at Rice University. He is the author of *Advanced Logic for Applications* (Reidel, 1977) and editor or coeditor of *Theories and Observation in Science* (Prentice-Hall, 1973), *Readings in the Philosophy of Science* (Prentice-Hall, 1989), and *Philosophical Grounds of Rationality: Intentions, Categories, Ends* (Oxford University Press, 1986). Grandy is the author of numerous articles in philosophy of science, philosophy of language, logic, metaphysics, and cognitive science. He is currently working on a book tentatively titled *Information, Semantics, and Ontology: Some Philosophical Implications of the Cognitive Sciences.*

GARY GUTTING is professor of philosophy at the University of Notre Dame. His books include *Religious Belief and Religious Skepticism* (University of Notre Dame Press, 1982), *Foucault's Archaeology of Scientific Knowledge* (Cambridge University Press, 1989), *Pragmatic Liberalism and the Critique of Modernity* (Cambridge University Press, 1999), and *French Philosophy in the Twentieth Century* (Cambridge University Press, 2001). He has edited *Paradigms and Revolutions: Applications and Appraisals of Thomas Kuhn's Philosophy of Science* (University of Notre Dame Press, 1980) and *The Cambridge Companion to Foucault* (Cambridge University Press, 1994). Gutting is a former editor of the *American Philosophical Quarterly.*

HELEN E. LONGINO is Professor of Philosophy and Women's Studies at the University of Minnesota. She is author of *Science as Social Knowledge* (Princeton University Press, 1990) and of many articles in philosophy of science and feminist philosophy. She is a coeditor of *Feminism and Science* (Oxford University Press, 1996), *Gender and Scientific Authority* (University of Chicago Press, 1996), and *Osiris 12: Women, Gender, and Science* (History of Science Society) and is a member of numerous editorial boards, including those of *Philosophy of Science* and *Perspectives on Science*. Her most recent book is *The Fate of Knowledge* (Princeton University Press, 2002).

NANCY J. NERSESSIAN is Professor of Cognitive Science and Coordinator of the Cognitive Science Program at Georgia Institute of Technology. Her research focuses on the nature and processes of conceptual innovation and change in science, specifically, the role of model-based reasoning in conceptual change. She is author of numerous publications in philosophy and history of science, including *Faraday to Einstein: Constructing Meaning in Scientific Theories* (Nijhoff, 1984). Nersessian is editor of *The Process of Science* (Nijhoff, 1987) and coeditor of *Model-Based Reasoning in Scientific Discovery* (Kluwer, 1999). She is also the editor of Kluwer's "Science and Philosophy" series. She is currently finishing a book tentatively titled *Creating Science: A Cognitive-Historical Approach to Conceptual Change*.

THOMAS NICKLES is Foundation Professor and chair of philosophy at the University of Nevada, Reno. He is editor of *Scientific Discovery, Logic, and Rationality* and *Scientific Discovery: Case Studies* (both Reidel, 1980) and coeditor of *PSA 1982*. He has authored numerous articles on scientific explanation, theory and problem reduction, problem solving, and the relations of philosophy of science to history of science. He is currently working on problem solving by evolutionary computation and on the history and philosophy of the idea of scientific method.

JOSEPH ROUSE is professor of philosophy and chair of the Science in Society Program at Wesleyan University. In addition to his numerous articles, he is the author of *Engaging Science: How to Understand Its Practices Philosophically* (Cornell University Press, 1996) and *Knowledge and Power: Toward a Political Philosophy of Science* (Cornell University Press, 1987). His most recent book is *How Scientific Practices Matter: Reclaiming Philosophical Naturalism* (University of Chicago Press, 2002).

JOHN WORRALL is professor of philosophy of science at the London School of Economics and codirector of the Centre for Philosophy of Natural and Social Science there. He was the editor of the *British Journal for the Philosophy of Science* from 1974 to 1983 and the managing editor of Imre Lakatos's posthumous works. He is the author of numerous papers on general philosophy of science and the history and philosophy of nineteenth-century physics. Worrall is completing a book titled *Reason in Revolution: A Study of Theory-Change in Science* and is working on topics in the methodology of medicine.

Preface

Every essay in this book has been written especially for this volume. While the book is aimed at a general educated audience, each author aspires to say something sufficiently substantial about one or more dimensions of Kuhn's work to interest experts. Moreover, this is more than a retrospective on Kuhn's work. It is forward-looking as well, with an eye on ongoing developments in philosophy of science, epistemology, social studies of science, and especially the cognitive sciences. Given our space limitations, we focus on Kuhn the philosopher of science rather than Kuhn the historian, and we devote more attention to Kuhn's relation to cognitive science than to social studies of science.

I owe the idea for the project to Terry Moore, Publishing Director for Humanities at Cambridge University Press, New York. Terry conceived the timely new series Contemporary Philosophy in Focus, with this book being one of the first offerings. I appreciate his guidance as to what sort of book it should be. Thanks to production editor Louise Calabro and to copyeditor Helen Greenberg, who gave the volume its final form. Thanks also to my wife, Dr. Gaye McCollum-Nickles, for helpful comments on my own contributions to the volume.

The decision of which authors to include in such a volume is always difficult and somewhat arbitrary. Several outstanding expositors and/or critics of Kuhn had to be passed over in order to keep the volume to a manageable size and to achieve a wider diversity of perspectives on Kuhn's work. Nonetheless, I am delighted that the particular authors represented here have joined me in the project, and I hope that you, the reader, find their work as stimulating as I have.

Thomas Nickles
Philosophy Department
University of Nevada, Reno

Introduction

THOMAS NICKLES

Whether one is pro-Kuhn, anti-Kuhn, or neutral, no one can deny that the work of Thomas Kuhn has been a lightning rod for debates about science, culture, and policy across many academic fields – and even in the political arena and the business world. This is especially true of Kuhn's best-known work, *The Structure of Scientific Revolutions*, originally published in 1962 and expanded in 1970. By now the book has sold over a million copies in two dozen languages – numbers almost unheard of for an academic book about abstract philosophical topics. The wide reception of his work, which greatly surprised Kuhn himself, has elevated the terms "paradigm," "paradigm change," and "paradigm shift" to household phrases and the stuff of advertising slogans, corporate boardrooms, and Washington bureaucratese. Although diverse individuals and groups have read and used (or misused!) it very differently, each according to their own abilities and needs, Kuhn's work has the merit, in these fragmented times, of serving as a common reference point and of generating cross-disciplinary discussion.

When Kuhn began writing, philosophy of science, especially in England and the United States, was dominated by the logical positivists (Rudolf Carnap, Hans Reichenbach, Carl Hempel, and others) and by Karl Popper and his followers. In *The Structure of Scientific Revolutions* (*Structure* hereafter), Kuhn gave us a very different picture of science.[1] Kuhn contended that there are two types of mature physical science, "normal science" and "extraordinary" or "revolutionary science." In a given scientific field, long periods of conservative, tradition-bound normal science are punctuated by an occasional crisis and, still less frequently, by a revolution. Normal science is highly regimented work under a paradigm. It aims to extend and articulate the paradigm, not to test it, for the paradigm *defines* the research tradition, the scientific life, of a particular discipline and its practitioners. Normal research consists in attempting to solve research puzzles by modeling them and their solutions on exemplary problem solutions previously achieved. Good science is delimited not by rules such as Popper's criterion of falsifiability, or positivist meaning postulates, or even by more content-laden rules specific to the discipline, but by how practitioners perceive and apply these "exemplars" (as Kuhn termed them). In fact, there is no scientific method in the sense of a set of rules that guide inquiry. Surprisingly, Kuhnian normal science does not aim at essential novelty and, in that respect, is convergent rather than divergent. Yet its very focus on esoteric detail makes it almost inevitable that normal research will eventually disclose difficulties for the reigning paradigm. If these difficulties persist and turn critical, a crisis results.

During a crisis period the usual conservative strictures relax somewhat, and truly innovative ideas and practices may emerge as serious alternatives. The repeated failure of established normal scientists to handle the crisis situation, together with the emergence of a promising new approach, may trigger a revolution. What typically happens during the final phase of a scientific revolution is that a group of mostly younger practitioners advocating a new paradigm succeeds in shoving aside the old paradigm and its supporters and subsequently rewriting the history of the field to make their new paradigm appear to be the final stage in the progressive development of the field.

Clearly, paradigm change is not a rational process as understood by the traditional canons of rationality. For in revolutionary science, normal modes of decision making are no longer available. There is no longer universal agreement about a common archive of exemplars and their significance. Moreover, logic and empirical data alone are never sufficient to resolve paradigm debates, said Kuhn. Indeed, there is often disagreement about the problems, standards, and goals of research and a failure of the vocabularies of the two paradigms to match. Therefore two competing paradigms are "incommensurable," meaning, roughly, that they cannot be measured against the same standard. Yet in Kuhn's own view, paradigm decisions need not be irrational. However, in the more radical passages of *Structure*, he spoke of paradigm changes as akin to perceptual Gestalt switches, religious conversions, and political revolutions, comparisons that he later dropped. In *Structure* (and to the end of his life), he struggled to make sense of the claim that scientists working under competing paradigms "live in different worlds." Hence his conclusion that there is no point in saying that a paradigm change takes that scientific field closer to the truth about a fully determinate real world, waiting out there to be discovered.

While normal scientific results are largely cumulative, on Kuhn's account, science, overall, does not accumulate either empirical facts or theories in a long, progressive ascent toward truth; for revolutions can undermine bodies of fact and their observational vocabularies as well as entrenched theories and research practices. A revolution carries a science off in a different direction. Near the end of *Structure*, Kuhn likened this process to biological speciation. In science no more than in biological evolution does it make sense to speak of overall progress toward a preordained goal, although we can still trace historical lineages and note significant historical differences such as the increasing specialization and accuracy of latter-day science relative to its past. Thus Kuhn attempted to mesh the two great metaphors: science is evolutionary as well as revolutionary.

All the key terms in this précis of *Structure* are problematic, and all are discussed in the following essays, some in great detail. Kuhn himself added a "Postscript" to the 1970 edition of *Structure* in which he provided some clarification of the highly ambiguous notion of paradigm, explained his "different worlds" position more fully, and defended himself against some prominent criticisms. A paradigm in the primary sense, Kuhn told us, is an "exemplar," that is, an exemplary historical problem solution, an achievement that serves as a model for further work. But he admitted to using "paradigm" in a larger, more global, and more social sense that he now labeled "disciplinary matrix" (a term that he employed rarely thereafter). A disciplinary matrix consists of four kinds of shared commitments that together implicitly characterize a particular research discipline and community: (1) symbolic generalizations such as Newton's laws, (2) metaphysical models of what the world is supposedly really like (e.g., gases as consisting of zillions of billiard-ball-like elastic molecules in random motion), (3) values and standards, and (4) exemplars.

Early critics such as Israel Scheffler (1967) dubbed Kuhn a radical irrationalist, subjectivist, relativist, and irrealist for denying that science gives us the objective truth about reality, even at the perceptual-phenomenal level. More recent critics, such as Alan Sokal and Jean Bricmont (1998, chap. 4), view Kuhn as a principal source of postmodern relativism and of culture-theoretical treatments of science generally – and hence as an instigator of the so-called Science Wars.[2] Other critics view Kuhn as intellectually conservative in important ways. On their account, Kuhn (for good or ill) differed rather little from the logical positivists on crucial issues, especially assumptions about language and meaning. Dudley Shapere's reviews of *Structure* are an early case in point.[3] For Steve Fuller (2000), Kuhn's work is also *politically* conservative and elitist, so much so that, owing to its great influence, it has destroyed any attempt to develop a more democratic science policy for the foreseeable future.

WAS KUHN POSTMODERN?

Since the relevance of Kuhn to postmodern culture studies is a topic that interests many readers, I offer a few suggestive remarks in that connection.[4] One ironic answer to the question "Why consider Kuhn postmodern?" is that he is so difficult to categorize. You simply cannot pin down Kuhn in your butterfly collection of intellectual positions. More seriously, postmodern is post *what*, exactly? What is commonly meant by the "modern era"? A simple answer is that there are at least two quite different referents.

The modern period in philosophy runs, very roughly, from 1600 to 1800, from Bacon and Descartes at one end to Kant at the other. It includes the Enlightenment as well as post-Kantian thinkers such as John Stuart Mill. The twentieth-century logical positivists and Karl Popper and their followers have continued to embrace Enlightenment conceptions and ideals. It was during the seventeenth and eighteenth centuries that epistemology or theory of knowledge replaced metaphysics as "first philosophy" on the ground that, before we can say what the world is really like, we must critically examine the nature and limits of knowledge itself. According to the modern philosophers and many of their successors, knowledge consists in individuals having correct mental representations (e.g., ideas, conceptions, theories) of the world, representations subject to rules or laws such as the association of ideas. Many moderns believed that there is a scientific method the discovery of which explains the seventeenth-century Scientific Revolution and subsequent progress as well as practically guaranteeing future scientific progress – and hence the social progress attendant upon the scientific banishment of ignorance and superstitious folk traditions.

A quite distinct development was modernism in literature, music, painting, and architecture, a multifaceted international avant-garde movement that occurred a century after the Kantian era, roughly from the time of Nietzsche to World War II. Modernism in this sense is also too rich to be described briefly, but it is characterized by free experimentation with alternative (nontraditional) forms – indeed, deliberate breaks with tradition and the discipline it imposes – yet also by the sometimes shameless and heterodox appropriation of traditional materials in ways that transgress artistic, gender, and cultural boundaries and by the desire to construct a future not dictated by the past. Some prominent examples of modernism are stream-of-conscious novels, Bauhaus architecture, atonal music, and cubist painting. Since by their very nature modernism and postmodernism (in this second sense) do not admit of precise definition, and since they vary from one artistic community to another, one is on safer (but never safe) ground in considering modernism one genre at a time, an endeavor obviously inappropriate here.

Some tendencies in Kuhn's work are postmodern in both senses of "postmodern," others in neither sense. Since Kuhn is far more concerned with the philosophical tradition than with the arts, I shall confine myself to that dimension of the postmodernist debate.

Jean-François Lyotard (1984, p. xxiv) defines postmodern as "incredulity toward metanarratives." Kuhn is best known for challenging the master narrative of modern science, a narrative that became a fixture of the Enlightenment.[5] This is the grand story of human progress toward the ultimate truth about the world and the resulting emancipation from ignorance and from the social problems that it engenders. This progress is to be achieved by the hard labor of our brightest citizens studying the natural world intensely. In some respects it is complementary to, or a secular parallel to, the grand Judeo-Christian religious narrative of the fall and redemption.

Kuhn famously (or notoriously) denied that the history of science tells one linear, continuous, cumulative, unified story. Rather, like other cultural institutions, science (or, rather, the historical succession of sciences) is (are) beset by discontinuities, incommensurabilities, and disunities; and its products are as much constructed or invented as discovered. In this respect, Kuhn decentered the Enlightenment account. The history of science provides no master text of reality, nor is there any reason to think that there is one privileged language of nature. In some passages, Kuhn suggested that science is not so much a self-legitimating project as a diverse but overlapping cluster of alternative forms of life. In deconstructing deep modernist myths about the nature of science, he unintentionally opened the door to attacks upon science itself.

Kuhn's work challenges traditional epistemology in several ways. Clearly, his "historical Kantian" relativism and his rejection of strong realism and traditional conceptions of truth, rationality, objectivity, and justification in science are relevant here. Kuhn dismissed all attempts to put knowledge on permanent foundations. He rejected both traditional rationalism and traditional empiricism, including the latter's sharp distinction between a neutral observational language and a theoretical language. There is no "given" in either experience or thought. Every feature of scientific experience and thought is acquired and, in principle, contestable (albeit not within normal science). He denied that explicit rules and representations exhaust what scientists know and that they even constitute the most fundamental dimensions of that knowledge. On the contrary, the most important knowledge is embodied in expert experimental and theoretical practice and in the learned but tacit cognitive similarity metrics upon which skilled practices depend. Kuhn denied that there is any such thing as the "scientific method" or even methods (plural) construed as sets of timeless rules of inquiry. Kuhn posited communities of specialists rather than solitary individuals as the bearers of knowledge and insisted that there is no higher form of justification than the assent of the relevant community of experts. Moreover, he noted that scientists, unlike most philosophers, are forward-looking problem solvers rather than backward-looking justifiers of claims about the world: justification of present commitments can be more a matter of future promise than of past success.

Kuhn can therefore be read as reversing some main tendencies of Enlightenment thought. There is no universal reason or intelligence distinct from the content of the specific disciplines. Here Kuhn was indebted to Quine's challenge to the analytic–synthetic distinction and to Quine's naturalism, fallibilism, and holism. However, Kuhn went on to reject Quine's view (which Quine held in common with many positivists) that symbolic logic provides a canonical language for understanding scientific work. There is no privileged language or logic that provides a royal road to clarity or truth, that adequately captures the real world or even our experience of it. In the old debate between logic and rhetoric, Kuhn came down on the side of rhetoric in the sense that, for him, human cognition is governed at bottom by rhetorical relations of similarity, analogy, metaphor, and modeling rather than by logical relations and rules. Scientific thinking does not consist in applying purely logical rules so much as matching present perceptions and problems to domain-specific exemplars; and a great deal of scientific work consists in the construction and use of models. The early Kuhn stressed both direct modeling and the importance of historical patterns of development over static logical patterns, while the later Kuhn expanded his cognitive themes at the expense of the historical ones. In any case, the history of science discloses not steady progress toward a universal, canonical language of science but rather a collection of diverse local discourse communities, all of which eventually find their linguistic and conceptual resources contested as anomalies begin to accumulate. In crisis and revolutionary periods, these irruptions produce the various linguistic and practical failures, failures of translation and of mutual intelligibility, that Kuhn labels incommensurability. These failures of what, previously, to its practitioners, seemed to be the language of nature can serve to open up new possibilities for description and action, new forms of intelligibility.

While the Enlightenment thinkers championed the science of their day for its cosmopolitan character, Kuhn stressed the local aspects of scientific communities. Kuhn was not an expressive Romantic in the sense of the Romantic poets and artists in their reaction to the Enlightenment; but, like the Romantics, he prized the wisdom and intelligence (and intelligibility) of local, discipline-specific, historical traditions over the claims for pure reason. Contrary to the Cartesian tradition, pure reason does not issue in self-intelligible, clear, and distinct ideas with their allegedly self-evident applications in context. Rather, traditions (in a broad enough sense to include established community practices) are what constitute the basis for intelligibility. Furthermore, Kuhn portrayed scientific specialist communities as surprisingly like medieval guilds, with their masters and apprentices learning by example. In this sense he was postmodern because premodern. And despite being an internalist intellectual historian and philosopher in his own work, Kuhn's religious and political metaphors in *Structure* challenged the traditionally sharp distinctions between fact and value, and between internal and external factors in science.

While some of these tendencies were radical, especially for their day, Kuhn's conception of science was also conservative in other ways. Unlike many contributors to present-day cultural studies, Kuhn was not at all antiscience. On the contrary, he considered modern science a good thing, something of great intellectual and social value; and he resisted any efforts to change it even with the intention of improving it. (This is one reason why Fuller charges Kuhn with cultural and political conservatism.) As for the new science studies that his work encouraged, Kuhn famously rejected the Strong Programme in Sociology of Knowledge as "deconstruction gone mad" (Kuhn 2000, p. 110). As indicated earlier, many critics have noted how close some of Kuhn's views about language and meaning were to those of positivists such as Carnap, an observation that is sometimes reversed to demonstrate that the positivists themselves were not the "conservative heavies" that they are often portrayed to be.

I have already mentioned the quasi-medieval, convergent, tradition-bound, authoritarian nature of normal science. Many prominent critics have rejected Kuhn's conception of paradigms themselves as dogmatic, to-talizing centers of scientific thought and practice. In addition, Kuhn's own perspective in *Structure* is not that of a committed normal scientist more or less imprisoned within his local Kantian world of experience. Rather, Kuhn pretends to stand outside the history of science as a godlike but skeptical observer and to declare that mature natural sciences must fit one simple, repeating pattern: normal science → revolution → new normal science, a pattern that must employ arbitrary assumptions in every cycle and hence can never hope to find the warranted truth about the world (Nickles 1998). So, in these particular respects, even Kuhn offers us a totalizing narrative.

However, Kuhn's narrative is nuanced. For Kuhnian paradigms are not dogmatic creeds so much as forms of practical life. Paradigms are not rigid, deductive, logical structures that all practitioners must believe in, articulate, and justify in the same way. Each subspecialty develops its own local paradigm as well as its own practical understanding of the global paradigm that characterizes the scientific field as a whole.

KUHN'S LIFE AND CAREER

Thomas Samuel Kuhn was born in 1922 in Cincinnati, Ohio, the first child of a father who was a hydraulic engineer turned investment consultant and an educator mother who did professional editing.[6] The family soon moved to New York City and later to a country town an hour away up the Hudson River. Young Tom Kuhn attended various politically progressive private schools in the eastern United States. In 1940 he was proud to be admitted to Harvard, his father's college, as an undergraduate. Much later in life he was surprised and amused to learn that, in those days, nearly all qualified applicants were admitted to Harvard.

Kuhn's forte as a schoolboy had been mathematics and physical science, so he became a physics major. He also enjoyed literature and philosophy while having limited time to pursue them. He found Kant's philosophy a "revelation," a discovery that foreshadowed Kuhn's later intellectual development. It was surely his editorials in the *Harvard Crimson* that brought him to the attention of James B. Conant, the chemist president of Harvard and a national leader in science policy circles and in academe's response to the outbreak of World War II. Kuhn compressed his undergraduate work into three years in order to graduate and join the war effort. He worked in radar for the U.S. government in Boston and then in England, with bits on the Continent, work that he found increasingly tedious – certainly relative to the events unfolding around him. In 1945, with the war ending and having witnessed the liberation of Paris, he returned to enter Harvard Graduate School in physics.

Kuhn's academic career has been described in terms of "cumulative advantage" (Merton 1977, p. 89) and as "being there" (Fuller 2000), but it also had its rough side. Although Kuhn was a physics graduate student, he suspected that his heart was in philosophy; so he received permission to spend part of his first year taking philosophy courses. However, finding his background in philosophy too thin to consider switching fields at that point, he decided to finish his degree in physics, writing a dissertation in solid state physics under James Van Vleck, later a Nobel laureate. But by this time Kuhn's more important mentor had become Conant himself, who recruited Kuhn to teach his newly conceived undergraduate history of science course. This was the famous Harvard "case studies" course. Conant's purpose in organizing it, apparently, was not only to increase scientific literacy among nonscientists but also to lure talented undergraduates into the fields of science and technology, especially as policy makers (Fuller 2000).

During the dissertation stage of his graduate training, Kuhn finally decided to switch fields. He boldly persuaded Conant to support his appointment as a Junior Fellow of Harvard's Society of Fellows in order to transform himself into a historian of science as a route to the philosophical issues he really wished to investigate. Kuhn, who had not liked the history course he took as an undergraduate and who would never relish careful archival research, thus became, in his own words, "a physicist turned historian for philosophical purposes" (Kuhn 2000, p. 320). A high-strung, rather nervous and impatient person, Kuhn was never completely comfortable in any professional field any more than he had felt fully at home in any discipline as a student. Indeed, Kuhn was always something of an amateur, largely self-taught in philosophy and even in history of science. The latter is not surprising, however, since in those days history of science was only beginning to emerge as a professional discipline.

After three years as a Fellow, Kuhn became an instructor and then an assistant professor at Harvard. But it was still not smooth sailing, for it eventually became clear that he would not be awarded tenure at Harvard. So Kuhn accepted an assistant professorship post on the opposite coast, at the University of California, Berkeley. The position was initially offered by the Philosophy Department but was then turned into a joint appointment with History. Kuhn's job was to teach history of science and intellectual history from a scientific point of view. Not long after heading west, he spent a year at the Institute for Advanced Study in the Behavioral Sciences in Palo Alto working on the material that would eventually become *Structure*. Then, some years later, it happened again. When he came up for promotion to full professor, having published *The Copernican Revolution* and *Structure* as well as numerous historical essays, the Philosophy Department supported his promotion only in History, not in Philosophy. This was a severe blow to a man who considered himself a philosopher first and whose abiding interest was the philosophical consequences of the history of science.

While spending a year in Copenhagen working on an archive for the history of quantum mechanics,[7] Kuhn received an offer from Princeton to join the new Program in History and Philosophy of Science, a position that seemed ideally suited to his aspirations. He moved to Princeton in 1964 and remained there until 1979, when he returned to Cambridge – but now to MIT rather than Harvard, as the Laurence S. Rockefeller Professor of Philosophy. He retired from MIT in 1991.

Thomas Kuhn died of cancer in 1996 at the age of seventy-three.

While at Berkeley, Kuhn had published two books, *The Copernican Revolution* (1957) and *The Structure of Scientific Revolutions* (1962). The former emerged from Kuhn's lectures and already challenged orthodox understandings of science in various ways. Among other things, this book was the first major expression of Kuhn's abiding interest in revolutionary cognitive shifts arising out of his own earlier epiphany in making sense of Aristotle[8] and his still earlier encounter with Kant. Indeed, all of Kuhn's work was deeply personal.

Structure was solicited by none other than Rudolf Carnap, the leading positivist philosopher and logician, for the *Encyclopedia of Unified Science*, the large encyclopedia project of the logical positivists, originally conceived by Otto Neurath and published by The University of Chicago Press. The Press agreed to publish *Structure* also as a separate volume.

A crucial event in Kuhn's gaining a major reputation was the International Colloquium in the Philosophy of Science, held at Bedford College, London, in July 1965. Kuhn was invited as a rising young historian of science whose ideas had philosophical implications. He left as a major player among the competing "big systems" in methodology of science. Among the other players were Karl Popper, Imre Lakatos, Paul Feyerabend, Stephen Toulmin, and, of course, the positivists collectively, including Kuhn's new colleague, Carl Hempel. The proceedings of this conference, with many of the contributions appearing in revised form in order to respond to Kuhn's challenge, appeared in 1970 as *Criticism and the Growth of Knowledge*, edited by Lakatos and Alan Musgrave.

The Essential Tension, a collection of Kuhn's more influential historical and methodological essays, appeared in 1977, followed a year later by *Black-Body Theory and the Quantum Discontinuity: 1894–1912*, an unorthodox history of the emergence of the early quantum theory. Kuhn's central thesis in that book was that, contrary to the received view, Max Planck was not the founder of quantum theory in 1900, for he was then still working in a well-established classical tradition. Rather, it was Einstein's and Ehrenfest's misreading of Planck's work as an attempt to solve *their* problems that initiated the early quantum theory. Although Kuhn makes a plausible case for his contentions, and although more confirming evidence has since come to light, physicists have strongly resisted his revisionist history, and historians of science have largely ignored it (Brush 2000).

By 1978 Kuhn's style of doing history was already professionally passé. For Kuhn was an intellectual historian, an "internalist" historian of ideas with idealist tendencies, whose goal was to "get inside the heads" of the major figures he studied. Yet, as Joseph Rouse brings out in his essay in this volume and in previous publications, Kuhn also attended to the practical skills of scientists. In studying major figures such as Aristotle, Copernicus, Carnot, Planck, and Bohr, Kuhn always devoted a great deal of attention to their problem situations, as they supposedly understood them, and to the tools and skills available to them from the research traditions and communities within which they worked.[9]

Surprised by the huge sales of *Structure*, but also perplexed and even stung by the philosophical critiques of it, Kuhn always intended to write a sequel containing the definitive statement of his position, a statement less inviting of critical misunderstanding.[10] Unfortunately, he did not finish this project during his lifetime, and his conception of it gradually changed over the years, as will become apparent in some of the essays in this volume. Before his death, Kuhn arranged for John Haugeland and James Conant (philosopher grandson of James B. Conant) to prepare the unfinished manuscript for publication, with the tentative title *Plurality of Worlds: An Evolutionary Theory of Scientific Discovery*. Meanwhile, in 2000, The University of Chicago Press issued a second collection of Kuhn's essays (also edited by Conant and Haugeland) entitled *The Road Since Structure: Philosophical Essays 1970–1993, with an Autobiographical Interview*. The interview is by three Greek philosophers, Aristides Baltas, Kostas Gavroglu, and Vassiliki Kindi. In this book the reader may also find a complete list of Kuhn's publications.

In his obituary notice for Kuhn, former student and collaborator John Heilbron (1998, p. 515) aptly characterized Kuhn the philosopher-historian as follows:

[H]e drew the portrait of science in the manner of the Impressionists. At a distance, where most viewers stand, the portrait appears illuminating, persuasive, and inspiring; close in, where historians and philosophers stare, it looks sketchy, puzzling, and richly challenging.

It is ironic that Kuhn, the internalist intellectual historian, should have done so much to stimulate contemporary social studies of science and that Kuhn the fervent seeker after philosophical and scientific truth should have done so much to encourage postmodern characterizations of science as based upon anything but the rational assessment of evidence and argument. For on both counts he insisted, in effect, "Je ne suis pas Kuhnien."

THE INDIVIDUAL ESSAYS

Our aim in this volume is to present the leading ideas, problems, and influences on, and of, Thomas Kuhn in a manner that is accessible to the general reader while also provoking discussion among specialists. We cannot, of course, pretend to provide complete coverage. The bias of this volume is toward Kuhn's work in relation to the cognitive sciences. In this area, Kuhnian ideas would seem to have a future as well as a past. Although he explicitly limited the account of science in *Structure* to the "mature" sciences (principally the physical sciences), his account of normal scientific cognition and some of his examples therein, as well as a good deal of his later work, suggest a far wider application.

The ten essays that follow can be read in any order, as each is a standalone essay. However, I have grouped them to begin with the more general "background" essays reporting influences on, or developments parallel to, Kuhn, namely, the logical positivists, French thinkers, and then Popper and Lakatos. Next, the reader will find more specialized essays on scientific practices within communities of practitioners, on normal science, revolutionary science and incommensurability, on Kuhn's relation to the cognitive sciences, and on his impact on the feminist movement.

Michael Friedman, in "Kuhn and Logical Empiricism," gives us an intellectual feast in his exploration of the intellectual background of both the logical empiricists and Kuhn. In the process he corrects popular misconceptions of positivism, brings out the striking commonalities of Kuhn's view of paradigms and paradigm change with Schlick's, Reichenbach's, and Carnap's logic of science, and traces both their commonalities and their differences to the debate between neo-Kantians and their critics (specifically, Cassirer, Meyerson, and Koyré) over the nature of scientific progress and the proper interpretation of non-Euclidean geometry and of Einstein's relativity theory. Friedman's essay features the philosophical debates underlying Kuhn's approach to history of science and philosophy of science.

In "Thomas Kuhn and French Philosophy of Science," **Gary Gutting** explores parallels between Kuhn's account of science and those of the prominent French historico-philosophical tradition, including Brunschwicg,

Bachelard, and Canguilhem. The French took a historical approach to the intellectual appraisal of science long before Kuhn and post-Kuhnian historical philosophy of science. In several instances the French thinkers anticipated postmodern insights commonly attributed to Kuhn in the Anglophone world. Gutting suggests that the French tradition provides resources for solving Kuhnian problems concerning objectivity, rationality, and realism. Gutting edited a previous collection of essays about Kuhn's work (Gutting 1980).

John Worrall, in "Normal Science and Dogmatism, Paradigms and Progress: Kuhn 'versus' Popper and Lakatos," deals with the clash of the titans. Worrall follows the issues arising out of the previously mentioned London conference of 1965, when Kuhn challenged Popper and Lakatos on their home ground, with Feyerabend, Toulmin, Watkins, and others participating as well. Worrall, himself one of Lakatos's most distinguished students, evaluates the Kuhn–Popper debate, and Lakatos's own methodology of scientific research programs as well, as a compromise between Popper and Kuhn.

In his essay on normal science as a distinctive sort of practice, **Joseph Rouse**, in "Kuhn's Philosophy of Scientific Practice," provides an alternative, more pragmatic reading of Kuhn that subtly undermines and transforms the usual understandings of Kuhn given us by admirers and critics alike. Paradigms or exemplars are better conceived as sets of skills than as sets of propositions or beliefs or as idealist *Weltanschauungen*, contends Rouse. On this reading, gone are the old distinctions between theory and experiment, theory and application, theory and practice, realism and antirealism, and context of discovery and context of justification. A standard technique of linguistic philosophers, including the logical positivists, has been "semantic ascent," Willard Van Orman Quine's term for reformulating substantive disagreements as disagreements over the use of language. Against this, Rouse, following Kuhn, says, in effect, that we must employ semantic "descent" if we are to understand scientific practice. Verbal agreement and disagreement (over how to state or interpret a theory) are not as important as scientists' common identification of which puzzles are important and accessible and their agreement about how to deal with them by means of the standard tools and practices of the workworld of that scientific specialty.

As an example of how Kuhn's account alters philosophy of science: for the positivists and Popper, there is little more to philosophy of science than study of the relations between finished theories and evidence. Kuhn almost totally rejects standard retrospective "theories of justification" of this sort and instead focuses on how scientists choose puzzles, techniques, and so on, based on the future promise of extending the paradigm. Hence his remarks about how he blurs the traditional discovery–justification distinction.

Nowadays, science studies experts, including those philosophers (such as Rouse) who focus on scientific practice, often make the point that shared practices do not presuppose or require fully shared beliefs and/or norms. This was, in fact, one of Kuhn's central points about normal science. But then we are left with the problem of understanding how it is possible that these shared practices can be constituted and maintained. This is the problem addressed by **Barry Barnes**, a leading sociologist of science and a founding member of the Edinburgh Strong Programme in the 1970s and 1980s, as well as the author of a well-known book on Kuhn (Barnes 1982). In "Thomas Kuhn and the Problem of Social Order in Science," Barnes frames this challenge as the application to the sciences of the problem of social order, long a staple of the sociological tradition. Barnes credits the functionalist sociology of Robert Merton as first seriously addressing this problem for the sciences. Kuhn then advanced the discussion a step further. But no one, Barnes says, has dealt at all adequately with this problem. Worse still, even sociologists have recently joined philosophers in retreating to an individualistic position. Yet understanding the sociology of expert communities is crucial to a wise and efficient science policy in a democratic culture ambivalent about exclusionary communities of experts.

Thomas Nickles, in "Normal Science: From Logic to Case-Based and Model-Based Reasoning," presents the central features of normal science and their implications for methodology of science and for learning theory. Normal science is conservative and tradition bound yet has radical implications. Kuhnian normal science anticipated later developments in cognitive and social psychology and artificial intelligence. Specifically, Kuhn's use of exemplars anticipates case-based and model-based versus rule-based reasoning; and schema theory in psychology is relevant to our assessment of Kuhn's tantalizing remarks about what he called the "acquired [or learned] similarity relation." Attention to these later developments, in turn, helps to bring out ambiguities and lacunae in Kuhn's account.

Kuhn's publication and revision of *Structure* coincided with the revolution in cognitive science in the 1960s and early 1970s. Why, then, did Kuhn not take more notice of these developments? **Nancy Nersessian**, in "Kuhn, Conceptual Change, and Cognitive Science," addresses this issue, based on her interviews of Kuhn and others and her interpretations of some of his latest work. She shows how work in cognitive science on mental models illuminates Kuhn's account of scientific concept formation, meaning change, and incommensurability. These cognitive devices are *social* resources, not merely structures hidden in the heads of individuals. The role of the perceptual system in mental modeling somewhat rehabilitates the early Kuhn's emphasis on perception. And research on revolutionary conceptual change in science seems to bring lessons both for science education and for human learning and problem solving in general.

Kuhn was the first major thinker since Wittgenstein to attack the traditional view that concepts are specified by sets of individually necessary and jointly sufficient conditions or rules. **Peter Barker, Xiang Chen, and Hanne Andersen**, in "Kuhn on Concepts and Categorization," explore the problem of concepts and concept learning in detail, arguing that a large body of empirical research in cognitive psychology, initiated by Eleanor Rosch, supports Kuhn's intuitive account in *Structure* and later works, so much so that a currently adequate account of concepts is better grounded in cognitive psychology than in history of science. If true, this would justify Kuhn's later turn away from history of science to linguistic studies of conceptual development as the main prop for his views about revolution and incommensurability. In fact, Barker, Chen, and Andersen maintain that Kuhn's new account of concepts rehabilitates his long-disputed claims about incommensurability. A scientific revolution can display incommensurability and yet develop gradually and permit rational appraisal of competing positions. The authors conclude that, ironically, incommensurability – the very notion that always gave Kuhn the most trouble – not only exists but that an adequate account of it also provides "a complete answer to the sociological critique of philosophy of science."

In "Kuhn's World Changes," **Richard Grandy** addresses Kuhn's most controversial claims about scientific revolutions and his ambivalence over whether to locate revolutionary change in the minds of practitioners or in the world. Grandy discusses Kuhn's work in the context of the debate over the nature of scientific theories (the logical "statement" view of the positivists versus the "nonstatement" view of the semantic interpretation) and the old problems concerning the relation of theoretical terms to observation terms and the theory-ladenness of observation. From this point of view, Grandy says, Kuhn's later attempts to understand incommensurability in linguistic terms is a bit retrograde. Grandy suggests that Kuhn could have focused on interpretive practices rather than rules for interpretation. Alternatively, he might have moved even further in the direction of embodiment of skills and employed physical motor metaphors such as the different gaits of a horse.

Science was long held to be immune to the kinds of critical examination engaged in by sociologists of knowledge and feminist scholars. Given Kuhn's own rejection of sociological and postmodern applications of his work, did he help or hinder feminist understandings of science? In her essay, "Does *The Structure of Scientific Revolutions* Permit a Feminist Revolution in Science?," **Helen Longino** shows how Kuhn's early work on the intertwining of theory and observation and on the inseparability of scientific description, metaphysical commitments, values, and goals both demonstrated the possibility of a feminist treatment of science and, nevertheless, ultimately inhibited the positive development of feminist alternatives. For feminist critiques soon outran Kuhn's conservative reluctance to make any changes in normal science as currently constituted. After discussing the work of feminists such as Ruth Hubbard, Donna Haraway, Kathyrn Addelson, and Evelyn Fox Keller, Longino sketches her own view of a pluralistic "contextual empiricism."

Notes

1. For a detailed account of the "received view" of the positivists and (to some extent) Popper and its critics, including Kuhn, see Suppe (1974). The authoritative scholarly account of Kuhn's development is Hoyningen-Huene (1993), hammered out in close consultation with Kuhn himself.

2. For some notable "Science Wars" responses to post-Kuhnian science studies, including sociology of science and feminist philosophy of science, see Gross and Levitt (1994), Gross, Levitt, and Lewis (1996), Sokal and Bricmont (1998), and Koertge (1998). Sardar (2000) is an introduction to the issues, from the social constructionist side, with many references to the constructionist literature. See also the special journal issues of *Social Text* (Spring–Summer 1996) and *Social Studies of Science* 29 (1998), no. 2.

3. These reviews and related essays, such as "Meaning and Scientific Change," are reprinted in Shapere (1984). Larry Laudan (1996 and elsewhere) is another who locates some of Kuhn's difficulties in the linguistic assumptions he allegedly took over from the positivists. See also Michael Friedman's essay in this volume.

4. My web browser returned over 4,000 items for the search string "kuhn+postmodern."

5. Bruno Latour (1993) characterizes the modern as the mendacious conjunction of three projects: the domination of nature, the emancipation of humanity, and the rigid separation of nature and society. See also Rouse (1996). There is, of course, no characterization upon which scholars agree.

6. My biographical sketch draws upon Andersen (2000), Andresen (1999), Buchwald and Smith (1997), Caneva (2000), Heilbron (1998), Hoyningen-Huene (1997), Merton (1977), and the Greek autobiographical interview-discussion in Kuhn (2000), among other sources.

7. This work eventuated in the publication of Kuhn et al. (1967).

8. Kuhn repeatedly stressed the importance of the Aristotle episode to his own understanding of history and scientific change – and to his own career. See, e.g., Kuhn (1977, Preface) and the interview by Aristides Baltas, Kostas Gavroglu, and Vassiliki Kindi, reprinted in Kuhn (2000, pp. 255–323).

9. See Buchwald and Smith (1997, 369ff.). See also the chapter by Barry Barnes.

10. I was a graduate student in the History and Philosophy of Science Program at Princeton from 1965 to 1969 and participated in the seminar in which Kuhn attempted to work out his ideas for the sequel to *Structure* as well as seminars more strictly on history of science. Although he developed few disciples, Kuhn was very accessible to students and helpful to them.

References

Andersen, Hanne. 2000. *On Kuhn*. Belmont, CA: Wadsworth.

Andresen, Jensine. 1999. "Crisis and Kuhn." *Isis* (supplement) 90: S43–S67.

Barnes, Barry. 1982. *T. S. Kuhn and Social Science*. New York: Columbia University Press.

Brush, Stephen. 2000. "Thomas Kuhn as a Historian of Science." *Science & Education* 9: 39–58.

Buchwald, Jed Z., and George Smith. 1997. "Thomas S. Kuhn, 1922–1996." *Philosophy of Science* 64: 361–76.

Caneva, Kenneth. 2000. "Possible Kuhns in the History of Science: Anomalies of Incommensurable Paradigms." *Studies in History and Philosophy of Science* 31: 87–124.

Fuller, Steve. 2000. *Thomas Kuhn: A Philosophical History for our Times*. Chicago: University of Chicago Press.

Gross, Paul, and Norman Levitt. 1994. *Higher Superstition: The Academic Left and Its Quarrels with Science*. Baltimore: Johns Hopkins University Press.

Gross, Paul, Norman Levitt, and Martin Lewis, eds. 1996. *The Flight from Science and Reason*. New York: New York Academy of Sciences.

Gutting, Gary, ed. 1980. *Paradigms and Revolutions*. Notre Dame, IN: University of Notre Dame Press.

Heilbron, John. 1998. "Thomas Samuel Kuhn, 18 July 1922–17 June 1996." *Isis* 89: 505–15.

Horwich, Paul, ed. 1993. *World Changes: Thomas Kuhn and the Nature of Science*. Cambridge, MA: MIT Press.

Hoyningen-Huene, Paul. 1993. *Reconstructing Science: Thomas Kuhn's Philosophy of Science*. Chicago: University of Chicago Press.

1997. "Thomas S. Kuhn." *Journal for General Philosophy of Science* 28: 235–56.

Koertge, Noretta, ed. 1998. *A House Built on Sand: Exposing Postmodernist Myths about Science*. New York: Oxford University Press.

Kuhn, Thomas. 1957. *The Copernican Revolution*. Cambridge, MA: Harvard University Press.

　　1962. *The Structure of Scientific Revolutions*. 2nd edition, enlarged, 1970. 3rd edition, 1996. Chicago: University of Chicago Press.

　　1977. *The Essential Tension: Selected Essays in Scientific Tradition and Change*. Chicago: University of Chicago Press.

　　1978. *Black-Body Theory and the Quantum Discontinuity, 1894–1912*. New York: Oxford University Press. Reprinted with an afterward, "Revisiting Planck" (a response to critics), in 1987.

　　2000. *The Road Since Structure: Philosophical Essays, 1970–1993, with an Autobiographical Interview*. Edited by James Conant and John Haugeland. Chicago: University of Chicago Press.

Kuhn, Thomas, John Heilbron, Paul Forman, and Lini Allen. 1967. *Sources for the History of Quantum Physics: An Inventory and Report*. Philadelphia: American Philosophical Society.

Lakatos, Imre, and Alan Musgrave, eds. 1970. *Criticism and the Growth of Knowledge*. Cambridge: Cambridge University Press.

Latour, Bruno. 1993. *We Have Never Been Modern*. Cambridge, MA: Harvard University Press. The original French edition was published in 1991.

Laudan, Larry. 1996. *Beyond Positivism and Relativism*. Boulder, CO: Westview Press.

Lyotard, Jean-François. 1984. *The Postmodern Condition: A Report on Knowledge*. Minneapolis: University of Minnesota Press. Translated by Geoff Bennington and Brian Massumi. The original French edition was published in 1979.

Merton, Robert. 1977. *Sociology of Science: An Episodic Memoir*. Carbondale: Southern Illinois University Press.

Nickles, Thomas. 1998. "Kuhn, Historical Philosophy of Science, and Case-Based Reasoning." *Configurations* 6: 51–85 (special issue on Thomas Kuhn).

Rouse, Joseph. 1996. *Engaging Science: How to Understand Its Practices Philosophically*. Ithaca, NY: Cornell University Press.

Sardar, Ziauddin. 2000. *Thomas Kuhn and the Science Wars*. New York: Totem.

Scheffler, Israel. 1967. *Science and Subjectivity*. Indianapolis: Bobbs-Merrill.

Shapere, Dudley. 1984. *Reason and the Search for Knowledge*. Dordrecht: Reidel.

Sokal, Alan, and Jean Bricmont. 1998. *Fashionable Nonsense: Postmodern Intellectuals' Abuse of Science*. New York: Picador.

Suppe, Frederick. 1974. "The Search for Philosophic Understanding of Scientific Theories." In F. Suppe, ed., *The Structure of Scientific Theories*. Urbana: University of Illinois Press, pp. 3–241. Second edition, 1977.

1 Kuhn and Logical Empiricism

MICHAEL FRIEDMAN

Conventional wisdom concerning twentieth-century philosophical approaches to scientific knowledge has held that Kuhn's theory of scientific revolutions is diametrically opposed to the philosophical movement known as "logical positivism" or "logical empiricism." Logical positivism has been portrayed as a naive version of empiricist foundationalism, according to which all knowledge is to be reduced to an epistemically certain basis in observational reports. And it follows, on this view, that there can be no genuine scientific revolutions in the Kuhnian sense: scientific progress must rather follow the "development-by-accumulation" model (in this case, development by accumulation of observable facts) that Kuhn explicitly rejects at the outset.[1] If we accept Kuhn's theory, by contrast, it follows that the progress of science is marked by radical discontinuities quite incompatible with such naive empiricism. So it is no wonder that Kuhn's theory of scientific revolutions is standardly taken as a major factor in the demise of logical empiricism.[2]

Over the past twenty-five years, however, a growing body of active research has been devoted to detailed study of the rise and decline of the logical empiricist movement. And this research has shown, not surprisingly, that the accepted conventional wisdom concerning the relationship between Kuhn's theory of scientific revolutions and logical empiricist philosophy of science is seriously oversimplified and fundamentally misleading. Perhaps the most striking results of this research appear in an article by George Reisch (1991) entitled "Did Kuhn Kill Logical Empiricism?" Beginning with the well-known fact that Kuhn's *The Structure of Scientific Revolutions* first appeared, in 1962, as a volume of the *International Encyclopedia of Unified Science* (the official monograph series of the logical empiricist movement in exile), Reisch presents two previously unpublished letters written to Kuhn by Rudolf Carnap in the latter's capacity as editor of this series. There Carnap expresses enthusiastic approval of Kuhn's ideas, which, he says, "will be very stimulating for all those who are interested in the nature of scientific theories and especially the causes and forms of their changes."

Carnap also states, while admitting that his own "knowledge of the history of science is rather fragmentary," that he especially "liked your [Kuhn's] emphasis on the new conceptual frameworks which are proposed in revolutions in science, and, on their basis, the posing of new questions, not only answers to old problems."[3]

These expressions of approval by Rudolf Carnap – the generally acknowledged leading representative of logical empiricism – are certainly striking, and they must give serious pause to expositors of the conventional wisdom. But even more striking, as Reisch also explains, are the deep affinities between Carnap's underlying philosophical perspective and Kuhn's ideas. Natural science, for Carnap, is to be conceived as represented within a particular formal language or linguistic framework. And perhaps Carnap's most fundamental thought is that there are a plurality of essentially different, nonintertranslatable such frameworks. Thus, for example, there are linguistic frameworks in which the rules of classical logic are taken to be valid, and there are also linguistic frameworks in which we instead adopt the rules of intuitionistic logic (wherein the law of the excluded middle is no longer universally valid). For Carnap, moreover, there is no sense in which one such framework can be "correct" while another is "incorrect." Rather, all standards of logical correctness are relative or "internal" to a particular choice of linguistic framework. "External" questions concerning which linguistic framework to adopt are not similarly adjudicable by already established logical rules but rather require a "conventional" or "pragmatic" choice based on suitability or adaptedness for one or another given purpose.[4] Such external questions, involving the change from one linguistic framework to a different one, are precisely what is at issue, for Carnap, in scientific revolutions.[5]

The affinities between Carnap's philosophy of linguistic frameworks and Kuhn's theory of scientific revolutions are therefore pervasive indeed. According to Kuhn, there are two essentially different kinds of periods in the history of science: periods of normal science in which the relevant community operates unquestioningly within a generally accepted paradigm "committed to the same rules and standards for scientific practice" (1970, p. 11), and periods of revolutionary science in which precisely such an underlying consensus is then undercut. Similarly, for Carnap, there are two essentially different kinds of activities associated with the linguistic frameworks within which our theories in natural science are formulated: the adjudication of internal questions on the basis of the accepted logical rules of a single given linguistic framework and the adjudication of external questions that, by hypothesis, do not and cannot presuppose such logical rules.[6] Just as, for Carnap, the logical rules of a linguistic framework are constitutive of the notion of correctness or validity relative to this framework, a particular paradigm governing a given episode of normal science, for Kuhn, yields generally agreed upon – although largely tacit – rules constitutive of what counts as a valid or correct solution to a problem within this episode of normal science. Just as, for Carnap, external questions concerning which linguistic framework to adopt are not similarly governed by logical rules but rather require a much less definite appeal to conventional and/or pragmatic considerations, changes of paradigm in revolutionary science, for Kuhn, do not proceed in accordance with generally agreed upon rules, as in normal science, but rather require something more akin to a conversion experience.[7]

It is especially noteworthy, then, that Kuhn, toward the end of his career, explicitly acknowledges these parallels. Kuhn expresses embarrassment, to begin with, that "[w]hen I received the kind letter in which Carnap told me of his pleasure in the manuscript [one of the letters concerning the initial publication of *Structure* cited by Reisch], I interpreted it as mere politeness, not as an indication that we might usefully talk."[8] But Kuhn then goes on to explain the "correspondingly deep difference" between Carnap and himself that he thinks survives the acknowledged parallels. This does not consist, as one might first expect, in the circumstance that Carnap's linguistic rules must always be explicitly formulated, whereas Kuhn's "rules and standards for scientific practice" are largely tacit and are thus enforced by implicit convention rather than explicit formal legislation. Kuhn rather emphasizes that he, unlike Carnap, is concerned from the start with historical *development*, so that, in particular, "[l]anguage change is *cognitively* significant for me as it was not for Carnap" (1993, p. 314). The point, I take it, is that change of language involves an external question for Carnap and is therefore merely pragmatic, and not cognitive or epistemic in the only sense of "epistemology" Carnap recognizes. For, although Carnap, as Reisch emphasizes, does connect his notion of change of language with scientific revolutions, he never discusses such revolutions in any serious way. Such a historical investigation could never be a part of what Carnap himself preserves of epistemology, namely, *Wissenschaftslogik* [the logic of science] – the formulation and examination of a variety of possible linguistic frameworks within which the results of the special sciences may be represented. What is crucial, for Carnap, is that the only remaining properly philosophical problems are purely formal – belonging to the application of logic to the language of the special sciences. Although many interesting *empirical* questions may arise in analyzing the historical transitions from one theory to another during a scientific revolution (and Carnap expresses keen interest in such questions in his letters to Kuhn cited by Reisch), the only properly _philosophical_ questions here concern the (purely timeless) articulation of the logical structures of the two different languages under consideration.[9] For Kuhn, by contrast, as the very first chapter of _Structure_ makes clear, the point is precisely that historical examination of scientific change can, above all, be genuinely philosophical.

We can deepen our appreciation of the parallels between Carnap and Kuhn – and also their important differences – by looking a bit more closely into the development of both views. I consider first the development of logical empiricism.

Conventional wisdom portrays logical empiricism as directly descended from the classical empiricism of Locke, Berkeley, and Hume, with a more recent boost from the scientific positivism articulated by Ernst Mach at the end of the nineteenth century.[10] And it is true, of course, that the influence of Mach – and, more generally, of broadly empiricist currents of thought – is certainly important. (Indeed, as is well known, the logical positivism of the Vienna Circle was first formulated as an official movement under the rubric of the _Verein Ernst Mach_.) Nevertheless, there are equally important influences on the development of logical empiricism that lie quite outside the classical empiricist tradition. Two such influences are especially important in the present context: developments in non-Euclidean geometry and its philosophy that formed the indispensable background to Albert Einstein's formulation of the theory of relativity and developments in early-twentieth-century neo-Kantian epistemology – especially within the tradition of the Marburg School represented by Hermann Cohen, Paul Natorp, and Ernst Cassirer.[11]

The crucial figures in the development of non-Euclidean geometry, for the logical empiricists, were Hermann von Helmholtz and Henri Poincaré. And neither of these two thinkers defends a straightforwardly empiricist conception – such as was then standardly identified with John Stuart Mill – of either geometry in particular or scientific knowledge more generally. Whereas it is true, for example, that Helmholtz views the choice between Euclidean and non-Euclidean geometries as empirical, he also suggests that the more general structure of space common to both Euclidean and non-Euclidean systems (that of constant curvature or what Helmholtz called "free mobility") is a necessary presupposition of all spatial measurement and thus a "transcendental" form of our spatial intuition in the sense of Kant. Helmholtz's own approach to scientific epistemology is therefore Kantian insofar as space indeed has a "necessary form" expressed in the condition of free mobility; his approach is empiricist, however, insofar as which of the geometries of constant curvature actually holds is then determined by experience. So what we find here, in the end, is an attempt to *combine* Kantian and empiricist ideas so as to be as faithful as possible to the new scientific (and philosophical) situation.[12]

We find an analogous attempt to adapt both Kantian and empiricist ideas to the new scientific situation in the thought of Henri Poincaré, although here there is even less emphasis on traditional empiricism. According to Poincaré, whereas no particular geometry – neither Euclidean nor non-Euclidean – is an a priori condition of our spatial intuition, it does not follow that the choice between them, as Helmholtz thought, is empirical. For there remains an irreducible gulf between our crude and approximate sensory experience and our precise mathematical descriptions of nature. Establishing one or another system of geometry, Poincaré argues, therefore requires a free choice, a *convention* of our own – based, in the end, on the greater mathematical simplicity of the Euclidean system. And this notion of convention (which, as we shall see, is central to the development of logical empiricism) is explicitly adopted as a substitute for Kant's original, necessarily fixed notion of the a priori (represented by the laws of specifically Euclidean geometry), intended to respect Kant's insight into the "experience-constituting" role of geometry while simultaneously accommodating the new scientific developments showing that Euclidean geometry, in particular, is in no way uniquely forced upon us.[13]

As I suggested, these mathematical and philosophical developments formed the indispensable background to Einstein's formulation of the theory of relativity, and they were taken as such by Einstein himself and by the logical empiricists.[14] Indeed, the earliest philosophizing of those thinkers later to be identified most closely with logical empiricism arose directly from an attempt to assimilate both Einstein's new theory and the epistemological reflections of Helmholtz and Poincaré. Moritz Schlick, the founder and guiding spirit of the Vienna Circle, began this process in his *Space and Time in Contemporary Physics* (Schlick 1917), which went through four editions between 1917 and 1922. (Indeed, it was on the basis of this work, enthusiastically endorsed by Einstein, that Schlick gained the Chair for the Philosophy of the Inductive Sciences previously occupied by Mach and Ludwig Boltzmann at the University of Vienna in 1922.) Here Schlick argues that the lesson of the theory of relativity is not, as one might expect, that Euclidean geometry is a false description of physical space. It is rather, following Poincaré, that there is no fact of the matter about the geometry of physical space: choosing one or another physical geometry is not forced upon us by any observable facts but rather depends on a prior convention or stipulation without which the question of physical geometry is simply undefined. In particular, we can, if we wish, retain Euclidean geometry in the context of Einstein's theory, but this choice would result in formidable complications in our total system of geometry plus physics that make it pragmatically inexpedient (but not false).[15]

Carnap, in his doctoral dissertation (1922), explicitly follows Schlick in this Poincaré-inspired interpretation of the status of physical geometry in Einstein's theory. But here, in contrast to Schlick, there is a more positive estimation of the Kantian theory of space. Indeed, Carnap began his doctoral work under the guidance of the neo-Kantian philosopher Bruno Bauch at Jena, and, after taking a year-long seminar on the *Critique of Pure Reason* with Bauch, Carnap "was strongly impressed by Kant's conception that the geometrical structure of space is determined by the form of our intuition" (Carnap 1963, p. 4). Of course, one cannot now maintain Kant's original conception of the fixed synthetic a priori status of specifically Euclidean geometry; so Carnap rather defends a generalization of Kant's conception of spatial intuition according to which only the *infinitesimally* Euclidean character of physical space is a priori determined by the form of our intuition. Only this merely "topological form," for Carnap, is necessary, whereas the choice of specifically "metrical form" (whether Euclidean or non-Euclidean) is "optional [*wahlfrei*]" – and is in fact determined by convention (on the basis of the overall simplicity of our total system of geometry plus physics) in precisely the sense defended by Schlick.[16]

But the most fully developed attempt to reconcile the Kantian conception of scientific knowledge and Einstein's theory of relativity within the logical empiricist tradition was undertaken by Hans Reichenbach in his first book, *The Theory of Relativity and A Priori Knowledge* (1920). Reichenbach there draws a distinction between two meanings of the Kantian a priori: necessary and unrevisable, fixed for all time, on the one hand, and "constitutive of the concept of the object of [scientific] knowledge," on the other.[17] Reichenbach argues, on this basis, that the lesson of the theory of relativity is that the former meaning must be dropped and the latter must be retained. Relativity theory involves a priori constitutive principles (which Reichenbach calls "axioms of coordination") as necessary presuppositions of its properly empirical claims ("axioms of connection"), just as much as did Newtonian physics, but these principles have changed in the transition from the latter theory to the former: whereas Euclidean geometry is indeed constitutively a priori in the context of Newtonian physics, for example, only infinitesimally Euclidean geometry is constitutively a priori in the context of general relativity. What Reichenbach ends up with is thus a *relativized* conception of a priori mathematical-physical principles (axioms of coordination), which change and develop along with the development of the mathematical and physical sciences but which nevertheless retain the characteristically Kantian constitutive function of making the empirical natural knowledge (axioms of connection) thereby structured and framed by such principles first possible. Thus, as Reichenbach points out in a prepublication footnote added in proof, his ideas have much in common with contemporaneous attempts by neo-Kantian philosophers to develop an analogous reconciliation between the theory of relativity and Kantian philosophy.[18]

That logical empiricism was significantly influenced by recent developments within neo-Kantian epistemology – and especially by the Marburg School of neo-Kantianism represented by Cohen, Natorp, and Cassirer – is therefore evident (see notes 16 and 18). This influence is seen most clearly, however, in the first work on epistemology produced within the Vienna Circle, Carnap's *Der logische Aufbau der Welt* (1928). Although conventional wisdom has portrayed Carnap's *Aufbau* as the epitome of the logical positivists' supposed empiricist foundationalism,[19] more recent historical research has shown that this picture, too, is seriously oversimplified and that the influence of Marburg neo-Kantianism, in particular, is perhaps even more significant.[20]

For Carnap, the neo-Kantianism of the Marburg School had been given its most satisfactory and significant formulation in Cassirer's *Substance and Function* (1910). The burden of this work is to argue that modern developments in logic, the foundations of mathematics, and mathematical physics show that the traditional theory of the concept, based on Aristotelian syllogistic logic, is entirely inadequate – and, as a result, that the traditional epistemological conceptions of both rationalism and empiricism are entirely inadequate as well. On the one hand, Aristotelian subject-predicate logic mistakenly privileges the relation between substance and accident, and it is the attempt to develop an a priori ontology based on this privileged relation that is characteristic of traditional rationalism. On the other hand, however, traditional empiricism is equally dependent on Aristotelian logic in mistakenly privileging the procedure of concept formation by abstraction, whereby we inductively ascend from sensory particulars to ever higher superordinate concepts (genera and species) predicated of these particulars. Modern logic has shown the poverty of both views, according to Cassirer, by developing a new theory of the concept based on the mathematical notion of function or relation – a theory of what we would now call "abstract relational structures" (the series of natural numbers, for example, or the abstract structure exemplified by Euclidean space).[21] In developing an alternative theory of knowledge and reality, Cassirer then rejects empiricist and inductivist accounts of scientific knowledge in favor of the so-called genetic conception of knowledge characteristic of the Marburg School. Empirical science proceeds by progressively embedding natural phenomena in an ordered sequence of relational structures as we successively articulate and refine mathematical representations of these phenomena in the historical development of our theories. This procedure results in an infinite, never-ending sequence of relational structures, but one that is nonetheless converging on a limit structure or limit theory representing the ideal completion of scientific progress. The object of scientific knowledge is thus never completely given: it is only successively approximated in the limit as the ideal X toward which our mathematical representations of nature are converging.[22]

Carnap, in the *Aufbau*, shares the ambition of replacing all forms of traditional epistemology – theories of knowledge and its relation to reality – with a new approach based on the modern logical theory of relations. Indeed, Carnap (1928, §3) initially characterizes the method to be followed as "the analysis of reality with the help of the theory of relations." Moreover, when Carnap first introduces the question of the basic or fundamental relations on which his "constitutional system of reality" is to be erected, he cites Cassirer (1910) as showing the necessity of formally defined relational concepts for ordering the "undigested experiential given" favored by "positivism."[23] Carnap thus hopes to achieve a synthesis of empiricism and Kantianism – a synthesis that emphasizes, as does the Marburg School, the absolute indispensability of logico-mathematical formal structures for underwriting the clarity, precision, and intersubjective communicability of empirical scientific knowledge.[24]

Carnap also follows the Marburg School in representing empirical knowledge by a serial or stepwise sequence of formal logical structures, depicting, in an idealized fashion, how our scientific methods for acquiring knowledge actually play out in practice. This sequence does not represent the historical progression of mathematical-physical successor theories, however, but rather the epistemological progress of a single individual or cognitive subject as its knowledge extends from the initial subjective sensory data belonging to the *autopsychological* realm, through the world of public external objects constituting the *physical* realm, and finally to the intersubjective and cultural realities belonging to the *heteropsychological* realm. Carnap's methodological series is thus a "rational reconstruction" of the actual present state of scientific knowledge intended formally to represent the "actual process of cognition."[25] For Carnap, moreover, this is not a series of successor theories in the historical progress of mathematical natural science, but rather *a sequence of levels or ranks in the hierarchy of logical types* of Whitehead's and Russell's *Principia Mathematica* (1910–13),[26] a sequence of levels *ordered by type-theoretic definitions*. Objects on any level (other than the first) are thus formally defined as classes of objects (or relations between objects) from the preceding level.

The "logicization" of empirical scientific knowledge undertaken by the Marburg School is thereby implemented in an even more radical fashion. For the historically oriented epistemology of the Marburg tradition – which proceeds largely by the methods of intellectual history – is here transformed into a purely formal exercise: the project of formally presenting the logical definitions of all objects of (current) scientific knowledge subsisting at the various levels of Carnap's constitutional system. And, in the course of this formal exercise, Carnap is able, by means of the theory of types, to transcend the Marburg doctrine of the essentially incomplete character of the object of scientific knowledge – its character, that is, as a never to be completed X. For Carnap, all objects whatsoever are defined or "constituted" at *definite finite ranks* within the hierarchy of logical types, and it is only the further empirical specification of these objects that remains essentially incomplete. As a result, Carnap is also able to reject the Kantian conception of synthetic a priori principles, for objects are defined or constituted by *stipulation* and then further investigated by *experience*: "[a]ccording to the conception of constitutional theory there are no other components in cognition than these two – the conventional and the empirical – and thus no synthetic a priori [components]."[27]

In a direct engagement with neo-Kantian epistemology, Carnap thereby arrives at the same point that was reached in the context of the logical empiricists' earlier engagement with the foundations of geometry and relativity theory: Kant's original conception of fixed synthetic a priori principles governing our empirical scientific knowledge is to be replaced by Poincaré's notion of convention, so that, in particular, the principles in question are no longer necessarily fixed but become "optional," subject to choice, and relative or internal to a specific scientific context. Thus Carnap here stands on the brink of his mature philosophy of linguistic frameworks,[28] which, as we saw at the outset, has deep affinities with the Kuhnian theory of scientific revolutions. This philosophy, as we now see, can be viewed as a kind of generalization and logicization of the conception of relativized a priori principles developed by Reichenbach (1920),[29] resulting from Carnap's simultaneous engagement with both the details of neo-Kantian epistemology and the most recent developments in modern mathematical logic.[30]

It is noteworthy, once again, that Kuhn, toward the end of his career, explicitly acknowledges the Kantian and neo-Kantian background to the development of logical empiricism and the resulting parallels with his own views. In particular, commenting on Reichenbach's distinction between two meanings of the a priori (fixed and unrevisable versus constitutive relative to a theory), Kuhn remarks that "[b]oth meanings make the world in some sense mind-dependent, but the first disarms the apparent threat to objectivity by insisting on the absolute fixity of the categories, while the second relativizes the categories (and the experienced world with them) to time, place, and culture." And he continues in an important passage worth quoting in full:

> Though it is a more articulated source of constitutive categories, my structured lexicon [Kuhn's late version of "paradigm"] resembles Kant's a priori when the latter is taken in its second, relativized sense. Both are constitutive of *possible experience* of the world, but neither dictates what that experience must be. Rather, they are constitutive of the infinite range of possible experiences that might conceivably occur in the actual world to which they give access. Which of these conceivable experiences occurs in that actual world is something that must be learned, both from everyday experience and from the more systematic and refined experience that characterizes scientific practice. They are both stern teachers, firmly resisting the promulgation of beliefs unsuited to the form of life the lexicon permits. What results from respectful attention to them is knowledge of nature, and the criteria that serve to evaluate contributions to that knowledge are, correspondingly, epistemic. The fact that experience within another form of life – another time, place, or culture – might have constituted knowledge differently is irrelevant to its status as knowledge.[31]

Kuhn, like the logical empiricists, has thus adopted a relativized conception of Kantian a priori principles. However, since Kuhn's perspective, unlike that of the logical empiricists, is essentially historical (their a priori is relativized to a theory or linguistic framework, not to a "time, place, or culture"), he also raises (and here rather abruptly dismisses) the central historicist problem concerning the social and cultural relativity of scientific knowledge that dominates post-Kuhnian work in science studies.[32]

Let us now take a brief look at the background to Kuhn's theory of scientific revolutions. Although there has not yet been much study of the development of Kuhn's views, Kuhn has left some intriguing hints.

Thus, in the Preface to *Structure*, Kuhn portrays how he shifted his career plans from physics to the history of science, and, in explaining his initial intensive work in the subject, he states that he (1970, pp. v–vi) "continued to study the writings of Alexandre Koyré and first encountered those of Emile Meyerson, Hélène Metzger, and Anneliese Maier [; more] clearly than most other recent scholars, this group has shown what it was like to think scientifically in a period when the canons of scientific thought were very different from those current today." Then, in the introductory first chapter on "A Role for History," Kuhn explains the background to his rejection of the development-by-accumulation model:

> [H]istorians of science have begun to ask new sorts of questions and to trace different, and often less than cumulative, developmental lines for the sciences. Rather than seeking the permanent contributions of an older science to our present vantage, they attempt to display the historical integrity of that science in its own time. They ask, for example, not about the relation of Galileo's views to those of modern science, but rather about the relationship between his views and those of his group, i.e., his teachers, contemporaries, and immediate successors in the sciences. Furthermore, they insist upon studying the opinions of that group and other similar ones from the viewpoint – usually very different from that of modern science – that gives those opinions the maximum internal coherence and the closest possible fit to nature. Seen through the works that result, works perhaps best exemplified in the writings of Alexandre Koyré, science does not seem altogether the same enterprise as the one discussed by writers in the older historiographic tradition.[33]

Kuhn, not surprisingly, thus places himself squarely within the historiographical tradition initiated by Koyré in his works on Galileo first published in 1939 – a tradition that established the history of science as an independent discipline in the immediate postwar period.[34]

In a survey article on the development of the history of science, Kuhn (1968) again explains the initial break with the development-by-accumulation model, which began, according to Kuhn, with "the influence, beginning in the late nineteenth century, of the history of philosophy." We here learned an "attitude towards past thinkers," Kuhn explains, that

> came to the history of science from philosophy. Partly it was learned from men like Lange and Cassirer who dealt historically with people or ideas that were also important for scientific development.... And partly it was learned from a small group of neo-Kantian epistemologists, particularly Brunschvicg and Meyerson, whose search for quasi-absolute categories of thought in older scientific ideas produced brilliant genetic analyses of

concepts which the main tradition in the history of science had misunder-stood or dismissed.[35]

Finally, in a "Historiographic/Philosophical Addendum," concluding his response to criticisms of his work on Planck and black-body theory, Kuhn (1984) makes some further intriguing remarks. Responding to questions about the relationship between his work on Planck and the theory of scientific revolutions presented in *Structure*, Kuhn (1987, p. 361) explains that "[t]he concept of historical reconstruction that underlies [the Planck book] has from the start been fundamental to both my historical and my philosophical work[; it] is by no means original: I owe it primarily to Alexandre Koyré; its ultimate sources lie in neo-Kantian philosophy."

What does Kuhn mean here by "neo-Kantian epistemology" and "neo-Kantian philosophy"? It is not entirely clear. Whereas, as we have seen, Cassirer is certainly a leading figure in early-twentieth-century neo-Kantianism, and it is also very plausible to locate Maier, in particular, in the context of Kantian and neo-Kantian thought,[36] the other figures on Kuhn's list can be referred to as "neo-Kantians" only by making more or less of a stretch. To be sure, they agree in rejecting naive empiricist accounts of the development of modern science (and thus the development-by-accumulation model) and emphasize instead the fundamental importance of mind sets, conceptual frameworks, or "mentalities" contributed by thought itself.[37] At the same time, however, several of these figures make a point of taking issue with Kantian and neo-Kantian ideas, both philosophically and with reference to the interpretation of the history of science.[38] But perhaps there is, nonetheless, something importantly right in Kuhn's assertion that the "ultimate sources [of his concept of historical reconstruction] lie in neo-Kantian philosophy." For all the figures on his list, in one way or another, are taking inspiration from, and reacting to, Cassirer's seminal work on the history of modern science and philosophy, *Das Erkenntnisproblem* [*The Problem of Knowledge*] (1906–7).[39]

Das Erkenntnisproblem is the first work of intellectual history to develop a detailed reading of the seventeenth-century scientific revolution in terms of the "Platonic" idea that the thoroughgoing application of mathematics to nature (the so-called mathematization of nature) is the central and overarching achievement of this revolution.[40] Cassirer simultaneously articulates an interpretation of the history of modern philosophy as the development and eventual triumph of what he calls "modern philosophical idealism." This tradition takes its inspiration from idealism in the Platonic sense, from an appreciation for the "ideal" formal structures paradigmatically studied in mathematics, and it is distinctively modern in recognizing the fundamental importance of the systematic application of such structures to empirically given nature in modern mathematical physics – a progressive and synthetic process wherein mathematical models of nature are successively refined and corrected without limit. For Cassirer, it is Galileo, above all, in opposition to both sterile Aristotelian-Scholastic formal logic and sterile Aristotelian-Scholastic empirical induction, who first grasped the essential structure of this synthetic process; and the development of "modern philosophical idealism" in the work of Descartes, Spinoza, Gassendi, Hobbes, Leibniz, and Kant then consists in its increasingly self-conscious philosophical articulation and elaboration. Cassirer therefore interprets the development of modern thought as a whole from the point of view of the philosophical perspective of Marburg neo-Kantianism. In particular, he here anticipates his own systematic work in *Substance and Function* by interpreting the characteristically modern conception of nature as the triumph of the mathematical-relational concept of *function* – as expressed in the universal laws of mathematical physics – over the traditional Aristotelian concept of *substance*.

Yet Meyerson, who is clearly the next most seminal figure on Kuhn's list of inspirational precursors,[41] takes a quite different view. He agrees with Kant and the neo-Kantians on the necessity for a priori requirements of the mind to give meaning and structure to the results of empirical science. But he is vehemently opposed to the attempt to assimilate scientific understanding to the formulation of universal laws governing phenomena. Indeed, the central thought of his *Identity and Reality* (1930, first published in 1908) is that genuine scientific knowledge and understanding can never be the result of mere lawfulness (*légalité*) but must instead answer to the mind's a priori logical demand for identity (*identité*). And the primary requirement resulting from this demand is precisely that some underlying *substance* be conserved as absolutely unchanging and self-identical in all sensible alterations of nature. Thus, the triumph of the scientific revolution, for Meyerson, is represented by the rise of mechanistic atomism, wherein elementary corpuscles preserve their sizes, shapes, and masses while merely changing their mutual positions in uniform and homogeneous space via motion; this same demand for transtemporal identity is also represented, in more recent times, by Lavoisier's use of the principle of the conservation of matter in his new chemistry and by the discovery of the conservation of energy. However, in the even more recent discovery of what we now know as the second law of thermodynamics ("Carnot's principle"), which governs the *temporally irreversible* process of "degradation" or "dissipation" of energy, we encounter nature's complementary and unavoidable resistance to our a priori logical demands. In the end, therefore, Meyerson views the development of natural science as progressing via a perpetual dialectical opposition between the mind's a priori demand for substantiality and thus absolute identity through time, on the one side, and nature's "irrational" a posteriori resistance to this demand, on the other.

In the work of Cassirer and Meyerson, then, we find two sharply diverging visions of the history of modern science. For Cassirer, this history is seen as a process of evolving rational purification of our view of nature, as we progress from naively realistic "substantialistic" conceptions, focusing on underlying substances, causes, and mechanisms subsisting "behind" the observable phenomena, to increasingly abstract, purely "functional" conceptions, in which we abandon the search for underlying ontology in favor of ever more precise mathematical representations of phenomena in terms of exactly formulated universal laws. For Meyerson, by contrast, this same history is seen as a necessarily dialectical progression (in something like the Hegelian sense), wherein reason perpetually seeks to enforce precisely the substantialistic impulse, and nature continually offers resistance via the ultimate irrationality of temporal succession. It is by no means surprising, therefore, that Meyerson, in the course of considering, and rejecting, "anti-substantialistic conceptions of science," explicitly takes issue with Cassirer's characteristic claim that "[m]athematical physics turns aside from the essence of things and their inner substantiality in order to turn towards their numerical order and connection, their functional and mathematical structure."[42] And it is also no wonder, similarly, that Cassirer, in the course of his own discussion of "identity and diversity, constancy and change," explicitly takes issue with Meyerson's views by asserting that "[t]he identity towards which thought progressively strives is not the identity of ultimate substantial things but the identity of functional orders and coordinations."[43]

It is especially striking, in view of this sharp divergence, that Koyré, in particular, emphatically places himself on the side of Meyerson. Indeed, his *Galileo Studies* is dedicated to Meyerson, and Koyré's allegiance to Meyerson's position in the dispute with Cassirer clearly emerges, if only implicitly, in Koyré's criticism of Cassirer's "excessively Kantian" reading of Galileo's "Platonism."[44] That this criticism does not merely concern the interpretation of Galileo, however, is explicitly expressed in an earlier paper explaining and defending Meyerson's philosophy to a German audience. Specifically, Koyré (1931) defends Meyerson's conception against the "anti-substantialistic" pretensions of neo-Kantianism, according to which "science has nothing to do with substantial causes, but is occupied only with constructing functional dependencies, functional interconnections of the phenomena and clothing them in mathematical formulas."[45] While science does aim at mathematical laws, of course, this is not the ultimate goal of the rational comprehension of phenomena required by thought. Here Meyerson, following the ancient tradition initiated by Parmenides and Plato, is perfectly correct: the demand for rational comprehension can be satisfied only by absolute unity and self-identity. Yet, as Plato – and, following him, Hegel – clearly saw, the reality with which thought is confronted is essentially irrational. In particular, temporal succession is ultimate and irreducible, and reality itself is a necessary mixture of (rational) "sameness" and (irrational) "otherness." In the end, therefore, Koyré, despite his well-known emphasis on rationalism and the mathematization of nature, is a Meyersonian. His "Platonism" – in explicit opposition to the more Kantian version articulated by Cassirer – is clearly and firmly based on a recognition of the *limits* of mathematical thought.[46]

The historiographical tradition Kuhn attempts to assimilate in his theory of scientific revolutions (see note 33) is thus by no means unitary and uncontentious. On the contrary, it is characterized by a deep philosophical opposition between a mathematical idealist tendency taking its inspiration from Kant and a more realistic, substantialistic tendency taking its inspiration – via the thought of Meyerson – from a mixture of Platonic, Cartesian, and Hegelian ideas. The former tendency, following Kant, renounces the ambition of describing an ontological realm of substantial things subsisting behind the empirical phenomena in favor of a rigorous mathematical description of the lawlike relations among the phenomena themselves. It differs from Kant, however, in recognizing that no particular mathematical structures (such as those of Euclidean geometry and Newtonian physics) are necessarily instantiated in the phenomena, and, accordingly, it portrays the rationality and universality of scientific progress as a historical evolution marked by a continuous unfolding and generalization of the powers of mathematical thought.[47] The latter tendency, by contrast, maintains precisely an ontology of substantial things, and, accordingly, it emphatically rejects the attempt to reduce the task of science to the formulation of precise mathematical laws. It thus ends up with a more pessimistic reading of the history of modern science in which our demand for fundamentally ontological rational intelligibility is met by an inevitable resistance to this demand arising from the irrational, essentially temporal character of nature itself.[48]

If I am not mistaken, this deep philosophical tension is echoed in Kuhn's theory of scientific revolutions, particularly where he considers the question of continuity over time at the *theoretical* level. Here Kuhn shows himself, in this respect, to be a follower of the Meyersonian tendency, for he consistently gives the question an ontological rather than a mathematical interpretation. Thus, for example, when Kuhn considers the relationship between relativistic and Newtonian mechanics, in explicit opposition to what he calls "early logical positivism," he rejects the notion of a fundamental continuity between the two theories on the grounds that the "physical reference" of their terms is essentially different;[49] and he nowhere considers the contrasting idea, characteristic of the Marburg School, that continuity of relevant mathematical structures might be sufficient. Moreover, Kuhn consistently gives an ontological rather than a mathematical interpretation to the question of theoretical convergence over time: the question is always whether our theories can be said to converge to an independently existing "truth" about reality, to a theory-independent external world.[50] By contrast, as we have seen, the Marburg School rejects this realistic reading of convergence at the outset: our theories do not (ontologically) converge to a mind-independent realm of substantial things; they (mathematically) converge *within* the historical progression of our theories as they continually approximate, but never reach, an ideally complete mathematical representation of the phenomena.

Our examination of the development of both logical empiricism and Kuhn's theory of scientific revolutions took its starting point from the affinities between Kuhn's theory and Carnap's philosophy of linguistic frameworks. We have now seen that these affinities are in no way accidental but rather reflect an early-twentieth-century intellectual situation encompassing both the history and the philosophy of science. All the thinkers we have considered agreed, on broadly Kantian grounds, in rejecting naive empiricist epistemology in favor of an emphasis on demands set by the mind itself, and virtually all (with the possible exception of Meyerson) departed from Kant in recognizing that the resulting mind sets, conceptual frameworks, or mentalities significantly evolve throughout the development of the sciences and are thus relative to or dependent on a given stage of theoretical progress. The logical empiricists, in particular, were closest, in this respect, to the Marburg neo-Kantianism articulated in the work of Cassirer, wherein the conceptual frameworks in question are exemplified in their purest form in the development of modern mathematics, mathematical physics, and mathematical logic. The logical empiricists went one step further than Cassirer, however, in their ambition to formulate philosophy, too, as a branch of exact mathematical science – that is, as *Wissenschaftslogik*. In this way, as we have seen, they removed the history of science from the purview of philosophy. And it was then Kuhn's great merit, against this common background, to have reinstated the history of science as perhaps the most important object considered in the philosophy of science. As we have also seen, however, this very "historicization" of the philosophy of science inevitably raised the problem of social and cultural relativism that dominates post-Kuhnian discussion today. The question arises, then, of whether it is possible to address this problem in a more satisfactory way by continuing to emphasize the importance of developments in modern mathematics, mathematical physics, and mathematical logic (as in both logical empiricism and the Marburg School) while simultaneously recognizing the importance of the factual historical evolution of the sciences (as in both the Marburg School and the historiographical tradition leading up to, and including, the work of Kuhn). But a further consideration of this question will have to wait for another occasion.[51]

Notes

1. Kuhn (1970) begins by rejecting this model in chapter 1, "A Role for History," although he does not there explicitly associate it with logical empiricism. In chapter 9, "The Nature and Necessity of Scientific Revolutions," however, he rejects the view, "closely associated with early logical positivism," that "would restrict the range and meaning of an accepted theory so that it could not possibly conflict with any later theory that made predictions about some of the same natural phenomena" (p. 98). Logical positivism is supposed to do this, of course, by holding that the meaning of a theory is exhausted by its logical implications within a class of theory-neutral observation sentences.

2. See, for example, Giere (1988, p. 32): "Kuhn's *Structure of Scientific Revolutions*... was a major contributor to the decline of logical empiricism beginning in the 1960s.... Of course, already in 1962 other works even more directly critical of logical empiricism had been published, including some appealing to the history of science. But Kuhn was the only theorist at the time to provide an alternative overall framework in which to investigate the nature of science." A similar viewpoint is found in the Introduction to Suppe (1977), where logical empiricism is characterized as "the Received View" to which more recent views (including Kuhn's) are opposed. See also Rorty (1979, pp. 59, 332–3).

3. For both of these quotations see Reisch (1991, pp. 266–7).

4. This philosophy of linguistic frameworks, including the sharp distinction between internal and external questions, is formulated most explicitly in Carnap (1950). The basic ideas go back to Carnap (1934).

5. For discussion and references see Reisch (1991, pp. 270–4).

6. For Carnap, the standard procedure of testing a scientific theory by the deduction of observational predictions fails, in the end, to be entirely governed by "established rules." For, as Carnap (1934, §82) explains, when faced with a conflict between theoretical predictions and observational results, we have three options open to us: reject the theoretical sentences from which the unsuccessful predictions are derived, reject the observational reports that conflict with the theory in question, or alter the logical rules of the language so that there is no longer an inconsistency between observation and theory. In the same section, Carnap explicitly links his viewpoint with the epistemological holism he associates with Duhem and Poincaré. This makes it especially clear, in particular, how far Carnap's philosophy is from traditional empiricist foundationalism.

7. These affinities between Carnap and Kuhn are discussed by several authors in addition to Reisch. See Friedman (1992a), Earman (1993) – which follows Reisch – and Friedman (1993).

8. Kuhn (1993, p. 313). Kuhn is here responding to the second two papers cited in note 7.

9. Carnap (1936) explicitly proposes *Wissenschaftslogik* as a replacement for all forms of traditional epistemology. See also Carnap (1934, §72): "The alleged peculiarly philosophical point of view, from which the objects of science are supposed to be considered, is abolished, just as the alleged peculiarly philosophical stratum of objects was already previously eliminated. Aside from the questions of the individual special sciences, the only questions that remain as genuinely scientific questions are those of the logical analysis of science – its sentences, concepts, theories, etc. We will call this complex of questions *Wissenschaftslogik*. . . . Taking the place of the inextricable tangle of problems that is known as philosophy is Wissenschaftslogik.*"

10. Again, one finds this picture in the three representatives of the conventional wisdom cited in note 2. Ayer (1936) is largely responsible for its initial formulation and promulgation. In general, this view of the background to logical empiricism is most frequently articulated, by both defenders and critics, within the Anglo-American philosophical tradition – including, for example, the sympathetic commentaries and criticisms of Nelson Goodman and W. V. Quine (see note 19).

11. Suppe (1977, pp. 6–15) notes the importance of the Marburg School within the scientific epistemology of the time, but he then goes on to associate the origins of logical empiricism exclusively with Machian positivism and other more empiricist tendencies of thought.

12. A good selection of Helmholtz's papers on geometry and scientific epistemology can be found in Cohen and Elkana (1977). For further discussion see Friedman (1997, 2000a).

13. Poincaré (1902, 1905, 1908) is the classical source of his scientific epistemology. For further discussion see Friedman (1996, 2000a).

14. For further discussion see Friedman (2002).

15. For further discussion see Friedman (1983, 2002).

16. Carnap retrospectively sums up his position as follows (1963, p. 12): "Knowledge of intuitive space I regarded at that time, under the influence of Kant and the neo-Kantians, especially Natorp and Cassirer, as based on 'pure intuition' and independent of contingent experience. But, in contrast to Kant, I limited the features of intuitive space grasped by pure intuition to certain topological properties; the metrical structure (in Kant's view, the Euclidean structure)...I regarded not as purely intuitive, but rather as empirical. Knowledge of physical space I already considered as entirely empirical, in agreement with empiricists like Helmholtz and Schlick." As we have seen, the "entirely empirical" in the last sentence is actually quite misleading – and signifies only that Carnap here follows "empiricism" in rejecting Kant's original conception of the fixed synthetic a priori character of the metric of physical space. For further discussion see Friedman (1995; 2000b, chapter 5).

17. See Reichenbach (1920, chapter 5).

18. See Reichenbach (1920, note 20), which refers to Cassirer (1921). (Similarly, Cassirer acknowledges Reichenbach's work in a prepublication note added in proof to his book.) The relationships among Schlick's, Carnap's, and Reichenbach's developing conceptions of the foundations of geometry are quite complex. In particular, following Schlick's insistence, both Carnap and Reichenbach came to drop all references to Kant and to characterize their views under the simple rubric of "empiricism" (compare note 16). For further discussion see Friedman (1994).

19. See, e.g., Goodman (1951, 1963) and Quine (1951, 1969).

20. For growing awareness of the more Kantian roots of the *Aufbau* see Haack (1977), Moulines (1985), Sauer (1985, 1989) – Sauer gives particular emphasis to the influence of the Marburg School – Friedman (1987, 1992b), and Richardson (1992, 1998). See also Friedman (2000b, chapter 5).

21. Cassirer refers, in this context, to the work of Richard Dedekind, Gottlob Frege, David Hilbert, and especially Bertrand Russell (1903).

22. For further discussion of Cassirer and the Marburg School see Friedman (2000b, chapters 3 and 6).

23. Carnap (1928, §75). For further discussion of this and other passages expressing Carnap's agreement with Cassirer and the Marburg School see the works of Sauer, Richardson, and myself cited in note 20.

24. Compare the description of his work as a synthesis of traditional empiricism and rationalism in the Preface to the second edition of Carnap (1928).

25. See Carnap (1928, §§100, 143).

26. This work, for Carnap and the logical empiricists, represented the definitive formulation of modern mathematical logic. Its theory of logical types went far beyond the theory of relations presented in Russell (1903), which alone was known to Cassirer (see note 21).

27. Carnap (1928, §179). Here Carnap also explains the corresponding divergence from the Marburg School: "According to the conception of the *Marburg School* [Carnap refers here to Natorp (1910)] the object is the eternal X, its determination is an incompleteable task. In opposition to this it is to be noted that finitely

many determinations suffice for the constitution of the object – and thus for its univocal description among the objects in general. Once such a description is set up the object is no longer an X, but rather something univocally determined – whose complete description then certainly still remains an incompleteable task."

28. As I indicated in note 9, Carnap's mature standpoint adopts *Wissenschaftslogik* as the substitute for all forms of epistemology, including the epistemology of the *Aufbau* – which, from Carnap's new standpoint, is still inappropriately committed to a basis in "private experience." For further discussion see Richardson (1996) and Friedman (1992b, §IV).

29. For further discussion of the relationship between Carnap's philosophy of linguistic frameworks and Reichenbach (1920) see Friedman (1994).

30. In particular, whereas the *Aufbau* deals only with the theory of types, *Logical Syntax* is responding to the so-called foundations crisis of the late 1920s involving logical systems differing essentially from the "logicist" system of Whitehead and Russell, such as the intuitionistic logic of Brouwer and the "formalism" of Hilbert. Carnap's conclusion is that, just as the earlier crisis in the foundations of geometry had been resolved through the insight that no particular geometry – whether Euclidean or non-Euclidean – is the true one, there is now similarly no question of a single true logic. For further discussion see Friedman (1999, chapter 9). Here especially see also Coffa (1991), which is a posthumous publication of Coffa's pioneering work on the history of logical positivism specifically oriented around the parallel between conventionalism in the foundations of geometry and Carnap's philosophy of linguistic frameworks.

31. Kuhn (1993, p. 331). (Kuhn is here responding to the last article cited in note 7.) There is a special irony in the circumstance that it is precisely the logical positivists' engagement with Einstein's theory of relativity that led, as we have seen, to the affinities between their conception and Kuhn's; for Kuhn (1970, chapter 9) appeals to Einstein's theory, in particular, to combat the supposedly naive empiricism of "early logical positivism" (compare note 1).

32. For discussion of this problem in its historical and philosophical context see Friedman (1998).

33. Kuhn (1970, p. 3). The passage concludes: "By implication, at least, these historical studies suggest the possibility of a new image of science. This essay aims to delineate that image by making explicit some of the new historiography's implications."

34. See Koyré (1978). Kuhn (1970, p. vi) also cites Meyerson (1930, first published in 1908), Metzger (1923, 1930), and Maier (1949).

35. Kuhn (1977, pp. 107–8). In the same pages Kuhn cites the work of E. A. Burtt and A. Lovejoy and refers to "the modern historiography of science" founded by "E. J. Dijksterhuis, Anneliese Maier, and especially Alexandre Koyré." (I am grateful to Alan Richardson for calling my attention to this passage.)

36. Maier's father was an influential Kantian philosopher of the time, and her first published work, her dissertation (1930), is a historical examination of a Kantian

topic culminating in a defense of her father's interpretation. See the Introduction to Sargent (1982), which is a useful selection from Maier's writings.

37. The concept of "mentality" is especially important in Metzger, and she derives it, in turn, from the work of Lucien Lévy-Bruhl on "primitive mentality." For a discussion of Metzger's historiography see Golinski (1987).

38. Thus Koyré, for example, while articulating his well-known interpretation of Galileo's "Platonism," explicitly criticizes Cassirer's analogous reading as being excessively Kantian. See Koyré (1978, note 123 on p. 223): "E. Cassirer, in his *Erkenntnisproblem*, vol. I, expresses the opinion that Galileo resurrected the Platonist ideal of scientific knowledge; from which follows, for Galileo (and Kepler), the necessity for mathematising nature.... Unfortunately (at least in our opinion) Cassirer turns Plato into Kant." In general, Koyré takes philosophical inspiration from his teacher Edmund Husserl, from Plato, and from Hegel, rather than from Kant.

39. Despite the disagreement mentioned in note 38, for example, Koyré (1978, p. 1) begins with these words: "Fortunately it is no longer necessary nowadays to insist on the interest of the historical study of science. It is no longer even necessary – after the magisterial work of those such as Duhem and Emile Meyerson, Cassirer and Brunschvicg – to insist on the *philosophical* interest and fruitfulness of this study." Meyerson (1930) – beginning in the second, 1912, edition – often refers to *Das Erkenntnisproblem*, as does Brunschvicg. Metzger, in turn, was substantially influenced by Meyerson and also by Brunschvicg (who was naturally much influenced by Meyerson as well). Indeed, virtually all the historians who initiated the study of modern science in the twentieth century, including especially Dijksterhuis and Burtt (compare note 35), drew significant inspiration from Cassirer's work.

40. In his recent historiographical study of the literature on the scientific revolution H. Floris Cohen acknowledges Cassirer's influence, of course, but he nonetheless contends (1994, note 175 on p. 543) that "only Burtt, Dijksterhuis, and Koyré were to elaborate such views [on the mathematization of nature] into detailed examinations of the birth of early modern science." This contention is gainsaid by the text of *Das Erkenntnisproblem* itself, however, which treats Kepler, Galileo, Descartes, Bacon, and Newton (along with Copernicus, Bruno, Leonardo, Gilbert, Gassendi, Hobbes, Boyle, and Huygens) in considerable detail.

41. See note 39. Meyerson enjoyed a close philosophical friendship with both Brunschvicg and Lévy-Bruhl, and his weekly intellectual salon was also attended by Metzger and Koyré.

42. See Meyerson (1930, pp. 388–9) (the quotation is from vol. 2 of *Das Erkenntnisproblem*). Compare also Meyerson's criticism of the "mathematical idealism" of the Marburg School on pp. 437–8 and his reference to both Cassirer (1910) and Natorp (1910) on p. 423.

43. See Cassirer (1910, chapter 7, pp. 323–5 of the translation). The passage continues: "But these ['functional orders and coordinations (*Ordnungen und Zuordnungen*)'] do not exclude the moments of difference and change but only

achieve determination in and with them. It is not manifoldness as such that is annulled [*aufgehoben*] but [we attain] only a manifold of another dimension: the mathematical manifold takes the place of the sensible manifold in scientific explanation. What thought requires is thus not the dissolution of diversity and change as such, but rather their mastery in virtue of the mathematical *continuity* of serial laws and serial forms."

44. See note 38. The passage quoted continues: "Thus, for him [Cassirer], Galileo's 'Platonism' is expressed by his giving priority to function and law over being and substance."

45. Koyré (1931, pp. 207–8). Koyré's argument against this view echoes Meyerson's argument in the passage cited in note 42: whatever scientific philosophers (or scientists themselves speaking philosophically) may claim about "proper" scientific method, science *in fact* proceeds by looking for underlying substantial causes.

46. This recognition, for Koyré, harmonizes with Plato's original insistence on the unbridgeable gulf between ideal mathematical forms and the empirical realities given by sense, and also with Hegel's emphasis on the essentially dialectical nature of time (compare note 38; Koyré [1931] likens Meyerson's method to Husserl's as well). Koyré's conception of the mathematization of nature is thus ultimately *Cartesian*, in that it takes as its ideal the reduction of all physics to pure geometry and thus to space – infinite and unchanging, uniform and homogeneous. And here Koyré again explicitly follows Meyerson, particularly where he asserts (1978, note 34 on p. 113) that "[s]pace is rational – at least in form – whereas time is dialectical." On Kant's conception, by contrast, empirically given nature – including, centrally, its temporal dimension – is necessarily (and perfectly accurately) describable by precise mathematical laws. For Kant, it is the great achievement of specifically *Newtonian* science to have attained a full mathematization of time parallel to the Euclidean mathematization of space (whereas, for Koyré, the Newtonian conception of force introduces an essentially irrational element into our understanding of nature).

47. See the passage from Cassirer (1910) cited in note 43. This section concludes with a characteristic statement of the (Marburg) genetic conception of knowledge: "[T]he inexhaustibility of the scientific task is no indication of its unsolvability in principle, but rather contains within itself the conditions and the stimulus for its ever more complete solution."

48. In the thought of Brunschvicg, despite his clear debts to Meyerson, we find a point of view more sympathetic to Marburg neo-Kantianism. Whereas Meyerson comes from chemistry, Brunschvicg comes from mathematics (Brunschvicg [1912] is a celebrated study of the history of mathematical thought); and Brunschvicg's divergence from Meyerson is clearly expressed in his discussion of "the duality of the principles of thermodynamics" in (1922, §168): here Brunschvicg criticizes Meyerson's conception of causality for failing to appreciate the Kantian discovery that both substance and causality express *relations* between phenomena and, more generally, for giving an excessively ontological interpretation of these categories. Moreover, although Metzger was a student of Meyerson's, she nevertheless disagrees with him on several significant

points – most notably, perhaps, in recognizing explicitly that "the demands of thought" are not rigidly fixed but rather depend on the given stage of science and the form of scientific mentality. See again Golinski (1987) and also Metzger (1937).

49. Kuhn (1970, pp. 101–2). Compare notes 1 and 31 for Kuhn and "early logical positivism."

50. See especially (1970, pp. 206–7), where Kuhn rejects all talk of convergence over time on the grounds that "[t]here is, I think, no theory-independent way to reconstruct phrases like 'really there'; the notion of a match between the ontology of a theory and its 'real' counterpart in nature now seems to me illusive in principle." He continues (now speaking "as a historian"): "I do not doubt, for example, that Newton's mechanics improves on Aristotle's and that Einstein's improves on Newton's as instruments for puzzle-solving. But I can see in their succession no coherent direction of ontological development." Once again, he simply fails to consider the question of purely mathematical development.

51. For a first approximation to such a consideration see Friedman (2001).

References

Ayer, Alfred Jules. 1936. *Language, Truth, and Logic*. London: Gollancz.

Brunschvicg, Léon. 1912. *Les étapes de la philosophie mathématique*. Paris: Alcan.

   1922. *L'expérience humaine et la causalité physique*. Paris: Alcan.

Carnap, Rudolf. 1922. *Der Raum*. Berlin: Reuther & Reichard.

   1928. *Der logische Aufbau der Welt*. Berlin: Weltkreis, 1928. 2nd ed. Hamburg: Meiner, 1961. Translated from the 2nd ed. as *The Logical Structure of the World*. Los Angeles: University of California Press, 1967.

   1934. *Logische Syntax der Sprache*. Wien: Springer. Translated as *The Logical Syntax of Language*. London: Kegan Paul, 1937.

   1936. "Von der Erkenntnistheorie zur Wissenschaftslogik." In *Actes du Congrès international de philosophie scientifique*, vol. 4. Paris: Hermann.

   1950. "Empiricism, Semantics, and Ontology." *Revue Internationale de Philosophie* 11: 20–40. Reprinted in *Meaning and Necessity*, 2nd ed. Chicago: University of Chicago Press, 1956.

   1963. "Intellectual Autobiography." In Schilpp (1963), pp. 3–43.

Cassirer, Ernst. 1906–7. *Das Erkenntnisproblem in der Philosophie und Wissenschaft der neueren Zeit*. 2 vols. Berlin: Bruno Cassirer.

   1910. *Substanzbegriff und Funktionsbegriff*. Berlin: Bruno Cassirer. Translated as *Substance and Function*. Chicago: Open Court, 1923.

   1921. *Zur Einsteinschen Relativitätstheorie*. Berlin: Bruno Cassirer. Translated as *Einstein's Theory of Relativity*. Chicago: Open Court, 1923.

Coffa, J. Alberto. 1991. *The Semantic Tradition from Kant to Carnap*. Cambridge: Cambridge University Press.

Cohen, H. Floris. 1994. *The Scientific Revolution*. Chicago: University of Chicago Press.

Cohen, Robert and Yehuda Elkana, eds. 1977. *Hermann von Helmholtz: Epistemological Writings*. Dordrecht: Reidel. Translation of P. Hertz and M. Schlick, eds. *Hermann v. Helmholtz: Schriften zur Erkenntnistheorie*. Berlin: Springer, 1921.

Earman, John. 1993. "Carnap, Kuhn, and the Philosophy of Scientific Methodology." In Horwich (1993), pp. 9–36.

Friedman, Michael. 1983. "Critical Notice: Moritz Schlick, Philosophical Papers." *Philosophy of Science* 50: 498–514. Reprinted (with a Postscript) in Friedman (1999), pp. 17–43.

    1987. "Carnap's *Aufbau* Reconsidered." *Noûs* 21: 521–45. Reprinted in Friedman (1999), pp. 89–113.

    1992a. "Philosophy and the Exact Sciences: Logical Positivism as a Case Study." In J. Earman, ed. *Inference, Explanation, and Other Frustrations*. Berkeley: University of California Press, pp. 84–98.

    1992b. "Epistemology in the *Aufbau*." *Synthese* 93: 15–57. Reprinted (with a Postscript) in Friedman (1999), pp. 114–62.

    1993. "Remarks on the History of Science and the History of Philosophy." In Horwich (1993), pp. 37–54.

    1994. "Geometry, Convention, and the Relativized a Priori." In W. Salmon and G. Wolters, eds. *Logic, Language, and the Structure of Scientific Theories*. Pittsburgh: University of Pittsburgh Press, pp. 21–34. Reprinted in Friedman (1999), pp. 59–70.

    1995. "Carnap and Weyl on the Foundations of Geometry and Relativity Theory." *Erkenntnis* 42: 247–60. Reprinted in Friedman (1999), pp. 44–58.

    1996. "Poincaré's Conventionalism and the Logical Positivists." In J.-L. Greffe, G. Heinzmann, and K. Lorenz, eds. *Henri Poincaré: Science and Philosophy*. Berlin and Paris: Akademie Verlag, 1996, pp. 299–314. Reprinted in Friedman (1999), pp. 71–86.

    1997. "Helmholtz's *Zeichentheorie* and Schlick's *Allgemeine Erkenntnislehre*." *Philosophical Topics* 25: 19–50.

    1998. "On the Sociology of Scientific Knowedge and Its Philosophical Agenda." *Studies in History and Philosophy of Science* 29: 239–71.

    1999. *Reconsidering Logical Positivism*. Cambridge: Cambridge University Press.

    2000a. "Geometry, Construction, and Intuition in Kant and His Successors." In: G. Sher and R. Tieszen, eds. *Between Logic and Intuition: Essays in Honor of Charles Parsons*. Cambridge: Cambridge University Press, pp. 186–211.

    2000b. *A Parting of the Ways: Carnap, Cassirer, and Heidegger*. Chicago: Open Court.

    2001. *Dynamics of Reason*. Stanford: CSLI Publications.

    2002. "Geometry as a Branch of Physics: Background and Context for Einstein's 'Geometry and Experience'." In D. Malament, ed. *Reading Natural Philosophy: Essays in Honor of Howard Stein*. Chicago: Open Court.

Giere, Ronald. 1988. *Explaining Science*. Chicago: University of Chicago Press.

Golinski, Jan. 1987. "Hélène Metzger and the Interpretation of Seventeenth Century Chemistry." *History of Science* 25: 85–97.

Goodman, Nelson. 1951. *The Structure of Appearance*. Cambridge, MA: Harvard University Press.

1963. "The Significance of *Der logische Aufbau der Welt*." In Schilpp (1963), pp. 545–58.

Haack, Susan. 1977. "Carnap's *Aufbau*: Some Kantian Reflexions." *Ratio* 19: 170–6.

Halsted, George, ed. 1913. *The Foundations of Science*. Lancaster: Science Press.

Horwich, Paul, ed. 1993. *World Changes: Thomas Kuhn and the Nature of Science*. Cambridge, MA: MIT Press.

Koyré, Alexandre. 1931. "Die Philosophie Emile Meyersons." *Deutsch-Französische Rundschau* 4: 197–217.

1978. *Galileo Studies*. Atlantic Highlands, NJ: Humanities Press. Translation of *Etudes Galiléenes*. 3 vols. Paris: Hermann, 1939.

Kuhn, Thomas. 1968. "The History of Science." In *International Encyclopedia of the Social Sciences*. New York: Crowell Collier and Macmillan. Reprinted in Kuhn (1977), pp. 105–26.

1970. *The Structure of Scientific Revolutions*, 2nd ed. Chicago: University of Chicago Press. Original edition published in 1962.

1977. *The Essential Tension*. Chicago: University of Chicago Press.

1984. "Revisiting Planck." *Historical Studies in the Physical Studies* 14: 231–52. Reprinted as Afterward in Kuhn (1987), pp. 349–70.

1987. *Black-Body Theory and the Quantum Discontinuity, 1894–1912*. 2nd (paperback) ed. Chicago: University of Chicago Press.

1993. "Afterwords." In Horwich (1993), pp. 311–41.

Maier, Anneliese. 1930. *Kants Qualitätskategorien*. Berlin: Metzner.

1949. *Die Vorläufer Galileis im 14. Jahrhundert*. Rome: Edizioni di Storia e Letteratura.

Metzger, Hélène. 1923. *Les doctrines chimique en France du début du XVIIe à la fin du XVIIIe siècle*. Paris: Les Presses Universitaires de France.

1930. *Newton, Stahl, Boerhaave et la doctrine chimique*. Paris: Alcan.

1937. "La méthode philosophique dans l'histoire des science." *Archeion* 19: 204–16.

Meyerson, Émile. 1930. *Identity and Reality*. London: Allen & Unwin. Translation from 3rd ed., 1926 (identical to 2nd ed., 1912), of *Identité et réalité*. Paris: Alcan, 1908.

Moulines, C. Ulises. 1985. "Hintergründe der Erkenntnistheorie des frühen Carnap." *Grazer Philosophische Studien* 23: 1–18.

Natorp, Paul. 1910. *Die logischen Grundlagen der exakten Wissenschaften*. Leipzig: Teubner.

Poincaré, Henri. 1902. *La Science et l'Hypothèse*. Paris: Flammarion. Translated as *Science and Hypothesis*. In Halsted (1913), pp. 27–197.

1905. *La Valeur de la Science*. Paris: Flammarion. Translated as *The Value of Science*. In Halsted (1913), pp. 205–355.

1908. *Science et Méthode*. Paris: Flammarion. Translated as *Science and Method*. In Halsted (1913), pp. 359–546.

Quine, Willard van Orman. 1951. "Two Dogmas of Empiricism." *Philosophical Review* 60: 20–43. Reprinted in *From a Logical Point of View*. New York: Harper, 1963, pp. 20–46.

1969. "Epistemology Naturalized." In *Ontological Relativity and Other Essays*. New York: Columbia University Press, pp. 69–90.

Reichenbach, Hans. 1920. *Relativitätstheorie und Erkenntnis Apriori*. Berlin: Springer. Translated as *The Theory of Relativity and A Priori Knowledge*. Los Angeles: University of California Press, 1965.

Reisch, George. 1991. "Did Kuhn Kill Logical Empiricism?" *Philosophy of Science* 58: 264–77.

Richardson, Alan. 1992. "Logical Idealism and Carnap's Construction of the World." *Synthese* 93: 59–92.

1996. "From Epistemology to the Logic of Science." In R. Giere and A. Richardson, eds. *Origins of Logical Empiricism*. Minneapolis: University of Minnesota Press, pp. 309–32.

1998. *Carnap's Construction of the World*. Cambridge: Cambridge University Press.

Rorty, Richard. 1979. *Philosophy and the Mirror of Nature*. Princeton: Princeton University Press.

Russell, Bertrand. 1903. *The Principles of Mathematics*. London: Allen & Unwin.

Sargent, Steven, ed. 1982. *On the Threshold of Exact Science*. Philadelphia: University of Pennsylvania Press.

Sauer, Werner. 1985. "Carnaps 'Aufbau' in Kantianischer Sicht." *Grazer Philosophische Studien* 23: 19–35.

1989. "On the Kantian Background of Neopositivism." *Topoi* 8: 111–19.

Schilpp, Paul Arthur, ed. 1963. *The Philosophy of Rudolf Carnap*. La Salle, IL: Open Court.

Schlick, Moritz. 1917. *Raum und Zeit in der gegenwärtigen Physik*. Berlin: Springer. 2nd ed., 1919. 3rd ed., 1920. 4th ed., 1922. Translated from the 3rd ed. as *Space and Time in Contemporary Physics*. Oxford: Oxford University Press, 1920. Expanded to include changes in the 4th ed. in H. Mulder and B. van de Velde-Schlick, *Moritz Schlick: Philosophical Papers*, vol. 1. Dordrecht: Reidel, 1978.

Suppe, Frederick. 1977. *The Structure of Scientific Theories*. 2nd ed. Urbana: University of Illinois Press.

Whitehead, Alfred and Bertrand Russell. 1910–13. *Principia Mathematica*. 3 vols. Cambridge: Cambridge University Press.

2 | Thomas Kuhn and French Philosophy of Science

GARY GUTTING

There is very little to be said about direct influences of twentieth-century French or German philosophers on Kuhn's work (or vice versa, for that matter). He did strongly appreciate Émile Meyerson's approach to the history of science but expressed distaste for Meyerson's idealism; and, as we will see, he had a brief but unproductive encounter with Gaston Bachelard. Beyond this, Kuhn seems to have had very little direct contact with European philosophy.[1]

It is, of course, possible to plot various parallels between Kuhn's philosophy of science and the general trend of European thought from Heidegger through Derrida. Post-Kuhnianism and postmodernism oppose a similar range of Cartesian theses and pose the standard skeptical threats of a radically historicized reason. But beyond the broadest generalizations, there is little substantial overlap between Kuhn's philosophical interests and inclinations and those of, say, Heidegger and Derrida.

The one movement in twentieth-century European thought that has substantive affinities with Kuhn's work is the French tradition of philosophy of science. This begins with the classic writings of Poincaré, Duhem, and Meyerson but takes on its distinctive character (and its strongest similarities to Kuhn) in the work of Léon Brunschvicg, Gaston Bachelard, and Georges Canguilhem. Kuhn himself, unfortunately, had only a glancing contact with this tradition and no serious understanding of it. The main contact came through Koyré, who had urged him to meet Bachelard and provided a letter of introduction. The upshot, as Kuhn tells the story, was more a comedy of errors than a meeting of great minds. To begin with, Kuhn had the idea – no doubt vaguely based on information about Bachelard's interest in the literary imagination – that he was an expert on English and American literature and so would surely speak English. "I assumed he would greet me and be willing to talk in English." But, although Kuhn opened with "My French is bad, may we talk English?," the "large burly man in his undershirt [who] came to the door . . . made me talk French."

We can well understand that, as Kuhn puts it, "this all didn't last very long."[2]

Kuhn says he later read a bit more of Bachelard and thought he was on to something but that his thought was too constrained by preset categories: "he had categories, and methodological categories, and moved the thing up an escalator too systematically for me." Nonetheless, Kuhn concluded, "there were things to be discovered there that I did not discover, or did not discover in that way."[3] Here, at least, Kuhn's judgment of Bachelard was correct. There are substantial similarities in the approach and problems of Kuhn's philosophy of science and those of Bachelard's tradition, and these similarities can sustain a mutually fruitful dialogue, even though the exigencies of history prevented it from actually occurring between Kuhn and Bachelard.

In fact, the exigencies of history had much wider effects. Outside of France, after the rise of logical positivism, philosophy of science took a formal, nonhistorical turn for which the French tradition was uncongenial. The French, in turn, were disdainful of what they saw as the naive epistemological foundationalism of logical positivism and its insensitivity to the actual practice of science. Later, when the historicist reaction against positivism took hold, English-speaking philosophers of science rediscovered major themes articulated long before by the French tradition, such as the theory-ladenness of observation and the irreducibility of scientific rationality to logic. But by then the two approaches were too far apart for fruitful interaction. The French could hardly share the excitement of what they rightly saw as old news; and the British and Americans had scant interest in discussions that, if they read them at all, lacked the analytic clarity and rigor to which they were accustomed and that ignored logical positivist philosophy of science as hardly worth refuting. When George Steiner chided Foucault for (in *Les mots et les chose*) not mentioning Kuhn, Foucault responded that he had instead cited a thinker who had anticipated Kuhn: Georges Canguilhem.[4]

As a result, the dialogue in which I am here interested must be constructed, not reported. But the construction, as I hope to show, is not without interest. It will, in particular, shed useful philosophical light on three topics of philosophy of science that have endured in both the Francophone and the Anglophone worlds: scientific progress, scientific rationality, and scientific realism. Part I sketches some of the main lines of French philosophy of science in Brunschvicg, Bachelard, and Canguilhem; Part II reflects on the issues of progress, rationality, and realism through a comparison of the French tradition and Kuhn.

PART I: FRENCH PHILOSOPHY OF SCIENCE

Léon Brunschvicg

Brunschvicg's philosophy is idealistic in that it is based on a thorough rejection of the thing-in-itself. He finds no sense in the idea that we could
have any knowledge of something as it exists entirely apart from its relation to our knowledge. "Knowledge is not an accident that is added on
from outside a being" but rather "constitutes a world that is the world for
us," for "a thing outside of knowledge would be by definition inaccessible,
indeterminable, that is to say equivalent for us to nothing."[5]

Whereas natural sciences are concerned with the objects of thought,
philosophy is concerned with thought itself, the intellectual activity through
which objects are presented to (constituted for) us. It may seem that characterizing the activity of thought as "intellectual" begs important questions about its nature, but Brunschvicg is prepared to argue that thinking
is identical to judging, the quintessential intellectual activity. Given that to
think is to judge, Brunschvicg turns to the question of what a judgment is.
He begins by noting that, in some cases, judgment seems to be a matter
of our awareness of the internal connection between two ideas. When,
for example, I judge that *the sum of the interior angles of a triangle is two
right angles*, the "is" of my judgment expresses the necessary intellectual
connection between the two terms connected. Such a judgment expresses
the unity that the mind finds between two notions that are only verbally
separated and are in themselves mutually implicated. Here Brunschvicg will
say that judgment takes the "form of interiority," since its "is" expresses the
internal unity of ideas. In other cases, however, my judgment seems to
have nothing to do with the internal connections of ideas but rather expresses the brute fact that something exists in reality, that, for example,
"this thing exists here and now." In such a case, "is" does not express a
unity required by the mind's understanding but a "shock of reality" that
the mind must simply accept without understanding: "it is the impossibility of the intellect's penetrating to the interior of what it represents in
order to analyze and understand it that obliges [the intellect] to stop short
[*s'arrêter*], to posit being, that is, to recognize the fact that *that is*."[6] Here
judgment takes the "form of exteriority," its "is" expressing not the internal
necessity of intelligible thought but the undeniable givenness of an external
reality.

Brunschvicg's acceptance of this givenness does not mean that he is
abandoning idealism. Like Fichte (from whom he takes the expression

"shock of reality"), he is prepared to argue that the very exteriority of external objects is just the way they are given to (constituted by) the mind. But there nonetheless remains an unbridgeable epistemological gap between what can be known simply through the mind's internal reflection and what requires the jolt of external experience.

Brunschvicg emphasizes that pure interiority and pure exteriority are merely ideal forms, limiting cases of judgment, which in reality is always a mixture of the two. This means that our effort to discover the truth of reality cannot be a matter, as some idealists have thought, of the mind's reflectively intuiting or deducing its own intellectual content. Such an enterprise will yield only fragile abstractions that cannot sustain the shock of reality. At the same time, Brunschvicg, of course, rejects the empiricist error of believing that the truth lies simply in what the mind passively receives from outside. Truth and reality are rather expressed in "mixed judgments" through which what has been given so far in experience is interpreted through the best intellectual framework so far developed by the mind. Since both the most precise experience and the most accurate interpretations of it are achieved by science, it follows that the philosophical pursuit of truth and reality must take the form of historical reflection on science's development of increasingly adequate judgments. The truth is derived from reflection on the life of the mind, but the mind itself is encountered as a positive reality in human history of science, not as an esoteric ahistorical object of philosophical insight.

Brunschvicg's basic views on judgment, truth, and reality provide the guiding thread for the three massive historical studies that constitute the bulk of his life's work. The first was *Les étapes de la pensée mathématique* (1912), which follows the entire history of mathematics and of mathematically inspired philosophy from the ancient Greeks through twentieth-century logicism and intuitionism. Brunschvicg rejects the idea that mathematics is a pure study of merely ideal relations and instead views it as essentially tied to our efforts to understand the world. His history shows how novel mathematical ideas emerge from the mind's creative efforts to make sense of our experience of the world: "nature puts the mind to the test; the mind responds by constituting mathematical science."[7] At the same time, Brunschvicg follows the work of philosophers – particularly Plato, Descartes, Leibniz, and Kant – inspired by the mathematical achievements of their times. He acknowledges the resulting advances in philosophical understanding but denounces the philosophical systems that present those results as the final word on the nature of reality, arguing that the subsequent history of mathematics always creates new ideas that undermine the old systems. The only philosophical conclusion supported by the history of mathematics is Brunschvicg's own antisystematic view of the mind responding to ever new and unpredictable "shocks" of nature with its own new and unpredictable interpretations.

A second volume, *L'expérience humaine et la causalité physique* (1922), develops the same general viewpoint, this time through a study of scientific and philosophical conceptions of causality. It concludes that history undermines the pretensions of both the philosophies of nature of absolute idealists such as Hegel and the philosophies of science of other modern philosophers such as Descartes and Kant, but supports the more modest claims of Brunschvicg's "philosophy of thought" (*philosophie de pensée*). As he uses the term, a philosophy of nature offers a view of the natural world, derived entirely from philosophical insight and reasoning, that claims to be independent of and superior to the empirical constructions of natural scientists. Whereas both ancient and early modern philosophers saw an intimate connection, if not identity, between philosophical and scientific efforts to understand the world, the philosophy of nature, first fully developed by German idealists of the early nineteenth century, claimed to be able to "achieve, on its own, through original procedures, the system of things that scientists have not been able to achieve" with their mathematical and experimental methods. Brunschvicg rejects this project as "a chimera," refuted by its obvious inconsistency with scientific truths and explained by the human desire for "dogmatic speculation that seeks simple and definitive systems."[8]

By contrast, a philosophy of science quite properly does not seek "truths beyond the plane of scientific verification; it limits the horizon of human knowledge [*connaissance*] to the results furnished by science [*savoir scientifique*]" (EH, 546). Such philosophies – especially in the form of Kant's critique or Comte's positivism – effectively oppose systems of dogmatic metaphysics. But they go wrong in thinking that, from the de facto science of their time, they can extract final truths that must define the framework of all subsequent science. Brunschvicg notes how often, during the nineteenth century, developments in pure mathematics – and even more in mechanics and physics – "have blithely ignored [*jouées comme à plaisir*] the alleged limits imposed on them in the name of [Kantian] criticism or of positivism."[9] (In this regard, Brunschvicg finds Einstein's general theory of relativity particularly revolutionary.)

Brunschvicg's own "philosophy of thought" balances the claim that only science can provide the definitive account of reality with a realization that the content of its account cannot be extracted from the science of any given

time. What is required instead is historical reflection on the full sweep of
science as it has developed over the last 2,500 years: "science considered
apart from its history [*devenir*] is an abstraction." The philosophy of thought
hopes to show that this history is not a mere "aggregate of disparate and
diverging opinions." Its project is to employ a "total knowledge of the curve
followed [by science] up to now . . . to project the light of a new reflection
onto the previous phases of thought and . . . in particular to clarify the
relative position of the present." The result will be "a philosophy of human
history" that will "define the direction [*sens*] of the drama in which humanity has found itself engaged since it first became aware of its contact with
things."[10]

Gaston Bachelard

Bachelard's work, with its deep roots in detailed knowledge of the history and current practice of science, immediately associates him with the
tradition of Poincaré, Meyerson, and Boutroux. But his basic view of the
relation of science and philosophy derives most directly from Brunschvicg,
who (along with Abel Rey) directed his doctoral work. Like Brunschvicg,
Bachelard sees philosophy as having to work out an understanding of reason by reflection on the historical development of science; and, again like
Brunschvicg, his work is based on case studies in the history of mathematics and the physical sciences.[11] On the other hand, Bachelard emphasizes
far more than Brunschvicg the role of discontinuity in the development of
science and at least tries to avoid a wholehearted endorsement of idealism
over realism.

Bachelard's picture of scientific development centers on his notion of
"epistemological break" (*coupure épistémologique*). Science requires, first of
all, a break from our common sense experiences and beliefs, since it places
everyday objects under new concepts and shows them to possess properties not revealed by ordinary sense perception (or even in contradiction
to sense perception, as when what seem to be intrinsic qualities, such as
color, are reinterpreted as relations to sense organs). But scientific progress
also requires breaks from previous scientific conceptions, which, as much
as common sense, can become obstacles to our attaining scientific truth.
Thus, the viewpoint of Newtonian mechanics became, in the twentieth
century, a major obstacle to Einstein's formulation of an adequate account
of space, time, and gravitation. Breaking with the Newtonian view initiated a "new scientific spirit" that involved not only new conceptions of the
physical world but also new criteria of scientific methodology.[12] (Bachelard's

treatment of this subject precedes Thomas Kuhn's treatment of "scientific revolutions" by more than thirty years.)

Since for Bachelard philosophical conceptions of knowledge and reality are, quite properly, derivative from the best science of their time, epistemological breaks in scientific thought require corresponding revolutions in philosophy. Much of his work is devoted to developing new philosophical views to replace those "outdated" by the progress of science. He proposes, for example, a "non-Cartesian epistemology" (a notion meant to parallel "non-Euclidean geometry"), based on a rejection of Descartes's (and many subsequent philosophers') foundationalist privileging of the "givens" of immediate experience. This epistemology will, of course, also be "non-Kantian" in its denial of the eternal validity of categories that in fact are contingent expressions of Newtonian science. Bachelard further suggests the need for a "psychoanalysis of knowledge" that will expose the unconscious role that outdated common sense and scientific concepts play in our thinking.[13]

Bachelard's insistence on breaks and discontinuity might seem to reject Brunschvicg's view of science as an essentially progressive enterprise. Bachelard, however, maintains that progress does not require continuity. Even though there are sharp conceptual and methodological breaks from one scientific worldview to another, we are still justified in speaking of progress because some specific achievements of past science are preserved as special cases within later theories. Once again, Bachelard invokes the analogy with non-Euclidean geometry, which, for example, denies the Euclidean claim that all triangles have 180 degrees as the sum of their interior angles while admitting a special class of triangles ("Euclidean triangles") for which this is true. In the same way, concepts such as specific heat (developed by Black in terms of the now superseded caloric theory) and mass (as understood by Newton) have been reformulated in the context of later theories.

There is deeper tension between Bachelard and Brunschvicg on the issue of idealism. Bachelard does criticize a position he calls "realism," characterized as believing "in the prolix richness of the individual sensation and in the systematic impoverishment of abstractive thought."[14] Realism in this sense asserts the epistemic and metaphysical primacy of ordinary sense objects over what it regards as abstract accounts in terms of the theoretical entities of science. Bachelard's critique of realism is in effect an assertion of the ontological primacy of theoretical entities as concrete realities. To this extent, it amounts to a defense of what analytic philosophers of science nowadays call "scientific realism."

Bachelard does not, however, understand this scientific realism as implying a traditional metaphysical realism, which asserts that the objects of our knowledge are entirely mind-independent. He maintains a "rationalism" that emphasizes both the active role of the mind in the construction of the scientific concepts with which we describe reality and the richness and specificity of these concepts in contrast to the vagueness and generality of sensations. At the same time, he tries to stay clear of an idealism that would see the world as constituted by pure thought. Truth is not a matter of the mind's creating or constituting the world. It is, rather, the result of the mind's "revision" (*rectification*) by scientific concepts of a world that is already there. Bachelard says, accordingly, that his rationalism is "applied"; that is, the mind never produces its objects ex nihilo but rather applies its concepts to pregiven objects. However, he also emphasizes that objects are not "pregiven" in any absolute sense but are the results of previous applications of concepts. Later, we will discuss the viability of this effort to forge a path between realism and idealism.

Whatever its relation to realism and idealism, Bachelard's applied rationalism also introduces the crucial idea that scientific instrumentation has a central role in the constitution of the physical world. Instruments are, he says, "theories materialized," and a concept is truly scientific only to the extent that it receives concrete reality through a "technique of realization."[15] Husserl's phenomenology describes how the mind constitutes the objects of everyday experience, but we also require a "phenomeno-technics" that will describe the constitution of scientific objects by instrumental technology.

Georges Canguilhem

Although Georges Canguilhem starts from an essentially Bachelardian view of science, the foci of his work are different from Bachelard's: philosophical history rather than historical philosophizing, the biological and medical sciences rather than physics and chemistry. Further, his results suggest a number of important modifications in Bachelard's position.

Canguilhem's most important methodological contribution is his distinction between concepts and theories. In much twentieth-century philosophy of science, concepts are functions of theories, deriving their meaning from the roles they play in theoretical accounts of phenomena. Newtonian and Einsteinian mass, for example, are regarded as fundamentally different concepts because they are embedded in fundamentally different physical theories. This subordination of concept to theory derives from the view that the interpretation of phenomena (that is, their subsumption under a given set of concepts) is a matter of explaining them on the basis of a particular theoretical framework. For Canguilhem, by contrast, there is a crucial distinction between the interpretation of phenomena (via concepts) and their theoretical explanation. According to him, a given set of concepts provides the preliminary descriptions of a phenomenon that allow the formulation of questions about how to explain it. Different theories (all, however, formulated in terms of the same set of basic concepts) will provide competing answers to these questions. Galileo, for example, introduced a new conception of the motion of falling bodies to replace the Aristotelian conception. Galileo, Descartes, and Newton all employed this new conception in their description of the motion of falling bodies and in the theories they developed to explain this motion. Although the basic concept of motion was the same, the explanatory theories were very different. This shows, according to Canguilhem, the "theoretical polyvalence" of concepts: their ability to function in the context of widely differing theories. His own historical studies (for example, of reflex movement) are typically histories of concepts that persist through a series of theoretical formulations.

Taken seriously, Canguilhem's emphasis on the history of concepts as opposed to the history of theories requires important modifications in Bachelard's view of science. Epistemological breaks, for example, must be construed as due to conceptual rather than theoretical innovation. Since successful conceptualizations tend to reappear in even quite diverse theories, epistemological breaks are, for Canguilhem, less frequent and, in many cases, less radical than Bachelard had suggested. The priority of concepts also requires us to rethink the notion of an epistemological obstacle. The same piece of scientific work may be an obstacle in terms of the theoretical context in which it is formulated and a creative breakthrough in terms of some of its conceptual content. Thus, Joseph Black, the eighteenth-century chemist, even though he worked in the now outdated context of phlogiston theory, introduced the enduring concept of specific heat. The notion of an epistemological obstacle is more ambivalent than Bachelard suggests. Canguilhem makes particularly effective use of this ambivalence in his discussion of vitalism, so often abused as an enemy of progress in biology. Canguilhem admits that vitalistic theories have generally impeded the development of more adequate mechanistic accounts, but he maintains that the concept of vitalism, through its insistence on the uniqueness of biological phenomena, has served as a valuable protection against unfortunate reductionist tendencies of mechanistic theories.

Canguilhem's refinement of the notions of epistemological breaks and obstacles also suggests a weakening of Bachelard's sharp distinction between science and nonscience. Science is what overcomes epistemological obstacles and effects epistemological breaks. To the extent that the notions of obstacle and break have become ambivalent, so has the notion of science. As a result, Canguilhem is reluctant to say more than that, in a given context, a given idea or approach is "more scientific" than another (e.g., more fully integrated into current experimental procedures). Further developing this line of thought, Canguilhem (influenced here by his students, Althusser and Foucault) introduced the notion of "scientific ideology" as an intermediary between science and nonscience.[16]

A scientific ideology (Herbert Spencer's philosophy of evolution is a good example) is scientific in the sense that it models itself on a successful scientific theory. It is ideological, however, because it makes claims about the world that go beyond what the science contemporary with it is able to establish; it has, in other words, pretensions that are not scientifically grounded. Such pretensions may very well function as obstacles to the development of science. But Canguilhem also sees a positive role for scientific ideologies: They provide an essential, if not entirely responsible, dimension of intellectual adventure, without which many scientific advances would not occur. Scientific ideologies are a prime example of the ambivalence of epistemological obstacles.

Like other antifoundational philosophers of science, Canguilhem pays particular attention to the problem of rationality and objectivity. If there are no Cartesian certainties grounding science, if its development is a contingent historical process, what guarantee do we have that it is a reliable source of truths about the world? Bachelard tries to ground the objectivity of science through social norms. Contrary to Descartes, he holds that objectivity is not found in the individual self's intuitions (which will always remain obstacles to scientific progress) but in a move to considerations that convince not just a given individual but all rational minds. This move, which Bachelard characterizes as from the isolated *cogito* (I think) to the social *cogitamus* (we think), takes us, he maintains, from the subjectivity of the merely psychological to the objectivity of the epistemological.

Canguilhem offers a much more extensive treatment of norms, rooted in his analysis of biological norms.[17] He notes that, whereas modern physics has rejected any distinction between normal and pathological states of its entities, biological systems (organisms) require a distinction between states that enhance their functioning and those that impede it – in other words, a distinction between health and disease. However, Canguilhem maintains, we cannot define health as simply life in accord with the relevant biological norms. In any state, even one that is clearly pathological, there will be norms specifying the proper functioning of the organism in that state. (For example, a person who has lost a kidney is in a pathological state, even though the norms for proper functioning in this state are the same as for someone with both kidneys.) The pathological must, accordingly, be understood rather as a reduction in the range of circumstances in which an organism can function properly. Correspondingly, health is a state in which an organism is not only able to survive in its current circumstances but is capable of surviving in a significant range of varying circumstances.

Canguilhem emphasizes that, according to his account, biological norms are not objective in any scientific sense. Physiology can describe the states that we call "normal" or "pathological," but their normative status as such derives not from the physiological description but from the meaning of those states for the organism. Put another way, biological norms are subjective in the sense that they are constituted by the organism itself. On the other hand, this constitution is not a matter of individual idiosyncrasy but corresponds to the essential nature of the organism in question. Biological norms are not objective in the sense of being derived from value-neutral scientific inquiry, but they are rooted in the biological reality of the organisms that they regulate.

Turning to the question of social norms, such as those Bachelard sees as governing scientific practice, Canguilhem notes that there are important ways in which societies are similar to organisms and that social norms can have the same sort of necessary force that biological norms do. The biological analogy works, however, only for so-called traditional societies, where there is a set of norms that defines, once and for all, the essential nature and purpose of the society. Modern societies have no such "intrinsic finality," since the question of what should be their fundamental direction is contested in principle. A distinguishing feature of a modern society such as ours is dissent regarding basic norms. Canguilhem does not conclude, however, that a consensus, no matter how formed, would legitimately establish norms in a modern society. He criticizes, for example, Kuhn's account of scientific norms because, in his view, it derives them from a contingent, merely psychological agreement that has no genuine regulative force. Canguilhem makes a similar criticism of Bachelard, who, he suggests, poses but does not solve the problem of finding a middle ground between grounding scientific norms in the illusion of Cartesian foundations and reducing them to the merely descriptive realm of empirical psychology. Canguilhem himself is never entirely clear about just how to solve this problem, but, as we shall see, his emphasis on norms provides the key to a resolution of the difficulty.

PART II: PROGRESS, ONTOLOGY, AND RATIONALITY

Like the French thinkers we have just been discussing, Kuhn sees science as an essentially historical process that involves fundamental discontinuities ("revolutions") that raise serious questions about its linear progress (and, correspondingly, ontological significance) and rationality.

The obvious basis for claims of scientific progress is that later theories are typically closer to the truth than earlier ones. Scientific progress is problematic for Kuhn because he sees no plausible way of judging that a given scientific paradigm is true (or truer than another). There are two sources in Kuhn's account of science for this distrust of truth. First, he sees competing paradigms as assigning different meanings to key scientific terms, so that, for example, Newtonian and Einsteinian statements about mass are only apparently in conflict with one another and cannot be said to compete as assertions of truth. (This is one aspect of what Kuhn calls "incommensurability.") Second, Kuhn thinks there is no way around the "vexing problems" of correspondence between thought and reality that he sees implied by the very notion of truth. "There is, I think, no theory-independent way to reconstruct phrases like 'really there'; the notion of a match between the ontology of a theory and its 'real' counterpart now seems to me illusive in principle."[18] Unable to appeal to truth, Kuhn appeals to puzzle-solving: the ability of a new paradigm to provide answers to questions (how to do certain calculations, how to explain certain experiments, etc.) to which previous paradigms were not able to respond.

But what puzzles require solving and what counts as a solution to them is itself a matter of dispute among rival paradigms. Galileo could point to the superiority of his mechanics for the mathematical calculation of the rates at which heavy bodies fall to earth, but Aristotelians could see such calculation as marginal to the central issue, entirely ignored by Galileo, of explaining *why* heavy bodies fall to earth. Also, even given agreement on the set of problems and the criteria of their solution, there are intractable difficulties in determining the relative puzzle-solving power of rival paradigms. There seems to be no way of rationally counting the number of puzzles a paradigm solves, and, even if there were, there would remain the difficulty of judging whether some puzzles are more important to solve than others.

All such problems would disappear if we could find a way around Kuhn's difficulties with comparing rival paradigms in terms of their truth. Here the French tradition provides a very helpful perspective. Whereas Kuhn sees the discontinuities of scientific development – focused on the fact of incommensurability – as posing an insuperable obstacle to progress toward truth, Bachelard suggests that such progress is compatible with discontinuity. This is because some scientific achievements have a perennial status: "One may smile at the dogmatism of a rationalist philosopher who writes 'forever' regarding a scholastic truth. But there are concepts so indispensable in scientific culture that we cannot conceive being led to abandon them."[19] This does not mean that the concepts in question are not altered as science progresses. But it does mean that a condition on the progress of science is that the concept – and key truths expressed in terms of it – be reformulated so as to be preserved in subsequent accounts. So, for example, Black's discovery of specific heat, although initially formulated in terms of phlogiston theory, has reappeared in one guise or another in Newtonian and quantum accounts of heat.

Bachelard's approach is reinforced by Canguilhem's distinction between concept and theory. Kuhn sees the meanings of terms in rival paradigms as incommensurable because he thinks concepts vary with the use made of them in theoretical formulations. But Canguilhem shows that the same concept can occur in quite different theoretical contexts; for example, the concept of a reflex action in an organism was first introduced by Thomas Willis in the context of a vitalistic theory based on traditional ideas of the animal soul. Later, however, this same concept was employed in the mechanistic theories of Descartes and his followers. Concepts bridge the discontinuity between successive paradigms and allow us to speak of truths persisting from theory to theory and of progress in the sense of the increase of persisting truths over time.

This Bachelard–Canguilhem picture of scientific progress is not the naive positivist one of a linear accumulation of truths within a single conceptual framework that defines an unchanging "scientific view" of the world. As in Kuhn's account, the overall conception at one time may well be rejected later as erroneous. The history of science is a history of error as well as of truth. Progress occurs nonetheless because each successive scientific standpoint (corresponding to a Kuhnian paradigm) represents a more general perspective from which previous perspectives can be assessed and, to the extent that they remain valid, be incorporated in the current formulation.

There remains Kuhn's second reason for distrusting the idea of truth: its apparent connection with an untenable notion of correspondence. Here the French tradition, at least in Brunschvicg, also offers a straightforward solution: reject the realism of the correspondence theory of truth in favor of idealism. Such a response has to have a certain resonance for Kuhn, whose analysis of scientific development leads to the idea that, after a scientific revolution, scientists "live in a different world." As Paul Hoyningen-Huene makes particularly clear, Kuhn is thereby committed to a view of the scientific mind as somehow constituting the phenomenal world.[20] Kuhn, however, like most Anglophone philosophers of science, regards idealism as a threat rather than a refuge and is at pains to reconcile his view with a core of realism about scientific theories. Similarly, Bachelard, despite the influence of Brunschvicg and the idealistic tendencies of his own thought, struggled to maintain key realistic insights. Some reflection on this struggle will provide a helpful approach to Kuhn's problem of the ontological significance of science.

Bachelard labels his position an "applied rationalism." It is a rationalism because it recognizes, as does Kuhn, the active role of the mind in the constitution of the concepts whereby science describes the world. It is applied because scientific concepts do not literally create the objects they describe; these objects exist prior to and are independent of the concepts (and the mental acts that constitute them). Bachelard presents his applied rationalism as a way between traditional idealism and realism, accepting idealism's emphasis on the mind's active role in knowledge without at the same time denying realism's emphasis on the independent existence of the known object.

Applied rationalism is open to the objection that it merely evades the basic ontological issue. Bachelard tries to maintain realism by saying that any scientific concept is applied to an object that exists independently of that application. But his accommodation with idealism further requires that the object as preexistent was nonetheless constituted by previous applications of other concepts. Unless there is an unintelligible infinite regress of applications and objects, there must be an initial object that is the starting point of our knowledge. This object is either entirely constituted by the mind – which amounts to the most implausible idealism – or it is a conceptually inaccessible thing-in-itself – which amounts to the most implausible realism.

This objection, however, depends on taking applied rationalism as a full-blooded alternative to traditional idealism and realism. It depends, that is, on the assumption that applied rationalism offers a new solution to the traditional metaphysical problem of the ultimate nature of reality in its relation to mind. It is entirely possible that Bachelard himself sees his view in this way. But it is also possible to understand applied rationalism as a refusal to take sides in the traditional metaphysical dispute. The idea would be to maintain a healthy skepticism about the deep global issues posed by this dispute and to content ourselves with a (finite) series of regional claims about the nature of specific scientific objects. For each case, applied rationalism says that the given object is constituted in a distinctive way by the mind's creative conceptualization but that this constitution presupposes the prior givenness of the object relative to that constitution. In each case, it is the task of a philosophically reflective history of science to sort out what is given and what is constituted. As Bachelard suggests, one theme of such a history of modern physical science will surely be the role of instruments in the constitution of scientific objects. But applied rationalism assiduously avoids taking any position on the question of the ultimate relation of the mind to the world of objects. In this way, Bachelard can assert a sophisticated scientific realism (sophisticated in its accommodation with key idealist themes) and at the same time avoid taking a position on the question of metaphysical realism. My suggestion, of course, is that exactly the same strategy is open to Kuhn. He can maintain a realism about scientific objects (and the truth of assertions about them) while maintaining a healthy metaphysical skepticism about the "vexing problems" of the correspondence theory of truth.

Rationality

Despite his vigorous denials, Kuhn is thought to question the rationality of science because he gives such a central role to the judgment of the scientific community. Canguilhem is in accord with many Anglophone critics when he accuses Kuhn of eliminating rationality in favor of merely shared opinions. The point is this: By making the judgment of the scientific community the ultimate justification of scientific claims, he makes reason-giving nothing more than a social practice. But surely I can have perfectly good reasons for believing something that everyone else thought was false and unjustified. Why should enough recalcitrant Athenians be able to put Socrates in the wrong? Kuhn seems to erase the boundary between objective knowledge and subjective opinion. His doctrine of incommensurability rejects the idea that there is any necessarily shared epistemic ground (e.g., a neutral observation language or a priori methodological rules) that we can use to resolve scientific disagreements, and the result is that he must locate the ultimate source of science's cognitive authority in the consensus of the scientific community.

The problem becomes particularly clear when we reflect on Kuhn's distinction of normal and abnormal science. Normal science occurs when scientists are in sufficient agreement on fundamentals to allow the evaluation of contested claims by shared standards. Such discourse is the "behavioral" equivalent of the discourse that would be possible if there were standards of rationality independent of our judgments. Kuhn denies that there are any such standards, but in normal science the agreement of investigators allows them to proceed as if there were. Abnormal science arises when someone, for whatever reason, speaks in a manner counter to the consensus of normal science (as when a Galileo says that the earth is not at rest). This typically occurs in response to a perceived "crisis" in the paradigm guiding normal science. Sometimes the crisis turns out to be judged illusory, and the abnormal approach simply falls by the wayside as mere foolishness or eccentricity. But sometimes the new approach is gradually picked up by the rest of the community and effects a radical change to a new paradigm. Then the innovators are hailed as revolutionary geniuses. But of course, on Kuhn's account, this means only that the community has accepted their new discursive standards. Given this, critics ask how Kuhn can preserve any meaningful epistemological distinction between objective knowledge and subjective belief. Scientists know that the earth moves relative to the sun; but for Kuhn this seems to mean merely that all members of the relevant scientific community agree that the earth moves. Group consensus – which in fact is no different from what Imre Lakatos called "mob psychology" – has become the only standard of knowledge.[21]

The objection – and possible responses to it – can be sharpened by reflecting on the distinction between "objective" and "subjective." Kuhn in effect distinguishes three cases. Sometimes "subjective" refers to what is a matter of individual preference and "objective" to what is generally accepted. In this sense, "Chateau Lafite is Bordeaux" is objective, whereas "Chateau Lafite 1959 is the best Bordeaux" is subjective. Kuhn obviously does not make all knowledge subjective in this sense. The consensus of a scientific, literary, or political community is not a matter of personal opinion. It is objective at least in the sense of being *inter*subjective. Sometimes "subjective" refers to what is a matter of judgment as opposed to what can be unequivocally demonstrated (e.g., proven algorithmically). Kuhnian consensus is subjective in this sense, but then so is virtually every form of knowledge available to us outside of the most rigorous mathematical demonstrations. (Indeed, even mathematical demonstrations involve ineliminable acts of judgment regarding, for example, the applicability of a general principle to a particular case.) So for these first two cases, Kuhn can respond to the charge of subjectivism with, respectively, "Not guilty" and "So what?"

The third sense of the distinction takes "subjective" to mean "how things appear to us" as opposed to "how things really are." This is surely the sense of "subjective" Kuhn's critics have in mind. If knowledge is nothing more than group consensus, then it expresses only how things seem to us, which may well not be how they really are. This version of the distinction is, however, ambivalent. It may be taken as merely a distinction between how things appear to us (that is, how they appear in first impressions, before serious inquiry) and how things appear after the fullest possible scrutiny. But then Kuhn's understanding of knowledge is obviously objective, since it surely does not require that we rest content with anything less than the most thorough investigation. Critics, however, may rather take the distinction as being between how things are described by our most careful and thorough inquiries and how things are just in themselves, entirely apart from how we describe them. But then the objection is presupposing the metaphysical realism that our preceding discussion showed us we can dispense with.

But even if we agree that Kuhn can deploy an intelligible sense of scientific objectivity, it does not follow that he has an answer to the Socrates-versus-the-Athenians objection. A consensus derived from the sustained investigations of a trained group of inquirers may still be wrong, and a maverick who rejects it may be right.

It is at this point that the French tradition once again becomes relevant to Kuhn's problematic. Where Kuhn emphasizes consensus as the ultimate epistemological category in our understanding of science, Bachelard and especially Canguilhem give pride of place to norms. Admittedly, these are *social* norms, ultimately constituted by the practices of the groups that they govern. But understanding the nature of scientific (or any other sort of) rationality requires that we avoid confusing social practice with group consensus. As Canguilhem emphasizes, the fact that a norm has no objective reality outside the group it regulates does not entail that it expresses the mere opinions or whims of the group (and much less of individuals within it). Just as biological norms are rooted in the organic reality of organisms they regulate, so social norms derive from the "social reality" of the groups for which they are valid. Belonging to a community means coming under the norms that constitute that community, but not every opinion shared by all or most members of a community expresses a communal norm. It is, in fact, quite possible for a single individual to be in accord with a community's norms when the rest of the community is not. I could, for example, be the only person who pronounces my name correctly or the only person who knows that the twenty-first century did not begin until 2001. Of course, enough changes in the views and practices of the members of a community will eventually lead to changes in its norms, since norms have no basis outside of the community itself. But this does not mean that norms are changeable at the whim of a group, even if the group includes everyone.

Even if we all *say* something different, we may not all be able to believe it or be able to reflect it in our practices.

It is easy to fall into confusion on this point. Consensus is closely tied to reason-giving in both origin and outcome. Like any social practice, reason-giving proceeds from an intersubjective acceptance of a set of norms, and it tends toward agreement on claims that have been justified by the practice. We tend to collapse these two points into the misleading claim that consensus is what justifies a proposition. But this is true only in a very indirect sense. At some ultimate point, further demands for justification of the norms governing our reasoning-giving no longer make sense; and we can do no more than point out that these *are* the norms that we accept. But this acceptance is by no means an optional choice by individuals. It is the outcome of the deep-rooted and complex process whereby they have become reason-givers. In Canguilhem's terms, this is the process that forms a community as a social reality. At the other end, consensus is (at least in ideal cases) the outcome of successful reason-giving: the process of discussing the evidence, presenting arguments, and answering objections leads, when things go right, to widespread agreement on what to believe. So consensus about norms is the ultimate source of the practice of reason-giving, and consensus in specific beliefs is often the outcome of the practice.

None of this, however, implies that our beliefs are justified only to the extent that we agree on them. This is the basis of Canguilhem's criticism of Kuhn's focus on consensus as opposed to norms. As he reads Kuhn, "A paradigm is the result of a choice by those who use it. The normal is what is common, over a given period, to a collectivity of specialists in a university or other academic institution. We think we are dealing with concepts of a philosophical critique, only to find ourselves on the level of social psychology" (IR, 23).[22] Canguilhem may not be entirely justified in forcing on Kuhn a purely psychological reading of consensus, but he is right in suggesting that Kuhn needs to make a clearer distinction between the roles of norms and the roles of individual and group judgments governed by norms. Given such a distinction, we can see that an individual might have good reasons to believe that everyone else in the community is ignorant of, misinterpreting, or simply incapable of understanding the relevant community norms appropriate for evaluating a given claim. Perhaps, for example, the rest of the community has lost the ability to understand the millennial significance of the fact that there is no year zero. In such a case, the individual will be justified against everyone else – not necessarily *sub specie aeternitatis* but in light of his superior understanding of norms implicit in his community.

Literal justification by consensus occurs only in special cases. When astrophysicists accept the existence of black holes, their justification is a complicated body of evidence and arguments based on it, not on the fact that they agree that black holes exist. Nonexperts who accept the results of astrophysics on authority may justify their belief in black holes by the consensus of astrophysicists. But this is a derivative sort of justification that does not define the nature of the practice.

Rethinking Kuhn's position in terms of the French tradition of philosophy of science, then, there is no need to assimilate rational justification to voluntary consensus as though norms of belief depended on the majority vote at the next epistemic town meeting. There is, in other words, no need to formulate the view of reason-giving as a social practice in this decisionistic way. Admitting that rationality is ultimately a matter of sharing a practice rather than, say, attaining self-evident insights does not make the routine results of ordinary epistemic deliberations a matter of arbitrary choice. Thomas McCarthy has rightly maintained that " 'our' culture is shot through with transcultural notions of validity." As he says, our actual practices of justification "involve constructing arguments that claim to be universally valid," not appealing to our agreement on a given claim. "In general, it is not *because* we agree that we hold a claim to be valid; rather, we agree because we have grounds for granting its validity."[23] But in giving epistemic priority to the judgment of the scientific community, Kuhn need not reject this point. The issue is not about the content of the norms involved in our practice of justification, but only about the ultimate basis of these norms. His claim is that, in the final analysis, there is nothing underlying these norms other than the practice that they define. This is not a contradiction of our practice, but merely a rejection of an indefensible philosophical interpretation of that practice.

Notes

1. Kuhn was, like so many historians of science of his generation, strongly influenced by Alexandre Koyré, but the influence was primarily historiographical, not philosophical. He did not, for example, share Koyré's interest in Hegel.
2. "A Discussion with Thomas Kuhn," in James Conant and John Haugeland (eds.), *The Road Since Structure*, Chicago: University of Chicago Press, 2000, pp. 284–5.
3. "A Discussion with Thomas Kuhn," p. 285.
4. "Foucault responds 2," *Diacritics* I, 2 (Winter 1971), p. 60.
5. *La modalité du jugement*, 2, Paris: Presses Universitaires de France, 1964.
6. *La modalité du jugement*, p. 88.

7. *Les étapes de la pensée mathématique*, Paris: Alcan, 1912, p. 569.

8. *L'expérience humaine et la causalité physique*, Paris: Alcan, 1922, pp. 544–5.

9. *L'expérience humaine et la causalité physique*, p. 546.

10. *L'expérience humaine et la causalité physique*, p. 552.

11. On the similarities of Bachelard's thought to Brunschvicg's, see Michel Vadée, *Gaston Bachelard*, Paris: Éditions Sociales, 1975, especially pp. 229–35. Vadée maintains that Bachelard's debt to Brunschvicg has been ignored by his followers and commentators (in particular, Canguilhem). See also Bachelard's paper "La philosophie scientifique de Léon Brunschvicg," *Revue de métaphysique et de morale* 50 (1945), pp. 77–84; reprinted in *L'engagement rationaliste*, Paris: Presses Universitaires de France, 1972, pp. 169–77.

12. See Gaston Bachelard, *Le nouvel esprit scientifique*, Paris: Alcan, 1934 (*The New Scientific Spirit*, translated by A. Goldhammer, Boston: Beacon, 1984), as well as his earlier detailed discussion of relativity theory, *La valeur inductive de la relativité*, Paris: Vrin, 1929.

13. In this regard, see his *La psychoanalyse du feu*, Paris: Gallimard, 1938 (*The Psychoanalysis of Fire*, translated by G. C. Waterston, New York: Orion, 1969).

14. *La valeur inductive de la relativité*, p. 206.

15. *The New Scientific Spirit*, pp. 13, 16.

16. Georges Canguilhem, *Idéologie et rationalité*, Paris: Vrin, 1977 (*Ideology and Rationality in the History of the Life Sciences*, translated by A. Goldhammer, Cambridge, MA: MIT Press, 1988).

17. Georges Canguilhem, *Le normal et le pathologique*, Paris: Presses Universitaires de France, 1966 (*On the Normal and the Pathological*, translated by C. R. Fawcett, Dordrecht: Reidel, 1978).

18. *The Structure of Scientific Revolutions*, 2nd ed., Chicago: University of Chicago Press, 1970, "Postscript," p. 206.

19. *L'activité rationaliste de la physique contemporaine*, Paris: Presses Universitaires de France, 1951, p. 26.

20. Paul Hoyningen-Huene, *Reconstructing Scientific Revolutions*, Chicago: University of Chicago Press, 1993, chap. 3.

21. Imre Lakatos, "The Methodology of Scientific Research Programmes," in I. Lakatos and A. Musgrave, eds., *Criticism and the Growth of Knowledge*, Cambridge: Cambridge University Press, 1970, p. 178.

22. *Idéologie et rationalité*, p. 232.

23. Thomas McCarthy, "Philosophy and Social Practice: Richard Rorty's 'New Pragmatism,'" in *Ideals and Illusions*, Cambridge, MA: MIT Press, 1991, pp. 17, 19.

3 | Normal Science and Dogmatism, Paradigms and Progress: Kuhn 'versus' Popper and Lakatos

JOHN WORRALL

One sixties' summer, shortly before the 'Summer of Love', probably the two most widely influential philosophers of science of the twentieth century – Karl Popper and Thomas Kuhn – met at a conference in 'swinging London' to compare and contrast their views on the nature of theory change in science.

The debate was recorded (and extended) in an influential book called *Criticism and the Growth of Knowledge*.[1] Although Kuhn was at pains to begin his paper (1970) by stressing similarities between his own views of scientific development and those of 'Sir Karl', and although Kuhn's official line was that the differences between Popper and himself were 'comparatively secondary', it soon became clear that those differences were in fact sharp and apparently rather deep. Kuhn claimed, for example, that 'Sir Karl has characterized the entire scientific enterprise in terms that apply only to its occasional revolutionary parts' (p. 6). And he suggested that to accept his own account of science was, in effect, 'to turn Sir Karl's view on its head' by accepting that 'it is precisely the abandonment of critical discourse that marks the transition to a science' (ibid.). Popper responded[2] by, amongst other things, admitting that Kuhn's 'normal science' is a real phenomenon and that he had indeed hitherto failed fully to recognise it – but he did so reluctantly in the way that a starstruck lover might be brought to admit that he had hitherto been blind to an imperfection in his inamorata. Normal science is, said Popper, 'a danger to [presumably 'proper', critical] science and, indeed to our civilization [!]' (p. 53), adding for good measure that '[i]n my view, the 'normal' scientist . . . is a person one ought to be sorry for' (p. 52).

Although, of course, conducted in the best academic traditions of (at any rate, professed) mutual respect, this was, then, and despite the tenor of the times, no swinging love-in. It more than merits the name 'Popper–Kuhn controversy'. Underlying the specific points of disagreement is, as we shall see, what many philosophers at least took to be a fundamental difference over the 'objectivity' of scientific knowledge and the 'rationality'

65

of scientific change. Several other eminent philosophers of science contributed to the discussion in London, among them Paul Feyerabend,
Stephen Toulmin, John Watkins, and especially Imre Lakatos, whose
'methodology of scientific research programmes' was explicitly developed
as an attempted 'synthesis' of Kuhn's and Popper's opposing views. Kuhn's
exasperation with at least some of his critics shines through his long and
revealing 'Replies to Critics'. The controversy grumbled on for a number of
years.

In this essay, I review what was at stake in the Popper–Kuhn controversy,
and I try to assess the success or otherwise of the Lakatosian synthesis.
Although Kuhn raised a number of interrelated issues – many of which merit
detailed discussion – I shall focus the treatment in this essay sharply on the
question of theory change in science and the role of criticism and testing
in theory change. To avoid the danger of excessive rational reconstruction,
I begin in fairly close contact with Kuhn's London paper and Popper's
response to it. Having set them at odds with one another, I shall then, to
avoid the danger of overscholasticism, analyse in a general way what I think
was, and was not, at issue in the central part of the Kuhn–Popper debate.
The debate is, as I hope to show, of more than merely historical interest.
Involved in it were important problems that remain unresolved by current
philosophy of science.

DISAGREEMENTS – THE ROLE OF 'TRADITION' AND
THE ROLE OF 'FALSIFICATION'

Kuhn begins his paper by stressing the extent of his agreement with Popper.
They are, for example, united in rejecting the view that science develops
by 'accretion' and in emphasising instead that change at the level of fun-
damental theory in science has sometimes been radical or 'revolutionary'.
The disagreements are about the extent and mechanics of such changes.
Kuhn identified

> two comparatively secondary issues about which my disagreement with
> Sir Karl is most nearly explicit: [1] my emphasis on the importance [in
> science] of deep commitment to tradition and [2] my discontent with the
> implications of the term "falsification." (p. 2)

The two disagreements are in fact deeper than Kuhn's emollient rhetoric
suggests and are very closely related, as we shall see. Let's begin by focussing
on the second.

What exactly were Popper's views of the role of tests, and particularly of 'falsifications', in science? One side effect of this controversy, at least in some circles, was a series of heated debates on what Popper's views on these issues really were. The position that most commentators would take as the definitively Popperian one, however, is surely that articulated by Popper himself in his *Conjectures and Refutations* (1963). There Popper relates how, 'in the winter of 1919–20', he had responded to the confirmation of Einstein's General Theory of Relativity by the (just-published) results of the Eddington Eclipse Expedition. This striking success for Einstein's theory forced a comparison in Popper's mind with other theories, such as those of Freud and of Adler, which many of his contemporaries also saw as impressively (and multiply) confirmed but which he thought essentially worthless. The problem was that the supposed 'confirmations' in the case of those latter theories came too easily. Indeed, said Popper:

> I could not think of any human behaviour which could not be interpreted in terms of either [Freud's or Adler's] theory. It was precisely this fact – that they always fitted, that they were always confirmed – which in the eyes of their admirers constituted the strongest argument in favour of these theories. It began to dawn on me that this apparent strength was in fact their weakness. (p. 35)

The confirmation of Einstein's theory was 'strikingly different':

> The impressive thing about this [Einstein] case is the *risk* involved. . . . If observation shows that the predicted effect is definitely absent, then the theory is simply refuted. The theory is *incompatible with certain [possible] results of observation* – in fact with results which everyone before Einstein would have expected. This is quite different from the . . . situation [in the Adler and Freud cases], when it turned out that the theories in question were compatible with the most divergent human behaviour, so that it was practically impossible to describe any human behaviour that might not be claimed to be a verification of these theories.

On the basis of this comparison, Popper succinctly characterised his basic position in the form of seven propositions:

1. It is easy to obtain confirmations, or verifications, for nearly every theory – if we look for confirmations.

2. Confirmations should count only if they are the result of *risky predictions*; that is to say, if, unenlightened by the theory in question, we should

have expected an event which was incompatible with the theory – which would have refuted the theory.

3. Every 'good' scientific theory is a prohibition: it forbids certain things to happen. The more it forbids, the better it is.

4. A theory which is not refutable by any conceivable event is non-scientific. Irrefutability is not a virtue of a theory (as people often think), but a vice.

5. Every genuine test of a theory is an attempt to falsify it, or to refute it. Testability is falsifiability; but there are degrees of testability: some theories are more testable, more exposed to refutation, than others; they take, as it were, greater risks.

6. Confirming evidence should not count *except when it is the result of a genuine test of the theory*; and this means that it can be presented as a serious but unsuccessful attempt to falsify the theory....

7. Some genuinely testable theories, when found to be false, are still upheld by their admirers – for example by introducing *ad hoc* some auxiliary assumption, or by re-interpreting the theory *ad hoc* in such a way that it escapes refutation. Such a procedure is always possible, but it rescues the theory from refutation only at the price of destroying, or at least lowering its scientific status.... (pp. 36–7)

Popper does not explicitly include in this list his view on the correct scientific attitude to take when a theory fails a test. However, he does explicitly say in the preamble that 'If observation shows that the predicted effect is definitely absent, then the theory is simply refuted'. And this is a message very strongly endorsed elsewhere in his writings – bold conjectures and hard refutations followed by new bold conjectures. Notice – it will be important later – that, as he emphasised in point 7, Popper *did* take into account the possibility of a theory's 'admirers' continuing to 'uphold' a theory, even when refuted, that is, 'found to be false'[3], but he claimed that such a move carries the 'price of destroying, or at least lowering its scientific status'.

Kuhn argued, contrary to Popper's view, that there is only one straightforward sense in which a scientist can be said to be testing a theory. This is within the context of normal science – within a context in which the scientist simply postulates, and so takes for granted, his basic theory and basic methods; what *can* then be tested are 'statements of an individual's best guesses as to how to connect his own research problem with [that] corpus of accepted scientific knowledge' (p. 4). Kuhn insisted that

[i]n no usual sense, however, are such tests directed to current theory. On the contrary, when engaged with a normal research problem, the scientist must *premise* current theory as the rules of his game. His object is to solve a puzzle, preferably one at which others have failed, and his current theory is required to define that puzzle.... Of course the practitioner of such an enterprise must often test the conjectural puzzle solution that his ingenuity suggests. But only his personal conjecture is tested. (pp. 4–5)

In fact, as he notoriously went on to suggest,

if [this 'personal conjecture'] fails the test, only [the scientist's] own ability not the corpus of current science is impugned. In short, though tests occur frequently in normal science, these tests are of a peculiar sort, for in the final analysis it is the individual scientist rather than current theory which is tested. (p. 5)

As Kuhn, of course, recognised, the 'tests' that Popper had in mind were, on the contrary, ones that (allegedly) *do* challenge fundamental theory. Kuhn listed, on Popper's behalf, 'Lavoisier's experiments on calcination, the eclipse expedition of 1919, and the recent experiments on parity conservation'. Rather perplexingly, he conceded that 'classic tests' such as these can be 'destructive in their outcome' and concentrated initially on the criticism that such tests, contrary to Popper's claims, are extremely rare in the history of science. This led to the already quoted remark that 'Sir Karl has characterized the entire scientific enterprise in terms that apply only to its occasional revolutionary parts' (p. 6).

Given the position developed in *The Structure of Scientific Revolutions* (1962), however, Kuhn could hardly have meant that the outcomes of these 'classic tests' were 'destructive' in the sense of directly knocking out the theories underlying the older paradigms concerned. In that book, he made it clear that no one experimental 'anomaly' is ever the single crucial piece of evidence that 'refutes' a theory. He can only have meant here, then, that these 'classic tests' were, *given the context of a feeling of 'crisis' induced by other anomalies and problems*, the final straw, or, more explicitly, that, *with liberal helpings of hindsight*, we can now see that they were the final straw. At the time when the test was actually performed, as he emphasised in *Structure* and again stressed elsewhere in his London paper, the negative outcome can only be the 'final straw' for *some* – perhaps most, but certainly not all – members of the community. The whole rhetoric of 'refutation' and 'falsification' suggests disproofs or at least results that will 'compel assent from any member of the relevant professional community' (p. 13). But there are, Kuhn was clear, no such things. His real position, then, was that what Popper seemed to be saying about tests *never* really applies – either in normal *or* in extraordinary science.

The fundamental flaws in Popper's position on testing and 'falsification' stem, according to Kuhn, from his complete misconception (or perhaps lack of any conception) of the role and importance of 'normal science'. That is, of Kuhn's two 'comparatively secondary' points of disagreement with Popper, the first – his 'emphasis on the importance of deep commitment to tradition' – was indeed the more important. Popper's misconception of the role and importance of normal science led him, in Kuhn's view, *both* to an incorrect demarcation criterion between science and pseudoscience *and* to a misappraisal of the merits of holding on to a basic theory when it (or rather, as we shall see shortly, the latest theoretical system based on it) runs into experimental difficulties.

Popper's view was that astrology, for example, is a pseudsoscience because it is unfalsifiable. Kuhn argued that this is incorrect – at least if unfalsifiability involves never making predictions that were agreed, on the basis of evidence, to fail. (Kuhn here cited Thorndike for mainly sixteenth-century examples of failed astrological predictions.[4]) The real reason astrology fails to be scientific, according to Kuhn, is that it has not yet developed, and of course may never develop, a puzzle-solving tradition; it has not progressed to the stage of sustaining normal science. For the sixteenth-century *astronomer*, the failure of an individual prediction was a fertile source of research problems. He had a whole armoury of ideas for reacting to failure: there were clear-cut ways in which the 'data' might be challenged (and 'improved') and, if that was unsuccessful, clear-cut suggestions for modifying theory by manipulating epicycles, eccentrics, equants, and so on. No such puzzle-solving ideas were available to the sixteenth-century astrologer. There were 'too many possible sources of difficulty, most of them beyond the astrologer's knowledge [or] control...' (p. 9), and hence a predictive failure was entirely 'uninformative'.

On the *central* issue of reacting to falsifications (or rather, according to Kuhn, 'anomalies') by continuing to defend the central theory, Kuhn argued that Popper's account is again quite wrong. Popper always acknowledged that it is possible to defend a theory against a potential refutation by, for example, 'introducing' an auxiliary or by questioning the data. But, as we just saw, he suggested that although undoubtedly possible, any such manoeuvre is automatically under suspicion: '[Such a 'defensive' move] is always possible, but it rescues the theory from refutation only at the price of destroying, or at least lowering its scientific status.'

Kuhn argued that, to the contrary, not only is it true that 'all theories can be modified by a variety of *ad hoc* adjustments without ceasing to be, in their main lines, the same theories', but it is moreover 'important... that this should be so, for it is often by challenging observations or adjusting theories that scientific knowledge grows' (p. 13).

Popper's response to Kuhn in his paper in *Criticism and the Growth of Knowledge* (Lakatos and Musgrave 1970) was very strange. He reiterated and re-emphasised his standard line that the scientific attitude, and indeed the rational attitude in general, requires that all assumptions be always open to criticism (and indeed requires a constantly questioning attitude; we must not only be open to criticism should it come along, but must constantly strive to ensure that good criticisms *do* come along). And yet he had, he stated, 'always' agreed with one aspect of Kuhn's view – that 'dogmatism' has an important role to play:

> I believe that science is essentially critical. . . . But I have always stressed the need for some dogmatism. The dogmatic scientist [this should surely be an oxymoron for Popper] has an important role to play. If we give in to criticism too easily, we never find out where the real power of our theories lies. (p. 55)

It is difficult to think of any passages that would support Popper's claim that he had 'always' stressed the need for a whiff of dogmatism, but, much more importantly, it seems difficult to make sense of the position he now adopted. Are we supposed to believe that the success of the true critical scientist depends on the existence of others who are not properly scientific because they are dogmatic? Why this unnecessarily bipartite view? Since Popper now accepted that being somewhat dogmatic may help reveal the 'true power' of our theories, it seems that the right move for him would have been instead to agree that the idea of *effective* criticism is somewhat more nuanced than he earlier allowed (which, although he didn't put it exactly that way, was essentially Kuhn's line). Moreover, the dogmatism at issue presumably involves at least sometimes reacting to a negative test result for – a potential 'falsification' of – a theory by holding on to it, despite that result. But then what happened to Popper's claim that this was the hallmark of pseudoscience or, at least, that such a move was always to be viewed negatively because it reduces, and perhaps even 'destroys', the scientific character of the theory? How can a move that reduces the scientific character of a theory at the same time perhaps reveal its 'true power'?

A (LARGE) PART OF THE RESOLUTION – DUHEM'S ANALYSIS OF THEORY TESTING

Despite the major impact of the work, many of the points Kuhn made in *Structure* about the role of tests and especially 'anomalies' are in fact – and, of course, unrecognised by Kuhn himself – easy consequences of Duhem's analysis of the logic of theory testing in science. Despite the fact that he explicitly cited him on occasion, Popper never seems to have fully absorbed the simple lessons of Duhem's analysis. A sizeable portion of the debate between the two on the issues raised so far can be resolved simply by thinking through Duhem's points.[5]

Duhem remarked that the sort of claim that is usually taken as a 'single theory' in science – Newton's theory, Maxwell's theory, 'the' wave theory of light, for example – never has any empirical consequence 'in isolation' (or even when conjoined with other empirical statements taken as 'initial conditions'). Instead auxiliary assumptions are always needed. So, for example, Newton's theory (of mechanics plus universal gravitation) taken on its own has, of course, no testable implications about planetary positions – not even ones of a conditional kind such as that if Mars is at (x,y,z) at time t, then it will be at (x',y',z') at time t'. In order to draw such consequences, we need to make an assumption about the total force acting on the planet. This will, in turn, be based on assumptions about the number, masses, and positions of the sun and other planets in the solar system, together with a 'closure assumption' – to the effect that forces other than the gravitational interactions between Mars and the sun and other planets are negligible. The minimum testable unit in science always consists, then, of what might be termed a 'central' theory together with a (sometimes quite large, though of course finite) set of auxiliary assumptions. (This set often includes some 'idealising' assumptions such as the closure assumption just mentioned.)

Moreover, in some cases – such as 'the' wave theory of light, analysed at length by Duhem – the central theory itself naturally breaks down into a 'core' component (light consists of *some sort* of periodic disturbance transmitted through *some sort* of elastic medium) together with a whole series of more specific assumptions (associating particular kinds of monochromatic light with waves of specific wavelengths, specifying the precise properties of the elastic light-carrying medium, how those properties differ in the 'free' ether as opposed to the ether as constrained within transparent substances such as glass, and so on).

A trivial, but vital, result in metalogic says that if some conclusion C is validly derivable only from some finite set of premises $\{P_1, \ldots, P_n\}$, and if C is false, then all that follows is that *at least one* of $P_1, \ldots, P_n$ must be false. Duhem's analysis tells us that the full deductive structure of any test of some 'single' 'central' theory is at least as complicated as the following:

Central Theory (maybe ⇔ core claim and specific assumptions)
Auxiliaries

Therefore, testable consequence.

Two results follow straightforwardly concerning the points at issue between Popper and Kuhn. *Firstly*, contrary to Kuhn, scientists can, at least sometimes (the qualifications are spelled out in the next section), be regarded as involved in testing, and testing a chunk of theoretical material, not an individual scientist's capability. It is just that the unit being tested is not a single isolated theory but a sometimes quite complex theoretical system. This means, in turn, that a negative outcome may be of little significance since it seems overwhelmingly probable that it will be dealt with by changing some relatively secondary (and perhaps so far not very well thought-through) specific or auxiliary assumption. *Secondly* – it's really just the other side of the coin, but this time contrary to Popper – it becomes clear why a scientist may perfectly properly, without any hint of dogmatism, regard some negative result as a Kuhnian anomaly rather than a Popperian falsification. The falsity of the central theory does *not* follow from the falsity of the empirical conclusion. Moreover, even if it were decided that the central theory rather than some auxiliary was more likely to be at fault (remember: this decision cannot be based on logic alone, from what has already been said), it would still not follow that it was the core of the central theory that was false rather than some specific assumption. If a scientist is doing anything that resembles testing, then she is always – whether she is fully aware of it or not – testing a *theoretical system* rather than a single isolated theory. It follows that if the empirical consequence entailed by some initially accepted theoretical system turns out to be false, then it would be just as dogmatic to argue – in the way that Popper's rhetoric seems to endorse – that it must be the central theory or the core theory within the central theory that is false, as it would be to argue that the fault cannot be with the central theory but instead with some auxiliary. Similarly (responding to Popper's concession about the possibility of holding on to a theory despite a refutation) there is no reason to think that questioning a specific or an auxiliary assumption in the light of a refutation of a whole theoretical system is *automatically* under any more suspicion from the point of view of good scientific practice than would be questioning the central theory.

Looked at in this way, the dispute about testing between Kuhn and Popper seems remarkably easy to resolve. As we shall see in the next section, there is in fact rather more to the dispute than my treatment so far has revealed. Before coming to this extra content, however, the Duhemian analysis that we already have on the table helps to clarify what was at issue in one point of apparent *agreement* between Kuhn and Popper that has played a significant role in the further debate and that we need to clarify.

Kuhn himself pointed out in his London paper that he and Popper agreed not just on the non-'accretional' nature of (some) scientific change, but also on the thesis that all so-called observation statements are 'theory-laden'. One consequence of that now widely adopted thesis would seem to be that a further possible reaction for the scientist seeking to 'hold on to' a favoured central theory is opened up. Not only could such a scientist seek to replace some auxiliary in the Duhemian theoretical system necessary for the derivation of the observational or experimental 'result', she could also question and seek to replace that empirical result itself. (As Kuhn hinted, the fact that Popper elsewhere enthusiastically endorsed this point makes it still more mysterious why he should also claim that 'rescuing' a theory by challenging a theory-laden empirical result should always reduce the theory's scientific status.)

I believe that, although of course directed at a real methodological phenomenon in science, the theory-ladenness thesis is *at best* a misleading way of representing it. There can, of course, be no doubt that every statement (at any rate every statement about the external world), no matter how 'observational', must count, in principle, as fallible; even claims like 'the needle in this meter points to around the mark "5" on the scale' presuppose, for example, that we are not being systematically deceived by a malign Cartesian demon. But Kuhn's argument (or rather claim) that there are, in any genuine case of intratheoretic rivalry, no theory-*neutral* (notice: not theory-*free*) observation statements to act as arbiters between the rivals seems to me entirely unconvincing. What *is* true is that in order to get down to the level of such effectively incorrigible observation statements – ones whose truth value is agreed to on all sides and that can, therefore, pace Kuhn and *perhaps* pace Popper, act as neutral arbiters between rival theoretical systems – we need to augment those theoretical systems still further; and that further augmentation naturally makes the 'Duhem problem' (which of the many statements in such systems to 'blame' for a refutation) still more complex.

One incident that is sometimes cited as illustrating the significant theory-ladenness of observation statements was the dispute between Newton and Flamsteed (the first Astronomer-Royal). As told by Imre Lakatos, the story went roughly as follows.[6] Newton sent some predictions about planetary positions made on the basis of his theory to Flamsteed and asked him to check their correctness. Flamsteed replied that Newton's predictions were incorrect. But Newton responded that in fact the predictions were correct and that it was Flamsteed's data that were in error. Told in this way, it sounds like a real case of Newton indeed being dogmatic in defence of his theory, and it seems to illustrate both the necessity for some dogmatism (since Newton was, we now believe, right) and the inevitable dependence of data on theory.

But neither in Lakatos's version nor in the real version was there was ever any dispute between Newton and Flamsteed at the level of what Duhem (1906) called 'practical' (as opposed to 'theoretical') facts. Newton did not charge Flamsteed and his assistants with misobserving or misrecording the angles of inclination of their telescopes or the reading on their clocks when certain characteristic spots of light could be observed sitting at the centre of the visual field of those telescopes. (Even such assertions are obviously fallible in the trivial sense that a slip could have been made, or one of the assistants could have been drunk, and so on. But such mere slips can always be controlled for by independent checks.) Newton's real suggestion was that Flamsteed had 'miscalculated' his data – on the basis of an incorrect assumption about the amount by which light is refracted in the Earth's atmosphere and the dependence of the amount of refraction affecting the light entering a particular telescope on the air temperature in the locality of the telescope.

The best way to see what is going on is again through a Duhem-style analysis. Although assertions about planetary positions deductively follow from the – relatively slim – theoretical system discussed earlier (containing Newton's four laws and some auxiliary assumptions), nothing follows even from that theoretical system, let alone from Newton's four laws alone, about characteristic spots of light at the centre of visual fields of telescopes. In order to have a theoretical system that *is* testable at this very 'low level' of observationality, we need further assumptions – ones that link real planetary positions to these telescopic phenomena. This link clearly requires the articulation of optical theories about the properties of telescopes, and it equally clearly requires an assumption about the amount of refraction that light undergoes in passing through the Earth's atmosphere. So, if we require our observation statements to be undisputed (I would suggest indisputable, at least *via serious* considerations), then the full deductive structure of this observational test is

Central theory
Auxiliary theories
Instrumental theories

Hence, observational consequence (about angles of inclination of telescopes rather than planetary positions).

From this – altogether more revealing – viewpoint, Newton again treated Flamsteed's results as anomalies: that is, he suggested some other part of the overall theoretical system (specifically, the assumption about atmospheric refraction from within the set of 'instrumental theories') as the primary target for replacement rather than his own central theory.

Despite occasional references to it, Popper seems never really to have taken Duhem's point on board, and so, assisted by the fact that Kuhn did not express the challenge as clearly as he might have had he explicitly exploited Duhem's analysis, Popper entirely misconstrued Kuhn's challenge on the issue of tests. For his part, Kuhn failed to see that at least some of the Popperian testing rhetoric could readily be accommodated within his own view. Scientific tests *can* be analysed – in line with Popper's general views – as the deduction of observation statements from a set of theoretical claims; if the test proves negative – that is, if the inferred statement is shown by experiment or observation to be false (and, unlike Popper, I think this latter process is essentially incorrigible if the observation statements are of sufficiently low level) – then the set of theoretical claims taken as a whole is falsified and needs to be replaced. Genuine tests are important, just as Popper claimed. However, the units of science that are tested in this way consist not of single scientific theories (these – again: Newton's theory, Maxwell's theory, 'the' wave theory of light, and so on – are, despite Popper's rhetoric, unfalsifiable), and neither are they best seen, as Kuhn claimed, as tests of individual scientists rather than of any claims about the world. Instead, tests in science are of whole sets of statements organised in 'theoretical systems'. The replacement theoretical system may – in principle – differ from the original in *any* of its parts – core, specific but still central, auxiliary, or instrumental. The only scientist who could reasonably be charged with dogmatism is one who refused to modify any part of her initial overall theoretical system – but, of course, no scientist would ever do this. In advance of consideration of *further* tests (a crucial consideration, as we shall soon see), no particular type of reaction is under more suspicion from the epistemic point of view than any other, and none need be more dogmatic than any other. There is no prior reason why seeking to replace an auxiliary and retain the central theory should be judged any more dogmatic than the alternative strategy of retaining the auxiliaries and looking for a new central theory.

Recall that Kuhn specified two respects in which his own view differed from Popper's. The second of these was his 'discontent with the implications of the term "falsification"'. A major step in resolving this 'discontent' is again made once we accept that falsifications are of theoretical systems rather than central theories. Kuhn's anomalies are, then, at least in the simplest case, falsifications of overall theoretical systems that scientists regard – at any rate for the time being – as likely to be resolved by replacing that theoretical system with another one that shares the same central theory and differs only over some auxiliary or instrumental assumption. Most Newtonians in the nineteenth century regarded the observations of Uranus's orbit as anomalies for, rather than falsifications of, Newton's theory because they expected that the best replacement theoretical system that predicted the correct orbit for Uranus would also be built around Newton's theory and would differ from the current one 'only' over some auxiliary. This attitude was, of course, dramatically vindicated by Adams and Leverrier, who, 'holding on to' Newton's theory, replaced the auxiliary assumption about the number of other gravitational masses in the solar system and hence produced an overall system that not only correctly accounted for Uranus's orbit, but also predicted the existence of a new planet – Neptune. This success, in turn, made it more plausible to regard the difficulties with Mercury's orbit (known about, of course, long before Einstein) as similarly anomalous (rather than falsifying). It seemed likely that, by working within the basic Newtonian approach (that is, revising some auxiliary within the theoretical framework based on Newton's theory), a successful account of Mercury's motion could eventually be found.

WHAT KUHN ADDED TO DUHEM

Kuhn added at least two important points to anything that can be found at all explicitly in Duhem. *Firstly*, although it is sometimes reasonably clear what the 'best available' auxiliary assumptions are, so that we can, without too much rational reconstruction, see a particular scientist, or particular group of scientists, as testing a given, fairly clear, theoretical system built around whatever central theory is at issue, in other circumstances – perhaps the majority of circumstances – such clearly preferred auxiliary assumptions are not to hand. The same point holds – perhaps still more importantly – in cases where the central theory breaks down into a core theory and a set of 'specific assumptions'. Sometimes in such cases scientists who are working on the core theory may not know which specific assumptions are the best candidates for acceptance. What exact assumption should an eighteenth-century upholder of the corpuscular theory of light, for example, make about what differentiates the corpuscles that produce violet light from those that produce red light? No obvious answer was to hand. Such scientists are more naturally analysed not as *testing* any particular theoretical system at all (let alone, of course, as directly testing the central theory within that system), but rather as *working towards* the best candidate theoretical system based on that central theory. *Secondly* (and relatedly), the core idea behind a central theory will generally not only be an assertion about the universe, but will also be associated with a set of ideas (a 'heuristic') that can be used in working towards that best candidate theoretical system. Both of these additional features are connected with Kuhn's insistence on the importance in science of 'commitment to tradition'.

The first point is straightforward. Duhem showed that scientists only ever test complex theoretical systems built around core theories. It is by no means obvious, however, that there will always be natural candidates for 'best available auxiliary theories' within such a system. Indeed, it would be amazing if this were always the case. Where it is not, Kuhn is surely right that it is a stretch to speak of testing at all. Suppose that no value for the index of atmospheric refraction of light and its temperature dependence was taken as known in the late seventeenth century. It would, in that case, be foolish simply to make a Popperian bold conjecture about that index and test the resulting theoretical system based on Newton's theory against astronomical data. Conjecturing would be almost bound to fail. Instead, given that we have independent reason to accept the central Newtonian theory (through its accounts of the precession of the equinoxes and other phenomena), it is clearly more reasonable to *premise* that central theory and address the question of which account of atmospheric refraction would, when added to that central theory (plus, of course, other accepted assumptions), produce an overall system that yields the observed results. The central theory is premised in order to use the observed phenomena to indicate an accredited value of this theoretical parameter.[7]

An especially clear-cut version of this sort of process had been de-scribed long before Kuhn – in fact by Isaac Newton – under the name 'deduction from the phenomena'. Suppose, to take an especially clear-cut example, the general wave theory that light consists of waves transmitted through some mechanical medium is already accepted. That general theory itself, of course, specifies no particular wavelengths for light from particular monochromatic light sources (the latter *are* characterised by the general theory as those that emit light that undergoes no dispersion in refractive media). Such wavelengths – for example, of light from a sodium arc – are clearly *theoretical* parameters. Because the general theory does not specify the values of those parameters, it entails no precise values for the fringe distances in interference and diffraction experiments. In order to have such observational consequences, the general theory needs to be augmented by further specific assumptions about the wavelengths. Again, it would be absurd to make a bold Popperian conjecture at this point. Instead, a scientist will take the general theory as a premise and look for a consequence of it that identifies wavelengths of monochromatic light in general as some one-to-one function of measurable quantities, like fringe distances and slit separations. Thus, for example, the general wave theory, together with some approximating assumptions, entails the following functional relationship between, on the one hand, the wavelength λ and, on the other, the slit separation d, the distance from the two-slit screen to the observational screen D, and the distance X between the central bright fringe and the first bright fringe on either side of the centre in Young's famous two-slit experiment:

$$X = \frac{D\lambda}{d}$$

Hence since d, D ('initial conditions'), and X ('experimental outcome') can all be determined experimentally, the scientist can deduce a value for the theoretical parameter λ from the phenomena. This is, of course (and as always), really deduction from the phenomena *plus background knowledge* (here principally the general wave theory of light).[8]

Other cases in which background knowledge informs further scientific developments are rather less sharply delineated but are none the less important (and can, I believe, always be analysed in more clear-cut terms than Kuhn manages). Consider again the 'classical' wave theory of light. Fresnel produced, in 1819, a wave theory that accounted satisfactorily for a range of diffraction and interference results. Since the luminiferous aether, whatever its precise constitution, had to allow the planets to pass through it with negligible frictional effects (Newton's theory already very successfully accounted for planetary motions purely on the basis of gravity), Fresnel

took it that the aether is in fact a highly attenuated fluid and that the waves
of light are, correspondingly, longitudinal pressure waves. (A longitudinal
wave – the only kind that a fluid can transmit – is one in which the particles
whose motions constitute the wave oscillate in the same direction as the
overall transmission of the disturbance. An example is provided by sound
waves in air.) Polarisation effects, known about at least since Huygens, remained an outstanding problem. Naturally, since the general wave theory
had been impressively successful when augmented to supply a precise theory of diffraction, Fresnel and others 'premised' that same general wave
theory in attempting to build an account of polarised light (and of crystal
optics more generally). Fresnel quickly ran into a major problem, however.
As he and his friend Arago discovered, if the famous two-slit experiment
is performed in such a way that the light coming through the two slits is
polarised in mutually orthogonal planes (by interposing suitably oriented
quartz plates), then the interference fringes disappear. And yet, if the waves
were longitudinal, then near the centre of the pattern where the beams of
light coming from the two slits are nearly parallel, the general theory dic-
tates that there *must be* interference; and in particular, when the beams from
the two slits travel distances that differ by a half-wavelength, there should
be destructive interference and hence a dark band. Yet no such bands are
observed in Fresnel and Arago's experiment. Again, background knowledge
saved Fresnel from a theoretical limbo. It specified another type of wave,
a transverse wave (in which the particles of the waving medium oscillate at
right angles to the overall transmission of the disturbance). If the two beams
from the two slits in his modified experiment were transverse waves and,
being orthogonal to one another, hence oscillated in orthogonal planes,
then no destructive interference would be expected. As always, taking the
general wave theory as given, Fresnel inferred that since the experiment
showed that the waves could not be longitudinal, they are transverse, and
he began to work on the problems that this assumption produces. Hence
Fresnel *deduced*, rather than conjectured, the elastic solid theory of the luminiferous aether.[9]

Notice, however, that the sort of heuristic guidance exemplified in these
cases is available only once science has become sufficiently mature to possess background knowledge of this powerful kind. In particular, this sort of
heuristic guidance is available only once science possesses a general framework theory sufficiently well supported and sufficiently powerful to guide
work in this way. This was surely the chief phenomenon that Kuhn was
attempting to highlight using his notion of normal science. Although what
is involved can at least in some cases be described much more sharply than

Kuhn managed (as I hope the preceding brief analyses show), there is surely no doubt that the phenomenon he was pointing to is of exceptional importance and had hitherto been 'analysed' by philosophers of science at best in a hand-waving way.

Popper seems to have been as good as blind to this important phenomenon. Of course, no one who thought about science as much as Popper did could be *totally* blind to it and – as he reminded Kuhn in his London paper – he had written in his *Logic of Scientific Discovery*:

> A scientist engaged in a piece of research, say in physics, can attack his problem straight away. He can go at once to the heart of the matter, that is, to the heart of an organized structure. For a structure of scientific doctrines is already in existence; and with it a generally accepted problem-situation. (Popper 1958, p. 13)

There are also a couple of other passing remarks in Popper's work about the importance of background knowledge and of a scientist's being 'immersed in a problem-situation'. But he seems to have done nothing towards developing this outline idea into a systematic account of the precise ways in which background knowledge can inform the further development of science. (Indeed, his well-known insistence that, while there is a logic of the appraisal of already-articulated theories, there can be, despite the English title of his best-known book, no such thing as the logic of scientific *discovery*, a 'logic' of how good theories get to be articulated in the first place, seems to indicate that he sometimes thought that no such development is possible.) And, of course, it follows that Popper never gave systematic thought to how such an account would affect his claims about falsification and refutation.[10]

On the other hand, Kuhn's account of the puzzle-solving tradition that comes as the benefit of buying into a paradigm, and his insistence on the importance of exemplars, were both attempts to put some flesh on this outline idea of mature science 'building on itself'.

In sum, then, Kuhn, contrary to Popper's interpretation (and that of others such as Feyerabend), should be seen *not* as advocating dogmatism, but rather as advertising the fact that 'commitment' to the sort of framework supplied by well-developed science brings enormous epistemic benefits; without such commitments, mature science would be incapable of making the progress it has in fact made. Popper's claim that normal science is 'a danger to [real] science and indeed to our civilisation' betrayed complete misunderstanding.

On the other hand, surely some of Kuhn's claims gave Popper legitimate cause for concern. Kuhn did often seem to advocate a view altogether stronger than the one I have just articulated and endorsed: that the commitments involved in adopting a paradigm are absolute, brooking no question; that it is in fact impossible for a scientist, no matter how hard she might try, to stand outside of her framework so that she can articulate or recognise those commitments; and clearly, if the commitments cannot be recognised, it follows that they cannot be questioned. Nothing in the preceding analysis endorses this extension of the view. It may be a psychological necessity for some scientists, in order to get themselves to put in the enormous effort necessary to develop specific theories within an accepted framework, to believe unquestioningly – at least *pro tem* – in the truth of the general principles that constitute the framework. But if so, this is indeed a purely psychological phenomenon and need not, and should not, be endorsed by any normative account of how science ought to proceed. And there are, after all, clear-cut examples of distinguished scientists who made contributions to theories in whose basic tenets they did not believe: Maxwell and the statistical-kinetic theory and Einstein and the quantum theory are two examples that spring immediately to mind. Although it may not sit very well with certain types of mind set, there seems to be no logical reason at all why it should be impossible for a scientist to ascend to the metalevel and stand outside her theories and perhaps have the view that, whatever may be their ultimate fate, they are the most interesting theories around, so that developing them will constitute a genuine contribution to science (if only perhaps by showing in which respects they need to be replaced).

Kuhn's – apparent – claims about the 'paradigm dependence of everything', the inability of a scientist to be able to step outside a paradigm and take part in a critical debate about its epistemic virtues and failings, of course achieve their sharpest focus and highest importance when it comes to the issue of theory – or paradigm – *change*, that is, when it comes to scientific 'revolutions'.

THE RATIONALITY OF 'REVOLUTIONARY' THEORY CHANGE IN SCIENCE

Whatever Popper's particular claims and occasional oversights, what really drove his resistance to Kuhn's account was surely what he, and many other commentators, perceived as a threat to the objectivity of science and the rationality of scientific progress. The simple account of scientific revolutions that Popper sometimes seemed to endorse – involving outright refutations of the older theory – may not supply the necessary rationale, but one should not, of course, jump from the failure of that particular simple account to the conclusion that there is *no sort* of rationale for (revolutionary) theory change. Yet that is exactly the conclusion that many people saw Kuhn as espousing: successive theories are not comparable but instead 'incommensurable'; the switch to the newer paradigm is a 'conversion experience' rather than a process governed by general rules of theory superiority; 'hold-outs' for older paradigms who do not accept the superiority of the revolutionary new paradigm are 'neither illogical nor unscientific'. Popper, like many others, saw Kuhn as committed to historical relativism, to the claim that critical discussion always presupposes a framework, and therefore to the view that those who operate within different frameworks (support different paradigms) are incapable of fruitful critical interaction (the famous 'dialogue of the deaf'). Hence Popper's charge that Kuhn had succumbed to 'the myth of the framework'; and hence also the charge of many other philosophers of science – Scheffler and Shapere included – that Kuhn had given up on any idea of objective *progress* in science.[11] (At any rate, he had given up on the idea of any progress through revolutionary change of paradigm, as opposed to 'progress as judged within, and by the standards of, a paradigm'.) The charge was put in its bluntest form by Imre Lakatos, who suggested that Kuhn had reduced radical theory change in science to a matter of 'mob psychology'. Elaborating on the point by contrasting what he took to be Kuhn's views with Popper's, Lakatos wrote (p. 93):

> For Popper scientific change is rational or at least rationally reconstructible and falls within the realm of the *logic of discovery*. For Kuhn scientific change – from one 'paradigm' to another – is a mystical conversion that cannot be governed by rules of reason and which falls within the realm of the (*social*) *psychology of discovery*. Scientific change is a kind of religious change.[12]

Did Kuhn really hold the views he is here charged with? Are whatever views he did in fact hold well supported by argument and historical evidence? And do those views indeed challenge the idea that the progress of science has been – at bottom – a 'rational' affair? Did Kuhn win *this* – crucial – part of the argument against Popper (and others)?

Radical sociologists of science influenced by Kuhn seemed to take it that the answer to all four of these questions is 'yes'; and therefore that Kuhn had opened the way to a 'symmetrical', naturalistic explanation of theory choice in science purely in terms of social and psychological factors – an explanation that eschewed any talk of the 'correct' rational choice underwritten by some logic of evidence. On the other hand, 'rationalists' about scientific progress, like Shapere and Lakatos, seemed to take it that Kuhn really did hold the views at issue, that those views really do challenge the idea of scientific change as a rational process, but that they are not in fact convincingly argued and hence that there is no need to reject the older view to which Popper (amongst others) was committed. Matters are not as straightforward as either side imagined.

Kuhn was always insistent that the 'mob psychology' gibe was grotesquely misplaced. And there are indeed passages in his London paper, and more especially in his 'Replies to Critics', that seem to put him quite clearly on the side of those philosophers who took themselves to be his opponents and against those sociologists who took themselves to be drawing and endorsing the 'antirationalist' conclusions of his own analysis. He expressed his belief, for example, that science 'is our surest example of sound knowledge' (p. 20). Again, while accepting that his own account of the development of science shares a good deal with that of Feyerabend, Kuhn added that describing that account (as Feyerabend, of course, did) 'as a defence of irrationality in science seems to me not only absurd but vaguely obscene' (p. 264). And, more extensively and more strikingly, he took the following 'evolutionary' account of scientific knowledge to be very much part of his overall view:

> Imagine . . . an evolutionary tree representing the development of the scientific specialities from their common origin in, say, primitive natural philosophy. Imagine . . . a line drawn up that tree . . . to the tip of some limb without doubling back on itself. Any two theories found along this line are related to each other by descent. . . . [C]onsider two such theories each chosen from a point not too near its origin [i.e., after the science concerned has achieved 'maturity']. I believe it would be easy to design a set of criteria – including maximum accuracy of predictions, degree of specialization, number (but not scope) of concrete problem-solutions – which would enable any observer involved with neither theory to tell which was the older, which the descendant. For me, therefore, scientific development is, like biological evolution, unidirectional and irreversible. One scientific theory is not as good as another for doing what scientists normally do. (p. 264)[13]

Except that he described as 'easy' the central task that 'traditional' philosophers of science have been working on for years and have still far from unambiguously achieved – that of articulating the criteria for one theory to be scientifically superior to another in the light of the evidence – and except perhaps for the striking qualification, to which we shall need to return, that the outside observer judging the two theories must not be 'involved' with either theory, Kuhn in this passage seems to have conceded to his philosophical 'opponents' such as Popper and Lakatos all that they could want. Kuhn here acknowledged that there has been genuine progress in science, not simply mere change; later theories (at least in the mature sciences) are objectively superior to their predecessors. So what could all the fuss have been about?

One issue is, of course, whether the 'pro-objectivity' sentiments that Kuhn expresses here are really consistent with the main thrust of the position developed in *Structure*. A number of questions arise. How can the unambiguous assertion that theory change has been from good to better theories – better according to the sorts of criteria that philosophers have standardly endorsed – be consistent with claims that successive theories (or theoretical systems or paradigms) are incommensurable? How can that assertion be consistent with the famous claims about theory change, so far as an individual scientist is concerned, being a 'conversion experience'? It would seem possible, according to the view just quoted from Kuhn, simply to show such a scientist that the new theory was better than the one he currently held based on the criteria at issue. Again, how is the view just quoted consistent with the famous claim that 'hold-outs' – scientists who continue to endorse the older paradigm in what turns out to be a revolution – cannot be judged 'either illogical or unscientific'? Given that Lavoisier's oxygen theory lies closer to the top of the scientific-evolutionary tree than the phlogiston theory, doesn't it follow that, on the contrary, Priestley, in 'holding out' for the phlogiston theory, *was* unscientific, at least in the sense of continuing to somehow prefer a theory that was objectively inferior to an available rival?

Perhaps not all of these mysteries can be solved, but some of them can be if we go slowly concerning the difficult issues they raise. Let's first return to the question of Kuhn's account of scientists' reactions to anomalies. We saw earlier that Kuhn's disagreement with Popper over the impact on theories of negative experimental results is significantly clarified by recognising – with acknowledgments to Duhem – that the minimum unit of theoretical claims that can come into direct logical conflict with observation statements is not a single 'isolated' theory (such as Newton's theory or Maxwell's theory) but rather a theoretical system, built around such a theory but also involving a range of auxiliary assumptions. It follows that no such isolated theory is ever directly, logically refuted. Kuhn's claim that scientists standardly do treat apparently negative evidence as anomalies rather than refutations, and that there is nothing 'illegitimate' in their so doing, is then, underwritten – at least to the extent that it is indeed always possible, so far as purely logical constraints are concerned, to hold on to the central theory and regard any negative evidence, any anomaly, as requiring some change in the auxiliary assumptions. However, although Popper's blanket assumption that any such move (any such 'immunising stratagem', as he called it elsewhere) is automatically under scientific suspicion was misjudged, it is easy *both* to see what motivated Popper here *and* to empathise with that motivation.

Kuhn stressed in *Structure* that what sustains hold-outs to revolutions is their conviction that the evidence of their revolutionary opponents could be 'shoved into the box' provided by their preferred (older) paradigm.[14] As a statement of mere deductive logical possibility, the claim that Kuhn makes on behalf of his hold-out is definitively underwritten by Duhem's analysis. However, a distinction in terms of scientific value between two quite separate types of case of 'shoving' erstwhile negative evidence into the paradigm's 'box' surely cries out for articulation.

Suppose, contrary to historical fact but for the sake of a simple illustration, that Priestley, in the face of the experimental result that burning mercury in a certain way produces a substance heavier than the original mercury, had held on to the phlogiston theory (whose core assumption was that, whenever anything burned, a substance, namely phlogiston, was given off) by assuming that phlogiston has 'negative weight'. (Hence, removing phlogiston from a substance increases its weight.) Contrast that with the case in which Newtonians insisted that the apparently negative observational results concerning Uranus's orbit can be shoved into the Newtonian box; and Adams and Leverrier postulated a hitherto undiscovered planet whose gravitational interaction with Uranus explained the initial apparent anomaly. Although both instantiate the Kuhnian 'holding on to an existing paradigm' scheme, the first seems purely defensive, while the second was regarded (surely correctly) as one of Newtonian theory's most impressive successes.

The difference between the two is not far to seek. The first was indeed *purely* defensive, ad hoc in the pejorative sense: at best, the move reconciled the preexisting framework with the initially negative-seeming evidence. As such, it stands on a par with the 'reconciliation' with the fossil record of the fundamental creationist claim that God created the world in 4004 B.C. with essentially the same 'kinds' as presently inhabit it. That record *apparently* attests to the existence of very many now-extinct species, but reconciliation can easily be achieved by postulating that God happened to choose to paint pretty pictures in the rocks that *look like* the imprints of the skeletons of animals from extinct species and to mix in with the desert sands some *bonelike* structures. In the Adams and Leverrier case, too, mere reconciliation is fairly cheap. It is always possible to produce a total force function that will account for any observed motion of Uranus, and it may be possible to work back to what assumptions about an extra massive body in the solar system will, in concert with the effects of already known planets, produce that total force. However, there is a crucial difference: in all cases the initially negative experimental result is accommodated, but in the Adams–Leverrier case, quite unlike the phlogiston and creationist ones, the new assumption leads to independent tests. If there is an extra planet in the universe and if its mass and motion are such as to account for the initially anomalous motion of Uranus, then we ought to be able to observe that planet. And indeed, so it was (roughly speaking) that Neptune was discovered.

What distinguishes the scientifically impressive cases from those that are 'mere accommodations' is independent testability and independent empirical success. The new version of the theory, or rather the new theoretical system based on the same central theory, not only accommodates the initial anomaly, it also successfully predicts some new fact. This is exactly the distinction between progressive and degenerating research programmes that lies at the heart of Lakatos's attempted synthesis of Popper and Kuhn: his 'methodology of scientific research programmes'. Although the point is already essentially in Duhem, it is not one that Kuhn acknowledged (at any rate in any clear way) in *Structure*.

Lakatos accepted that not every move in response to erstwhile anomalies would be met with success even within programmes (or paradigms) that are scientifically in good shape. A well-known example concerns stellar parallax and the Copernican theory. If, as Copernican theory centrally postulates, we are on a moving observatory, the Earth, then two 'fixed' stars ought to appear to us at least a little closer together at certain times (when we are relatively far from them) than they do at others (when we are relatively close). Hence Copernican theory predicts stellar parallax: the apparently relative motion of any one fixed star relative to any other close to it. On the other hand, of course, Ptolemaic theory, since it postulates a stationary Earth, predicts no such motion. At the time, and indeed well into the nineteenth century, no stellar parallax was observed. The response of Copernicans was essentially that there must indeed be such apparent parallactic motions, and that the explanation of the failure to observe them must be that they are so small (since the radius of the Earth's orbit is so small compared to the distance between the sun and even the nearest star) that they were invisible even to the best available telescopic observations. The new theoretical system does make a prediction that is, at least in principle, independently testable: that increasingly accurate telescopes will eventually reveal stellar parallax. But clearly in this case there was no question of an immediate independent *success*. Hence Lakatos characterised a research programme as progressive if its successive versions (some, though not all, produced in response to negative evidence for their predecessor) are (i) consistently independently testable (they make testable predictions over and beyond those of the previous version about phenomena other than those that refuted the predecessor system) and (ii) at least now and then (and preferably often) are independently confirmed – that is, are successful in those independent tests. Otherwise, and particularly when successive versions do no more than accommodate what had been anomalies for their predecessors, the programme is degenerating.

According to Lakatos, progressive programmes are objectively scientifically superior to degenerating rivals. His characterisation of progress and degeneration is what inserts 'hard objective elements' into Kuhn's account. It revises in a radical way the view expressed by Popper in clause 7 of his account of tests. Reacting to a negative result by modifying the theory (really creating a new theoretical system with the same central, or at any rate core, theory) need not in general 'destroy or at least reduce' the scientific character of the (central) theory. Instead such a reaction actually *increases* its scientific value, and hence the value of the research programme that it underpins, if the modification is independently testable and independently confirmed, and decreases its scientific value only if the reaction is purely ad hoc, that is, merely accommodatory, with no independent testability.

Lakatos's claim was, of course, that scientific revolutions invariably consist of the – at least eventual – replacement of a degenerating research programme by a progressive one based on a rival central theory. This is what explains the development of science as a 'rational' process. By the early nineteenth century, the programme based on the particulate theory of light (that light consists of tiny material particles affected by various forces) had a long history of consistent degeneration; Fresnel produced a rival programme (or rather significantly developed an existing programme) based on the idea that light consists of periodic disturbances transmitted through an all-pervading elastic medium and made that programme impressively progressive. For example, in response to the initial difficulty produced by the observation that the interference fringes disappear when the two-slit experiment is performed with orthogonally polarised beams of light coming through the two slits, Fresnel shifted to a new theoretical system (involving transverse rather than longitudinal waves) that made exciting new predictions about crystal optics, and these predictions were empirically confirmed. This is why the revolution was rational.

Any Kuhnian hold-out to this revolution would have been trivially correct – courtesy again of Duhem – in claiming that the successful empirical results pointed to by the wave revolutionaries could, *somehow or other*, be shoved into the corpuscular box (some scientists were tempted to explain interference fringes, for example, as physiological phenomena caused by two streams of light particles hitting the eye in such a way as to create interference at the retina); but they would have been quite wrong – as Kuhn at least in *Structure* failed to recognise – if they believed that such shoving automatically balances the evidential scales. A programme gets more scientific brownie points, higher confirmation, from data that it predicts than it does from data that it merely accommodates: if the wave theory predicts the interference fringes, then a hold-out would be quite wrong to think that producing an ad hoc not-further-testable accommodation of the fringes by invoking physiology, for example, automatically balances the evidential scales.[15]

Although Kuhn did not, either in the original London address or in his 'Replies to Critics', explicitly accept this point, he *did* express agreement with at least the broad outlines of Lakatos's 'often admirable' paper. And he seems quite explicitly to have held that the difference between their basic views is little more than terminological: 'Though [Lakatos's] terminology is different, his analytic apparatus is as close to mine as need be: hard core, work in the protective belt, and degenerative phase are close parallels for my paradigms, normal science and crisis' (p. 256).

This brief passage hides significant concessions.[16] In particular, if Kuhn accepted that his 'analytic apparatus' is essentially the same as Lakatos's, then he seems now to stand committed to an altogether more objective view of 'crisis' than most commentators had believed. It is not just a sociological fact that a scientific community is suddenly gripped by a feeling of crisis involving a loss of confidence in the ability of the paradigm to deal with the anomalies it faces, nor is it an internal paradigm-dependent matter whether a particular anomaly has been properly, scientifically resolved. Whatever the paradigm, the rules – at least at the abstract, general level – for what counts as an adequate resolution of an anomaly are always the same: the theoretical framework within the paradigm that resolves the anomaly should count as a 'progressive shift'; the resolution, in other words, should not just resolve the anomaly, it should also produce independently testable predictions, some of which are confirmed. A crisis for a paradigm again seems to have a cross-paradigm characterisation: a paradigm is in crisis if it hits a consistently degenerating phase in Lakatos's sense.

So Kuhn made two concessions to what we might term the 'objectivists': the 'progress concession' (the evolutionary tree) and the 'same as Lakatos concession'. Whether he ever seriously thought through the question of how far these concessions cohere with the main body of the views he expressed in *Structure* is unclear to me. Indeed, it is not even clear if he thought through the question of whether the two different concessions – for all that they undoubtedly point in the same direction – are themselves fully coherent. Consider again Kuhn's list of objective factors that in combination will invariably distinguish the newer from the older theory on the evolutionary tree of scientific knowledge. The only one that might be thought to be Kuhn's version of the crucial Lakatosian criterion of *independent* predictive success is 'maximum accuracy of predictions'; and there Kuhn in fact seems to have been using 'prediction' just in the sense of empirical consequence and hence referring simply to the empirical adequacy of the theory. (Lakatos's problem, following Duhem, was, of course, the ever-present possibility of producing specific theories based on different cores that are equally adequate empirically in the straightforward sense of entailing all the same empirical consequences and yet that, intuitively speaking, do not at all stand on a par with respect to the evidence.) The fact probably is, I suggest, that Kuhn had little interest in what he thought of as a relatively trivial issue; it was clear to him that later theories in the mature sciences are in objective ways superior to earlier ones. He was willing to concede entirely to the philosophers that there are objective cross-paradigm standards for when one theory is scientifically superior to another, and was happy to leave it to them to take their best shot at the – 'relatively easy' – task of articulating the details of those standards. He himself was interested in the question of 'theory choice' in some other, and for him more challenging, sense.

What exactly was this sense, and what exactly were Kuhn's claims about it? As preliminaries to tackling this question, two issues require investigation. The first is Kuhn's reaction in his London 'Replies' to Popper's charge that he was guilty of historical relativism. Kuhn insisted that there are two senses in which he might be accused of relativism: in the first sense he is no relativist, and although he is guilty of relativism in the second sense, this is not a charge that anyone should worry about. Relativism of the first kind denies that science has made progress according to cross-paradigm criteria, and his remarks about the evolutionary tree are his explicit denial of guilt on that charge. What is the second sense of historical relativism? Kuhn explained:

> [T]here is another step . . . which many philosophers of science wish to take and which I refuse. They wish, that is, to compare theories as representations of nature, as statements about 'what is really out there'. Granting that neither theory of a historical pair is true, they nonetheless seek a sense in which the later is a better approximation to the truth. I believe nothing of that sort can be found. On the other hand, I no longer feel that anything

is lost, least of all the ability to explain scientific progress, by taking this position. (pp. 264–5)

In other words, Kuhn explicitly rejected any form of scientific realism but insisted that this did not imply the rejection of the thesis that science has made progress according to objective criteria. His argument against scientific realism was simply that he found it impossible to see in actual cases of successive theory changes from the history of science anything like a consistent movement towards greater 'approximate truth'.

Whether or not the argument is convincing, his view that the realism issue and the rationality/progress issue can be treated separately surely ought to have been uncontroversial. Suppose that philosophers of science had succeeded in producing the correct 'inductive logic' (in the broadest sense) – the rules, common across the whole scientific endeavour, for how evidence relates to theories and for how, in some instances at least, the evidence may establish a preference for one theory over its rivals. And suppose that philosophers had shown that the actual progress of science could be fully explained according to these rules; each change of theory in the history of the mature sciences constituted a move to a theory that was (at least eventually – see later) better 'supported' by the evidence than its predecessor. They would then have shown that there is one set of rules (at least at the abstract level) that characterises the whole 'game of science'.

The further question could still be raised of what *justifies* those rules: why play *that* game? Why prefer theories that are better supported by the evidence rather than, say, theories that show greater consistency with holy writ? One obvious (attempted) justification – no doubt the first we would think of – is the 'realist' one that playing the scientific game will (or, more plausibly, is more likely to) lead towards the truth. But one can clearly reject that answer, and perhaps substitute another, without at the same time questioning that the 'right' rules have been identified. An instrumentalist or another kind of antirealist, who denies that scientific theories are true or approximately true, can still hold that the way scientific theories are judged on the basis of the evidence is an objective matter, satisfying very general rules that remain the same throughout science (usually, in the case of instrumentalists, rules to do centrally with empirical adequacy and simplicity). Such an antirealist would continue to hold that there has been progress in science towards better and better theories, and would simply deny that 'better and better' here means 'truer and truer'.[17]

This is certainly not a point on which Kuhn was in conflict with either Popper or Lakatos. Popper encouraged the *conjecture* that successive theories accepted in science, each of which is (allegedly) an improvement over its predecessor according to the criteria he favoured, also have montonically increasing 'verisimilitude' – but this was clearly an 'optional extra', not something that is inherent in rationality on his view.[18] And similarly, Lakatos talked explicitly and often about *linking* what, using Popperian terms, he took to be judgments of corroboration, on the one hand, and judgments of verisimilitude, on the other. Science makes progress, scientific theory change is rational, because successive theories have greater corroboration. The link to scientific realism, via verisimilitude – that is, to the issue of whether, by preferring better corroborated theories, we are being taken closer and closer to the truth – is an independent, and philosophically challenging, matter.[19]

The second issue over which Kuhn still thinks of himself as in some conflict with 'the' philosophers despite the progress concession is aimed more directly at the rationality issue. Kuhn's remarks in his London 'Replies to Critics' about theory choice presage those in Chapter 13 of his *Essential Tension* (1977). Conceding that there are indeed 'objective factors' (simplicity, empirical scope, and the like) that undoubtedly play an important role in theory, choice and conceding that these factors may all *eventually* point in the same direction and thus declare that the same one of two rival theories is superior, Kuhn none the less insisted that *at the time that the debate between the two theories was a live one in the history of science*, it is generally the case (i) that the objective factors are not univocal – some will favour one theory, while others favour its rival – and (ii) that different scientists may – legitimately – differ in their judgments as to which of the two theories is favoured, even with respect to a single objective factor. As Kuhn himself put it in his London 'Replies' concerning point (i): '[I]n many concrete situations, different [epistemic] values, though all constitutive of good reasons, dictate different conclusions, different [theory] choices' (p. 262).

And he suggested, as an illustration, that 'one theory [may be] simpler, but the other . . . more accurate' (ibid.) Concerning point (ii), he wrote:

> More important, though scientists share these values and must continue to do so if science is to survive, they do not all apply them in the same way. Simplicity, scope, fruitfulness, and even accuracy can be judged quite differently (which is not to say that they can be judged arbitrarily) by different people. (Ibid.)

The objectivist should surely have no problem with point (i): it may well be – in fact, it would be amazing were it not the case – that a clear judgment about which of two theories is objectively superior emerges only after a protracted period of rivalry and development. Once we have the picture, not of complete theories springing in final form out of the heads of their creators, but rather of developing paradigms or research programmes (together, of course, with a developing evidential basis), this comes as little surprise. Moreover, the sensible objectivist will have some way of combining the various criteria, and so having two criteria point in opposite directions need not prevent her from pronouncing one theory superior to the other in an overall sense. (Indeed, for the ultrasensible objectivist, the criterion of independent empirical success is dominant.)

Point (ii) raises more difficulties. Indeed, it is not at all easy to see how to reconcile Kuhn's claim here with the progress concession quoted earlier. The image of the evolutionary tree involves an observer who stands back from the scientific process and is always capable of making seemingly definitive judgments about the overall scientific merit of competing theories (given, of course, the evidence that has accumulated up to a certain point). This seems to require clear-cut criteria, and yet now we are told that these objective factors operate instead as 'values' that, without being arbitrary, may none the less be 'judged quite differently ... by different people'. This presumably has something to do with Kuhn's qualifying remark that the observer who judges which is the later (and better) of two theories must be 'involved' with neither; what exactly this is, however, is not clear. Adding to the confusion is Kuhn's continued insistence on the existence of incommensurability. Admittedly, Kuhn suggested in his 'Replies' that he had only ever regarded this as an 'obstacle' to adequate communication across a paradigm divide rather than as something that showed that such communication is impossible.[20] But it is not clear how the progress concession can be consistent with *any* claim of incommensurability.

I am more than happy to leave it to others to decide what, if anything, Kuhn really meant by this total package of remarks about progress, theory choice, incommensurability, and the rest. Here is my best shot concerning what he *may* have been getting at – a view that, although inevitably revisionary to some extent, is (i) consistent with *some* of the things he wrote, (ii) reasonably interesting, and (iii) arguably true.

It is a seductive idea that philosophers of science should be centrally concerned with explaining the attitudes taken towards rival theories by particular scientists. Was Priestley's choice to continue to favour the phlogiston theory irrational, while, say, Einstein's choice to abandon classical physics was rational? Were Kepler and Galileo rational in choosing to develop Copernican theory, while those who continued to espouse some sort of Aristotelian–Ptolemaic view were irrational? After all, it might be thought, a scientific revolution consists at root of scientists making the decision to choose some newer theory in preference to a previously established one, and how could such a revolution be explained as rational except by exhibiting the choices made by the individual scientists, or by a large majority of them, as rational?

However, the primary concern of philosophy of science is surely not with the decisions of scientists at all but rather with the relationships between theory and evidence, and in particular with judgments about the strength of support provided by various pieces of evidence for particular rival theories. These judgments concern the abstraction that might be called the 'intellectual state of the debate at a given time'; they are logical judgments in a broad sense and make no reference to individuals at all.[21] There is then the *further* issue of how such (inductive) logical judgments – the result of the two-slit experiment strongly favours the wave theory of light compared to its rivals, the fossil record is strong evidence for Darwinian theory despite the fact that creationists can accommodate that record by writing it into God's creation, and so on – relate to the decisions and preferences of individual scientists. It ought always to have been clear that this issue is a complex and difficult one. It is blindingly obvious – at least once the issue is addressed head on – that nothing as simple as 'the rational person chooses the evidentially best-supported theory' will work.

If choosing a theory involves choosing to work on it (or advocating that others work on it), then, as has often been recognised, such a link would automatically declare the great revolutionary scientists irrational. After all, these are the innovators who choose to work on some theory *before* it is 'the best available in the light of the evidence', and indeed through whose work that theory assumes that mantle. Suppose we could, for example, explain Kepler and Galileo as having made rational choices to adopt the Copernican theory in preference to the Ptolemaic or Tychonic theory because the evidence available to them favoured the former. Even so, we clearly could not produce such an explanation in the case of Copernicus himself. No doubt in this case, as in all others, there was a preexisting reason to object to the prevailing theory – here the Ptolemaic one – but the latter was, of course, none the less the best-supported theory available to Copernicus at the time that he started to work on his own theory. It was only through the latter's efforts that the evidential tables *began* to be turned.

On the other hand, if choosing a theory means regarding it as true or as established by the evidence (and there is no doubt that some scientists have chosen theories in this sense), then it is not at all clear that such choices ought to be sanctioned by any adequate normative account of the relationship between theory and evidence in science. It has been clear at least since the time of Hume (and in fact since the time of the ancient Greeks) that no amount of evidence ever deductively entails a general scientific theory. But it is not immediately obvious that we need to take seriously the mere possibility that a theory *might* turn out to be false, no matter how well established it might appear in view of the evidence accumulated at a particular time. That possibility might have been just a philosopher's fancy. The history of radical theory change in science – highlighted above all by Kuhn himself and earlier by Popper – shows that the possibility cannot be dismissed in this way. No theory seemed better established than Newton's theory of motion plus universal gravitation – to the extent that eighteenth- and nineteenth-century scientists were wont to lament that there was only one truth about the universe, that Newton had discovered it, and that all that was left to them was to fill in a few details and footnotes. Yet the Einsteinian revolution, while showing that Newton's theory is indeed a highly adequate empirical approximation in the case of relatively slow-moving bodies, also showed that the whole framework on which it is based – involving absolute space, absolute simultaneity, and action at a distance – is totally false. It seems that a scientist had better choose no theory at all, if choosing it implies believing it to be true.

Kuhn's notion of 'theory choice', employed both here in his London 'Replies' and in Chapter 13 of his *Essential Tension*, clearly requires clarification.[22] One clear-cut way in which a scientist might choose a theory is by choosing to try to develop it (or, speaking our Sunday, or Duhemian, best, choosing to try to replace the currently best available theoretical system built around the theory with a still better one based on the same core). As we saw, there can be no rule always to choose to work on the core theory that presently gets most support from the evidence, and in fact, a scientist clearly might choose to work on a theory for a variety of reasons that have no uniform relationship to her (degree of) belief in the theory or in its current epistemic virtues. (So, for example, Newton worked on Descartes's vortex theory, which already looked highly problematic and had little empirical support, in order to show once and for all that it was hopeless. Einstein contributed significantly to the quantum theory, through his account of the photoelectric effect, while famously rejecting the idea that quantum theory could be, at any rate, the *complete* truth about its domain. Much of Einstein's attitude is captured by the judgment that, although quantum theory clearly had more support from the evidence than any other alternative, it needed to be replaced by a theory with quite different metaphysical commitments that would nonetheless recapture – and indeed extend – the empirical success of quantum mechanics.)

Nonetheless, it may well be true, sociologically speaking, that as a broad statistical generalisation, most scientists who make significant contributions to a theory have 'taken it to their hearts' in a stronger sense than the *apparently* rather anemic one of simply regarding it as currently best supported by the evidence.[23] The great innovators no doubt believe that they can turn the theory they have chosen into the best-supported theory in its field – a belief that cannot, by definition, be justified by the current evidence. And no doubt the 'normal' scientists who choose to develop some theory have attitudes towards it that, if generally vague and sometimes misguidedly strong (such as outright belief in its truth), clearly go beyond that of merely regarding it as currently better supported empirically than any rival. It may also be true, as Kuhn, following Planck, suggested, that scientists who have contributed to one theory find it especially difficult to commit themselves in the same way to a newer theory even when, assessed on the objective factors, that newer theory looks superior.

It was this extra, and rather ill-defined, 'oomph' – the commitment factor, if you like – that chiefly fascinated Kuhn. And concerning *it*, it is unclear whether an orthodox rationalist philosopher such as Popper, Lakatos, or the others need object to talk of conversion experiences, only partial mutual understanding, or even incommensurability. This commitment involves, in all cases, at least a judgment made on the basis of the current state of the theory and the evidence for it about how some modified version of that theory will look in the light of *future* evidence – and such judgments obviously and inevitably lie outside of the purview of the sort of 'inductive logic' judgments that philosophers have traditionally sought to articulate and defend.

Here then is one way to understand Kuhn's final position. *Firstly* there is, just as 'the' philosophers of science have insisted, always an objectively correct judgment to be made about how various rival theories, at a given time, stand in relation to the evidence. There is (this is the undeniably revisionary part, since Kuhn explicitly said the opposite) no leeway, no room for (informed) subjective disagreement, concerning judgments about the objective factors that go into making that overall judgment about what might be called the 'state of the intellectual debate' between the various rival theories at any given time in the light of the evidence available at that time. (In so far as there are genuine differences between individual scientists about these matters, they either result from a mistake by one of them or – no doubt more often – are best interpreted as views about how some *future* version of one or more theories, the outlines of which the scientist may feel she has in mind, will look with respect to the objective factor concerned.) That state of the intellectual debate sets the context within which the individual scientist operates. However, *secondly*, there is *clearly* a lot more to the process of science than simply the state of the intellectual debate, much more to the choices and decisions of scientists; for one thing, because those scientists are engaged in *changing* that state of the debate. It is here that flesh-and-blood decisions, conversion experiences, disagreement, and failure fully to communicate all may come in.

On this interpretation, then, laying aside the (important) issues about falsification, there was no real need for Popper and Kuhn to be at odds. Popper could concede that the points that Kuhn made about theory choice all belong in the context of discovery (rather than the context of justification or, better for Popper, the context of appraisal). And Popper always insisted that only the latter context is ruled by logic. Popper needed to have no quarrel with Kuhn's claim that psychological and sociological factors play ineliminable roles in theory choice if that is construed as essentially a context of discovery notion. The issue of whether this analysis of theory choice reconciles Kuhn's views with those of Lakatos is altogether more difficult. Lakatos was always troubled by Feyerabend's charge that philosophy of science was rather empty if it *simply* laid down rules of appraisal and hence allowed any theory choice in this Kuhnian sense I have attributed to Kuhn, as long as the chooser correctly acknowledged the current 'state of the intellectual debate'. Moreover, Lakatos saw (if not always clearly) one element of the appraisal of the *current* state of a research programme as a measure of its current heuristic power – essentially of how many related ideas for constructing specific theories within the programme remained unexhausted. Even more than thirty years on, I believe that the issues raised by this suggestion and the related question of how much of the process of theory change in science can be explained as a rational process remain both pressing and unanswered.[24]

Notes

1. Lakatos and Musgrave (1970). Unadorned page references throughout this essay are to this book.
2. In fact, Popper took the chair at the symposium led by Kuhn, but made several contributions to the discussion and, of course, developed his response in his (1970) paper.
3. This is, of course, based on a confusion. The problem, as we shall see in detail later, is exactly that the sort of theory that Popper had in mind: 'single' scientific

theories, such as those of Newton or Maxwell, are not refutable 'in isolation' (as Duhem put it) and hence are never directly 'found to be false'. It would be irrational indeed for a scientist to continue to hold a theory that had been 'found to be false'. The fact rather is that such scientists are claiming that the theory may still be true and that the apparently negative evidence is explained by the falsity of some other theoretical assumption.

4. Kuhn's reference is to Thorndike (1923–58), 5. In fact, astrology's so-called failed predictions are unimpressive. Of course, there is an implicit assumption in talking about the predictive success of science that the predictions are properly derived from a theory (or rather theoretical system) and not just thrown out more or less at random, with little or no connection with any theory. But, so far as I can tell, the 'predictions' that Thorndike cites are all of the latter sort. But that means that if the prediction fails, that failure supplies no refutation of any set of astrological theories. Hence Thorndike's examples seem to underwrite Popper's point rather than challenge it.

5. Duhem (1906). Although it is often nowadays referred to as the 'Duhem–Quine thesis', Quine in fact added nothing of substance.

6. In fact, the real historical story was very different and much less confrontational. However, as so often happens, the rationally reconstructed account helps make the methodological issues much sharper.

7. In fact, contrary to the Lakatos version, this is basically what happened historically.

8. See my (2000b) article for an account of, and references to, the recent revival of the old Newtonian idea of deduction from the phenomena.

9. See my (1996) work and especially my (2002b) article.

10. See my (1996) work for references and discussion.

11. See Scheffler (1967) and Shapere (1964).

12. Lakatos here uses the term 'logic of discovery' in the Pickwickian sense that makes Popper's book a real contribution to that field. What he really meant, of course, was 'logic of theory appraisal'.

13. Although the message is clear, Kuhn did not explain himself as clearly as he might have. Obviously, if the tree has already been drawn, one can tell which theory is the later one. What Kuhn clearly really meant was that such an outside observer could use the 'objective factors' to *construct* the evolutionary tree.

14. See *Structure*, pp. 151–2: 'The source of resistance is the assurance that the older paradigm will solve all its problems, that nature can be shoved into the box the paradigm supplies.'

15. I have tried to clarify and extend the earlier treatments of the 'prediction versus accommodation' debate by Lakatos, Zahar, and myself in my (2002a) work.

16. Again, this means 'concessions relative to the position that most philosophers initially took Kuhn to be adopting'. It seems to me an unclear, and relatively uninteresting, issue whether they are concessions relative to Kuhn's 'real' initial position or merely clarifications.

17. Indeed, the main thesis of van Fraassen's later – and very influential – (1980) book is precisely that the phenomenon of the rational acceptance of a theory in science can be explained without any assumption about the theory's truth.

18. Kuhn made a repeated mistake concerning Popper's notion of verisimilitude. He supposed that Popper (and Lakatos following him) intended it as an 'effective' notion: that there should be some algorithm for arriving at a value of a theory's verisimilitude. See in particular p. 238, where Kuhn explicitly talked about Popper attempting to provide 'an algorithm for verisimilitude'. But Popper was quite explicit that he was attempting to do for approximate truth what Tarski had done for full-blown truth – namely, providing a 'metaphysical' account of *what it would mean* for one theory to be a closer approximation to the truth than another in a way that need not (and did not) carry any 'epistemological' component – instructing one how to arrive at actual judgments about verisimilitude in particular cases.

19. For one thing, it involves a 'whiff' of induction. See in particular Lakatos (1974).

20. Kuhn talks, on pp. 231–2, of incommensurability as amounting to 'partial or incomplete communication'; and he acknowledges that those accepting incommensurable frameworks are *not* left without recourse – 'there must be recourse.... Given what they share, they can find out much about how they differ. At least they can do so if they have sufficient will, patience and tolerance of threatening ambiguity....' (pp. 276–7).

21. Admittedly, Bayesianism, currently perhaps the most popular systematic philosophy of science, blurs the distinction by talking in terms of the degrees of belief of Bayesian *agents*. But this, in turn, is a logical abstraction. There is no such thing as a real Bayesian agent, since she would have to be, amongst other things, a perfect deductive logician. For a systematic treatment of the relationship between Kuhn's analysis of science and personalist Bayesianism, see my (2000a) work.

22. For systematic attempts to clarify this notion see Earman (1993) and my (2000a) work.

23. It isn't in fact so anemic; see my (1978) and (2000a) works.

24. I have tried to provide some important preliminary clarifications in my (2000a) essay.

References

Duhem, P. 1906. *The Aim and Structure of Physical Theory*. (English translation of the second [1914] edition, 1954). Princeton: Princeton University Press.

Earman, J. S. 1993. 'Carnap, Kuhn and the Philosophy of Scientific Methodology'. In: P. Horwich, ed. *World Changes: Thomas Kuhn and the Nature of Science*. Cambridge, MA: MIT Press, pp. 9–36.

Kuhn, T. S. 1962. *The Structure of Scientific Revolutions*. Chicago: University of Chicago Press.

1970. 'Logic of Discovery or Psychology of Research?' In: Lakatos and Musgrave (1970), pp. 1–23.

1977. *The Essential Tension*. Chicago: University of Chicago Press.

Lakatos, I. 1970. 'Falsification and the Methodology of Scientific Research Programmes'. In: Lakatos and Musgrave (1970), pp. 91–195.

1974. 'Popper on Demarcation and Induction'. In: P. A. Schilpp, ed. *The Philosophy of Karl Popper*. La Salle: Open Court, pp. 241–73.

Lakatos, I., and A. Musgrave, eds. 1970. *Criticism and the Growth of Knowledge*. Cambridge: Cambridge University Press.

Popper, K. R. 1958. *The Logic of Scientific Discovery*. London: Hutchison.

1963. *Conjectures and Refutations*. London: Routledge.

1970. 'Normal Science and Its Dangers'. In: Lakatos and Musgrave (1970), pp. 51–8.

Scheffler, I. 1967. *Science and Subjectivity*. Indianapolis: Bobbs Merrill.

Shapere, D. 1964. 'The Structure of Scientific Revolutions'. *Philosophical Review* 73: 383–94.

Thorndike, L. 1923–58. *A History of Magic and Experimental Science*. 8 vols. New York: Columbia University Press.

Van Fraassen, B. 1980. *The Scientific Image*. Oxford: Oxford University Press.

Worrall, J. 1978. 'Against Too Much Method'. *Erkenntnis* 13: 279–95.

1996. ' "Revolution in Permanence": Popper on Theory-Change in Science'. In: A. O'Hear, ed. *Karl Popper: Philosophy and Problems*. Cambridge: Cambridge University Press, pp. 75–102.

2000a. 'Kuhn, Bayes and "Theory-Choice": How Revolutionary Is Kuhn's Account of Scientific Change?' In: R. Nola and H. Sankey, eds. *After Popper, Kuhn and Feyerabend. Recent Issues in Theories of Scientific Method*. Dordrecht: Kluwer, pp. 125–51.

2000b. 'The Scope, Limits and Distinctiveness of the Method of "Deduction from the Phenomena": Some Lessons from Newton's "Demonstrations" in Optics'. *British Journal for the Philosophy of Science* 51: 45–80.

2002a. ' "Heuristic Power" and the "Logic of Scientific Discovery": Why MSRP Is No More Than Half the Story'. In: G. Kempis, ed. *The Impact of Lakatos's Philosophy*. Dordrecht: Kluwer.

2002b. 'New Evidence for Old'. In: P. Gardenfors, K. Kijania-Placek, and J. Wolenski, eds. *Proceedings of the 11th International Congress in Logic, Methodology and Philosophy of Science*. Dordrecht: Kluwer.

4 | Kuhn's Philosophy of Scientific Practice[1]

JOSEPH ROUSE

The opening sentence of *The Structure of Scientific Revolutions* is often thought to be prophetic. Kuhn proclaimed that "history of science . . . could produce a decisive transformation in the image of science by which we are now possessed" (1970, p. 1). In the decade or so after the book was published in 1962, the dominant philosophical conception of science, logical empiricism, was indeed substantially transformed. Moreover, although Kuhn's book at the time was only one among a half dozen prominent challenges to logical empiricism, it has in retrospect become the symbol for its own revolution, marking a transition to a postempiricist era in the philosophy of science.[2] Citations of Kuhn are now ubiquitous in various contrasts between the supposedly bad old days and some more enlightened present conception of science.

Proclamations of revolution are often succeeded by revisionist debunking. That fate may well befall Kuhn's book. In the past decade or so, a number of scholars have convincingly called attention to important continuities between Kuhn's book and the work of his logical empiricist predecessors.[3] Others note that Kuhn and his most sympathetic readers have repudiated the most radical-sounding claims associated with the book.[4] In a still different vein, one scholar has argued that Kuhn's book was reactionary rather than revolutionary: Fuller (1999) claims both that Kuhn aimed to insulate science from public scrutiny and democratic control, and that, contrary to its public image, the philosophical and social scientific work most influenced by Kuhn has had just that effect.

In what follows, I propose a different revisionist response to the opening proclamation of Kuhn's book. I shall argue that there was indeed implicit in Kuhn's book a potentially revolutionary transformation in the predominant conception of science. This revolution has not (yet) occurred, however. Philosophers and other theorists of science have not yet grasped, let alone achieved, a Kuhnian transformation in their conception of science. To say this is not to deny that important conceptual changes occurred in the wake of Kuhn's book, or that these actual developments in the philosophical understanding of science were important or illuminating. Rather, I would argue that these philosophical developments reflect attempts to accommodate Kuhn's claims and arguments within familiar conceptions of the philosophy of science. On my reading, however, *The Structure of Scientific Revolutions* is best understood as challenging the conceptual frame within which the book itself has been influentially read and interpreted. Thus, a truly decisive Kuhnian transformation in the current image of science will also transform the most familiar accounts of that book.

The pivotal question in my rereading of Kuhn concerns the subject matter of the philosophy of science. Traditionally, philosophy of science has been conceived epistemologically. Its subject matter is scientific knowledge, and the relevant philosophical questions concern the aim, structure, sources, methods, and justification of scientific knowledge. In his opening chapter, Kuhn derided the conception of scientific knowledge as the subject matter of philosophical reflection as one derived from the presentation of science in pedagogical textbooks. An "image [of science] drawn mainly from the study of finished scientific achievements . . . is no more likely to fit the enterprise that produced them than an image of a national culture drawn from a tourist brochure or a language text." Most readers of Kuhn have taken this claim to imply that we need a different conception of scientific knowledge. I take Kuhn to have proposed a more fundamental challenge to a textbook-driven image of science, aiming for "the quite different concept of science that can emerge from the historical record of the *research activity itself*."[5] Kuhn then went on to say that this aim requires different questions to be asked about science and its history, and not merely different answers to the familiar questions that arise from the textbook image of science.

The alternative I propose is that Kuhn articulated a philosophical conception of science as "the research activity itself," or in the terms I prefer, of science as a practice. Kuhn himself was not always fully clear in articulating this distinction between epistemological and practical conceptions of science. Thus, readers who have understood Kuhn as offering novel answers to old questions have not altogether misunderstood him. He did not always fully grasp just how deeply his approach challenged familiar views, and there are coherent readings of the book that assimilate him to the tradition. But Kuhn was also well aware that the traditional conceptions and the questions they generate did not serve him well in articulating the alternative understanding of science for which he aimed. His misgivings about the adequacy of the very terms available for framing his discussion sometimes came out quite explicitly:

> In the absence of a developed alternative [to the epistemological viewpoint that has guided Western philosophy for three centuries], I find it impossible to relinquish entirely that viewpoint. Yet it no longer functions effectively.... (Kuhn 1970, p. 126)

Even this claim was ambiguous; it could be read as calling for a different epistemological viewpoint rather than for a viewpoint on science that is no longer primarily epistemological. The best argument for the latter reading of Kuhn's misgivings is to show how his own book began to articulate such a more far-reaching alternative, and that is what I shall do here. This alternative is best recognized, however, by contrast to the more familiar epistemological interpretations. Hence, I shall begin with my best reconstruction of how Kuhn has been assimilated within a more traditional conception of science and use that as a foil for my own preferred interpretation of the book.

THE FAMILIAR KUHN

This section develops an interpretation of *The Structure of Scientific Revolutions* that I do not fully endorse. I nevertheless present it in my own voice, without further qualification. This presentation is not merely for rhetorical convenience. This reading of Kuhn offers a defensible interpretation of the book, and also presents a thoughtful and informative conception of science. Some aspects of it are surely worth retaining. I reject it not for any obvious inadequacy of its own, but for an alternative that offers a better reading of Kuhn in large part because it promises a better understanding of science.

Kuhn began by discussing "normal science," in which scientists forgo any dispute about the most fundamental concepts and theories in their discipline in order to extend and refine them. These concepts and theories function together as components of a paradigm, a set of theoretical commitments that had either originally established or subsequently reconstituted a whole field of inquiry. Challenges to the paradigm are rejected as a distraction from scientists' primary task of describing the world in these accepted terms. A paradigm offers a comprehensive worldview for those who accept it, and such worldviews serve crucial functions for normal scientific inquiry. Paradigms prescribe some core beliefs as essential to work in this field and proscribe others as unacceptable. They determine which facts would be important to know and what instrumental, methodological, and theoretical tools are worth acquiring. Paradigms also strongly suggest how to proceed with these tasks, but these suggestions require considerable creativity, ingenuity, and hard work to carry out successfully. They constitute the puzzles whose solutions are the primary aim of normal scientific research.

The analogy between scientific research and puzzle solving is illuminating for Kuhn in multiple respects. Like jigsaw or crossword puzzles, scientific puzzles focus attention on reasonably well-defined gaps or deficiencies within a comprehensive scheme. At the outset, the overall scheme may be only sketchily articulated, but as work proceeds successfully, other puzzles become more sharply and accessibly characterized. Yet such puzzle-solving can be intelligibly undertaken only through an unquestioned acceptance of the overall scheme. If one were to doubt the core commitments that define puzzles or otherwise question the existence of unique, accessible solutions to them, the characteristically focused, dogged efforts of puzzle solvers would be misplaced. Failures are taken to mark inadequate effort or ingenuity by the puzzle solvers rather than erroneous features of the paradigm. Paradigms provide both normative and heuristic guides to scientific puzzle solving. Normatively, they indicate which puzzles are worth solving, what is the point of their solution, and thus what standards govern the acceptability of proposed solutions. Heuristically, they offer model problem solutions ("exemplars") that provide analogical guidance for how to extend past successes to new situations.

Kuhn also made constructive use of what might initially seem to be a disanalogy between puzzle solving and science. Crossword or jigsaw puzzle-solving may seem trivial and self-absorbed by comparison to science, for they lack the intellectual and practical significance usually accorded to scientific achievements. But Kuhn found the more transcendent goals of science to be too remote from day-to-day work to be motivationally significant; the challenge of solving a difficult puzzle provides a more immediately relevant goal for most scientists. More important, Kuhn used the puzzle-solving analogy to explain why scientific work is (and perhaps should be) mostly insulated from the demand to satisfy externally defined goals. He thought scientific work could satisfy practical and intellectual goals defined by socially salient concerns only to the extent that these tasks could be recast as soluble puzzles within the terms provided by available paradigms. For Kuhn, this analogy thus explained and partly justified scientists' relatively insular specialization and partial professional indifference to larger social goals.

Paradigms are thus closely linked to inward-looking scientific communities that accept and use them. Indeed, Kuhn thought that neither paradigms nor research communities could be readily identified apart from one another: paradigms are the core commitments of scientific communities, whose boundaries are defined by their shared acceptance of a paradigm. Such definitions of communities are not just retrospective abstractions; Kuhn thought that scientists whose work does not conform to paradigmatic norms are effectively excluded from the activities of a normal scientific community. Their work is not seriously read or cited, and their objections to standard approaches are marginalized. The ability of normal science to proceed without extensive controversy over fundamental commitments is thus actively sustained through the exclusion of such dissent, rather than being dependent upon the absence of challenges. For Kuhn, such exclusions are constructive. They enable more focused inquiry using complex and sophisticated apparatus to investigate esoteric phenomena, as well as more effective communication through a specialized professional literature. Scientists can get on with such work by avoiding more far-reaching theoretical or evaluative disputes.

All active paradigms confront anomalies (apparent counterinstances or unexpected failures) at all times. Paradigms are usually first accepted more on the basis of their future promise than on the basis of their inevitably limited initial successes. Indeed, their achievements can be extended further only by the more widespread efforts that *result* from their initial acceptance by a community of researchers. Such successes then introduce new, more esoteric and refined anomalies, since paradigmatic expectations can be more extensively and sharply defined and more precisely assessed. This recurrent generation of new puzzles sustains the life of a research community. A paradigm without discrepancies or gaps would leave no role for further research. Recognizable anomalies are thus normally divided into accessible puzzles that should be solvable with sufficient ingenuity and not yet accessible puzzles that can be bypassed for the time being. Yet sometimes, Kuhn thought, the persistence, proliferation, centrality, or recalcitrance of some anomalies can erode a community's commitment to a paradigm. The typical result is not outright rejection of the paradigm, but a willingness to loosen some of its standards or modify one or more of its marginal commitments. Alas, such tinkering may further erode the community's confidence, since it can undermine the ability to work from common assumptions. Not everyone will make the same modifications or agree about which if any modifications are sufficiently marginal. It then becomes less clear what beliefs can be taken for granted, what work is important, and when a puzzle has or has not been been genuinely solved. Crisis thus to some extent dissolves the community itself by breaking down what it had in common scientifically.

It is, however, revolution rather than crisis that provides the most philosophically striking features of Kuhn's account. One possible response to crisis is to propose a more fundamental violation of a paradigm's constitutive commitments (or to begin to take seriously a previously ignored proposal) in order to resolve its outstanding difficulties. Such proposals may split what remains of a community in crisis. The disagreements between proponents of such a proposal and the defenders of paradigmatic orthodoxy are not readily resolvable. Paradigms incorporate the values, standards, methods, and relevant factual background that govern the resolution of scientific disputes, but these features of a paradigm are precisely what are now *in* dispute. There is hence no commonly accepted basis for assessing the alternative positions; the new proposal is "not merely incompatible, but actually incommensurable with what has gone before" (Kuhn 1970, p. 103).

Kuhn noted various possible manifestations of incommensurability between competing paradigms. Their proponents may employ different vocabularies or, worse, the same vocabulary with different meanings or referents. They can each appeal to empirical evidence, but they may not take the same evidence to be important, and may even see and/or describe it differently. What one proposes as a solution to an outstanding puzzle may seem to another simply to redescribe the problem or to assume what needs to be demonstrated. They may even disagree about what problems really need to be solved or at least about which ones are sufficiently important that their solution could settle the dispute. As a result, these proponents may "talk past one another," failing to grasp their opponents' arguments or even perhaps their conclusions. Without common standards or procedures, the reasons offered for each choice can at best be persuasive and not rationally conclusive. Kuhn sometimes even likened the acceptance of a new paradigm to a religious conversion or a Gestalt switch, which in different ways exemplify sudden, unreasoned changes of belief and perception. The more troubling comparison, however, is to coercion. Since reasons for choosing one paradigm cannot be conclusive, the outcome may be determined by whose proponents are sufficiently numerous or influential to be able to close ranks by ignoring and excluding their opponents. A new normal scientific community thereby emerges, with a new paradigm for its research.

Scientific revolutions thus complete a recurrent cycle from normal science, to crisis, to a revolutionary reconstitution of normal science under a new paradigm. In retrospect, and from within, this cycle inevitably appears progressive. The revolution's victorious faction can claim to have resolved the fundamental anomalies of the old paradigm and to have renewed the prospects for successful research governed by shared assumptions. Indeed, the new community typically rewrites the textbooks, and retells its own history, to reflect this point of view. But from the standpoint of the losers, or even of those who look on impartially, such rewritings might seem to mark change without any genuine claim to progress, because there is no neutral standard by which to assess the merits of the change. The resulting body of knowledge is in any case not cumulative, since much of what was previously known (or merely believed) had to be excluded without ever having been conclusively refuted. One likewise cannot plausibly talk about revolutionary reconstitutions of science as aiming toward truth, for similarly, there can be no impartial formulation of standards for its assessment. The available justification of scientific knowledge after revolutions, couched in new terms according to newly instituted standards, may well be sufficient, but perhaps only because these standards and terms are now perforce our own.

THE KUHNIAN REVOLUTION YET TO COME

Despite the familiarity and influence of the interpretation of Kuhn in the previous section, I believe there is a better way to understand Kuhn's account of science. This reinterpretation does not fundamentally reorganize the book, but it does revise many of its familiar concepts. The crucial underlying shift is toward a description of science as an activity, rather than of knowledge as a product derived from that activity. Thus, normal science is research in which scientists know their way around. Professional training and research experience give scientists a reliable sense of what they are dealing with, what can affect its relevant behavior, how it makes itself known, and what they can do with it. These abilities are held together by their practical grasp of one or more paradigms, concrete scientific achievements that point toward an open-ended domain of possible research. Paradigms should not be understood as beliefs (even tacit beliefs) agreed upon by community members, but instead as exemplary ways of conceptualizing and intervening in particular situations. Accepting a paradigm is more like acquiring and using a set of skills than it is like understanding and believing a statement.

Among the skills that might constitute the grasp of a paradigm are the appropriate application of concepts to specific situations; the deployment of mathematical tools (not just solving equations, but choosing the right ones, applying them correctly to the situation at hand, knowing their limitations and the ways those limitations can be circumvented, etc.); the use of instrumentation and experimental techniques and procedures; and the recognition of significant opportunities to extend these skills in illuminating ways to new situations. The reasoning most often involved in such work is analogical rather than deduction from general principles. Scientists must understand how to handle novel situations in ways modeled on familiar treatments. General principles may well be invoked, but typically the analogical extension from one application to another explicates the principles, rather than depending upon a *prior* grasp of the principles to understand their application. To put the same point differently, general principles are useful as relatively compact *expressions*, but the understanding they express is embedded within the disaggregated ability to grasp various situations in those terms. A parallel point in science education is quite familiar to science students: typically, one first comes to understand a chapter in a science textbook only by learning to solve the problems at the end, rather than learning how to solve the problems by first understanding the chapter.

Scientists *use* paradigms rather than believing them. The use of a paradigm in research typically addresses related problems by employing shared concepts, symbolic expressions, experimental and mathematical tools and procedures, and even some of the same theoretical statements. Scientists need only understand *how* to use these various elements in ways that others would accept. These elements of shared practice thus need not presuppose any comparable unity in scientists' beliefs about what they are doing when they use them. Indeed, one role of a paradigm is to enable scientists to work successfully without having to provide a detailed account of what they are doing or what they believe about it. Kuhn noted that scientists "can agree in their *identification* of a paradigm without agreeing on, or even attempting to produce, a full *interpretation* or *rationalization* of it. Lack of a standard interpretation or of an agreed reduction to rules will not prevent a paradigm from guiding research" (1970, p. 44). By recognizing analogies between a research project and the paradigmatic achievements that motivate it, scientists can develop their own research, as well as understand the work of others, without having to spell out just how these analogies are supposed to work.

Paradigms are thus first and foremost to be understood as *exemplars*, "accepted examples of actual scientific practice – examples which include law, theory, application, and instrumentation together – [that] provide models from which spring particular coherent traditions of scientific research" (1970, p. 10). In working with these shared models of successful work, scientists open a field of research possibilities, a "disciplinary matrix." This matrix is the context or situation within which shared concepts, symbols, apparatus, procedures, and theoretical models are used. It articulates a domain of phenomena as a field of research possibilities, which present opportunities, challenges, and dead ends. These opportunities and challenges are understood as the outcome of prior activities and achievements. Research science is always oriented toward the future, but it thereby continually reconstructs its past as having led toward the current matrix of possibilities.

There is room for considerable disagreement within such a research field. Even within normal science, scientists assess differently what is possible, plausible, or promising. They consequently go in different directions within the common field (even apart from the ways their research choices reflect their own distinctive strengths and limitations and their prospects within the discipline). Yet such divergence is always held in partial check, both by the use of common resources and by a more or less common sense of what is at issue in their field, why it matters, and what must be done to resolve these issues. The acceptance of a paradigm is thus not a matter of monolithic agreement within a community, but rather of sufficient common ground to make disagreement both intelligible and interesting. In retrospect, Kuhn even identified the concept of a paradigm with a move away from conceiving scientific communities as held together by common beliefs.

> I [once] conceived normal science as a result of a consensus among the members of a scientific community . . . in order to account for the way they did research and, especially, for the unanimity with which they ordinarily evaluated the research done by others. . . . What I finally realized . . . was that no consensus of quite that kind was required. . . . If [scientists] accepted a sufficient set of standard [problem solutions], they could model their own subsequent research on them without needing to agree about which set of characteristics of these examples made them standard, justified their acceptance. (Kuhn 1977a, xviii–xix)

The result of this recognition is to think of scientific communities as composed of fellow practitioners rather than of fellow believers. Such communities do not include everyone whose training has given them a shared background understanding. Those trained in a field who do not undertake front-line research are not members of Kuhnian communities, while some scientists with different backgrounds do become acknowledged participants by undertaking the right kind of research. Kuhn has often been misread as insisting that members of scientific communities are in substantial agreement about fundamental issues in their field. What he actually says is that normal science rarely engages in controversy about such fundamentals. A lack of controversy is quite consistent with extensive disagreement, however, if research can proceed coherently and intelligibly without having to resolve the disagreements. Shared paradigms enable scientists to *identify* what has or has not already been done, and what is worth doing, without having to agree on how to describe, just what those achievements and projects are. Scientists are ignored by or excluded from a community of researchers not because they disagree with others' beliefs, but because their work does not mesh constructively with what others are *doing*. Scientists can hold heterodox beliefs about fundamental issues in their discipline as long as their research can be taken into account and used by others. What matters is the relevance and reliability of their work. Scientific communities share concepts, problems, techniques, and references, not orthodoxy.

I now turn to the analogy between normal scientific research and puzzle-solving. This analogy highlights the fact that such research usually addresses well-defined tasks with the presumption that they have a definite, attainable resolution. Such work primarily calls for ingenuity to satisfy multiple pre-determined constraints, rather than unconstrained curiosity or skepticism toward received doctrines. But there is no single primary characterization of how puzzles arise. Kuhn mentions three common types of normal scientific research projects. Sometimes one seeks to determine (or improve on) facts, techniques, or procedures whose importance is highlighted by a paradigm. At other times, however, a problem can be important not for any intrinsic significance of the facts to be determined, but only because they provide an opportunity to assess paradigmatic expectations empirically. Such "tests" of the paradigm are diagnostic rather than evaluative. They show whether, where, and how a paradigm needs further articulation and re-finement, rather than whether it should be accepted or rejected altogether. Finally, normal scientific research aims to develop such refinements and articulations of a paradigm. Such work includes extending paradigmatic so-lutions to apply to other phenomena, further developing paradigmatic the-ories or concepts, devising new experimental procedures or instruments, or otherwise extending the scope and power of the discipline's know-how. Philosophical readers of Kuhn often identify puzzles with anomalous facts or conceptual conflicts, but that is a misleading oversimplification. Anoma-lies and conflicts can arise only after considerable paradigm articulation has taken place. Philosophical preoccupation with testing and evaluating hypotheses betrays a retrospective emphasis on the certification of knowl-edge. That emphasis contrasts with the prospective orientation of scientific research toward the *extension* of understanding.

All paradigms confront obstacles to the development of normal scientific research. Anomalies, that is, unexpected or unclear empirical results, are prominent among these obstacles, but it is a mistake to think of them as if they were *counterinstances* to a paradigm. Recognizing a counterinstance presupposes a clear understanding of what you are dealing with and its significance for your approach to the field. Recognizing an anomaly involves the more limited awareness that something significant is not yet adequately understood or dealt with. To understand *what* the problem is, rather than just where it is, is to have already gone a long way toward resolving it. That is why Kuhn concluded that "assimilating a new sort of fact demands a more than additive adjustment of theory, and until that adjustment is completed . . . the new fact is not quite a scientific fact at all" (1970, p. 53). Until the disturbance is more clearly characterized, one cannot know how it matters or what can be done with it and, hence, what it *is*. A great deal depends on whether the disturbance can be localized within the research field. An anomaly that shows up in only a limited range of circumstances can be easily bypassed or dismissed as likely an artifact. More pervasive anomalies, or ones that affect widely used instruments or experimental procedures, must instead be dealt with. Kuhn illustrates the latter point with Roentgen's recognition that a barium platinocyanide screen was glowing in the vicinity of his shielded cathode-ray tube (1970, p. 57). This unexpectedly glowing screen could not just be dismissed as a curiosity. Cathode-ray tubes were important research apparatus, and if the shielding used to prevent such effects was permeable, it meant that physicists did not really understand what was going on with their equipment. Until the nature and scope of that failure was clarified, further research *with* cathode-ray tubes was pointless (indeed, the impending worry was that previous research was also rendered pointless, since one no longer knew what it showed).

Clarifying an anomaly is closely linked with determining how to respond to it. Sometimes a revision of theory or theoretical concepts is called for. In other cases, what is needed is a revision of experimental procedures or instruments to bypass the difficulty without necessarily fully explaining it. This possibility highlights that anomalous phenomena are not yet in conflict with theory, but are instead *practical* difficulties (which, looked at from another angle, may also be opportunities to explore the world in revealing ways, as the Roentgen case illustrates). Such problems need to be resolved only to the extent that they continue to block meaningful research. If an anomaly is sufficiently obstructive, or if it offers interesting alternative possibilities for research, it can become a focus of subsequent work. More often, however, apparently anomalous facts can be construed as obstacles to be circumvented so as to get on with normal science without having to understand the anomaly more fully.

Anomalies may arise frequently, but most are resolved or circumvented quickly. Some nevertheless persist and resist sustained efforts to accommodate them. If the significance of a persistent anomaly cannot be circumscribed (so that most scientists can ignore it), the result is disconcerting. Such persistent and pervasive anomalies suggest not merely that this particular phenomenon is not understood, but that whatever causes it, and whichever situations in which it can show up, are not reliably understood. Under these circumstances, a field may undergo a Kuhnian crisis, in which the intelligibility, reliability, and significance of its practices and achievements come into question. Crisis does not result merely because scientists cannot agree about what to believe about some phenomena. Scientists readily accommodate such uncertainty because they expect it to be resolved eventually by further research. Crisis results only when scientists become unsure how to proceed – which research is worth pursuing, which background assumptions may be unreliable, and which concepts and models are reliable guides to further work. Crisis is always partial, for without some sense of how to proceed, research would collapse altogether. There would be no coherent field of possibilities to explore. But crisis expands and blurs the bounds of the field, and thereby makes uncertain the significance of one's own activity. It makes sense to try more and different things, but it is less clear *what* sense these explorations may have.

Many incipient crises are resolved in ways that sustain the dominant research paradigm. Some crises, however, yield alternative paradigms. Such alternatives take the form of specific achievements that could provide a new focus and a different model for research. They need not involve anything like an overarching worldview. New concepts and theories may well result from these exemplary achievements, yet even their proponents may not fully agree about how to specify them. The more basic issue between proponents of alternative paradigms concerns how to proceed with research: what experimental systems or theoretical models are worth using, what they should be used for, what other achievements must be taken into account, and what would count as a significant and reliable result. The conflict is not so much between competing beliefs as between competing forms of (scientific) life.

Such conflicts can be difficult to resolve precisely because the protagonists now *work* in different worlds. Kuhn's claims about changes of world are widely misunderstood and often mischaracterized because insufficient emphasis is placed upon his reference to scientific work. Yet Kuhn was quite careful to distinguish the obvious sense in which the world does not change from changes in the world of scientists' research (1970, p. 112), the setting in which they "practice their trade" (1970, p. 150). Indeed, when Kuhn also talked about scientists *seeing* the world differently, this claim is often presented as a consequence of differences in their workworld and what they would characteristically *do* (1970, pp. 111–12, 118–22). What do I mean by a different workworld? Think about the differences expressed by phrases like "the business world" or "the academic world." Their inhabitants may well hold different beliefs, but the more important differences are in how they comport themselves, what is expected of them, and what is at issue and at stake in their dealings with things. Otherwise similar situations may then look quite different as a result of these differences in practical orientation. We should regard the differences between paradigms similarly. They reorganize the world as a field of possibilities, offering differently configured challenges and opportunities. If proponents of different paradigms do not fully communicate, it is not so much that they cannot correctly construe one another's sentences or follow one another's arguments. The problem is more that they cannot grasp the *point* of what the others are doing or recognize the *force* of their arguments.

Kuhn's distinctions between normal science, crisis, and revolution are often misconstrued as a rigid periodization of the development of scientific disciplines. Normal science and crisis are instead ways of *doing* science. One or the other may typically predominate within a field at any given time, but they can also coexist. Some scientists may begin to articulate their fundamental assumptions explicitly, and tinker with the ones that seem less essential, in response to problems that do not greatly disturb their colleagues. Others may blithely go on with familiar ways of setting and solving puzzles, even though their colleagues are no longer sure what to make of the results. In retrospect, historical judgment may discern sharp breaks and crucial turning points, but these almost inevitably blur when looked at closely or without hindsight.

Revolution is likewise a matter of retrospective interpretation. Whether a new development amounts to a revolution rather than an articulation of a prevailing paradigm depends on how one interprets that paradigm; some interpretations would make the shift more dramatic than others. That is why Einstein could say that special relativity only worked out the implications of Maxwell's electrodynamics, whereas most commentators regard it as a revolutionary reconstruction of classical physics. Einstein and his contemporaries all started out from Maxwell's theory, but Einstein's reading of Maxwell pointed toward rather different ways of dealing with electromagnetic phenomena. Such possible ambiguities between normal paradigm articulation and revolutionary shifts are heightened by the retention of many familiar experimental arrangements, procedures, calculations, and other practices across scientific revolutions. Many of the same procedures are employed in different contexts but to somewhat different ends. The interpretive question is always whether to emphasize the continuities or the discontinuities, and that in turn is affected by where one foresees the next step to be.

Philosophical readers of Kuhn have tended to identify paradigm change first and foremost with theoretical change, despite the prominent example of Roentgen's discovery of X-rays, which revolutionized cathode-ray research without requiring fundamental changes in the underlying theory (Maxwell's). Such examples of instrumental and experimental revolutions abound, however. William Bechtel (1993) and Hans-Jörg Rheinberger (1997) have persuasively centered the shift in the 1940s and 1950s from classical cytology to modern cell biology on the introduction of ultracentrifuges and electron microscopes. These instruments enabled biologists to ask fundamentally different questions about cells, moving from a structural taxonomy of cell components toward a functional dynamics of intracellular processes. More recent examples of comparable shifts in research practice and goals can be found in the successive developments of recombinant DNA technologies, the polymerase chain reaction (PCR), and gene-activation arrays.[6] These were technical rather than conceptual achievements, but they have dramatically changed how biologists approach their work and to what ends.

Even revolutions that do initiate major theoretical change may do so only in concert with shifts in instrumentation and research practice. High-energy physics underwent a widely recognized revolution in the early 1970s. This shift has often been characterized in terms of the adoption of gauge field theories and the conception of particles such as protons and neutrons as composed of charmed quarks. But gauge theories go back to 1954, and the first quark models were proposed in 1964. What better coincides with the acknowledged revolution are the shifts in experimental practice and its associated theoretical modeling, which used beams of different kinds of particles (leptons like electrons, positrons, and neutrinos, often colliding two beams head on, rather than single beams of hadrons like protons and neutrons) or looked at different aspects of familiar particle beams (the relatively rare "hard" or sharp-angled scattering of hadrons, rather than the more common "soft" scattering in the vicinity of the beam).[7] Different phenomena were seen to be scientifically illuminating, and research practice was reorganized accordingly.

Whether initiated theoretically or experimentally, scientific revolutions mark progress in research. The most basic problem posed by Kuhnian crises is not inconsistent belief but incoherent practice. Revolutions succeed by giving renewed impetus to research. That is why the sciences are not normally impeded by incommensurable theoretical disputes. The disclosure of new ways to explore the world in revealing ways usually overrides contrary theoretical convictions. Perhaps with ingenuity, one could reconstruct a discarded paradigm such as phlogiston chemistry into a coherent system of beliefs and values, with its own reinterpreted body of supporting evidence. What one cannot so readily imagine is the reconstitution of phlogiston chemistry as a viable program of ongoing research. The insuperable objection to phlogiston theory was not its inconsistency or empirical falsification, but its inability to guide further inquiry into the new "airs" (gases) discovered in pneumatic chemistry. Scientific progress across revolutions is progress away from the impasse that initiated a crisis in normal scientific research.

Kuhn's conception of science as research practice offers a revealing insight into recent attempts to claim scientific credence for divine creation of species. Proponents of "creation science" have sought to place their views on a par with neo-Darwinist evolutionary theory by arguing that both are unproven theories. Even if such arguments were tenable, from Kuhn's perspective the wrong issue has been joined. Scientists' primary concern is not whether present beliefs are likely to be true, but instead whether available models of inquiry can effectively guide further research. If creationists claimed to offer not merely an internally consistent set of beliefs but also an ongoing research program that promises to advance beyond its current understanding, only then would they have begun to contest evolutionary biology on its own terrain. The epistemological orientation of "textbook" views of science has mistakenly encouraged a conception of science that highlights the retrospective justification of belief.[8] Kuhn emphasizes instead the futural orientation of scientific understanding. In that light, evolutionary biology is so central to modern biology not because its current formulations are likely to be correct, but because it provides the best available understanding of how to explore a wide range of biological phenomena. Science does also look back, not primarily to vindicate beliefs, but to better secure its orientation toward future disclosure.

CONCLUSION

What difference would it make to read Kuhn in this way as a philosopher of scientific practice? I have been arguing that Kuhn reorients the philosophy of science toward an account of scientific practices rather than scientific knowledge. This shift does not diminish the intellectual or cognitive significance of science but only reinterprets it. Kuhn encourages us to think about scientific *understanding* rather than scientific knowledge. Science aims not so much to produce justified beliefs as to transform human capacities to cope with the world practically and discursively. Biologists understand cells in the sense in which we say that a good mechanic understands cars. Biologists and mechanics can, if asked, produce many true sentences about what they work on, but that is hardly the point in either case.

That is why I have emphasized paradigms as achievements that one understands by *using* them as models for subsequent work. Scientific understanding is more a practical capacity to cope with an open-ended variety of relevant situations than it is the acceptance of purported truths. Indeed, Kuhn's view encourages us to think of verbal articulation as an ongoing activity rather than as an artifact of that activity. Moreover, Kuhn denied that concepts and theories could be understood in abstraction from the practical contexts in which they are articulated, including the relevant instrumentation and material practices. The sciences are not just a network of statements, which coincidentally have been applied in the laboratory. Concepts and their material realization go hand in hand. Kuhn thus insisted that

> [a]n acquaintance with the tables [comparing theory and experiment] is part of an acquaintance with the theory itself. Without the tables, the theory would be essentially incomplete. (Kuhn 1977b, 185–6)

To understand a theoretical claim is to understand how it is to be used in various situations, including the limitations on that use.

Such limitations are not simply accepted as given, however. A distinctive feature of modern science has been its relentlessly reflexive application: scientific understanding is often directed toward research that aims to extend and enhance scientific understanding. That reflexivity helps explain both the phenomenal growth of scientific research and the esoteric and apparently insular character of much scientific work.[9] Kuhn placed that reflexivity at the core of his conception of science; normal scientific research involves the further articulation of its own paradigms, while revolutions are the reconstitution of such research in response to its occasional breakdown. Thus, familiar readings of Kuhn that emphasize occasional revolutionary changes in scientific theory understate his point. Even normal science is oriented toward its own ongoing transformation, although its practitioners sometimes anticipate more continuity within that transformation than actually results.

Kuhn is often read as having challenged the "rationality" of science and as lending comfort to skepticism or relativism about scientific knowledge. Such readings are imposed on *The Structure of Scientific Revolutions*, however. Kuhn did not even ask such questions about the wholesale justification of scientific knowledge, let alone answer them. We can now see better why these questions did not arise for him. Such questions presuppose a retrospective, epistemological orientation, which stands back from scientific work to ask whether its achievements really are genuine. Kuhn adopted the implicit standpoint of scientific practitioners rather than that of philosophical spectators. Their questions concern *which* projects to pursue and *what* concepts, theories, and instruments to use, and these questions can be formulated only against the background of an extensive practical understanding of what one is dealing with, how it might function or break down, and what is at stake in its success or failure. To have doubts about the whole of one's grasp of the field is to doubt not just one's answers, but one's ability to ask intelligible questions or try to answer them.

Kuhn is more plausibly read as a critic of scientific realism, that is, as one who denies that science aims to provide a correct representation of a world independent of human concepts and practices. But antirealists often hold their view because they regard truth and reality as inaccessible, forever obscured by the effects of human language, culture, and perception. Such views are often ascribed to Kuhn, but they apply only if one reads him in the more familiar epistemological way. When Kuhn asks whether we should "imagine that there is some full, objective, true account of nature and that the proper measure of scientific achievement is the extent to which it brings us closer to that ultimate goal" (1970, p. 171), his objection is to the finality and completeness of this conception, not to its putative independence. He does indeed argue that scientific understanding engages the thoroughly human workworld of research practice rather than nature-in-itself, but that does not mean that paradigmatic concepts and perceptual Gestalts intervene between us and the world. The intelligibility of scientific concepts and ways of seeing are as much dependent upon ongoing interaction with the world as vice versa. The realist can posit a world "beyond" language and culture only by mistakenly thinking that we can have a definite language and culture distinct from how we engage the world.

Does Kuhn's thorough identification with a practitioner's standpoint then indicate an uncritical complacency on Kuhn's part, an uncritical commitment to the project of modern science? Perhaps. But that would be so only if it were possible for us in practice to disengage sufficiently from scientific understanding of the world in which we live and work so as to put it in question as a whole. If the practices, achievements, and norms of science are sufficiently integral to the workworld of everyone in modern scientific cultures, then critical questions about science might now be intelligible only from within a broadly scientific culture.

The difficulty of such wholesale detachment might well be reinforced if we take seriously the implications of Kuhn's concept of a paradigm. If paradigms are mistakenly identified with theoretical representations, worldviews, or "conceptual schemes," epistemological detachment and skeptical questions might seem perfectly plausible. But when we consider the extent to which materials, practices, and concepts from the sciences have been built into our everyday world, then wholesale detachment from scientific understanding might undermine the intelligibility of philosophical questioning rather than the justification of our answers.

That does not mean that Kuhn's philosophical perspective cannot accommodate far-reaching critical attitudes toward the sciences and their pervasive role in our world. Here are some examples. One might argue that the sciences have placed too much emphasis on the artificially controlled and simplified circumstances achievable in laboratories and have given inadequate attention to the more complex, messy, and uncontrolled aspects of the world outside. One might argue instead that the reflexive extension of scientific paradigms has increased both the costs and the benefits of scientific research in ways that have unjustly and dangerously reinforced intranational and international divisions of wealth and opportunity. Or one might argue that the extraordinary enhancement of those intellectual and practical capacities that can sustain traditions of normal-scientific puzzle-solving has led to the neglect of other human capacities in ways that leave many people's lives morally or spiritually impoverished. What is common to these, and many other critical perspectives one might take toward particular scientific practices and achievements, is that formulating the criticism and any adequate assessment of or response to it will extensively utilize the very scientific understanding whose alleged consequences are at issue. My point is not to endorse any of these hastily sketched critical concerns. Rather, it is to emphasize that a Kuhnian shift in philosophical focus from scientific knowledge to scientific practice might transform not just what we think science is, but how we think philosophically about science. Epistemological conceptions of science have led to debates that are largely disconnected from issues within particular sciences, and from the larger contexts in which science matters to us as human beings or as scientists. To understand sciences as practices might help reorient philosophical discussion toward questions of how science matters and what kinds of science we ought to do.

Notes

1. Rouse (1987, ch. 2; 1998) provides earlier articulations of many of the claims and arguments developed in this essay, aimed at different audiences.
2. Other roughly contemporary challenges to logical empiricism included Hanson (1958), Polanyi (1958), Toulmin (1962), Feyerabend (1962), and Popper (1957) (the first English translation of a then-forgotten work written in German in the 1930s). In the background were three extraordinarily influential challenges to the broader philosophical conception underlying logical empiricism: Quine (1953), Wittgenstein (1953), and Sellars (1963; first published in 1956).
3. Earman (1993) explicitly emphasizes the similarities now apparent between Kuhn and Carnap. Other work on logical empiricism that might encourage greater rapprochement between Kuhn and his predecessors is collected in Giere and Richardson (1996) and Friedman (1999).
4. Kuhn (1977c, 2000), Musgrave (1980), Hacking (1984).
5. All citations are from Kuhn (1970, p. 1); the emphasis is mine, however.
6. For a book-length argument that multiple fields of biology have been more fundamentally reorganized by recombinant DNA technology rather than by any theoretical reconceptualization, see the widely used textbook *Molecular Cell Biology* (Darnell, Lodish, and Baltimore, 1990); for the impact of PCR, see Rabinow (1996); gene-activation arrays are too recent an innovation to have been chronicled in this way.
7. For accessible accounts of these transformations in high-energy physics, see Crease and Mann (1986) and Pickering (1984).
8. Ironically, given Kuhn's challenge to the "textbook view" of science, the most prominent controversies over the status of "creation science" have concerned its presence in or absence from science textbooks and curricula. Despite their almost uniform hostility to creation science, the dominant philosophical models of science have encouraged creationists' underlying fideistic conception of science education as a matter of imparting beliefs (or "information"). Taking more seriously the conception of science as oriented toward future disclosure rather than retrospective justification could constructively reorient science education.
9. The reflexivity of research does not by itself explain why modern societies have provided the resources necessary to sustain the phenomenal growth of science. Nor does it explain the differences between successful and unsuccessful attempts to extend scientific understanding. It does, however, show how the aspiration to such growth has been built into much of scientific practice.

References

Bechtel, William. 1993. "Integrating Sciences by Creating New Disciplines: The Case of Cell Biology." *Biology and Philosophy* 8: 277–99.

Crease, Robert, and Charles Mann. 1986. *The Second Creation: Makers of the Revolution in 20th Century Physics*. New York: Macmillan.

Darnell, James, Harvey Lodish, and David Baltimore. 1990. *Molecular Cell Biology*. New York: W. H. Freeman.

Earman, John. 1993. "Carnap, Kuhn, and the Philosophy of Scientific Methodology." In: P. Horwich, ed. *World Changes: Thomas Kuhn and the Nature of Science*. Cambridge, MA: MIT Press, pp. 9–36.

Feyerabend, Paul. 1962. "Explanation, Reduction and Empiricism." In: H. Feigl and G. Maxwell, eds. *Scientific Explanation, Space and Time* (Minnesota Studies in the Philosophy of Science, Vol. 3). Minneapolis: University of Minnesota Press, pp. 28–97.

Friedman, Michael. 1999. *Reconsidering Logical Positivism*. Cambridge: Cambridge University Press.

Fuller, Steve. 1999. *Thomas Kuhn: A Philosophical History for Our Times*. Chicago: University of Chicago Press.

Giere, Ronald, and Alan Richardson, ed. 1996. *Origins of Logical Empiricism* (Minnesota Studies in the Philosophy of Science, Vol. 16). Minneapolis: University of Minnesota Press.

Hacking, Ian. 1984. "Five Parables." In: R. Rorty, J. Schneewind, and Q. Skinner, eds. *Philosophy in History*. Cambridge: Cambridge University Press, pp. 103–24.

Hanson, Norwood R. 1958. *Patterns of Discovery*. Cambridge: Cambridge University Press.

Kuhn, Thomas. 1970. *The Structure of Scientific Revolutions*. 2nd ed. Chicago: University of Chicago Press.

1977a. *The Essential Tension*. Chicago: University of Chicago Press.

1977b. "The Function of Measurement in Modern Physical Science." In: Kuhn (1977a, pp. 178–224).

1977c. "Objectivity, Rationality, and Theory Choice." In: Kuhn (1977a, pp. 320–39).

2000. "The Trouble with the Historical Philosophy of Science." In: J. Conant and J. Haugeland, eds., *The Road Since Structure*. Chicago: University of Chicago Press, pp. 90–104.

Musgrave, Alan. 1980. "Kuhn's Second Thoughts." In: G. Gutting, ed. *Paradigms and Revolutions*. Notre Dame, IN: University of Notre Dame Press, pp. 39–53.

Pickering, Andrew. 1984. *Constructing Quarks*. Chicago: University of Chicago Press.

Polanyi, Michael. 1958. *Personal Knowledge: Towards a Post-Critical Philosophy*. Chicago: University of Chicago Press.

Popper, Karl. 1957. *The Logic of Scientific Discovery*. New York: Harper & Row.

Quine, Willard v. O. 1953. "Two Dogmas of Empiricism." In: *From a Logical Point of View*. Cambridge, MA: Harvard University Press, pp. 20–46.

Rabinow, Paul 1996. *Making PCR: A Story of Biotechnology*. Chicago: University of Chicago Press.

Rheinberger, Hans-Jörg. 1997. *Toward a History of Epistemic Things: Synthesizing Proteins in the Test Tube*. Stanford, CA: Stanford University Press.

Rouse, Joseph. 1987. *Knowledge and Power: Toward a Political Philosophy of Science.* Ithaca, NY: Cornell University Press.

1998. "Kuhn and Scientific Practices." *Configurations* 6: 33–50.

Sellars, Wilfrid. 1963. "Empiricism and the Philosophy of Mind." In: *Science, Perception, and Reality.* London: Routledge & Kegan Paul, pp. 127–96.

Toulmin, Stephen. 1962. *Foresight and Understanding.* New York: Harper & Row.

Wittgenstein, Ludwig. 1953. *Philosophical Investigations.* London: Routledge & Kegan Paul.

5 Thomas Kuhn and the Problem of Social Order in Science

BARRY BARNES

Scientific knowledge, like language, is intrinsically the common property of a group or else nothing at all. To understand it we shall need to know the special characteristics of the groups that create and use it. Kuhn (1970, p. 210)

PREAMBLE

Any attempt to evaluate the contribution of Thomas Kuhn's work to the history and sociology of science has to take care not to undermine the significance of the work itself; for the more respect we have for it, the less we will be inclined to attribute decisive significance to it as an individual contribution to these fields. Kuhn helped to undermine the view that cultural traditions like those of the sciences could be analysed into so many discrete individual contributions. Indeed, the part he played in correcting the excessive individualism that once characterised studies of the natural sciences stands as an important part of his achievement, acknowledged even today, when individualism is once more rampant in the academic world.

It is worth recalling that, at the outset of Kuhn's career, the 'problem' of the nature of the 'discoveries' made by individual scientists still figured prominently in the thought of historians of science. In an early paper, Kuhn (1962) cited extensive evidence, and in particular the many documented cases of 'multiple' and 'simultaneous' discovery, in support of the view that discovery was actually a process wherein the members of the relevant scientific community reoriented themselves cognitively, over an extended period of time, to the states of affairs their research addressed. This account was the prelude to a whole series of further studies, by historians and sociologists, wherein attention was aligned on the community rather than the individual scientist, and the emergence of the 'discovery' at the focus of attention was addressed as a process and not as a bounded event.

A nice example of this subsequent work is that of Augustine Brannigan on *The Social Basis of Scientific Discoveries* (1981). This fascinating work included an extended reappraisal of the work of Gregor Mendel, according to which he was not the discoverer of genes and the founder of 'Mendelian genetics' at all, but a contributor to the understanding of variation in plant hybrids, which was already a well-established topic of study at the time. The Mendel of Mendelian genetics was actually a reconstruction, made decades later, as a number of 'rediscovers' of 'Mendelism' embarked on the process of aligning biological thought and practice according to their specifications rather than Mendel's. Ironically, Brannigan's own work on Mendel (1979) is also a candidate instance of 'simultaneous discovery', initially published in the same year as Robert Olby's equally penetrating 'Mendel: No Mendelian?' (1979). And Olby himself acknowledges the existence of a similar thesis in the contemporary work of L. A. Callender, as well as the existence of interesting, neglected 'precursors' who had proposed comparable interpretations.

In the light of instances of this kind, we now readily acknowledge that it is never possible precisely to delineate the effects, or the extent of the influence, of the work of an individual within a tradition. What would have appeared without that individual cannot be known. Nonetheless, in acknowledging the importance of the work of a 'major' figure, it is sensible to set aside undue concern for precision and to speak along conventional lines in praise of his or her individual contribution. And this is what I shall do in speaking of Kuhn, for all that his work is so sensitive to the limitations of an individualistic discourse and to the character of scientific and cultural change as a collective accomplishment.

TWO VIEWS OF KUHN'S IMPORTANCE

It is no more than conventional wisdom that Kuhn's account of scientific change, and particularly those very general concepts and ideas both deployed in his historical case studies and explicitly set out in his more reflective writings, has had an extremely important influence on subsequent work. But there is disagreement about the nature of that influence. One school of thought is impressed (or appalled) by what it regards as Kuhn's grand historical vision, wherein entire scientific worldviews are overthrown and replaced, in processes dramatising not the triumph of reason over entrenched tradition but rather the insufficiency of reason as a basis for scientific advance. This view of Kuhn has long been favoured by rationalist philosophers of science and has served as the basis of their largely negative evaluations of his work. It is a perspective that focuses on Kuhn's description of scientific revolutions, that highlights the incommensurability of scientific paradigms, and that tends to equate those paradigms with linguistically formulated scientific theories.

Against this 'large' view, others argue that the true value and significance of Kuhn's work lies in its revelatory treatment of scientific activity and the mundane details of everyday scientific practice. This perspective is mainly to be found amongst historians and sociologists, and amongst those philosophers of science suspicious of strong versions of rationalism and the 'statement view' of theories. It focuses on normal science, on paradigms as accepted exemplars of good practice, and on the extension of knowledge and competence through moves from one particular case to another in processes involving modelling, analogy, and induction. On this 'small' view, 'reason' is an insufficient guide to action at all points in the process of scientific research, and not just during those special episodes that are scientific revolutions. Thus, in many ways the nomenclature of large and small is misleading here; it is actually the small view that is more profound, iconoclastic, and far-reaching in its implications.

I shall give no more attention to the large view: no doubt justice will be done to it elsewhere in this volume. It is the alternative perspective that will guide and inform the argument of this essay, and indeed, I have long been a determined advocate of that perspective and have written extensively on its viability and its significance (Barnes 1982; Barnes, Bloor, and Henry 1996). The purpose of my essay is not, however, to say yet more by way of exegesis or defence of this view. It is now well entrenched in many academic contexts, and the role of Kuhn's work in exemplifying and encouraging it has been extensively documented, for example by Giere (1988). I hope and believe as well that some of the other contributions will focus on it in this volume. This leaves me in a position to presume the validity of the small view and to discuss its relevance to a topic that I have not previously addressed: the problem of social order in science. Such a discussion will serve as a reminder of the important connection between the functionalist sociology of science of Robert K. Merton and Kuhn's own thought. And it will allow reflection on how far current work in the sociology of science might have something to gain from a reading of Kuhn that situates his thought in this way.

THE SOCIAL ORDER PROBLEM

The social sciences have long been concerned with the problem of social order. Indeed, for the functionalist sociology that provided Kuhn's point of reference, it was the central problem. Talcott Parsons (1937/1968) referred to it as 'Hobbes's problem' and the reference was well chosen, for Hobbes made it abundantly clear that the problem encompassed not just order at the level of physical action but order at the level of knowledge and culture as well. What has to be understood is not simply the existence of coordinated, cooperative activity on the part of individuals with conflicting wants, but the existence of shared representations and coordinated understandings on the part of individuals with different perceptions and experiences. For this reason, the order problem in the context of the natural sciences had a special theoretical interest.

The sociologist who first addressed the order problem in this context was, of course, Robert K. Merton (1973), and his initial treatment, indeed his entire pioneering description of how scientific research had been institutionalised, was long treated as paradigmatic in sociology. Merton addressed research in traditional academic settings and noted how practitioners were related to each other as peers in a form of collegiate organisation. All were obliged to make their work freely available to the collective and to cede any individual rights in it. Their findings could then be scrutinised and evaluated by the collective, and those that stood as valid and significant could be made available to all. Every member of the collective was thus able rapidly to acquire and utilise the results of the entire field, which benefited the collective as a whole and was 'functional' in that it contributed to the achievement of the institutionalised goals of their field. Individual producers of those results, on the other hand, were not permitted to reap direct financial or extrinsic reward for their efforts, although they could expect honour and recognition for them from their peers and an enhanced standing within the field as a whole.

This simple account is extremely interesting when viewed from the general theoretical perspectives of the social sciences. Merton is in effect describing academic scientific communities as *status groups*, possessed of their own distinctive lifestyles and sharing a sense of their own special honour, as Max Weber (1968) famously described them. Crucially, as far as the social order problem is concerned, the activities of these groups are irrational when considered from a strictly 'economic' perspective, that is, in terms of the standard assumptions of rational choice individualism. It is not the absence of extrinsic rewards and incentives for individual scientists that is decisive here. A rational choice perspective could seek to argue that the honour and recognition of colleagues is in itself an incentive, indeed an extremely potent one, and that evidence of the motivating power of honour on individuals is available from practically every field of human endeavour. What is decisive, what a rational choice perspective cannot plausibly rationalise, is the practise of *honouring*. If honour is an incentive to individuals to do what benefits the collective, then honouring furthers the collective good; but that does not make the activity individually rational, and indeed, a calculative individual would surely leave it to others to offer honour and recognition to colleagues, and enjoy the ensuing collective benefits without incurring the individual costs of undertaking that activity (Barnes 1995).

All this is perhaps no more than an indirect way of saying that Merton described scientific communities as genuine communities, moral communities that were unintelligible in narrowly utilitarian terms as aggregates of individuals moved to action by independent calculations of their own benefit. But the interesting question is how they should be characterised as moral communities. Merton himself reckoned that all moral communities were defined by institutionalised commitments to social norms and values, and that scientific communities were defined by commitments to a number of very general social norms that were 'functional for science'. Thus, he believed, for example, that putative scientific findings were evaluated in terms of their 'consonance with experience', not because this was 'natural' but because institutionalised social norms of disinterest and skepticism in science enjoined evaluation of that kind. And more generally, he considered that the peculiar virtues of scientific knowledge as a representation of natural order derived from specific features of science as a moral order, and particularly from its central institutional norms.

If Kuhn's work is approached from this direction, then it can easily be made out as providing no more than a minor adjustment to Merton's theoretical perspective, and indeed, at one time it was widely understood in just this way. Institutionalised commitments remained essential to science as a collective enterprise, but instead of Merton's grand social norms, 'technical norms' embedded in Kuhn's scientific paradigms were identified as the necessary foci of commitment. Social order was sustained in science allegedly because research was evaluated according to how closely it conformed to specific rules and procedures, and how consistent its results proved to be with the 'implications' of accepted theories. Of course, this very minor adjustment to the form of Merton's sociological theory was perceived as a major innovation (and by some as a scandalous one) in other respects. For whereas scientists had previously been institutionally encouraged to respect experience and reason, now, it was said, they were encouraged to respect authority and tradition instead. And this brought into play the standard contrasts of Enlightenment dualism and all the tiresome formulaic debates and controversies associated with them.

This first response to Kuhn, however, was very much based on the large view of the import of his work. In particular, it derived from a view of paradigms that took them to be little different from theories, and took theories in turn to consist in linguistically formulable laws and rules with determinate implications. On this view, researchers could proceed in concert on the basis of a shared commitment to a paradigm/theory, since the commitment was to a clearly defined unitary entity, which would serve as a sufficient basis for agreement in their individual judgements and evaluations. The small view, it goes without saying, characterised paradigms in a radically different way and had radically different implications accordingly.

EXEMPLARS AND SOCIAL ORDER

Let us remind ourselves of the basics of the small view of Kuhn. His crucial insight, on this view, is that solved problems are the fundamental units of scientific knowledge. Particular problem solutions are accepted within a collective as valid achievements on the basis of which future work should proceed; these paradigms diffuse through the collective and are passed on down the generations as the elementary components of the scientific culture. By acquiring paradigms in this sense, scientists are equipped to do research, that is, to engage in the practice that Kuhn refers to as 'normal science'. Explicit warrant for this interpretation lies in Kuhn's definition of paradigms as achievements (1970, p. 10); his insistence that they are 'prior to the various concepts, laws, theories, and points of view that may be abstracted from' them (1970, p. 11); his further lengthy argument that actions based on paradigms cannot be understood as determined by rules (1970, ch. 5); and his account of paradigms as exemplars (1970, Postscript). Further, implicit warrant comes from his discussions of normal science and from the lengthy historical case studies that represent his finest scholarly achievements.

If Kuhn as interpreted on the small view is correct, then scientific research has to proceed on the basis of moves from instance to instance wherein solved problems provide the points of reference in addressing still unsolved ones. The scientist is guided by an existing exemplar and proceeds in analogy with it; the exemplar is the model for the practical activity focused on the unsolved problem. And in evaluating the outcome of this activity, the putative new problem solution resulting from it, the scientific collective is also guided by analogy, the analogy between the new solution and their repertoire of existing ones. What appertains at the level of practice also appertains at the level of epistemology, as it were; processes of knowledge production and knowledge evaluation are not discrete and different processes.

The crux of the small view of Kuhn is this: scientific research proceeds, and in the last analysis can do no other than proceed, by instance-to-instance moves involving modelling and analogy. This is germane to the social order problem because there is no single definitively correct way of making an analogy between model and problem or of extending existing practice in the light of such analogy: in truth, there are always innumerable formally defensible ways of doing so. Independent individuals may reasonably extend analogies in diverse ways, yet they actually extend them, most of the time, in ways sufficiently closely related to permit reference to a continuing agreement in their practice. Thus, the social order problem, the problem represented by the continuing existence of this agreement, arises everywhere, and looms anew, pro forma, every time an inference is made or a reasoned action is undertaken.

In Robert Merton's sociology the order problem is solved in two stages. Firstly, a shared respect for a specific set of social norms is engendered. Secondly, the norms themselves encourage enough action in accordance with their implications for order to be discernible. No doubt faith in the power of norms themselves to enforce their particular implications encouraged Merton to believe that just a few very general social norms would suffice to shape the reasoned activities of scientists into a functional institutionalised order. And on the large view, Kuhn's work is not inconsistent with this faith: it offers but a small adjustment to Merton's picture by positing that order ensues from conformity with the technical norms embedded in paradigms.

On the small view, however, neither norms nor paradigms, nor indeed theories or concepts or rules or principles, can engender order by themselves, however much they are respected, since they lack 'logical' implications, and nothing follows unproblematically from their acceptance. Paradigms are resources, for use as models and as points of reference for analogies; they do not fix and determine how they are used; any manifest orderliness in how they are used by the members of a collective remains a problem in search of a solution. That a paradigm is generally accepted and respected can only be the beginning of an explanation of the existence of order and coherence in the research of the field wherein it is accepted. Normal science, we might say, continues to count as a problem even after Kuhn's insightful account of its character.

Merton's account does not suffice to solve the social order problem, and indeed, no account that simply cites norms will do so, because norms cannot fix how people apply them, and it is at the level of their application that the problem arises in its most profound form. Kuhn's work makes this vividly apparent. It shows that the proper use of exemplars, and the correct application of the rules and norms incarnate in them, is itself a matter of collective agreement; hence, it raises the question of how and on what basis that agreement is secured. Kuhn provides a finitist vision of the use of concepts, norms, rules and laws, models and theories, and so forth, in the context of science, rather as Wittgenstein had done in the context of everyday life and ethnomethodologists and sociologists of knowledge were later to do in both contexts. And the import of this finitism to an understanding of scientific research is that the social order problem has to be confronted all the time and everywhere therein.

To say this, of course, is not to dismiss the traditional approach of Merton and sociological functionalism. On the contrary, it is to accept that the problem of order they highlighted does indeed exist and demands a solution. And it is to agree with them that no solution built on rational choice individualism is possible: it is moral action that has to be understood here, just as the functionalist tradition has always claimed. Indeed, when orthodox functionalism lost its dominant position in sociology and first came under sustained attack, its critics readily acknowledged all this. Harold Garfinkel (1967), for example, was deeply interested in the nature of moral order and was responsible for the interesting suggestion that it might consist not in conformity to norms, but rather in recognition of, and willingness to use and trust, members' shared knowledge as the basis of practical action and mutual accountability.

It is hard to imagine bodies of work more different in style than those of Kuhn and Garfinkel, yet in other ways they were closely analogous. Kuhn's work called into question Merton's solution to the social order problem in science, just as Garfinkel's called Parsons's similar solution into question in the context of social life generally. But at the same time, both writers remained appreciative of the work they at once depended on and undermined, and were seriously exercised by the fundamental problems that work had tried to resolve. In contrast, the work that has followed in their footsteps has been much more inclined to ignore or finesse these problems. In particular, neither in macrosociology since Garfinkel nor in sociology of science since Kuhn has any decisive resolution of the order problem been proffered, nor has it been convincingly exposed as a spurious problem or a pseudoproblem. It remains legitimate even now to address the problem much as it was conceptualised by Parsons and Merton, old hat though that conceptualisation is currently taken to be.

A SOLUTION

Functionalist sociologists saw social order as normative order, and accounted for it as the consequence of a shared nonrational respect for the relevant social norms. One view of Kuhn is that he reconceptualised this order as a paradigm-based order and accounted for it in terms of a specific shared respect for paradigms. In truth, however, what is made visible in Kuhn is an order pervading the whole of scientific practice, an order in how scientists apply, and evaluate the application of, paradigms as exemplars. The existence of a ubiquitous deference to the authority of paradigms does not account for an order such as this. And what we know empirically of scientific research indicates that deference to the authority of powerful persons does not account for it either. What then will account for this order? To account for such a ubiquitous and pervasive order in what scientists do, an orientation of respect and deference comparably ubiquitous and pervasive would seem to be required. And from a sociological perspective, the obvious conjecture would be that the respect that scientists have for *each other* is what is involved. Such a conjecture would link the primordial tendency of scientists to move into coordination and agreement to the respect and deference implied by the existence of social relations between them. And it would link their ability to operate coherently as distinct paradigm-sharing communities to the special respect and deference they accord each other as members thereof.

The project of the natural sciences can be formulated perfectly satisfactorily in the language of naive empiricism as a systematic attempt to learn from experience and to predict future experience on the basis of what has gone before. But the project is a collective one, and individual contributions to it must be coordinated and integrated so that a shared culture is carried forward by participants. As part and parcel of the practice intrinsic to their culture, scientists must perform the work involved in establishing agreed-on conventions, and in reifying the conventions into obligatory assumptions about the underlying nature of the physical world itself. This is work for the collective good of the sciences, and it can be carried out only by scientists respectful of each other and thereby moved by more than their own individual good.

There are many sources of insight into the conventional dimension of science and scientific knowledge, some of which deal with the topic more incisively than Kuhn. But Kuhn's recognition of conventions as intrinsically collective phenomena and, even more, his treatment of them as what ethnomethodologists call 'collective accomplishments' give his work a special sociological interest. This way of understanding convention, which is, of course, apparent throughout his work, is especially nicely articulated in his early paper on 'The Function of Measurement in Modern Physical Science' (1961). Here Kuhn draws attention to the comparisons between theoretical predictions and experimental findings offered as paradigmatic presentations in scientific textbooks, and he remarks how the 'agreement' asserted here can never be a matter of self-evident identity between the one and the other.

Agreement between theory and experiment or observation is always 'reasonable agreement', and what constitutes a reasonable agreement, rather than a significant divergence, between two different sets of numbers varies considerably with the scientific context. Physicists may require agreement to eight significant figures, for example between theory and spectroscopic data, whereas to get theoretical predictions within a factor of 10 of empirically based estimates may count as reasonable agreement where the masses of astronomical objects are concerned. What then are the criteria that fix what texts count as reasonable agreement? The question rests on a misconception. It is the predictions and findings cited by textbooks as 'in agreement', Kuhn tells us, that show what reasonable agreement consists in, in the contexts where the textbooks are authoritative. The cited predictions and cited data provide a model of what constitutes reasonable agreement, an authoritative model that those in the field will follow in subsequent research. Research is expected to align itself with that model not because any algorithm is available to legitimate the agreement it displays and exemplifies, but because it is that agreement that the collective backs with its authority.

The need to characterise the relationship between theoretical expectations and empirical findings arises all the time and everywhere in science, but prior to Kuhn it had generally been perceived as a purely technical problem of no profound significance. Kuhn addressed it with genuine curiosity and offered what at the time was a radical redescription of it. Reasonable agreement was identified as agreement by convention. And the basis of the convention was a specific exemplary instance that could only be emulated in further practice through processes of modelling and analogy. Thus, the continued existence of reasonable agreement can be seen to demand the continual connivance of the scientists following the initial instance of it: every instance of reasonable agreement, without exception, has to be accepted as in proper analogy with precedent. However many displays and descriptions of agreement are incarnate in it, something more than precedent itself is necessary, all the time, in order to dispose scientists to relate their practice to it in an adequately coordinated way. The textbook presentation of agreement will not in itself show how to distinguish what is agreement within 'acceptable error' from what is significant disagreement or serious anomaly. If scientists move collectively to the one view or the other in a given case, that is an interesting fact about them and their social behaviour.

As an aside, it is intriguing to find Kuhn drawing attention to the use of 'reasonable' to refer to something that is in truth accepted by convention. 'Reasonable' may indeed, so the dictionary assures us, denote what is sensible, or what conforms with fair expectations, both renderings that hint that what is reasonable may be a matter of convention. But notwithstanding this, to describe something as reasonable is often heard as an assertion that it rests on a rational *rather than* a conventional foundation. This makes our intuition that science is, whatever else, reasonable incline us toward the deeply misleading accounts of science propounded by rationalist philosophers. It is indeed a consistent virtue of Kuhn's work that he never permits a vision of research as oriented at once to convention and experience to metamorphose into the Enlightenment formula that renders it a synthesis of reason and experience.

To return to the main theme, it is argued that Kuhn's work bears on the social order problem above all because it displays science as the continuing open-ended elaboration of exemplars, and thereby exposes its continual dependence on the sociability of scientists and the mutual deference they accord to each other in their social relations. In one sense, this confirms Kuhn's own conviction that something special about scientific collectives is necessarily implicated in their success as producers of reliable knowledge, but in another sense it goes against it. There is indeed something special operative in scientific collectives in the shape of the deference that scientists accord only to each other; it is this mutual deference that permits movement to an agreed-on practice and a shared culture to unfold only amongst and between trained scientific specialists. On the other hand, the existence of mutual deference between scientists as members of a distinctive collective is in no way remarkable: wherever human beings sustain a shared culture or subculture, this appertains.

As collectives, traditionally organised academic scientists constitute typical Weberian status groups, wherein the particular mutual deference that members accord only to each other, the special honour of status as Weber called it, redounds to the collective good of the group. In according this honour only to each other, scientists, like other status-group members, both encourage each other to act in coordination and exclude outsiders from involvement in what they are doing, thereby securing a degree of collective autonomy. The importance of this special honour was clear to Merton and was emphasised in his brilliant studies of reward and recognition in academic science. Moving from these studies to Kuhn, the latter can be read as offering a still deeper and more far-reaching appreciation of the role of honorific relations. From Kuhn we can infer their importance in the creation and sustenance of the esoteric technical practice of science. He offers us a glimpse of how the mutual deference that is a part of our basic nature as social animals has been essential at every level in the constitution of the most magnificent of all our technical accomplishments.

Sadly, however, not even Thomas Kuhn himself read Kuhn in this way, and his sense of the special character of scientific communities was never satisfactorily transformed from intuition to explicit description. Nor has later work succeeded in filling the gap here. On the contrary, there is no extant account of the natural sciences, whether in philosophy or the social sciences, that does not beg the question where social order is concerned.

AN UNWANTED SOLUTION

Kuhn's wholly convincing account of the role of exemplars in science allows a greatly increased significance to be attached to the functionalist conjecture that the orderly character of science depends on the social relations between scientists. The mutual respect and deference intrinsic to those relations are now revealed not merely as necessary to the creation of a space for reason to work in, but as essential to the production of what will count as reasoned judgments and reasoned actions within that space. And the social order constituted by those judgments and actions stands revealed as the product of human sociability, even though it may also validly be described as scientists manipulating and interrogating the natural world. This, we might say, was Thomas Kuhn's unwanted solution to the order problem, a solution unwanted in the end even by Kuhn himself (Kuhn 2000).

Why was the solution unwanted? No doubt the problem of relativism furnishes part of the answer. An apologist for science does well to eschew relativism in all its forms, for the simple amongst her audience require a neat dualist scheme with a clear demarcation of good and evil and no equivocations or complications. But Kuhn's apologia permitted no such dualism, and indeed, the solution to the order problem it implied was profoundly monistic and relativistic. Kuhn described the technical practice of science as a social practice wherein what any scientist does is always bound up with and influenced by what other scientists are doing. And the influence in question is causally mediated: what brings about coordination and agreement is a causal relation with others that is part of the overall causal nexus surrounding the individual scientist as the occupant of a given external environment. The beliefs and practices of the scientist are thus made visible as the outcome of causal contingencies just like those of anyone else. If the beliefs and practices of human beings are explicable at all, then those of scientists are explicable along with those of everyone else, in the same causal frame and with reference to the same range of causes.

By way of another aside, here is the reason that Kuhn has been so important to the work of the Edinburgh School of sociology of science. Their project is precisely to seek a causal-scientific understanding of the entire sphere of human action that admits of no exceptions. The self-referential character of this inescapably relativistic project makes it at once a part of the overall explanatory project of science and an enterprise that, in seeking to observe and explain science 'scientifically' from the outside, must in that way be alienated from it. But indeed, there is no way of 'finishing' the scientific project that does not entail this kind of difficulty, as practising scientists are surely destined to discover for themselves fairly soon, as they continue to turn their curiosity more and more in upon themselves as knowing subjects (Barnes et al. 1996).

A solution to the social order problem that entails relativism of any sort must expect to be rejected by a significant body of academic opinion, responding in knee-jerk fashion to the word itself, as it were. But more needs to be said in the present instance. Sociologists, after all, are by no means all averse to relativism, and the problem of order has been of great importance in their tradition. It might be thought that they would have been keen to extend a line of thought leading from Max Weber, through Talcott Parsons and Robert Merton, and on to Thomas Kuhn, but it has proved not to be so. Although sociologists have become increasingly interested in the knowledge and culture of science in recent decades, and especially in scientific controversy, curiosity about the fundamental problem of order, agreement, and coherence in scientific communities has actually fallen away. Indeed, in a field that has increasingly embraced individualism and a metaphysics of free agency, there is now some reluctance to recognise order as a problem at all. Sociologists currently like to document creativity, knowledgeability, and individual autonomy in the actions of human beings, and are correspondingly reluctant to explain actions or to say what makes them patterned and orderly at the macro level.

The reception of the work of Bruno Latour in the 1980s will serve as a mark and symbol of this change. Latour (1987, 1988) wanted to erode the distinction between 'scientific' and 'political' actions, and began to speak as if all the actions of scientists without exception were political, which if the term is understood in a sufficiently broad sense was clearly so. What was surprising, however, at least to me, was that he went on to describe those actions using metaphors drawn from aggressively individualistic forms of economic and political theory, offering a picture of science as a form of Hobbesian war. And it was a still greater surprise when this particular aspect of Latour's work was acclaimed with enthusiasm by sociologists, for whom a tradition going back to Durkheim had decisively demonstrated (or so I had imagined) that not even war of the usual kind could possibly be Hobbesian war. Yet the successful advent of this radically unsociological sociology was no accident, and indeed, it is now the dominant approach to science, in a field where many have happily forgotten their Durkheimian inheritance and looked to fantasies of individual agency to relieve the tedium of their existence in comprehensively normalised societies.

DOES IT MATTER ANY MORE?

Prior to Kuhn, functionalist sociologists with an interest in social order as a formal theoretical problem had fruitfully extended their modes of thought to the natural sciences. In contrast, Kuhn remained exclusively concerned with the natural sciences and addressed the problem only in that context. This, however, did not preclude his furthering the project of his prede-cessors. Indeed, perversely perhaps, his most valuable insights bore on the fundamental problem of order, and not the specific one. Convinced that the distinctive character of scientific communities was crucial to their success, he developed our understanding of those communities as status groups, distinctive indeed, but distinctive only as status groups everywhere are dis-tinctive, by virtue of their claim to a special honour of membership. This might be thought a disappointing outcome to the career of an apologist for science like Kuhn; but from a sociological perspective, it actually increases the importance of his work. It makes it of interest not merely as a revelatory account of scientific practice but as a source of insight into social practices in general, and into the relationship between the esoteric practices of the natural sciences and those of its external audiences.

It is a strange feature of sociology and social theory that as time has passed, they have found it harder and harder to grasp, or perhaps to face up to, the way that human social relations are actually constituted. Anything that detracts from an imagined individual autonomy is found embarrassing.

In particular, many theorists shy away from the idea that persons must necessarily accord deference and honour to each other in and through their social relations, and that they profoundly affect each other thereby; they prefer to think of relations predicated on honour as optional and outmoded. Not even Erving Goffman, the sociologist who more than any other helped to uncover the essential role of deference, was able to do so in a direct and straightforward way. He did indeed quite brilliantly display its fundamental involvement in all kinds of social interactions, but he did so under cover of irony and predominantly by reference to unsavoury or pathological cases. It is true that in some ways this perversity is actually an advantage: Nobody who reads Goffman will make the error of believing that relations founded on honour and deference are ipso facto admirable or immune to corruption. Nonetheless, Goffman's sociology, as well as being the seminal resource for understanding the role of honour and deference in social interaction, is also a striking symbol of the difficulty we find in addressing that role at the level of conscious reflection (Goffman 1967; Scheff 1988).

Just as we have grown uncomfortable in reflecting on the role of honour, so we have grown less tolerant of systems that overtly rely on it. And this is especially the case with systems that rely on a special form of honour as a currency with which they can operate as differentiated semiautonomous entities. The special honour of status that Max Weber famously described is something we have become increasingly reluctant to acknowledge: We appear to have lost the knack of deferring to it whilst remaining fully secure in our own dignity. The change is clearly apparent in our current orientation to technical experts and independent professionals. We remain as ready as ever to reward them well for their services, but we increasingly insist on the reward's being monetary rather than honorific and deferential. Monetary reward denies or even inverts status relations, and erodes expert autonomy rather than reinforcing it, as deference does.

This move has increasingly eroded the taboo on direct external monetary reward formerly characteristic of the institutional arrangements of traditional academic scientific fields. But although many deeply harmful consequences have flowed from this, there is nothing to suggest that research has become less productive or innovative as a result of it, or that the reliability of its findings has been diminished thereby. This has served to reinforce a criticism long advanced against Merton's functionalist account of science: that institutional arrangements incorporating honorific rewards and a taboo on external monetary incentives cannot be functional necessities, since most science, and notably industrial science and military research, has always managed without them as a matter of history. And indeed, over a period when it has become ever clearer that even fundamental advances may readily emerge from 'applied' settings, Merton's account has lost its credibility.

Sociologists of science cannot be criticised for turning away from Merton's account. The traditional pseudoaristocratic institutional arrangements he described, admirable though they were and marvellously 'functional', were not necessary to the practice of scientific research and the engendering of reliable knowledge thereby. Nonetheless, to turn away from his thought entirely, and seek inspiration instead from individualistic modes of thought, is a mistake. For Merton was right in asserting the crucial role of honorific relations in science and wrong only in his judgment of where and how they were necessary to, not to say constitutive of, the activity.

With the benefit of hindsight and the insights bequeathed to us by Kuhn, the actual technical practice of science stands revealed as the location wherein these relations are essential. Situating Kuhn's work in continuity with that of Merton, we might say that it persists in the sociological conception of science of the latter, but moves away from a priestly vision of scientists toward a more generally applicable account of them as expert technical professionals. As such, they remain carriers of a shared esoteric culture and must carry it as a differentiated collective. But they are able to carry that culture as artists and musicians have long carried theirs, or engineers and craftspersons, or many other bearers of shared esoteric practices. And like them, they can perform successfully in the face of strong external expectations reinforced by extrinsic rewards and sanctions, given only that these do not intrude on the core of their shared technical practice and disrupt the social relations that permit its existence. Consistent with this vision of things, it is not to be wondered at if those who employ scientists in applied and industrial laboratories have learned that to allow them a certain kind of collective autonomy is very much in their interests. Indeed, perhaps this is why, in countries like Britain, where the autonomy of academic science has been radically suborned and its traditional carrier institutions systematically degraded, laboratories financed by industry and the military entirely out of utilitarian considerations are not infrequently regarded as the best available locations in which to pursue even nonapplied research.

At the same time, however, it requires but a small extension of Kuhn's basic vision to see why scientists should come to expect, in the normal way of things, an increasing amount of opposition and hostility. Simply to sustain their core technical practice, scientists need to operate as exclusionary status groups, wherein honour and respect for expertise impliy a corresponding contempt for the less informed opinions of the outsider. This easily engenders hostility amongst a lay public now increasingly prone to question any kind of collective status distinction and sensitive to the indignity of any form of exclusion. And precisely because a special respect for scientific expertise is manifested by the great institutions and sources of power, that hostility is confirmed and intensified amongst all those who distrust them and, more significantly, amongst all those groups of intellectuals who see it as their task to criticise them. Enjoying as they now do a near monopoly as suppliers of empirical knowledge and a correspondingly privileged position in the counsels of the powerful, they must expect to be attacked by those who would resist and neutralise that power, as well no doubt by those who envy its possessors and lament their own lack of it.

Kuhn's account of science is indeed of continuing relevance to the fundamental problem of how we might best relate to expertise, a problem currently attracting much attention in the social sciences. In a nutshell, the dilemma here is this: to pass the care of specific bodies of knowledge and skill to specialists is to reap what are in modern societies the vast efficiency benefits of the resulting division of labour; but at the same time, it is to cede powers to specialists, and thereby to engender an enduring dependence on them and on those with closest access to them.

The dilemma may also be formulated as that of how to control expertise. To monitor and evaluate technical judgments adequately, it is necessary to grasp the relevant technical considerations, but to move in this direction is to reverse the specialisation process itself and to lose its efficiency benefits. When all are competent to evaluate expertise, it is expertise no longer. To put the dilemma in this latter way is to highlight just how salient Kuhn's work is here. His account of scientific research is of a form of practice wherein continuing competence entails continuing participation, wherein 'to grasp the relevant technical considerations' entails no less than becoming a recognised practitioner in the relevant scientific field. On this account, adequate external evaluation of esoteric scientific knowledge and competence is not possible. This is why those who would challenge the claims of specialists from the outside, and who presume to contribute to the evaluation of their technical claims, are prone to read the account as an ideological justification of traditional attitudes to expertise. (No doubt a strongly rationalist vision would be more ideologically expedient for them. Inspired by a perspective of this kind, the interested layperson, or the civil servant, or the passionate protester could envisage mugging up a few laws and equations over the weekend and then running the rule over any amount of technical advice and information on the Monday.)

Nobody seriously engaged with the problem of expertise would deny the need for some kind of evaluation and regulation of scientists and technical professionals, but there are major differences about what this should consist in. For Kuhn, as for Merton, the presumption is that scientists and other experts should evaluate and regulate each other. In this way, evaluation is securely based on knowledge, and the consequences of incompetence or of a lack of proper disinterest will not go undetected due to ignorance or misunderstanding. These authors see no danger in having to trust a self-regulating collective of experts and no indignity in deferring to their judgements. For others, however, there is a danger here. And there is insult as well in the 'democratic deficit' they identify in decisions informed only by expert technical advice. For them, expertise ought to be externally controlled, and 'ought' implies 'can'. Accordingly, experts should not evaluate each other but should compete for the ear of external audiences and acquiesce in being evaluated by them.

These two orientations to esoteric knowledge and expertise, the 'hierarchy' and the 'market' orientation, as perhaps we should call them, have long existed and are easy to exemplify historically. But it is also clear as a matter of history that a secular trend away from hierarchy and toward market has long been underway. It is a trend currently being fuelled by an intensifying 'participatory impulse' in the populations of many democratic polities, and by populist politicians happy to attack any kind of independent professional activity. There is, of course, considerable variability in the constituents of the trend. A desire that greater access should be secured to important decision-making fora, and that experts should remain on tap as advisors and not metamorphose into decision takers in their own right, is all that moves some. And there are indeed good grounds for respecting concerns of this kind; the tendency of those experts who move into policy controversies to polarise into supporters of one or other side, and even to become polemicists on behalf of one outcome or another, is very well documented (Nelkin 1975, 1992). But what is more interesting here, as this discussion of Kuhn comes to an end, is the position of some of those who stand at the opposite extreme.

The existence of barriers between experts and laypersons, and the denial of any legitimate role to the latter in the evaluation of expertise, are now frequently perceived as intrinsic wrongs and are challenged uncompromisingly at a fundamental level. They have even come to be criticised on epistemological grounds. Knowledge in a modern society, it is said, will have to emerge from social interactions that cross existing lay–expert boundaries and encompass both the users of the knowledge and the many groups and interests affected by its use if it is to command sufficient credibility to count as knowledge at all. The 'institutionalised communication breakdown that euphemistically passes for "autonomous research communities"' will have to be overcome, so Steve Fuller claims, thereby nicely expressing an evaluation of the current organisation of science that could scarcely be more dissonant with Kuhn's (Fuller 2000, p. 7; see also Fuller 1988). The scope of traditional, esoteric, 'mode-one' forms of knowledge evaluated entirely within highly specialised collectives will diminish, and 'mode-two' knowledge sustained by more diverse and inclusive social relations will become of increasing importance, or so Mike Gibbons and his collaborators believe (Gibbons, Limoges, Nowotny, Schwartzman, Scott, and Tow 1994). The issues raised by assertions of this kind obviously lie far beyond the scope of this essay. But it is hard to think of work more apposite than that of Kuhn to the task of reflecting critically on them, reviewing their (truly far-reaching) implications in the imagination, and considering the consequences at the level of knowledge, culture, and practice of such a weakening of boundaries and reconstruction of social relations. In addressing this particular manifestation of the social order problem Kuhn should still be read, and indeed acknowledged as amongst the leading sources of insight. And whilst his general vision of scientific practice and his implicit epistemology may be the products of a context markedly different from our own, they are nonetheless extensively exemplified by the scholarly work of an outstanding historian, whereas some more recent competing visions have still not been properly exemplified at all.

References

Barnes, B. 1982. *T. S. Kuhn and Social Science*. London: Macmillan.
    1995. *The Elements of Social Theory*. Princeton: Princeton University Press.
Barnes, B., D. Bloor, and J. Henry. 1996. *Scientific Knowledge: A Sociological Analysis*. Chicago: University of Chicago Press.
Bloor, D. 1997. *Wittgenstein, Rules and Institutions*. London: Routledge.
Brannigan, A. 1979. "The reification of Mendel." *Social Studies of Science* 9: 423–54.
    1981. *The Social Basis of Scientific Discoveries*. Cambridge: Cambridge University Press.
Fuller, S. 1988. *Social Epistemology*. Bloomington: Indiana University Press.
    2000. *Thomas Kuhn*. Chicago: University of Chicago Press.
Garfinkel, H. 1967. *Studies in Ethnomethodology*. Englewood Cliffs, NJ: Prentice-Hall.
Gibbons, M., C. Limoges, H. Nowotny, S. Schwartzman, P. Scott, and M. Tow. 1994. *The New Production of Knowledge*. London: Sage.

Giere, R. N. 1988. *Explaining Science*. Chicago: University of Chicago Press.

Goffman, E. 1967. *Interaction Ritual: Essays on Face-to-Face Behavior.* New York: Doubleday.

Kuhn, T. S. 1961. "The Function of Measurement in Modern Physical Science." Reprinted in Kuhn (1977), pp. 178–224.

1962. "The Historical Structure of Scientific Discovery." Reprinted in Kuhn (1977), pp. 165–77.

1970. *The Structure of Scientific Revolutions*, 2nd ed. Chicago: University of Chicago Press.

1977. *The Essential Tension*. Chicago: University of Chicago Press.

Kuhn, T. S. 2000. *The Road Since Structure*. Edited by J. Conant and J. Haugeland. Chicago: University of Chicago Press.

Latour, B. 1987. *Science in Action*. Milton Keynes: Open University Press.

1988. *The Pasteurisation of France*. Cambridge, MA: Harvard University Press.

Merton, R. K. 1973. *The Sociology of Science*. Chicago: University of Chicago Press.

Nelkin, D. 1975. "The Political Impact of Technical Expertise." *Social Studies of Science* 5: 35–54.

1992. *Controversy*. London: Sage.

Olby, R. 1979. "Mendel: No Mendelian?" *History of Science* 17: 53–72.

Parsons, T. 1937/1968. *The Structure of Social Action*. New York: Free Press.

Scheff, T. J. 1988. "Shame and Conformity: The Deference-Emotion System." *American Sociological Review* 53: 395–406.

Weber, M. 1968. *Economy and Society: An Outline of Interpretive Sociology*. Berkeley: University of California Press.

6 Normal Science: From Logic to Case-Based and Model-Based Reasoning

THOMAS NICKLES

6.1 INTRODUCTION

The central distinction of Thomas Kuhn's *The Structure of Scientific Revolutions* (1962) is that between normal science and revolutionary science. He offered suggestive and provocative but sketchy accounts of both. Most historians and sociologists who have discussed Kuhn's work have maintained that his account of normal science is the more important, while philosophers and culture theorists – and Kuhn himself – have tended to regard his claims about revolutionary discontinuities and incommensurability as his truly original contribution.[1] In my judgment, the problems that Kuhn engaged in his account of normal science are more heuristically promising for understanding scientific inquiry and human inquiry more generally. Subsequent developments in cognitive psychology have vindicated Kuhn's departures from standard theories of cognition. It may even be the case that what is worth saving in Kuhn's treatment of revolutions depends on the account of cognition that he developed for normal science. After all, Kuhn's own most informative characterization of revolutionary science is that it is extraordinary – *non*normal. Accordingly, I shall examine Kuhn's account of normal scientific cognition as puzzle-solving practices guided by the exemplary problem solutions that he called "exemplars," together with what he termed "an acquired similarity relation." I shall center my discussion on that most basic problem concerning the very possibility of inquiry – the Meno paradox – and indicate how Kuhn's account of scientific inquiry attempts to solve it. Here I must limit myself to the "early" Kuhn of *Structure* and the related essays written in the 1960s and 1970s.[2] Kuhn's later work is taken up in detail in the essays that follow this one.

6.2 NORMAL SCIENCE AS ROUTINE

To what extent is scientific activity routine? Many issues, including our overall conception of what science is, who scientists are, and what they do, hinge on the answer to this question. At one extreme is the view that scientific work is methodical, dull routine and that scientists themselves are rather plodding people with tunnel vision. The overreaction to this view is the grand, romantic picture of science as the field of play of artistic geniuses. In the twentieth century, Karl Popper (1959, 1963) was a famous proponent of the romantic view.

The first view – that scientific work is highly routine or routinizable – suggests that we might be able to characterize modern scientific practice in terms of a *method*. There is, of course, a long history of such claims, beginning with Plato and Aristotle but dating especially from the time of Francis Bacon and René Descartes. Today the idea that there is a single general method that defines scientific inquiry ("the scientific method") remains popular among school administrators and the general public, but it has been virtually abandoned by historians, philosophers, and sociologists of science. However, on a smaller scale, routinization in the form of automation of many specific laboratory and computational procedures is not only possible but also actual, as becomes apparent when we step into a high-tech biochemistry laboratory or even when we observe social and behavioral scientists running semiautomated experiments and processing the data by means of computer programs.

Computer scientists are intensely interested in things routine, for they expect to find algorithmic programs for any activity to the degree that it is routinizable. In fact, most of the methodological work in scientific problem solving today occurs not in philosophy of science as traditionally understood but in computer science, some of it in artificial intelligence (AI).

Other professional groups also have a stake in the degree to which scientific work may be characterized as routine or at least tradition-bound. In order to answer key questions that arise in their professional disciplines, both historians and sociologists, including historians and sociologists of science, need to identify some degree of routine in the form of traditional or regularized cultural practices.[3] The highly romanticized view of major scientific advances as the intuitive creation *ex nihilo* of great geniuses leaves the historian and sociologist in the same boat as the logician and philosopher: there is not much that can be done to make such developments intelligible as the products of recognizable human practices. Hence, the romantic picture has been a professional obstacle to historians and sociologists seeking to treat scientific work in a way that conveys explanatory understanding, just as it has been an obstacle to philosophers of science seeking a better understanding of scientific innovation.

Now where does Thomas Kuhn himself fit into the spectrum between the two extremum positions? His standpoint looks paradoxical at first. Kuhn stated that nearly all mature science is normal science and that normal science is, in some sense, routine. Indeed, for Kuhn, the existence of routine problems (and problem-solving activity) is the hallmark of a mature science. This, if anything, is Kuhn's criterion of demarcation of mature science from immature science and nonscience.[4] Yet Kuhn strongly denied that scientific work, in its salient aspects, proceeds on the basis of logical or methodological rules. Scientists, he said, do not employ many rules explicitly, nor will any set of rules that captures past practice be reliably projectible onto the future of science (*Structure*, §V; 1970b, 1974).

In short, Kuhn confounded the Popperians, logical positivists, and others by claiming that scientific work is far *more* routinized yet far *less* methodical than they had imagined.[5] How is this possible?

The answer to this question is that Kuhn denied that routine scientific work is normally methodical in the sense of applying a set of rules. Rather, scientists directly model their current problem-solving efforts on concrete cases consisting of previous problem-solving achievements, which Kuhn termed "exemplars."

Kuhn repeatedly traced the provenance of most of his methodological ideas first to his experience as a physics student and then, as a young physics Ph.D., to his struggle to read, understand, and teach to Harvard undergraduates historical texts such as Aristotle's writings on motion. The importance of the fact that the course consisted in case studies in the history of science will become more apparent later.

The first step in understanding Aristotle, Kuhn remarked, is to stay within the immediate confines of his own text and the kinds of experiences routinely available to the Greeks of his day, with the aim of making that text internally coherent. Kuhn somewhat misleadingly termed this the "hermeneutic method."[6] The second step is to locate Aristotle's problems and solutions within a wider context of thought and action characteristic of his time rather than having them appear from nowhere like a deus ex machina. In both cases, it is crucial to avoid deploying cultural resources that were not available to the historical agents, certainly including present-day categories of description and standards of evaluation.[7]

Barry Barnes (1982) furnishes a good illustration of the second step from Kuhn's own historical treatment of Sadi Carnot (Kuhn 1960). In the 1820s, Carnot arrived at what we now call the "Carnot cycle" and an early form of the second law of thermodynamics (the law of entropy increase) while working within the old caloric tradition. If we look only at the work on heat theory being done at the time, such as it was, Carnot's results appear to drop from the sky, the insights of a prescient genius who, remarkably, achieved correct "modern" results from a badly mistaken theoretical standpoint. Accordingly, we get little idea of how he could have hit on them and recognized their importance. But if we place Carnot in the engineering tradition to which he in fact belonged, we gain a much better understanding of why he was working on his particular problems and in his particular manner.

Contextual location is everything, a theme that Barnes correctly identifies as running through Kuhn's career. Kuhn had dealt similarly with Copernicus in his first book, *The Copernican Revolution*. He later adopted the same historical-interpretive strategy in his history of the emergence of the early quantum theory, *Black-Body Theory and the Quantum Discontinuity, 1894–1912*. Once we locate Max Planck within the proper classical research tradition, we can understand him as a less radical, less iconoclastic thinker and explain his otherwise puzzling resistance to the very quantum ideas that he is usually credited with discovering. Of course, we then face the problem of explaining how Einstein, Ehrenfest, and others could have interpreted Planck's work so differently than Planck intended. The answer, briefly stated, is that they were working on a different problem than Planck was and misinterpreted his work as addressing their own, namely, the so-called ultraviolet catastrophe.[8]

6.3 HOW NORMAL SCIENCE IS ACHIEVED

Many practitioners of the nonphysical sciences have read Kuhn as providing a recipe for turning their own field into a fully mature science. The recipe is to agree on a paradigm that will make possible a routine problem-solving enterprise. Kuhn had little sympathy for such use of his work and disavowed any intention to extend his claims beyond the mature sciences (mainly the physical sciences and, to some degree, biology). Although Kuhnian normal science does depend heavily on its peculiar form of social organization and social cognition, we cannot create it at will. Why not?

First, Kuhn remained enough of a realist to say that the possibility of normal science depends on the way the world is, in some difficult-to-specify way (Hoyningen-Huene 1993, pp. 85, 94f). The world, or the aspect of it carved out by a successful normal scientific domain, cannot be totally chaotic. It must be patterned. Not only must there be some sort of natural regularity, but this regularity must be manifested in a certain degree of clustering of basic phenomena. Otherwise, the original acquisition and subsequent teaching of what Kuhn termed a "learned" or an "acquired similarity relation" could not get off the ground. Nature does not dictate the similarity relation, but neither is it completely arbitrary.

Second, the patterning must be humanly accessible, given the nature of our neural-psychological apparatus and social structure. And we must actually succeed in solving some basic problems that will become exemplars, achievements that can serve as models for dealing with new problems and, accordingly, can give rise to the problem-solving techniques or regularized problem-solving practices that enable normal science to take off. Kuhn assumed that human beings possess sufficient ingenuity to formulate problems and to propose interesting solutions for them, but he was not at all committed to the romantic genius view of scientific creativity. The point is that, in order to have normal science, you have to have some exemplary achievements on which to build. And the best way to explain where those come from is to regard them as variant products of more or less traditional activities that already exist. Not even Galileo's work on projectile motion and the pendulum emerged full-blown from his own feverish brain. In fact, Galileo's work became intelligible to us only whom Pierre Duhem and others revealed the existence of the rich medieval and renaissance traditions upon which Galileo drew (Hoyningen-Huene 1993, p. 17).

Here we begin to see the possibility of a step-by-step, evolutionary account of Kuhnian science.

Stated in another way, Kuhn's point is that traditions and established, successful practices cannot be invented overnight by an act of will on the part of an individual or a group (cf. Hobsbawm and Ranger 1992). Roughly speaking, Kuhn rejected the Enlightenment view that "rational" political societies and scientific communities can be created at will by simply sweeping away established traditions and replacing them by a rationally planned enterprise by means of a Popperian constitutional convention. His conception of science was pre-Enlightenment in several respects, including appreciation of the importance of tradition.

Despite his presuppositions about the natural world, however, Kuhn's main efforts, in explaining the emergence and maintenance of normal science, were devoted to the human, social-constructive side of normal science. Even given the right sort of world, it takes a very special sort of community to realize normal science. Kuhn's twin focus here was on the recruitment and training of new members of the community and on the maintenance of order within the community and the policing of its boundaries. In these and other respects, and rather like Polanyi (1958, 1966), Kuhn suggested that the scientific community operates surprisingly like a medieval guild: (1) It is a community of practitioners who possess expert knowledge. (2) The community sharply distinguishes itself from the nonexpert, lay public, including other expert scientific communities. Boundaries are maintained by the high costs of admission and expulsion, enforced by professors, journal editors, peer reviewers, and other "gatekeepers." (3) There is a standard training procedure for novices in a given specialty area. They are trained on the same problems, using the same or similar textbooks and laboratory exercises. At advanced stages, the training typically involves something akin to a master–apprentice relation. (4) The knowledge is imparted by example far more than by rule. (5) Hence, the crucial knowledge that distinguishes an expert from a well-read novice remains largely tacit, inarticulate, and more knowing-how than knowing-that. It involves teaching by showing and knowing by doing. (6) Strong personal commitment to the imparted tradition is expected. Being too critical of community presuppositions and practices threatens both the community and one's own career prospects.

Kuhn claimed an essential equivalence of training and research. Both require solving problems by modeling them on exemplars already in hand. However, what is a routine textbook exemplar already in hand for an expert will be a tough new puzzle for a student, amounting to a highly constrained student research experience. Thus the training ideally prepares students for later work as journeymen practitioners.

Unfortunately, Kuhn's account turns out to be too neat, as we shall see in §§6.8 and 6.9. The similarities here enticed Kuhn to overlook some important differences in the nature and function of exemplars.

6.4   HOW NORMAL SCIENCE WORKS

Kuhn popularized the view that scientific work is problem solving, not in Popper's grand sense but as a matter of routine. In order to secure their position in the community and thereby gain a professional reputation and access to more resources, normal scientists must pose and/or solve puzzles that further articulate the paradigm without breaking with its central thrust. The problems they tackle must be challenging and the work in solving them original but not radically innovative. Normal scientists must walk a tightrope, one held taut by Kuhn's "essential tension" between tradition and innovation (Kuhn 1977, chap. 9).

How is it that scientists can recognize their own kind, so to speak, that is, recognize a piece of work and its author(s) as belonging to their specialty area? More specifically, how is it that scientists can recognize that a problem falls within their domain of professional expertise and responsibility in the first place, and subsequently determine whether dealing with it is feasible, given current intellectual and socioeconomic resources? Similarly, how can they recognize a proffered solution as "the" correct solution or at least as an adequate solution? These are nontrivial questions. Anyone who has been involved in, or examined, frontier research knows that these recognition tasks – picking out significant features in a chaos of apparent noise – are crucial to success. There are always many faint trails, most of which lead nowhere. For example, which few of the hundreds of papers in recent volumes of *The Physical Review* will be significant for the future of physics?

Here we have a version of the old problem raised already by Plato in his dialogue *Meno*, namely, the Meno paradox. Briefly stated, the paradox takes the form of a dilemma that ultimately denies that inquiry and learning are possible. For you either know that which you seek or you do not. If you already have what you seek, you cannot inquire into it, for you already know it. But if you do not already possess it, then how will you recognize it even if you stumble on it accidentally?[9]

Not surprisingly, Kuhn's solution to the basic problem of inquiry, the Meno-recognition problem, was essentially identical with his solution to (what I call) the "problem of heuristic appraisal": given the vast and noisy field of possible options, how do scientists identify which problems, techniques, and other resources are more likely to be fruitful to pursue?[10]

Most attempts to solve the Meno problem "go between the horns" of the dilemma by contending that inquiry is possible in those cases in which we already know in one way but not in the desired way. Traditionally, this has meant that inquiry makes implicit, inarticulate, or otherwise imperfect knowledge verbally explicit in the form of statements, often rulelike declarations.

Now Kuhn himself did *not* couch his positive account of normal science in terms of the Meno problem; however, it is fruitful to read *Structure* §§II–V as his sketch of a solution to the Meno problem. Conversely, we can read his critiques of the positivists, Popper, Feyerabend, and others as pointing out their failure to solve the Meno problem. Kuhn's point was that scientific inquiry, as we know it, would be impossible if conducted in their fashion. What, then, was Kuhn's own, positive account?

First, normal science screens out as irrelevant the vast majority of potential problems that might present themselves. It further screens out many of those that do fall within the general domain of the particular specialty in question, on the ground that these problems are not yet solvable because there exist no suitable exemplars to indicate what a good answer would look like. Occasionally, however, a problem originally regarded as genuine will resist a solution so long that it will be set aside, without much immediate damage to the paradigm. The leading example is the nature of gravity within Newtonian mechanics.

This screening process does not consist in holding up every single possible problem and proposed solution for examination and then rejecting most of them, an uneconomical process reminiscent of Popper's methodology of the falsification of hypotheses. Rather, the paradigm makes a few problems salient in two related ways. The relevant scientific community selects problems the solutions of which would further articulate the paradigm, and the community actively seeks *doable* problems. The most doable problems will be precisely those that resemble exemplars already available. Moreover, it is training on these exemplars that tunes scientists to perceive the world in their terms in the first place. If the match is sufficiently obvious, the unsolved problems are left to graduate students and to the more pedestrian investigators.

It is worth emphasizing that the exemplars, as model solutions, include both axiological and normative-evaluative functions. They are something to be further articulated[11] and also emulated. They "show" what a good problem and solution look like and what sorts of practices produce them. They show what it is to do physics in specialty X. As such, they set the local goals of inquiry and the standards of evaluation. They also play a strong heuristic-directive role beyond this. This is why Kuhn largely abandoned the old invidious distinction between context of discovery (the search process) and context of justification (the logical "final" justification of the products of research). Epistemic justification, as traditionally understood, is important, of course, but it is rarely enough to determine the future promise of a candidate problem solution, model, theory, paradigm, or research technique. Heuristic appraisal is at least as important, because it is explicitly forward-looking.

Moreover, the exemplars are not merely abstract models but also contain the primary computational resources relevant to solving the new problems with which they are matched. One or more exemplars, suitably adapted, provide a model of one's current puzzle and the sought-for solution. One figures out how to solve the current puzzle by finding sufficiently close matches to puzzles solved previously.

Next, Kuhn made the strong claim that the paradigm of a mature science "guarantees," to the skilled practitioners, the solvability of legitimate problems. What could this mean? In a weak and rather uninteresting sense, this only means that scientists select problems that match the available repertoire. But there is a stronger sense, namely, that in a full-fledged, mature Kuhnian research program, there will exist one or more exemplars for every major problem type that is expected to arise at the present stage of development. (Solving these problems will likely produce more refined exemplars sufficient for proceeding to the next stage of articulation, and so on.) Borrowing a term from higher algebra, we might say that, in this sense, the set of exemplars "spans" the space of the problem domain, since every acceptable solution is expected to consist in the application of some combination of extant exemplars by means of standard practices. Second, previous work (notably, the set of available exemplars) indicates in advance what sort of answer can be expected. Wrote Kuhn about one sort of articulation problem:

> Perhaps the most striking feature of the normal research problems...is how little they aim to produce major novelties, conceptual or phenomenal. Sometimes, as in a wavelength measurement, everything but the most esoteric detail of the result is known in advance....(*Structure*, p. 35)

Herein lies Kuhn's solution to the Meno problem of recognition and learning. Problem solving involves a search of the unknown, but a very bounded one. The problems are well defined and highly constrained. So normal science is *not* science at the wildest epistemological frontier. Normal scientists committed to the paradigm believe not only that the paradigm guarantees the problems' solvability but also that it furnishes all the necessary resources to do so and, to some degree, points toward the correct solutions. The problems become challenges to the competence of the scientists. For these reasons, the problem-solving practitioners are highly motivated, competing to be the first to solve a solvable problem. For these same reasons, Kuhn termed the problems "puzzles" (as in crossword puzzles and jigsaw puzzles) rather than problems full stop. Remaining puzzles are lacunae in the developing structure of theory and practice.

In guaranteeing solvability, the paradigm assures scientists that they *already know* the solution implicitly in the sense that all the necessary resources are known and that the correct solution will be recognized quickly once it is expressed explicitly. (This is because exemplars and *genealogies* of exemplars in effect give rise to microtraditions or micropractices that make the work and its results intelligible in the manner described in §6.2.) And so, normal scientists "only" need to make the solution more explicit or more specific in practice (which can be a very challenging task). In Kuhn's terms, they need to "articulate" this implicit knowledge, a term that seems to resonate with Plato's own solution to the Meno problem.[12] Thus Kuhn's solution denies that the paradox expresses a genuine dilemma. Like most other attempted solutions, Kuhn's goes between the horns. However, Kuhn's attempted solution departs from the standard sort, including Plato's, which requires this implicit knowledge always to become fully, verbally explicit in propositional or rulelike form. For Kuhn, normal science not only begins from concrete cases but also, even when articulated, remains case-based rather than rule-based. Neither a fully articulated mathematical solution to a problem nor the statement of "method" (or experimental design) in the published write-up of a series of experiments expresses all that expert scientists know. For Kuhn, above all, solving the Meno problem in practical terms means just that – transforming implicit knowledge into standardized, useful practices, including cognitive recognition and analytical skills, and manual skills. Unlike the well-read amateur, the expert knows how to *do* science.[13]

I noted earlier that standard solutions to the Meno involve showing how potential knowledge can become actual knowledge – traditionally supposed to be fully explicit and articulated propositional knowledge, often rulelike knowledge. Kuhn (like others before him, such as Wittgenstein and Polanyi) pointed out the problem of going the other way as well – from articulated textbook statements of theories and methods, with sample problem solutions, to fluent practice. Fluent practice is what makes an expert, not simply an ability to read well. In effect, Kuhn articulated the Meno problem into three related subproblems. In addition to (1) the problem of recognizing relevant innovation, there are the problems of how inquiry can enable us to (2) transfer or transmit expert knowledge and practice from one person or community to another and (3) convert one form of knowledge or expertise into another form in either direction.

In sum, Kuhn challenged the traditional Leibnizean-Enlightenment conception of perfect, fully justified knowledge as verbally explicit,[14] including the reduction of procedures and skills to rules. Rule-based performance is often methodical in the pejorative sense – mechanical, plodding, inefficient, and nonintuitive, by contrast with the fluidity of expert performance.[15]

In the "Postscript" to *Structure*, Kuhn analyzed what he called "disciplinary matrices" (roughly, paradigms in the large sense) into four components, of which exemplars constitute only one. The other components also play significant roles in solving the problem of inquiry. These other components include metaphysical world pictures (or preferred metaphysical models such as the billiard-ball mechanistic model of gases), symbolic generalizations such as $F = ma$, and norms and values such as the value of clear, precise results ("Postscript," §2). Consider only the first. The (unproven) metaphysical worldview tells scientists what the world is like, what sorts of patterns to expect, what sorts of problems do and do not arise for such a world, and which problem-solving methods should or should not work. After all, which methods will work depend on the way the world is, to some degree. A crowbar will be a useless tool if the world is made of tomato soup (my example, not Kuhn's).

The reader will observe that we now have in place all the conditions for evolution to occur in Kuhnian normal science: a constant source of variation (competing candidates for recognizable puzzles and solutions), a selection mechanism (the assent of the expert community, deriving from the perceived similarity relation they have acquired in common), and a transmission mechanism (publication of papers and textbooks, education of the next generation of students, etc.). Under these conditions, evolution cannot fail to occur, assuming the slowly changing "environment" and selection pressures that normal science is supposed to furnish.[16] Notice also the connection to the Meno recognition problem and the heuristic appraisal problem. Variants will fail to be recognized as promising contributions to normal science insofar as they depart very much from normal scientific exemplars. On the other hand, slavishly copying those exemplars confers no selective advantage. Here we have Kuhn's "essential tension" between tradition and innovation (Kuhn 1977, title essay).

6.5 REVOLUTIONARY SCIENCE AND THE MENO PARADOX

If we take the preceding account of normal science seriously as a solution to the Meno problem, then we must expect that revolutionary science will provide difficulties for Kuhn's account of science; and it does. In a crisis period, as in preparadigm science, Meno recognition, transfer, and conversion problems become serious obstacles to routine work. Indeed, Kuhn's more radical claims for revolution make it unclear how scientific inquiry is even possible under such conditions, in other words, how scientists could possibly resolve the Meno dilemma.[17] In the title essay to *The Essential Tension*, Kuhn noted how scientific research (and, by implication, innovative developments in any field) must walk a tightrope between tradition and innovation. Insofar as one's work is completely tradition bound, it cannot be innovative, it cannot contribute to learning, and it cannot even count as a contribution to inquiry at the community level, since the community already knows the result. On the other hand, insofar as one's work is radically innovative, it runs the risk of not being recognized at all as a contribution to community-licensed projects. Admitting wild variations into scientific practice would destabilize it. Such efforts would fall so far afield as to be unrecognizable (or scarcely recognizable) as "variants" competing with other contributions to the field in question. Rather, they would be thought to change the subject insofar as they were intelligible at all. To take an extreme case, had a textbook on quantum mechanics happened to fall at Aristotle's feet, could he have had any inkling of what to do with it?

We have here precisely the two horns of the Meno paradox. The Popperian critics of Kuhn, who deplored the very existence of Kuhnian normal science, feared that it represented a degeneration of the scientific enterprise into something less than genuine inquiry. On the other hand, critics of Kuhn's and Feyerabend's accounts of incommensurable revolutions assert, in effect, that science, so conceived, impales itself on the other horn of the Meno dilemma. Kuhn himself made a similar charge against the Popperian slogan of "revolution in perpetuity."

So how is revolutionary scientific inquiry possible? This is indeed a serious difficulty for Kuhn, one with which he struggled to the end of his life. In *Structure* and related essays, he attempted to meet the objection by backtracking from some of his more radical-looking claims. For example, in the "Postscript" he allowed that there could be sufficient overlap in shared exemplars and values for some degree of communication to remain possible.[18] Already in the final section of *Structure*, "Progress Through Revolutions," Kuhn had sketched an account of scientific development that is explicitly *evolutionary* rather than revolutionary. Even revolutionary episodes grow out of normal science, so apparently, in his view, it remains possible to trace scientific lineages through a neo-Darwinian tree structure.

Therefore, in seeking to understand revolutions, we are drawn back to the nature of normal science (my central topic) and how tradition-bound inquiry, almost inevitably, leads to crisis. This is another aspect of the central tension and of Kuhn's response to the Meno problem. Focused, esoteric work cannot remain impaled on, or near, the first, "conservative" horn forever, for it eventually produces crisis situations so serious as to encourage some practitioners to impale themselves on the second, "radical" horn. To combine the metaphors, going between the horns means walking the tightrope of the essential tension.

6.6 NORMAL SCIENCE AND REVOLUTIONARY SCIENCE

"What is the fastest way to Carnegie Hall? . . . Slow practice!"

This musicians' joke, easily converted into a Darwinian joke about speciation and the creativity of evolution, parallels Kuhn's paradoxical point that the fastest way to divergent, revolutionary breakouts from the present paradigm is dogged, conservative, convergent normal science. Kuhn's point about normal science being the surest way to discover resistant anomalies that disclose the limits of a paradigm is by now familiar enough. There is a more positive point to be made, however, one that is richly illustrated in Kuhn's treatment of Planck's work in his book on the history of the early quantum theory.

The point is that even subtle developments, such as one can find in the tradition-bound work of normal science, can have revolutionary implications, once those implications are explored and explicitly embodied in theoretical and experimental practice. Even when purely deductive logical consequences are the issue, these consequences are not transparent unless completely trivial; and they must be worked out with effort, over many constructive iterations or "passes." (Otherwise, deep mathematical theorems and proofs such as Gödel's would be easy to construct, and we would not have to worry about the consistency of sets of propositions.) Scientific activity is "multipass" (my term, not Kuhn's[19]) in the sense that various practitioners keep cycling back to refine a seemingly important result, again and again, each time investing it with greater theoretical or experimental richness. This, together with normal interpretive variance, can develop a result in directions wholly unexpected by its original authors. Thus, according to Kuhn, the misreading of Planck's work by Einstein and Ehrenfest in 1905 resulted in a far more radical interpretation of it, one that eventually stuck in the relevant scientific communities. Einstein and Ehrenfest each invested Planck's empirical black-body radiation law with potentially radical theoretical content. In papers written over the next several years, both men deepened the significance of Planck's law (Kuhn 1978; Klein 1964, 1967, 1970). To mention some highlights: By analyzing Planck's formula in excruciating detail, Ehrenfest worked out his "adiabatic principle," which permitted extending the quantum conditions for the Planck oscillator (or any other known system) to additional kinds of physical systems. Einstein brought out the wave-particle duality implicit in Planck's formula when taken to the high and low frequency limits. Then Peter Debye and Einstein again each offered purified theoretical derivations of Planck's law, investing it with still more theoretical content. In 1924 Satyandra Nath Bose once again rederived Planck's law, on the basis of what became the Bose–Einstein statistics, and Einstein immediately extended Bose's analysis to a monatomic gas in a way that pointed toward the wave-particle duality even of material systems and that helped lay the groundwork for Schrödinger's wave mechanics. Meanwhile, Niels Bohr applied the emerging quantum ideas in still a different direction, much elaborated by Arnold Sommerfeld (1919) and his associates. And so on.

When we retrospectively telescope this two- or three-decade-long sequence of step-by-step achievements, we see revolution.

Epistemological enterprises, certainly including the various scientific enterprises, are "nonlinear" in the sense that a small tradition-bound result can have enormous, but largely unforeseen, consequences, themselves largely spelled out on the basis of further, heavily constrained work (Margolis 1993).[20] Such enterprises are nonlinear in the further sense that significant results do not just sit there as permanent Platonic models. Rather, research is recursive: it cycles back and refines such results, investing them with more meaning, as new developments occur on various fronts. Therefore, we should expect Kuhnian exemplars themselves (and the problems that they solve) to have a history, a point to which I return in §6.9.

Originally, Einstein and Ehrenfest were still working in somewhat the same tradition as Planck – classical thermodynamics enhanced by statistical mechanics. This case shows that even differences in problem choice can tune investigators to recognize and select exemplars somewhat differently, sometimes to great effect. Planck had trouble recognizing the use that Einstein and Ehrenfest had made of his work. Fortunately, he did recognize them to be serious young scientists on the basis of their other achievements, and this made it worthwhile for him to try to understand the basis of their misunderstanding.

This sort of genealogy of developmental stages of a "single" exemplar is rather different from the genealogy of problems of the sort that Kuhn notices in the "Postscript." (His example there is the pendulum-efflux problem or series of problems.) Had he given this first sort, as one key sort of paradigm articulation, as much play in *Structure* as he did in the quantum history, I believe that he would have found normal science to be not quite so rigid and more rapidly evolutionary, with the result that there would have been less need for the excessively radical, revolutionary breakouts from the old framework that his own epistemology of science failed to handle adequately. Here, too, to return to the theme of §6.1, "creativity may often be regarded as a kind of conformity" (Barnes 1982, p. 20).

6.7 SOME WIDER IMPLICATIONS FOR METHODOLOGY OF SCIENCE

Commentators and critics, sympathetic and otherwise, find Kuhn a puzzling figure. He wrote on traditions and paradigms, for instance, but he apparently never engaged in a systematic, scholarly study of those topics, both of which have significant intellectual and social histories. Still more puzzling, his work appeared during an explosion of work in the new cognitive sciences. In *Structure* Kuhn cited some available sources such as the old Gestalt theory and Jerome Bruner's experiments at Harvard, but in the ensuing decades he displayed remarkably little interest in the dramatic developments in cognitive psychology. Was this because, like many practitioners of present-day science studies, he held that sociology rather than cognitive psychology offered a more promising route to understanding scientific practice? Evidently not. Although *Structure* was of tremendous heuristic value to the founders of the Edinburgh Strong Programme in the Sociology of Knowledge, the Bath empirical program of methodological relativism, and other approaches to the sociology of science, Kuhn explicitly refused to recognize them as his legitimate offspring.

Kuhn was bothered by what he took to be the sociologists' denial that the natural world makes any contribution to the fabric of scientific knowledge and their corresponding assertion that everything is a product of human conventional construction. Yet Kuhn's own rejection of a sharp nature–convention distinction was something the sociologists could appreciate. Kuhn also chafed at the suggestion that scientific decisions are merely expressions of the social-power interests of individuals and groups and hence are nonrational or irrational. Yet, again, although Kuhn was identified as an "internalist" historian of ideas, his account in *Structure* allowed sociopolitical factors to play a significant role in resolving revolutionary paradigm debates. For him, unlike some other historians of ideas, history was not at all the inevitable logical unfolding of ideas.

Although Kuhn himself had sharply rejected the positivist and Popperian accounts of rationality of science, he insisted that he was sketching an alternative account of scientific rationality rather than abandoning the subject altogether. Similarly, although Kuhn never said this explicitly, to my knowledge, we can interpret *Structure* and the related articles as advancing an alternative conception of scientific methodology rather than as a complete abandonment of the idea of method. To be sure, if we define method as a set of rules, then there is no scientific method, according to Kuhn, or at most those ad hoc, local methods that emerge when a paradigm is in crisis. (An example of the latter is the emergence of explicit but not theoretically well motivated "selection rules" for state transitions during the waning years of the old quantum theory.) But insofar as exemplars largely replace rules in our best account of scientific practice, why not speak of a methodology based on puzzle matching, problem reduction, and the like?

An extension of this point to the metalevel illuminates some difficult questions regarding philosophers' and other methodologists' use of case studies. The work of Kuhn, Feyerabend, N. R. Hanson, Stephen Toulmin, and others spawned a whole generation of "historical philosophers of science" whose work was guided by historical case studies and the search for historical patterns rather than by efforts to recast scientific knowledge and method within a symbolic logical framework. But what is the status of such historical cases? Are they mere illustrations of the philosophers' (or the scientists') prior methodological commitments or do they have genuine evidential value, either as an inductive basis for generalization or as tests of methodological hypotheses? If the latter, why were the philosophers so cavalier and unsystematic in their selection of cases for discussion? How could general methodological rules be supported adequately by a few "cases" chosen at will? For, ironically, although inspired by Kuhn's work, few methodologists of that period were willing to dispense with methodological rules. An excuse for their playing fast and loose with historical evidence might be that this was the very first effort of professional philosophers of science to escape from pure conceptual analysis to the systematic use of empirical information about science.

A Kuhnian response to this predicament is to suggest that appropriately chosen case studies function, at the metalevel, much as Kuhnian exemplars function in normal science. In any case, there is often no sharp distinction between the levels, given the normative and computational resources of Kuhnian exemplars. And even in the sciences themselves we find metalevel studies and reviews of the primary literature. In any case, the idea here is that historical cases themselves can function as methodological exemplars, so there is usually no need to try to extract methodological rules from them at all. Of course, controls would be needed on the selection and treatment of cases, many of which should be discipline-specific, and on the tendency to overgeneralize their range of application. (Hence, here we face at the metalevel the counterpart to Kuhn's problem of where the original set of exemplars was supposed to come from.) Otherwise, a case-based counterpart to Popper (1963) could claim that his favorite collection of cases, from giants such as Newton and Einstein, together with the corresponding negative cases (Marx, Freud, Adler), provide a sufficient set of exemplars to provide all the methodology we can have.[21]

The difficulty is that Kuhnian exemplars work only for a suitably trained community of experts. Could there be any such community for science in general? Whether or not anyone could possess such broad expertise is doubtful, yet policy makers are often placed in this position. For them, the

Kuhnian suggestion is to take concrete historical examples more seriously than general rules. Perhaps this was Harvard President James B. Conant's original idea behind the case study-based history of science course that he developed and for which he consequentially recruited Thomas Kuhn as a graduate student (Fuller 2000).

6.8 KUHN'S RELATIONS TO COGNITIVE SCIENCE

Kuhn was practically the only major writer between philosopher Ludwig Wittgenstein (1953) and cognitive scientist Eleanor Rosch (e.g., 1973) to challenge the traditional view of concepts as defined by rules, specifically by individually necessary and jointly sufficient conditions. This is the burden of Kuhn's talk of acquired resemblance relations and direct modeling on exemplars, sans rules. For Kuhn, the shared similarity relations that made possible fullness of communication and unanimity of agreement never required that the individual practitioners agree on the answer to the question, Similar in respect to *what*? On the contrary, he allowed a significant degree of variation in the manner in which different individuals succeeded in identifying referents in the natural world (*Structure*, pp. 192ff). Up to a point, he said, such variation makes no difference to practice.

More generally, Kuhn can be read as attacking the leading modern theory of human cognition, which surely helps to explain why he did not draw more heavily on the new cognitive paradigm (De Mey 1982). On this theory, cognition consists in transforming explicit symbolic representations of the world by means or rules or laws, and knowledge consists of having warrantably correct internal representations of the world. An early version of this account is the familiar British empiricist doctrine of association of ideas. More recently, the theory has been developed in terms of digital computer models of the mind. In standard AI, symbol strings are transformed by computational rules: logical rules, heuristic rules, and rules or laws expressing empirical regularities. For example, a baseball player going back for a fly ball or a frog leaping from one lily pad to another is very rapidly (but subconsciously) solving equations of motion as perceptual data come in.

The remainder of my essay and the two that follow explore the crucial questions: What alternatives are there to rule-based accounts of science? How can these alternatives help us to interpret and extend Kuhn's suggestive but sketchy remarks? If we can reduce the importance of rules in understanding scientific practice, can't we do the same for symbolic mental representations, given that rules and representations are linked in the standard models of cognition? (See also the two preceding essays.)

I shall relate Kuhn's *Structure* to later work in case-based reasoning and schema theory, with a few added words about mental models and representations. Nancy Nersessian will focus on mental models, while Peter Barker, Xiang Chen, and Hanne Andersen will explicate the later Kuhn's account of concepts and categorization.

In §V of *Structure*, "The Priority of Paradigms," Kuhn argued that paradigms can and do function in the near absence of rules. He stated four related reasons for thinking so. First, their exemplars (paradigms in the small sense) are easily identifiable in the textbooks and practices of each mature scientific community, whereas rules are difficult to find. Second, students learn a theory mainly through its paradigmatic applications to standard problems, and rules are at a minimum in this process. Third, rules are prominent only in preparadigm science or during a crisis period – in other words, only when full commitment to a paradigm is lacking. Fourth, radical paradigm change can be very local to a specialist community, whereas rules, principles, and law statements are general or "cosmopolitan," as we might say.

Many have challenged Kuhn's fundamental claim that a research community can operate on the basis of exemplars rather than rules. However, the short history of AI provides evidence that Kuhn may be right. This is significant because AI is the field that has most strenuously studied methodological ideas with an eye to turning them into practical, automated, problem-solving procedures.

Among the founders of AI, Allen Newell and Herbert Simon identified inquiry with problem solving, and they made it their task to design programs that solved problems. However, the so-called General Problem Solver of Newell and Simon, based on logical rules and general, content-neutral heuristics, was disappointing in its limited problem-solving ability.[22] General rules provided only weak problem-solving power and applied only to well-defined, highly constrained problems. Artificial Reason was surprisingly limited in its problem-solving ability.

This limitation led to the idea that powerful problem-solving programs must incorporate knowledge from the domain in question. The late 1960s saw the advent of knowledge-based computation. The "expert systems" form of this idea was to transfer human expertise to a computer by first eliciting from scientific experts the specific knowledge and the rules that they used to solve problems.

While this approach produced some interesting results, the overall gain was again rather disappointing. Kuhn's "prediction" came true. It proved far more difficult to elicit a coherent set of problem-solving procedural rules, for the edification of either students or machines, than the AI proponents had imagined – in fact, much harder than to elicit sets of exemplary problems or cases, which, after all, textbook writers had been doing for a long time. The scientific experts sometimes had difficulty furnishing rules at all, and the rules they did supply often seemed to be post hoc rationalizations of their problem-solving moves. Sometimes they contradicted other rules that they had just reported in connection with a different problem solution. This difficulty has been dubbed "the knowledge elicitation bottleneck" or "Feigenbaum's problem," after one of the founders of the expert systems approach. Here, once again, we encounter the Meno transfer problem, in this case the problem of transferring expertise from human to machine rather than from human teacher to pupil or from human community to human community.

The resulting programs were problematic in the other ways as well. For example, the more knowledge they incorporated, the slower they ran (whereas the performance of human experts often speeds up), and the programs tended to be "brittle," that is, to be radically unstable under changes in the knowledge base.

During the 1980s and 1990s, case-based reasoning (CBR) emerged as a possible alternative to rule-based problem solving. The basic idea is that, instead of solving each newly presented problem from scratch, by appeal to fundamental rules, the system instead matches the new problem to one or more problems-plus-solutions already available in its case library. If it is important and distinctive enough, the solution to the new case can then be added to the case library. Moreover, these are to be real problems in context; hence, CBR is more holistic and supposedly closer to human practice. Proponents often draw an analogy to the use of precedents in case law. In some instances, case-based systems can solve difficult problems quite efficiently, although the performance of present-day systems still typically degrades slowly as more information is added (the so-called swamping problem). Everything depends on having an efficient indexing and retrieval system for cases. An alternative CBR strategy adapts previously successful methods or procedures rather than the concrete solutions themselves.

Like model-based reasoning (see later), CBR constitutes a potentially radical departure from traditional accounts of thinking, reasoning, and problem solving. In the case of human inference, CBR replaces the old faculty of Reason with experience. In place of general logical rules, we have exemplary cases, plus modes of accessing the cases and of adapting them to fit the current problem environment. On this view, our cognitive systems tend to organize our perceptions of present situations and our responses to them to match situations or scenarios with which we are already familiar. Thus are individual habits and social traditions born. Accordingly, it is not surprising to find genealogies of problems and solutions in the history of science, technology, and other fields of endeavor, a phenomenon that is not predicted by traditional rule-based accounts. For, on this CBR view, people solve problems not by trying to achieve a correct internal representation of the world and then generating a problem solution from scratch, by means of abstract rules, but rather by adapting a contextually rich, concrete experience from the past. Also, contrary to the received rule-based view of inquiry, CBR (and model-based reasoning) may occur without the use of language.

So, gone is the Enlightenment paradigm that makes reasoning a distinct, universal activity only contingently related to present context and previous domain-specific experience and that makes both language and logic essential to thinking and problem solving. Gone is the idea that there are general "program files" of Reason distinct from the "data files" of Experience, an a priori component of cognition clearly distinguishable from the empirical component. Rather, thought and experience are curiously interlaced. Intelligence and intelligibility both depend on expert domain knowledge. The model-based approach to reasoning goes still further and explicitly construes logical reasoning itself as a matter of pattern matching.[23]

Case-based reasoning is also an alternative to the so-called hypothetico-deductive method, sometimes called the "method of generate and test." Instead of generating a new hypothesis or candidate problem solution from first principles (or from who knows where, given the romantic conception of creativity), a CBR system selects from memory and adapts one or more nearby problem solutions already accomplished (cf. Riesbeck 1996, p. 383f). Innovation is modification. Thus, again, it automatically locates innovation within a kind of history or tradition of previous efforts rather than leaving it simply to fall out of the sky.[24]

Since exemplars play such a prominent role in Kuhn's account of problem solving, it is natural to reinterpret his work as a theory of case-based and/or model-based reasoning in normal science.[25] This fits well with his strategy of minimizing the problem of innovation or "scientific discovery," by contending that problem solving is more a matter of adaptively imitating or copying previously successful problem solutions than of copying reality (by generating theoretical representations of it from first principles), and by recognizing the importance of local traditions that depend on domain-specific acquired similarity relations for matching problems.[26] Learning may begin with something close to mechanical copying or slavish imitation, but it matures into learning by doing. CBR also makes more credible Kuhn's claim that he is not portraying scientific work (whether dogmatic normal science or radical, revolutionary science) as irrational but is instead sketching an alternative conception of scientific "reasoning."

Now viewing Kuhn's account in *Structure* through the lens of later work in CBR can be instructive not only in suggesting that an alternative to a rules account may be viable but also in pointing up difficulties in Kuhn's own treatment. One problem, already mentioned, is the origins problem: How can the set of initial cases and the similarity metric that indexes them be established? For this seemingly cannot be accomplished by the case-based system itself. It cannot construct itself using case-based reasoning. This chicken–egg problem is a specific form of the problem of where traditions come from, that is, of the "discovery" or "invention" problem for traditions. We seem to be faced with a vicious regress, for every novel problem solution is a modified copy or imitation of one or more prior problem solutions.

Kuhn's response to this difficulty was to apply, once again, his by now familiar strategy of locating all intelligible problem solving within some sort of tradition, that is, within an established practice, within an already extant approach with a history. If a piece of work does not seem to fit the tradition under study, look for another tradition where it does fit; and then study how the traditions could have intersected. Look also at how new traditions bud off old ones, at how old traditions divide into two or more. Kuhn's answer does not seem to be purely question begging. New traditions do seem to emerge from older ones by division, by the hybrid-forming crossing of two already extant traditions, and by related processes. (To be sure, the question requires a great deal of further study.) Kuhn expected the eventual result to resemble Darwinian lineages, apart from the nonbiological sort of intersection just mentioned.

Here is a second difficulty suggested by CBR in AI. If every newly solved case is added to the case library as a symbolic representation, we eventually get cognitive overload. So it cannot be the concrete cases in all their particular detail that are stored. (In the human case, memory studies deny this in any event.) Accordingly, the cases must somehow be abstracted into types or categories, with some loss of context, which raises a third difficulty.

Critics will object that CBR does not really abandon a rules approach but simply hides the rules in the abstraction procedure and the corresponding indexing and retrieval mechanisms. Advocates of CBR in AI acknowledge that this is true to some degree but insist that the cases remain primary. The advantages (and some disadvantages) of cases over rules are still there. What was Kuhn's response to this objection in the human case – that the rules are still there, operating below the level of easy conscious retrieval, so that the knowledge elicitation bottleneck is not a fatal problem after all? The early Kuhn did not deny that there might be rules, in the sense of deterministic laws, operating at the neural level.[27] His point was that expert scientists do not use such rules consciously and explicitly. He could have added that, even if such rules do exist and could be known, it is unlikely that they could be used as explicit methodological guides, for they are likely to be extremely complex and not formulatable at a conceptual level familiar to us and appropriate to our human problem domain. Today he would likely mention the subconceptual, parallel distributed processing of neural networks as an example. Suppose that there really are deep-structural grammatical and semantic rules for human natural language, for example. Would knowing these rules help us to speak more correctly in everyday conversation? To change the example, would intimate knowledge of the laws of mechanics have helped Willie Mays to hit a curve ball or to go back for a fly ball in center field? Not likely (Dreyfus and Dreyfus 1986). Furthermore, radical Kuhnians may reply that even the application of logical rules depends on a prior level of pattern matching, a view that finds support among several theorists investigating mental models today.[28] Logical reasoning, too, must be naturalized and not simply attributed to a faculty of Reason. Even when we are dealing with logical problems, write Rumelhart and coauthors (1986, p. 44),

> [t]he basic idea is that we succeed in solving problems not so much through the use of logic, but by making the problems we wish to solve conform to problems we are good at solving.

These issues remain far from decided, of course, but we face the Meno problem even in the context of trying to find purely deductive proofs.

Fourth, schema theory in cognitive psychology provides an alternative way to interpret what Kuhn wrote. Its basic idea is that our perceptions and thoughts do not come as atomic bits but are organized into larger structures (Bartlett 1932; Brewer and Nakamura 1984; Marshall 1995). Kuhn was sympathetic to anticipations of such ideas by the Gestalt theorists, with their "gestalt switches," and by Jean Piaget, with his discontinuous developmental schemas. Schemas are, roughly speaking, data structures of a part of the world or of an action sequence – for example, what a dentist's office is like or how to behave in a restaurant. They are sometimes conceived as frames in Marvin Minsky's sense, that is, as cognitive structures with many "slots" for various kinds of information, with some of the basic slots having default values. We take for granted that a dentist's office has a ceiling, for example, without having to take note of its existence explicitly. A schema induces something like what used to be called a "perceptual set" or a "learning set," although normally on a larger scale. In virtue of their training, normal scientists are primed to notice certain things as salient and to ignore others. Thus it is tempting to regard Kuhn's learned similarity relation as a kind of schema (or set of schemas) specific to a field of mature science.

Meanwhile, neural net modelers have attempted to design networks that exhibit schemalike behavior. Parallel distributed processing theorists Rumelhart, Smolensky, McClelland, and Hinton (1986) developed a dynamical model in which the schemata are not themselves symbolic, representational structures stored in memory but rather are implicit in the neural connections, which change over time. This idea, like the preceding quotation from their article, is broadly Kuhnian.

Now, finally, we can state the difficulty. With hindsight informed by recent developments in case-based reasoning, schema theory, and neural network theory, the question we should like to ask Kuhn is whether any one of these ideas articulates the account of cognition that he sketched in *Structure* and related articles. And, if so, does his account need *both* case-based reasoning (or model-based reasoning), *and* schema theory, or is one an alternative to the others? And is it possible that a neural net approach might dispense with the need for case-based or schema-theoretic representations? Or do different forms of cognition perhaps dominate different stages of cognitive development? For example, could the textbook exemplars used to train students be dispensed with, as permanent memory contents, once they have served their purpose of training the neural net that we call the central nervous system? Is this what it means to "internalize" examples (and rules, too, for that matter), so that expert behavior can proceed more intuitively and fluidly? I raise more questions of this sort in the next section.

Critics have complained that Kuhn's account of scientific cognition (and N. R. Hanson's before him) was too perceptual. Kuhn overused gestalt metaphors, and it seems naive to think that a young boy's learning to discriminate ducks, geese, and swans (Kuhn 1974) is of a piece with a physics graduate student's learning to discriminate "up" from "down" electron spin or a molecular biology student's learning to discriminate distinct chemical signaling pathways. As Dudley Shapere (1982) pointed out, the kind of observation employed in experimental scientific work and in testing theoretical models should not be identified with perception in the ordinary sense. In fact, the later Kuhn largely abandoned talk of episodic gestalt switches in favor of a more linguistic mode of discourse (Kuhn 2000).

Yet perception is making something of a comeback via its use in mental models. Some mental modelers take Kuhn's talk about perceptual recognition and direct modeling quite literally. One of many sorts[29] of mental models is a cognitive, analog (rather than digital) representation of a system. Such models may be dynamic, meaning that the agent can run simulations "in the head" of what the modeled system will do under various circumstances, and such simulations engage the visual system.[30] Like case-based reasoning, mental modeling does not necessarily require linguistic ability on the part of the agent. Prelinguistic infants and higher animals employ mental models as a form of thinking without language. Of course, in scientific work, symbolic thinking is required insofar as the model is used explicitly as a calculative resource. Case-based reasoning is more dependent upon prior experience than are some kinds of model-based cognition (and we are able to think, at least badly, about things we have not even approximately experienced), but this difference cannot be large for normal science.

Ronald Giere (1988, 1994; 1999, chaps. 6 and 7) explicitly links mental models to Kuhnian exemplars. For him, theories are, roughly, collections of models that are related in various ways. For example, a Newtonian particle system or a simple harmonic oscillator is an idealized model system, basically a definition. It is subsequently related to real-world systems by means of "theoretical hypotheses," as when we assert that a particular vibratory motion is simple harmonic motion, to a good approximation.

So what is the relation of models in this sense to mental models and to Kuhnian exemplars, schemata, and the perceived similarity relation?[31] Kuhn's original exemplars were particular sociohistorical achievements and, as such, not merely "in the heads" of one or more people.[32] He would allow that idealized textbook versions of these also merit the label "exemplars." With a little stretching, we can regard Giere's models as abstract structures of this sort. Some stretching is necessary because Giere talks in terms of abstract, idealized systems, whereas Kuhn speaks of exemplary problems-plus-solutions. As such, these are not *mental* models. Nonetheless, there is no incompatibility, it seems to me, between a case-based understanding of Kuhn and a model-based understanding, as long as we understand the cases to be models of the sort just indicated and the mental models to be internalized representations of them. However, case-based reasoning as so far implemented in AI is more disciplined and hence more narrowly focused than much of the work in mental models, where flexibility reigns and computer implementation of ideas is not a general requirement. The main problem with CBR is adapting cases to fit new cases (Leake 1996, chaps. 9–11 passim). Here is where the computational equivalent of Kuhn's perceived similarity relation would come into play, but designing a computational system that will do this, or simulate this, is a difficult task. We do not understand how human beings do it either, at a computational level, but much work in model-based reasoning does not yet address such computational questions.

6.9 FURTHER INTERNAL DIFFICULTIES WITH KUHN'S ACCOUNT OF NORMAL SCIENCE

Kuhn was aware of the incompleteness and imprecision of his treatment of normal (and revolutionary) science and continued working on various aspects of it to the end of his life. I myself am not particularly fond of the "linguistic turn," during his MIT years, that took him increasingly into philosophical disputes about the nature of reference and translation and away from history of science, but I must leave those topics to others.

In the preceding discussion, I have often gone beyond Kuhn's own account to suggest possible interpretations or lines of development that Kuhn did not explicitly offer. My purpose in this section is not to address the Popperian question of whether normal science is a good thing but rather to point out several gaps and ambiguities internal to Kuhn's account including those mentioned in §6.8.[33] The central difficulties are that Kuhn does not tell us precisely what an exemplar is or how it relates to the acquired similarity metric, and to mental representation of puzzles and potential solutions.

The issues here are notoriously difficult. My point is not that Kuhn failed to anticipate the cognitive and social science of thirty years later (where all these issues remain matters of controversy), only that what he says about exemplars and the resemblance relation, for all its suggestiveness, remains undeveloped in several crucial ways.

One difficulty is that "exemplar" remains ambiguous in both nature and function. There would seem to be different kinds of exemplars and/or different functions for them. For instance, the exemplars employed in concept learning (with their meaning-determining role) seem rather different from the exemplars involved in problem solving (with their heuristic and justificatory roles), although this distinction blurs at the level of theoretical terms. From the CBR point of view, the later Kuhn's turn away from historical cases to lexical matters was a mistake (but see the essays that follow for the positive import of Kuhn's "linguistic turn").

Second, in his essay in this volume, Joseph Rouse, for whom Kuhnian practice is primary, brings out the ambiguity between exemplars as representational structures such as beliefs and exemplars as nonrepresentational skills or idealized forms of practice. I agree with him (and with Rouse 1987, chap. 2) that, although Kuhn was not always clear, idealized skills and techniques are often the better interpretation. After all, Kuhn's point about the importance of working the problems at the end of the textbook chapters was not that students memorize little representations that correspond to reality but that they hone their own problem-solving skills, with these problems as models or precedents. Solving problems is one mode of practical-intellectual habit formation.

Third, the early Kuhn's scientific examples of exemplars were all, or nearly all, positive. In *Structure* the paradigms or exemplars are all achievements, not failures. The epistemologically interesting thing about Kuhn's account at this point is that it is the opposite of Popper's. Popper said that scientists learn from their mistakes, while Kuhn claimed, in effect, that they learn from their successes. Surely, however, neither extreme furnishes the whole story. In her influential text book on case-based reasoning, Janet Kolodner (1993) notes the importance of negative cases, things to avoid, the "war stories," as well as successes.[34] Meanwhile, in judicial practice, case law is normally adversarial. Kuhn himself later addressed the problem with his idea of "contrast sets," described in the following essays. A child learning to discriminate swans from geese and ducks thereby learns that geese and ducks are not swans.

Fourth, another epistemologically interesting feature of Kuhn's account also hides a difficulty. Kuhn strongly links the cognitive processes involved in training students with the cognitive processes puzzle-solving scientists employ in their research. Both engage in puzzle solving by means of exemplars rather than rules, supposedly the very same exemplars (according to the level of the student). Hence, this training is supposed to be peculiarly effective in the production of new members of the normal scientific community. Be that as it may, are the exemplars really identical? We may well imagine that struggling students hang on to the specific concrete examples worked in the text and in class. They are tyros, novice scientists at best. Are we really to imagine that seasoned veterans carry around these same concrete cases in their personal or group "case libraries"?

Fifth, to continue this line of questioning: Do experts in their completely routine work really need both a case library of exemplars as representational structures and the acquired similarity relation? Recall that learning exemplars is how students acquire the similarity relation in the first place. But once the community's practice of similarity recognition and response has been fully internalized, is there any need to burden the mind with dozens (or thousands) of concrete exemplars of this basic type? After all, any expert can now reconstruct them easily. Many studies suggest that human memory does not work by storing zillions of distinct representations, or historical "snapshots" of the agent's cognitive states, or even permanently fixed templates.[35]

The considerations just mentioned strongly suggest that human cognition is not like CBR, as exemplified by present-day computer systems. I do not doubt that exemplars (in some sense) are still important for expert work at the frontier, but these will typically be high-level exemplars from the technical literature, not those on which students are educated. (Graduate students doing research are in a transitional phase.) Nor will the latter constitute exemplars in the full social sense but simply results that happened to catch the attention of a particular individual or group as interestingly analogous to her or to its current research problem. Everything Kuhn says about concrete modeling still applies, but exemplars of this latter kind will be no part of the standard educational process. Sometimes the analogies come from outside the relevant scientific literature. Nils Jerne, walking through the streets of Copenhagen, realized that he could model the problem of how the immune system works on Plato's Meno paradox, of all things. But the Meno problem was not a standard part of the education of biochemists, and citation of Plato's Meno could hardly constitute an acceptable scientific reference.

Sixth, Kuhn said that exemplars are concrete historical achievements, but neither the exemplars that appear in science texts nor the exemplars to which scientists sometimes explicitly appeal are the original historical products. Rather, they are sanitized, idealized versions of those achievements, written up from a later point of view; and, unlike both historical cases and CBR cases in AI, the textbook examples tend to be decontextualized. Scientists are notoriously "whiggish" in their treatment of history, tending to interpret history in the light of their own current problems. Indeed, as practicing scientists, they must do so insofar as they view everything through the lens of their paradigm (Nickles 1992). Kuhn himself, qua historian, always pressed this point strongly. Even experts working at the frontier of research treat cited precedents whiggishly, unless those precedents are very recent and address exactly the same problems. More radically, some exemplars are likely to survive a paradigm shift, being inherited from the old paradigm, albeit somewhat transformed. Therefore, we need to distinguish exemplars in the historian's sense (so-called turning points in science) from exemplars as they are actually employed by the normal scientific community.

My final point is a continuation of the previous one. Kuhn could have more thoroughly incorporated into his account of normal science the multipass process that refines, sharpens, deepens, and applies further results. In particular, he could have brought his evolutionary account of "progress through revolutions" home to normal science. One thinks of progress as increasing fitness over time, including the fitness of the exemplars themselves. However, the fitness landscape keeps changing, even in normal science, as current problems (the frontiers of research) change. (Here "fitness" refers to consonance with the state of the art as defined by the scientific community, not directly to reality itself.) Fitting your current problem to available exemplars is a two-way street, since matching is a symmetric relation. It is a question of mutual fit, after all. You not only deform your problem so that it better fits an exemplar; you may also find a way to deform the exemplar in order to achieve a better fit with your problem. Successful work that stretches the exemplar in this way may result in a gradual reinterpretation of the exemplar itself.[36] Eventually the interpretation may be stretched practically out of recognition, as with Mendel's work on peas, if Brannigan (1981) is right, and Planck's work in 1900 on the so-called quantum theory, if Kuhn (1978) is right. Kuhn himself notes that while normal scientists agree on the set of historical exemplars, one can expect much variation in their interpretations and rationalizations of them (*Structure*, p. 44). In most cases these latter differences leave little trace on scientific practice. But cases like the reception of Mendel and of Planck are another story.

On the whole, however, Kuhn leaves us with the idea that exemplars are fixed historical achievements, permanent models, whereas they, too, historically evolve as normal science progresses. I am confident that Kuhn would agree with this latter contention. The static view stands in tension with his own claims about the whiggishness of scientists, arising in part out of his own experience in interviewing numerous eminent scientists during the quantum history archive project (Kuhn, Heilbron, Forman, and Allen 1967) and further documented by the unpopular reception of Kuhn's reinterpretation of Planck's work. Kuhn and his collaborators found that men such as Niels Bohr could not correctly recapture the historical problem situations of their own early work.

In short, Kuhn largely missed the opportunity to extend his evolutionary account to normal science. Even given the nature of normal science, he would surely agree that any scientific community that remembers its own past is doomed to repeat it.[37]

Notes

Parts of my essay derive from work supported by the U.S. National Science Foundation. See Nickles (forthcoming) for further discussion of some of the issues of this essay.

1. See Hoyningen-Huene (1993) for the most thorough and authoritative treatment of Kuhn's philosophy of science. For a helpful discussion of Kuhn's work and its reception, see Caneva (2000). For Kuhn's own position, see Kuhn (1993, p. 314f). Most of the authors of the present volume are philosophers, but they come down on both sides of this divide.

2. Besides the important "Postscript" added to the second edition of *Structure* in 1970, these essays include Kuhn (1970b, 1970c, and 1974). The last essay was first presented at the Illinois conference on the structure of theories in 1969 and later published in Suppe (1974).

3. See Barry Barnes, this volume, and Barnes (1982), for an expression of this point. I share this view and will develop it (in my own peculiar way) in ensuing sections. By implication, as Kuhn himself insisted, good historians and science studies professionals must be experts in the technical traditions that they study in order for the work to be intelligible to them. In a sense, they must be able to simulate membership in the tradition and to convey this, almost *per imposible*, to their readers.

4. Unfortunately, Kuhn never succeeded in making the idea of mature science crystal clear in a noncircular manner. His short answer is that normal science is science done under a paradigm. Yet it is the existence of normal scientific puzzle-solving practices that provide the social-behavioral evidence of the presence of a paradigm in the first place. See, e.g., Kuhn's "Postscript," where he tries to disentangle the ideas of paradigm and scientific community.

5. See the debate in Lakatos and Musgrave (1970). Popper and his followers responded by conceding to Kuhn the discovery of the existence of normal science, but they deplored normal science as uncritical, authoritarian, and boring, and they urged that future science take steps to eliminate it. For the Popperians, it is the Newtons and the Einsteins who make the story of science worth attending to. In short, the Popperians accepted Kuhn's descriptive claim about science but rejected his model of science as a normative model. Kuhn replied that to adopt Popper's recommendations would destroy natural science as we know it and make it too much like the social sciences and philosophy. (See the essay by John Worrall in this volume.)

6. Misleading because Kuhn was never a serious student of continental philosophical writings. (See Gary Gutting's essay in this volume and Hoyningen-Huene 1993, p. 21.) Nor, to anticipate what comes later, did he delve deeply into the ideas of tradition, genealogy, and lineage in a systematic, scholarly way. (See MacIntyre 1990 and Hull 1988a, 1988b.) Kuhn sometimes described himself as

a "physicist turned historian for philosophical purposes" (Kuhn 2000, p. 321) and admitted to being a philosophical amateur. On the other hand, *Structure* did much to undermine the received view that, in the natural sciences, objective observational facts of the "real" world are directly given by nature, by contrast with the social sciences, which are essentially interpretive. Kuhn's accounts of both normal and revolutionary science showed how interpretive (roughly, how paradigm-relative) even experimental practices in physics must be. And *Structure*, more than any other work, launched the historical approach to philosophy of science.

Ironically, Kuhn himself was not always forthcoming about his own intellectual influences or scholarly methods. For example, he claimed that neither Ludwik Fleck (1935) nor Stephen Toulmin (1961, 1972) had influenced him much, and that he had deliberately not read Michael Polanyi (1958, 1966). Martin Klein, the leading historian of quantum theory prior to Kuhn, is scarcely mentioned in Kuhn's quantum history (Kuhn 1978).

7. "Presentism" and "whiggism" or "whig history" are labels commonly given to the mistake of imposing our own knowledge and values on the past. They are mistakes not only because they involve false attributions and unfair evaluations but also because they prevent us from understanding what the historical actors themselves actually did – and how they could possibly have done it without the benefit of our hindsight. See Nickles (1992) for further dicussion.

8. See Brush (2000) as well as Klein (1970). Brannigan (1981) tells a similar story about Gregor Mendel's work and its reception. The history of science is full of fortunate (and unfortunate), but not entirely accidental, misreadings, misunderstandings, verbal slippages, and the like.

9. The problem runs deeper than the sometimes irritating word play of Plato's early dialogues suggests. As stated previously, the Meno problem is basically a problem of recognizing and selecting relevant items in an ocean of candidates competing for attention. Nor is the problem merely an impractical, abstract riddle. The vertebrate immune system faces one form of the problem: how to recognize a seemingly unlimited variety of antigens while discriminating them from the body's own cells and molecules, all on the basis of very slender resources.

10. Although Kuhn himself was certainly alive to it (witness the importance in *Structure* of promise over performance-to-date of a new paradigm contender), heuristic appraisal or "pursuit" may be the most neglected area in traditional philosophy of science. See Laudan (1977) and Nickles (1989).

11. Actually, I shall argue later that Kuhn gave insufficient attention to articulating a paradigm by means of articulating (deepening the significance of) the exemplars themselves rather than by extending the application of the paradigm.

12. Plato's solution supposed that we already know implicitly or tacitly the answers to basic questions about mathematics and the other Forms. Genuine inquiry into something totally new is impossible (except, apparently, for the disembodied souls between lives). What we call learning is really "reminiscence," a kind of remembering in which the tacit knowledge becomes fully articulated in the form of a universal definition, rule, or proof. (At this point, Kuhn departs from

Plato.) Concrete examples of, say, piety or justice or an equilateral triangle whose interior angles are also equal are epistemically useless except insofar as they can stimulate such reminiscence, say under Socratic questioning.

13. As Joseph Rouse (this volume and 1987, chap. 2) shows, it is fruitful to consider Kuhnian exemplars themselves as practices rather than as representations or sets of beliefs. From Plato's point of view, this is still worse than articulated examples, for it leaves scientific knowledge at the level of craft skill. Rouse (2002) develops a normative account of practice that does not require the existence of tight behavioral regularities.

14. This view has roots in the ancient Greek distinction of theory and practice and craft knowledge. For example, Aristotle distinguished sharply among theoretical reason, practical reason, and the kind of inferior productive knowledge exhibited by expert craftsmen.

15. See the following discussion, on case-based vs. rule-based reasoning. See also Margolis (1987, 1993), Dreyfus and Dreyfus (1986), Dreyfus (1992), Collins (1990), and Collins and Kusch (1998). There is a growing cognitive science literature on these issues.

16. It is possible to read Kuhn as anticipating a memetic theory of evolution of scientific culture distinct from biological evolution. Kuhnian exemplars are memelike, and puzzle solving amounts to a kind of adaptation of meme complexes. According to Blackmore (1999), for example, memes are transmitted only by imitation, which is a major form of meme replication and relevant to the Meno transfer problem. This ties in well with learning by example or case-based reasoning, as discussed later. See also Hull (1988a and 1988b).

17. Of course, Kuhn would reply that this is precisely his point, and that it is not his fault that crisis situations are so messy.

18. See the following essays in this volume for more detail on incommensurability and on Kuhn's later development.

19. My term "multipass" corresponds, in part but only in part, to Kuhn's account of genealogies of problems.

20. Indeed, any sort of history, including one's personal history, can all too easily be made to look "revolutionary" when we reflect on the major upshots of what once seemed minor contingencies. Consider Kuhn's autobiographical comments that "my attempt to come to terms with Aristotle's texts determined my future life. . . . What I'd encountered in reading Aristotle [one hot summer afternoon] was my first example of what I later called scientific revolutions" (Padua lecture, quoted by Caneva 2000, p. 100 n52). Compare note 25.

21. Laudan (1986) critiques case-based methodologies, including his own previous efforts. Barnes's essay (this volume) raises issues similar to mine.

22. See Newell and Simon (1972) for a detailed summation and extension of their earlier work and Crevier (1993) for a historical account of AI.

23. Kuhn was sympathetic with Quine's (1951) attack on the analytic–synthetic distinction. On CBR, see Kolodner (1993), Leake (1996, 1998). On habits of mind from a Kuhnian perspective, see Margolis (1987, 1993). On model-based

reasoning, see the later essays in this volume, Magnani, Nersessian, and Thagard (1999), Johnson-Laird (1983), and Johnson-Laird and Byrne (1991).

24. Compare Laura Snyder (1977) on William Whewell and "discoverer's induction."

25. And in his own life history as well, perhaps to a fault. Kuhn always wrote in a very personal style, as if his own experiences epitomized human history.

> While discovering history [during the 1947 summer afternoon eureka experience when Aristotle suddenly became clear to him] I had discovered my first scientific revolution [in his own experience, presumably!], and my subsequent search for best readings has often been a search for other episodes of the same sort. (Kuhn 1977, p. xiii)

The Copernican revolution, too, became an exemplar or model for Kuhn via Kuhn (1957).

26. In his "Postscript," §3, Kuhn sketches one such genealogy, from Galileo's rolling balls down inclined planes through the treatment of various kinds of pendula, by Huygens and others, to Daniel Bernoulli's solution to the speed of efflux problem of water from an orifice.

27. See Kuhn (1970a, p. 192; 1974, pp. 474ff.) and Andersen (2001, pp. 44ff). Kuhn is not, of course, positing a godlike consciousness independent of the neural processing.

28. See Johnson-Laird (1983) and Johnson-Laird and Byrne (1991). Margolis (1987) develops an intuitively attractive account of cognition, including logical reasoning, in terms of pattern matching. Insofar as logical rules are employed in cognition, they must be implemented in some kind of causal process.

29. Mental models may be persistent or evanescent, verbal or nonverbal, dynamic or nondynamic, analog or nonanalog, and so on.

30. Kelly Hamilton (2001a, 2001b) describes the importance of training on mechanical models (various combinations of gears, pulleys, levers, etc.) in standard German engineering education at the time when Ludwig Wittgenstein studied engineering at Berlin-Charlottenburg.

31. For a fuller discussion of schemes and mental models, see Brewer (1987).

32. There is a constant danger here, to which Kuhn himself sometimes succumbed, by his own admission, of conflating the individual and the social. It would seem that Kuhnian exemplars are social resources used to train individual students to have counterparts (mental models?) in their heads, in which case we can expect variation among individuals. Cases in CBR are similarly ambiguous. For Kuhn, we can treat a single individual as a CBR system but one whose existence derives from the CBR system represented by the expert community as a whole.

33. A somewhat fuller discussion of some of these issues can be found in Nickles (1998, 2000).

34. Henry Petroski, in several books, stresses the importance of learning from failure in engineering and urges that engineering students be taught a case library of historical exemplars of failure. See, e.g., Petroski (1994).

35. Vicente and Brewer (1993) provide empirical confirmation for the claim that memories of scientists are constructions that whiggishly distort historical findings to conform better to the agent's current theoretical views and also the claim, relevant to the issue of mutual fit, that human beings (via our cognitive functioning) seek as much coherence as possible in thinking and perception. In some cases we might speak of a "similarity bias" (my term). Antecedents include Bartlett's work on memory schemas and, perhaps also in a broader sense, Leon Festinger's work on cognitive dissonance and Jerome Bruner's on anomalous card recognition.

36. Notice that "exemplar" is often a retrospective or "historical" classification, for one usually does not know in advance which solutions will hold up and become particularly useful as models for future work. (Recall our opening discussion of the Meno recognition problem and of heuristic appraisal at the frontier of research.) Various forms of citation and co-word analysis have been developed, using databases such as the Science Citation Index to uncover patterns of linkages among papers, concepts, problems, etc.

37. The fact that written records in the form of textbooks and the reconstructive "historical" sections of later papers overwrite the historical record largely explains the working scientists' loss of historical memory. However, in any such enterprise, there is also something of an oral culture that is not anchored by any accessible historical record. Normal scientific communities (like some other kinds of communities) are conservative in this way also, in sharing some of the characteristics of a preliterate craft culture.

References

Andersen, Hanne. 2001. *On Kuhn.* Belmont, CA: Wadsworth.

Barnes, Barry. 1982. *T. S. Kuhn and Social Science.* New York: Columbia University Press.

Bartlett, Frederick. 1932. *Remembering.* Cambridge: Cambridge University Press.

Blackmore, Susan. 1999. *The Meme Machine.* Oxford: Oxford University Press.

Brannigan, Augustine. 1981. *The Social Basis of Scientific Discoveries.* Cambridge: Cambridge University Press.

Brewer, William. 1987. "Schemas versus Mental Models in Human Memory." In: Peter Morris, ed. *Modelling Cognition.* New York: John Wiley, pp. 187–97.

Brewer, William, and Glenn Nakamura. 1984. "The Nature and Function of Schemas." In: R. Wyer, Jr., and T. Srull, ed. *Handbook of Social Cognition.* Hillsdale, NJ: Lawrence Erlbaum, vol. 1, pp. 119–60.

Brush, Stephen. 2000. "Thomas Kuhn as a Historian of Science." *Science & Education* 9: 39–58.

Caneva, Kenneth. 2000. "Possible Kuhns in the History of Science: Anomalies of Incommensurable Paradigms." *Studies in History and Philosophy of Science* 31: 87–124.

Collins, Harry. 1990. *Artificial Experts: Social Knowledge and Intelligent Machines.* Cambridge, MA: MIT Press.

Collins, Harry, and Martin Kasch. 1998. *The Shape of Actions: What Humans and Machines Can Do.* Cambridge, MA: MIT Press.

Crevier, Daniel. 1993. *AI: The Tumultuous History of the Search for Artificial Intelligence.* New York: Basic Books.

De Mey, Marc. 1982. *The Cognitive Paradigm.* Dordrecht: Reidel.

Dreyfus, Hubert. 1992. *What Computers Still Can't Do.* Cambridge, MA: MIT Press. (First edition, 1972.)

Dreyfus, Hubert, and Stuart Dreyfus. 1986. *Mind Over Machine.* New York: Free Press.

Fleck, Ludwik. 1935. *Genesis and Development of a Scientific Fact.* As translated and reissued, with Kuhn's forward. Edited by Thaddeus Trenn and Robert Merton. Chicago: University of Chicago Press, 1979.

Fuller, Steve. 2000. *Thomas Kuhn: A Philosophical History for Our Times.* Chicago: University of Chicago Press.

Giere, Ronald. 1988. *Explaining Science: A Cognitive Approach.* Chicago: University of Chicago Press.

1994. "The Cognitive Structure of Scientific Theories." *Philosophy of Science* 61: 276–96. Reprinted in Giere (1999), pp. 97–117.

1999. *Science without Laws.* Chicago: University of Chicago Press.

Hamilton, Kelly. 2001a. "Some Philosophical Consequences of Wittgenstein's Aeronautical Research." *Perspectives on Science* 9:1–37.

2001b. "Wittgenstein and the Mind's Eye." In: James Klagge, ed. *Wittgenstein: Biography and Philosophy.* Cambridge: Cambridge University Press, pp. 53–93.

Hobsbawm, Eric, and Terence Ranger, eds. 1992. *The Invention of Tradition.* Cambridge: Cambridge University Press.

Hoyningen-Huene, Paul. 1993. *Reconstructing Scientific Revolutions: Thomas Kuhn's Philosophy of Science.* Chicago: University of Chicago Press.

Hull, David. 1988a. "A Mechanism and Its Metaphysics." *Biology and Philosophy* 3: 123–273 (including peer commentary and replies).

1988b. *Science as a Process: An Evolutionary Account of the Social and Conceptual Development of Science.* Chicago: University of Chicago Press.

Johnson-Laird, Philip. 1983. *Mental Models.* Cambridge, MA: Harvard University Press.

Johnson-Laird, Philip, and Ruth Byrne. 1991. *Deduction.* Hillsdale, NJ: Lawrence Erlbaum.

Klein, Martin. 1964. "Einstein and the Wave-Particle Duality." *The Natural Philosopher* 3: 3–49.

1967. "Thermodynamics in Einstein's Thought." *Science* 157: 509–16.

Klein, Martin.1970. *Paul Ehrenfest: Theoretical Physicist.* Amsterdam: North-Holland.

Kolodner, Janet. 1993. *Case-Based Reasoning.* San Mateo, CA: Morgan Kaufmann.

Kuhn, Thomas. 1957. *The Copernican Revolution*. Cambridge, MA: Harvard University Press.

1960. "Engineering Precedent for the Work of Sadi Carnot." *Archives Internationales d'Histoire des Sciences* 13: 251–5.

1962. *The Structure of Scientific Revolutions*. Second ed. with added "Postscript," 1970. Third ed., 1996. Chicago: University of Chicago Press.

1970a. "Postscript." Added to second edition of Kuhn (1962), pp. 174–210.

1970b. "Logic of Discovery or Psychology of Research?" In Lakatos and Musgrave (1970), pp. 1–23. Reprinted in Kuhn (1977), pp. 266–92.

1970c. "Reflections on My Critics." In Lakatos and Musgrave (1970), pp. 231–78.

1974. "Second Thoughts on Paradigms." In Suppe (1974), pp. 459–82. Reprinted in Kuhn (1977), pp. 293–319.

1977. *The Essential Tension: Selected Studies in Scientific Tradition and Change*. Chicago: University of Chicago Press.

1978. *Black-Body Theory and the Quantum Discontinuity, 1894–1912*. Oxford: Oxford University Press.

1993. "Afterward." In *World Changes: Thomas Kuhn and the Nature of Science*. Edited by Paul Horwich. Cambridge, MA: MIT Press.

Kuhn, Thomas, John Heilbron, Paul Forman, and Lini Allen. 1967. *Sources for the History of Quantum Physics: An Inventory and Report*. Philadelphia: American Philosophical Society.

Lakatos, Imre, and Alan Musgrave, eds. 1970. *Criticism and the Growth of Knowledge*. Cambridge: Cambridge University Press.

Laudan, Larry. 1977. *Progress and Its Problems*. Berkeley: University of California Press.

1986. "Intuitionist Meta-Methodologies." *Synthese* 67: 115–29.

Leake, David, ed. 1996. *Case-Based Reasoning: Experiences, Lessons, and Future Directions*. Cambridge, MA: MIT Press.

1998. "Case-Based Reasoning." In: William Bechtel and George Graham, eds. *A Companion to Cognitive Science*. Oxford: Blackwell, pp. 465–76.

MacIntyre, Alasdair. 1990. *Three Rival Versions of Moral Enquiry: Encyclopedia, Genealogy, and Tradition*. Notre Dame, IN: Notre Dame University Press.

Magnani, Lorenzo, Nancy Nersessian, and Paul Thagard, eds. 1999. *Model-Based Reasoning in Scientific Discovery*. New York: Kluwer.

Margolis, Howard. 1987. *Patterns, Thinking, and Cognition: A Theory of Judgment*. Chicago: University of Chicago Press.

1993. *Paradigms and Barriers: How Habits of Mind Govern Scientific Beliefs*. Chicago: University of Chicago Press.

Marshall, Sandra. 1995. *Schemas in Problem Solving*. Cambridge: Cambridge University Press.

Newell, Allen, and Herbert Simon. 1972. *Human Problem Solving*. Englewood Cliffs, NJ: Prentice-Hall.

Nickles, Thomas. 1989. "Heuristic Appraisal: A Proposal." *Social Epistemology* 3: 175–88.

1992. "Good Science as Bad History: From Order of Knowing to Order of Being." In: Ernan McMullin ed., *The Social Dimensions of Science*. Notre Dame, IN: University of Notre Dame Press, pp. 85–129.

1998. "Kuhn, Historical Philosophy of Science, and Case-Based Reasoning." *Configurations* 6: 51–85 (special issue on Thomas Kuhn).

2000. "Kuhnian Puzzle Solving and Schema Theory." *Philosophy of Science* 67 (special issue, PSA 2000 Proceedings): S242–S255.

Forthcoming. "Evolutionary Models of Innovation and the Meno Problem." In Larisa Shavinina, ed., *International Handbook on Innovation*. Hillsdale, NJ: Lawrence Erlbaum.

Petroski, Henry. 1994. *Design Paradigms: Case Histories of Error and Judgment in Engineering*. Cambridge: Cambridge University Press.

Polanyi, Michael. 1958. *Personal Knowledge*. Chicago: University of Chicago Press.

1966. *The Tacit Dimension*. Garden City, NY: Doubleday.

Popper, Karl R. 1959. *The Logic of Scientific Discovery*. (Expanded translation of *Logik der Forschung*, 1934.) New York: Basic Books.

1963. "Science: Conjectures and Refutations." In *Conjectures and Refutations*. London: Routledge, pp. 33–65. Originally published in 1957.

Quine, W. V. O. 1951. "Two Dogmas of Empiricism." *Philosophical Review* 60: 20–43. Reprinted with changes in *From a Logical Point of View*. Cambridge, MA: Harvard University Press, 1953, pp. 20–46.

Riesbeck, Christopher. 1996. "What Next? The Future of Case-Based Reasoning in Post-Modern AI." In Leake (1996), pp. 371–88.

Rosch, Eleanor. 1973. "Natural Categories." *Cognitive Psychology* 4: 328–50.

Rouse, Joseph. 1987. *Knowledge and Power*. Ithaca, NY: Cornell University Press.

2002. *How Scientific Practices Matter: Reclaiming Philosophical Naturalism*. Chicago: University of Chicago Press.

Rumelhart, David, Paul Smolensky, James McClelland, and Geoffrey Hinton. 1986. "Schemata and Sequential Thought Processes in PDP Models." In: James McClelland and David Rumelhart, eds. *Parallel Distributed Processing*. Cambridge, MA: MIT Press, vol. 2, pp. 7–57.

Shapere, Dudley. 1982. "The Concept of Observation in Science and Philosophy." *Philosophy of Science* 49: 485–525.

Snyder, Laura. 1997. "Discoverers' Induction." *Philosophy of Science* 64: 580–604.

Sommerfeld, Arnold. 1919. *Atombau und Spektrallinien*. Braunschweig: Vieweg. Many later editions.

Suppe, Frederick, ed. 1974. *The Structure of Scientific Theories*. 2nd ed., enlarged in 1977. Urbana: University of Illinois Press.

Toulmin, Stephen. 1961. *Foresight and Understanding*. New York: Harper & Row.

1972. *Human Understanding*. Princeton: Princeton University Press.

Vicente, Kim, and William Brewer. 1993. "Reconstructive Remembering of the Scientific Literature." *Cognition* 46: 101–28.

Wittgenstein, Ludwig. 1953. *Philosophical Investigations*. New York: Macmillan.

7 | Kuhn, Conceptual Change, and Cognitive Science

NANCY J. NERSESSIAN

7.1 INTRODUCTION

The research project outlined in Thomas Kuhn's *The Structure of Scientific Revolutions* seems intrinsically historical, philosophical, and psychological (Kuhn 1970). However, by and large, Kuhn never utilized research in the cognitive sciences that would have furthered his own paradigm in ways I think he would have found agreeable. Until his very last writings, psychology dropped out of Kuhn's post-*Structure* published articulations of his views just at the time that the cognitive revolution was beginning to provide accounts of representation, problem solving, and learning that I believe are pertinent to his intuitive insights.[1] With hindsight one can construct significant parallels between the views of knowledge, perception, and learning developed in each. In what follows I will discuss in what ways some of Kuhn's insights might be furthered today in light of cognitive science research. Seen through a cognitive lens, Kuhn's little book seems all the more remarkable and insightful. Many of the issues with which he grappled have been the subject of entire areas of research in cognitive science, especially cognitive psychology. In the course of this essay I can only give brief indications of how Kuhn's thinking and research in areas of cognitive science have been running along parallel lines and of how one might, through cognitive-historical analysis, create some intersecting lines.

In his Presidential Address to the Philosophy of Science Association, Kuhn expressed his abiding interest as being in "incommensurability and the nature of the conceptual divide between the developmental stages separated by . . . 'scientific revolutions'" (Conant and Haugeland 2000, p. 228). In this essay I will focus on three problems of conceptual change: the nature of the representation of a conceptual structure, the processes of learning a conceptual structure, and the processes of creating a conceptual structure. The problems of representation and learning were addressed by Kuhn. Although he recognized the problem of creation, he only briefly addressed it. The methodological approach I will employ in addressing all three problems is "cognitive-historical" (Nersessian 1992c, 1995b).

The underlying assumption of the cognitive-historical method is a "continuum hypothesis." The cognitive practices of scientists are extensions of the kinds of cognitive practices humans employ in coping with their environment and in problem solving of a more ordinary kind. Employed in analyzing problems relating to conceptual change in science, the "historical" dimension of the method uncovers the representational and reasoning practices scientists use and examines these over extended periods of time and as embedded within local communities and wider cultural contexts. The "cognitive" dimension factors into the analysis considerations of how human cognitive capacities and limitations could produce and constrain the practices of scientists. Thus cognitive-historical analyses, on the one hand, make use of the customary range of historical records and, on the other, draw on extensive scientific investigations into how humans reason, represent, and learn.

However, that ordinary and scientific representational and reasoning practices lie on a continuum does not rule out the possibility of differences. Differences can occur either because they are due to the inherent nature of the activity or because they are an artifact of the fact that much current cognitive science research has been conducted in artificial contexts and on problems of less complexity. My sense is that disparities largely arise because of the latter and that new insights into mundane cognition can be drawn from examining scientific cognition. Thus, the cognitive-historical method is reflexive. Cognitive theories and methods are drawn on insofar as they help interpret the historical cases, while at the same time theories of cognitive processes are evaluated concerning the extent to which they can be applied to scientific practices. Assessments of the fit between the cognitive theories and the scientific practices are fed back into cognitive science to be used in developing richer theories of cognition, which, in turn, will be applied and evaluated in further cognitive-historical analyses. The goal is to bring historical and cognitive interpretations into a state of reflective equilibrium so as to make the circularity inherent in the approach virtuous rather than vicious.

7.2 CONCEPTUAL CHANGE: REPRESENTATION AND PERCEPTION

Most of Kuhn's work after writing *Structure* centered on issues of what he called the scientific "lexicon," specifically, on how the language of a scientific community is acquired and how language change relates to incommensurability. I will begin with Kuhn's theory of concept representation and then move to the issue of the relation between representation and perception. It is in relation to the latter issue that Kuhn himself expressed interest in how research in cognitive science might further his project.

7.2.1 Concept Representation

In the account provided in *Structure* and in Kuhn's later work on the lexicon, concept representation is to be understood in terms of the notion that similarity and dissimilarity to problem exemplars is central to how one acquires the conceptual structure of a paradigm and how one resolves outstanding problems during the course of normal science. What one acquires in learning a conceptual structure are not sets of defining characteristics and specifiable rules for the concepts that participate in the problem exemplars comprised by the paradigm. Rather, one acquires sets of "family resemblances" that include both similarities and differences among instances. In presenting this view, Kuhn explicitly drew from the philosopher Wittgenstein, who in his *Philosophical Investigations* (Wittgenstein 1968) had argued against the "classical" view of concepts, originating with Plato and Aristotle and carried into twentieth-century philosophical analysis by Frege and Russell.

On the classical view, a concept is represented by a definition. A definition is a set of conditions that are singly necessary and jointly sufficient to delineate a concept. Wittgenstein argued that it is impossible to distinguish between "essential" properties of a concept, that is, those that must necessarily be contained in its definition, and "accidental" properties. For example, a flying creature is usually categorized as a 'bird', but 'flies' is a nonessential property, since not all birds fly. What unifies the category of bird is a set of family resemblances among the instances placed in that category. Further, Wittgenstein argued that the instances of some concepts such as 'game' not only cannot be defined by a list of necessary and sufficient conditions but may actually have no one feature in common, and thus each instance shows only a family resemblance to any other.

Kuhn referred to Wittgenstein's analysis in addressing the problem of what is required for there to be consistent application of a paradigm within the community when "the existence of a paradigm need not even imply that any full set of rules exist" (Kuhn 1970, p. 44). He extended Wittgenstein's analysis of concepts such as 'chair' and 'game' to argue that what a scientist knows when participating in a paradigm is not sets of defining criteria and rules, but "various research problems and techniques that...relate by resemblance and by modeling" (ibid., pp. 43–4). In support of his claim, Kuhn invoked the difficulty of formulating the rules that have guided any specific paradigm and the fact that scientists learn paradigms largely by working problem exemplars, not by learning rules and definitions in the abstract. In later work, he focused on the notion that a scientist acquires that part of the paradigm that constitutes its lexicon through a process of learning to discriminate similarities and differences among instances appearing in problem exemplars.

As I and others have noted (Andersen, Chen, and Barker 1996; Chen, Andersen, and Barker 1998; Nersessian 1984b, 1985, 1992b), research on categorization in cognitive psychology begun in the early 1970s by the psychologist Eleanor Rosch and her collaborators provides a cognitive underpinning for many of Kuhn's intuitive insights about concept representation and acquisition. To begin with, the psychological research lends empirical support to the position that in many instances people do not represent concepts by means of sets of necessary and sufficient conditions (see Smith and Medin 1981 for an overview). According to Rosch, this research, too, took its lead from Wittgenstein's critique of the classical view. Rosch began her research with investigations of color categorization and was led to the surprising conclusion that, irrespective of naming practices, the way individuals recognize (i.e., retrieve from memory) colors is not arbitrary, but seemingly is a function of the human perceptual system (Heider 1972). She then extended the research to other perceptual categories, including geometrical shapes, and semantic categories of natural and artificial kinds, such as birds, fruits, clothing, and sports (Rosch and Mervis 1975; Rosch 1987). Other researchers have established the same result for a variety of concepts, including mathematical concepts such as number and plane geometry figures (Armstrong, Gleitman, and Gleitman 1983). Based on the empirical findings, this research program has proposed that, rather than representing concepts by sets of defining criteria, humans represent both natural and artificial concepts by a prototypical example. Category membership is determined by similarity or dissimilarity to the features of the prototype.

Further, concepts show *graded structures*. That is, some instances of a given concept are better examples of the concept than other instances. The classical view cannot be reconciled with the existence of graded structures since, according to it, either a given object fulfills all conditions and therefore is an instance of the concept in question, or it fails to fulfill one or more conditions and therefore is not an instance. On a family resemblance account of concepts, however, some instances may be better examples than others, according to the degree of similarity the object shows to other instances or the degree of similarity the object shows to a prototypical instance. Of course, all instances are members of the category, but some are better exemplars than others. Additionally, categories possess an internal structure: basic level (e.g., bird), subordinate (e.g., Tweety), and superordinate (e.g., animal). The basic level provides the entry point for concept acquisition, naming, and remembering. This is the level at which the members exhibit the highest degree of similarity – especially visual similarity – for human observers. For example, members of the category 'bird' are more similar than those of the category 'animal' (superordinate), and there is no gain – and perhaps some loss – of similarity in the subordinate instances of birds, such as Tweety the canary and Fluffy the parakeet. The hierarchical structure shows that family resemblance concepts form taxonomies. That is, superordinate concepts decompose into more specific, subordinate concepts that may again decompose into yet more specific concepts, and so forth.

Finally, instances of a concept often show not only similarity to other instances of the same concept, but also dissimilarity to instances of other concepts to which the object could otherwise mistakenly have been assigned. To use Kuhn's favorite example, swans may be mistakenly categorized as geese, but instances of the category 'swan' are more similar to instances of the category 'goose' than they are to instances of the category 'dog'. That they can be mistaken for one another also indicates that they form a family resemblance class on the superordinate level. Such a group of concepts that together form a family resemblance class on the superordinate level is called a "contrast set," in this example 'waterfowl'.

The two main accounts of the representation of family resemblance concepts that have been suggested are feature lists and frames. Several varieties of feature-list representations have been proposed. However, these similarity-based representations have been criticized as not providing for well-known effects on categorization, such as context dependence and goals. For example, building nests and laying eggs are typical features of 'bird', but these features have complex relationships to one another, as well as to other features, such as having feathers. To learn what a bird is requires understanding some of these relationships. Thus, simply knowing how instances are similar or dissimilar to the prototype is not sufficient for learning and categorization. So, the empirical evidence strongly suggests that concepts are not represented simply by lists of features, but that the features are organized into more complex structures (Armstrong, et al. 1983; Barsalou 1987;

Medin 1989; Keil 1991). One such structure is a "dynamic frame" (Barsalou 1992), which has been utilized so successfully in the work of Andersen, Barker, and Chen (Andersen et al. 1996; Chen et al. 1998; Andersen and Nersessian 2000) on conceptual change and incommensurability. Since they have an essay in this volume, I will not elaborate on the implications of a dynamic frame-based account of concept representation for understanding conceptual change. It should be noted, though, that their analysis is limited to taxonomic concepts, and the case of science is complicated by the existence of many nontaxonomic concepts, such as 'force' and 'mass'.

Only a limited range of scientific concepts refer to things that can be picked out individually and that form contrast sets (family resemblance on the superordinate level), such as 'duck', 'goose', and 'swan' or 'planet', 'comet', and 'asteroid'. Most scientific concepts such as 'force' and 'electromagnetic field' refer to entities and processes that are learned by apprehending complex problem situations to which a given law applies and in which several concepts are used. For example, what are usually learned are instances of the application of a natural law, such as Newton's second law, $F = m\mathbf{a}$, in which the concepts 'force', 'mass', and 'acceleration' are involved simultaneously. Kuhn noted this problem on two occasions. In early work, he distinguished between taxonomic scientific concepts, called "basic", and nontaxonomic scientific concepts, called "theoretical" (Kuhn 1970). In later development, he referred to these as "normic" concepts and "nomic" concepts, respectively (Kuhn 1993). In both his earlier and later accounts of this distinction, Kuhn said nothing about how the referents of the individual concepts in such problem situations, here' force', 'mass', and 'acceleration', could be identified (see Andersen and Nersessian 2000 for a fuller discussion).

7.2.2 Concept Representation and Perception

Concept representation and perception are linked in *Structure* through the notion that scientists acquire a paradigm by learning similarity and dissimilarity relations among problem exemplars. Paul Hoyningen-Huene's (1993) analysis of Kuhn's philosophy of science is useful for understanding how this happens. His account provides new insights into Kuhn's views on perception, concept acquisition, and language that are especially useful in thinking about Kuhn's work from a cognitive perspective.

As Hoyningen points out, the account of family resemblance presented in *Structure* went beyond Wittgenstein in claiming that the "sort of world necessary to support the naming procedure" is one in which there must be what Kuhn called "natural families," that is, nonoverlapping or non-merging families, *and* one that depends for the observer on "the existence, after neural processing, of empty *perceptual space* between the families to be discriminated" (Kuhn 1970, p. 45, fn 2, italics in the original; see also Hoyningen-Huene 1993, p. 85). Kuhn's basic intuition was that the linkage among family resemblance concepts, natural families (or "kinds," as he later refers to them), and human perception creates linkage between conceptual change and perceptual experience. If we connect this intuition to his notion of 'the world' as being constituted by the conceptual structure of a paradigm, we can understand better what Kuhn had in mind in saying that in adopting a new paradigm, one experiences a different world. For him this was not a metaphorical way of speaking but the rudiments of a thoroughly nonrealist position that was never articulated fully.

Change in world-constitutive similarity relations is the hallmark of conceptual change in scientific revolutions. These world-constitutive relations are both learned through and constitutive of perceptual experience. When the representations through which we understand the world change, the world-constitutive similarities and differences that are the focal points of learning and problem solving change. Conceptual change entails perceptual change, and thus incommensurability of experience results as well as incommensurability of language. On Hoyningen's account, Kuhn's shift in focus from the early, largely "perceptual theory" in *Structure* to a focus on language came about for at least three related reasons: first, because of the need to talk about how communities are the agents of scientific activity and how they transmit paradigms and participate in normal scientific research; second, because of his post-*Structure* focus on incommensurability as untranslatability; and third, because of his inability to further articulate the perceptual theory. But, as Hoyningen intimates, the concern to articulate the perceptual theory remained a lifelong concern for Kuhn. The problem of the nature of the linkage between perceptual experience and conceptual change is central to incommensurability. The rudiments of this idea are elaborated in Chapter X of *Structure*, "Revolutions as Changes of World View," which many readers have found perplexing.

Kuhn began the chapter by stating that "The historian of science may be tempted to exclaim that when paradigms change, the world itself changes with them" (p. 111). In this chapter he gave many examples of how postrevolution scientists "lived" and "worked" in a "different world," such as "[a]t the very least, as a result discovering oxygen, Lavoisier saw nature differently. And in the absence of some recourse to that hypothetical fixed nature that he 'saw differently,' the principle of economy would urge us to say that after discovering oxygen Lavoisier worked in a different world" (p. 118). Here Kuhn invoked research in Gestalt psychology to support his insight. The world delimited by a scientific paradigm changes just as the perceived similarity relations change after one learns to conceptualize a Gestalt figure as, for example, a rabbit rather than as what one formally understood as a duck. Soon after the publication of *Structure*, Kuhn backed away from the Gestalt switch metaphor as a category mistake since he had applied to a community a notion that rightly applied only to an individual. He claimed to have relied too much on his own phenomenal experience as a historian attempting to understand Aristotle's worldview. Nevertheless, Kuhn continued to believe that an understanding of how the scientist's experience of the world changes in a revolution needed to be figured into the account of incommensurability. As he stated: "[t]hough the world does not change with the change of paradigm, the scientist afterwards works in a different world. . . . I am convinced that we must make sense of statements that at least resemble these" (p. 121). Kuhn's "linguistic turn" was a shift of focus and not an abandonment of the struggle to construct a viable perceptual theory. In his last published work he characterized the 'lexicon' as the mental "module in which members of a speech community store the community's kind terms" (Kuhn 1993). The lexicon engenders variable beliefs and expectations, depending on an individual's experience and learning. What the community holds in common he called 'lexical structure'. It is difference in lexical structure that creates incommensurability. Different lexical structures embody different kind relations, and these constitute different perceived realities.

On Kuhn's account, then, for conceptual change to take place, the human neural apparatus responsible for processing perceptual stimuli must be capable of being programmed and reprogrammed during the process of exposure to similarity and difference relations and must group perceptions into similarity classes in such a way that they are separated distinctly in perceptual space (Kuhn 1970, pp. 194–7). The Gestalt switch metaphor spoke to the phenomenal experience following a reprogramming through learning the postrevolution conceptual structure. The need to find a way to articulate this intuition accounted for the only interest Kuhn himself showed directly in cognitive science research. His one foray into computational modeling in 1969 was an attempt to model his view of the perceptual reprogramming aspect of conceptual change. In his later years he expressed interest in research on the evolution of the representational capabilities of the brain, cognitive development in children, and computational modeling of learning via neural nets.[2]

In what follows, I will speculate on how Kuhn possibly thought research on cognitive development would help him to articulate the perceptual theory. I say "speculate" since I have not had access to the draft manuscript in which he discusses the cognitive development literature. My account rests on some remarks made in his last writings, the 1990 lecture at UCLA (which he sent to me), "An Historian's Theory of Meaning," the two interviews with him conducted by Hanne Andersen, some discussions I had with him, and my interview with Susan Carey, in which I asked her about details of the material in the cognitive development literature she had discussed extensively with Kuhn and that he noted would play a major role in the analysis in his unfinished book.

The research he mentioned in the materials just noted and, in particular, discussed with Susan Carey concerned the psychological work on criteria for numerical identity and individuation. This research substantiates the existence of an innate representational system through which the brain places constraints on the way objects are individuated and tracked through space and time. Evidence for this system is found in infants as young as two months old in such research as Spelke's (Spelke, Phillips, and Woodward 1995) on object tracking and identification, in which infants show surprise if spatiotemporal continuity is violated for objects. This research provides evidence of tracking for individual objects, not kinds. It is not until around twelve months of age that information about features seems to play a role in object recognition. For example, until that time, when the researcher pulls objects from behind an occluded screen, it does not matter if in one case a boat is revealed and in the other a truck. Babies identify one object, indicating that they are using only spatiotemporal continuity criteria. At about twelve months of age they recognize that there are two objects behind the screen, indicating that they have developed the basis for kind identification. Additionally, research by Pylyshyn (2001) shows there is a midlevel perceptual system operative in adults that also tracks objects in the same way. This system of individuation is perceptually based and operates the same way whether or not the individuals are identifiable members of kinds. The twelve-month system that uses features to keep track of kinds plays a different role in individuation and is both maturation-based and involves learning to determine what kinds the language community discerns. Clearly this builds on the earlier system, and clearly it underlies language learning. In both systems there is a principled distinction between the processes that establish representations of individuals and those that bind features to individuals. The cognitive architecture starts with individuation and only later identifies objects as kinds (see Carey and Fei 2001 for a fuller discussion).

I believe Kuhn saw this work as having the potential to provide a means of furthering his intuition of "empty perceptual space" between the kinds established by a scientific lexicon. In his work on the lexicon, the early notion of "empty perceptual space between families to be discriminated" is related to what he called the "no-overlap principle" for taxonomic categories. According to this principle, no two categories can share a member unless one includes the other totally, such as superordinate categories and their subordinates. Swans and geese are members of the category 'waterfowl', but no swan is a member of the category 'goose'. No two kind terms can share a referent unless there is complete overlap in reference, so 'waterfowl' refers to both swans and geese, but 'swan' cannot refer to a goose. In the world so constituted by this lexicon, there is nothing that is both a swan and a goose. The similarity and difference relations grasped in the learning process constitute both the category and the kind in the world. The no-overlap principle is what makes complete translation impossible between conceptual systems on opposite sides of the revolutionary divide. In posing the problem of incommensurability, Kuhn most often discussed the principle in relation to individuating concepts. However, the psychological research is about constraints on numerical identity and individuation of objects. The function of the cognitive architecture as currently understood is to create *individuals* and track them through time in such a way as for there to be no overlap, not to individuate *concepts* and track them through time. Applying this literature to concepts would be a category mistake. But Kuhn's no-overlap principle has two aspects, one concerning language and the other concerning the world as constituted by that language. The term 'planet' in the Aristotelian lexicon cannot be translated by the term 'planet' in the Copernican–Galilean structure because they refer to different kinds. Kind terms support the categories necessary for describing and generalizing about the world, and different kinds provide for different descriptions and generalizations and thereby, experientially, different worlds.

Kuhn stated that his intention in the forthcoming book was to "suggest that this characteristic [no-overlap] can be traced to, and on from, the evolution of the neural mechanisms for reidentifying what Aristotle called 'substances': things that, between their origin and demise, trace a lifeline through space over time" (Conant and Haugeland 2000, p. 229). Here he referred to philosophical work on sortals (Wiggins 1980), which like the psychological literature on the early individuation system pertains only to substances, not kinds. How Kuhn might have seen the extension to kinds working out is as follows. There is an innate mechanism that embodies a no-overlap principle for tracking and individuation. This is a perceptually based system that works regardless of whether the individuals are kinds or not. On top of this builds the mature system, which plays a different role in individuation by means of kinds. It uses properties that enable discrimination (similarity and difference relations) to keep track of kinds and also embodies a no-overlap principle for kinds. Its development is a function of maturation and learning that is tied to language. But, as Kuhn noted, for his purposes a broader notion of 'kind' than is customary is needed, one that will "populate the world as well as divide up a preexisting population" (ibid., p. 229). In this case, the mature cognitive system would need to be capable of being reprogrammed to identify the new kinds created in a scientific revolution.

7.3   CONCEPTUAL CHANGE: LEARNING IN SCIENCE EDUCATION

As discussed in Section 7.2, Kuhn's theory of concepts derives from his insight that learning from problem exemplars provides entrée into the linguistic community of a science. The original insight involved more than learning concepts since problem exemplars also provide knowledge of other aspects of scientific practice such as knowledge of methods and analytical techniques and of how mathematical relations map to physical situations. Kuhn saw science education as a process of indoctrination in which textbook distillations and reformulations of current knowledge are the chief pedagogical tools. Repeatedly working problem sets and assimilating the similarities and differences among problem exemplars enables the learner to acquire the paradigm and thus the means for solving outstanding problems during the course of normal science. Kuhn also believed this pedagogical approach to be highly successful and one that should be continued since "[n]othing could be better calculated to produce 'mental sets' or *Einstellungen*" (Kuhn 1977, p. 229).

However, as Kuhn noted, there is something paradoxical about the apparent success of this pedagogical method. Consider the following problems. First, since textbook presentations do not represent the kinds of problems experts will need to solve and the range of methods for solution, how is the textbook method so successful at producing practitioners of "normal science"? Textbooks present problems analogous to paradigmatic examples of solved problems, and laboratory exercises largely present "canned" experiments related to these. In both cases, exemplars are not presented in the form practitioners will encounter or with many of the techniques needed to tackle the authentic problems. Yet the method seems to produce competent puzzle solvers for the existing tradition. Second, "followed by a term in an apprenticeship relation, this technique of exclusive exposure to a rigid tradition has been immensely productive of the most consequential sorts of innovation" (ibid., pp. 229–30) Although Kuhn is right in pointing out that there is an "essential tension" between innovation and tradition, what he failed to appreciate fully is that it is mitigated by the flexibility in the apprenticeship learning component of training practitioners. Cognitive science research indicates that there are no paradoxes with respect to the traditional pedagogical method. The textbook-type science education has *not* been successful in producing practitioners. Very few students learn the subject sufficiently well even to provide explanations and predictions of simple physics phenomena, never mind to go on to graduate school and become practitioners. Much of the credit for the success in creating practitioners goes to the apprenticeship – usually experienced first in graduate school – during which practices are learned in authentic situations. In apprenticeships, students learn the tacit as well as the explicit practices of the discipline. Within cognitive science such situated learning experiences have been called "cognitive apprenticeships" (Brown, Collins, and Duguid 1989; Collins, Brown, and Duguid 1989). In this form of training, science students learn, among other things, how to adapt problem exemplars to current research problems by observing how practitioners tackle these and participating in the research. In this process they are exposed directly to the formal and informal methodological practices, conceptual understandings, and interpretive structures that constitute the practice of the science.

7.3.1 Cognitive Research on Physics Education

If we focus just on the dimension of conceptual change, cognitive science research on learning in physics education shows that traditional undergraduate instructional techniques and textbooks are spectacularly *un*successful at facilitating the process of students learning the conceptual structure of physics. A substantial body of literature has established quite conclusively that even after training in physics, large numbers of students, including those who have learned to perform the requisite calculations, have not learned the scientific conceptual structure of the domain (Driver and Easley 1978; Viennot 1979; Champagne, Klopfer, and Gunstone 1982; Clement 1982; McCloskey 1983; McDermott 1984; Halloun and Hestenes 1985). In numerous studies of varying design, the qualitative explanations students give for various phenomena after instruction in science are at odds with those given by physics. The source of the difficulty is widely held to be the fact that students come to their physics classes with preconceptions about the nature and processes of such phenomena as motion that, though not fully developed and integrated, interfere with learning science. Thus, students are thought to have to undergo major conceptual change in the learning process.

Much of the research on learning in physics has focused on Newtonian mechanics since it is with mechanics that most students first encounter an abstract, formal scientific theory. Based on numerous studies of "restructuring," "conceptual change," and "naive physics" (Viennot 1979; Clement 1982, 1983; McCloskey 1983; McDermott 1984; Nersessian 1989; Nersessian and Resnick 1989; Chi 1992), it has been established that intuitive physical explanations, such as those of motion, differ from scientific explanations along several dimensions. These explanations employ concepts of a kind different from those used in scientific explanations, most notably with respect to ontological status and level of abstraction. For example, students conceive of objects, such as stones, rather than mathematical point masses; they think of force as a property of objects rather than a relation between objects; and they view motion as a process rather than as a state.

The intuitive conceptualizations of many of the phenomena present obstacles to learning. To see this, an example that I have discussed in some detail in previous work (Nersessian 1989; Nersessian and Resnick 1989) will be useful. From what we know thus far, in learning Newtonian mechanics students must change from believing that "motion implies force" to believing that "accelerated motion implies force." However, examining student protocols before and after-instruction reveals that their concepts of 'motion' and 'force' are not the same as the Newtonian concepts. In Newtonian mechanics, motion is a state in which bodies remain unless acted on by a force. Thus, rest and motion have the same ontological status: they are both states. Like rest, motion per se does not need to be explained, only changes of motion. Force is a functional quantity that explains changes in motion. Newtonian forces are relations between two or more bodies. Students, however, conceive of motion as a process that bodies undergo and believe that *all* motion needs an explanation. They conceive of force as some kind of power imparted to a body by an agent or another body. This makes force ontologically a property or perhaps even an entity, but not a relationship. On the whole, the concepts students intuitively employ to understand how objects move resemble more the Aristotelian/medieval concepts than the Newtonian understanding needed to acquire the science, which is most likely due to their experiences in a world of friction. And studies show that the intuitive conceptual structure is largely untouched by traditional science instruction.

From the cognitive research, it appears that learning a scientific conceptual structure requires the student to construct fundamentally new concepts and to build them into a new framework. By and large, Kuhn is correct that in the traditional textbook concepts are introduced by means of equations said to "define" them (such as " 'force' is defined as $\mathbf{F} = m\mathbf{a}$"), and these are accompanied by problem exemplars the concepts are instantiated by and by "canned" laboratory exercises that exemplify them. The expectation is that students will learn to apply the concepts by extracting them from the problem exemplars. The result of this pedagogical approach is that the majority of students leave their physics classes with their "intuitive" or "naive" conceptualizations of physical phenomena largely intact and without the ability to provide scientific explanations of these phenomena. One possible reason why it is difficult to learn the conceptual structure by this method is that, as discussed in Section 7.2, unlike concepts of ordinary language such as 'swan', most science concepts appear together in complex problem situations. Thus something more is needed for conceptual change than learning similarity and difference relations among problem exemplars.

Research on learning in science education and in cognitive development are areas of cognitive science where Kuhn's early views on scientific revolutions and incommensurability have had significant influence. Many researchers have proposed an analogy between the kinds of changes in conceptual structure required in learning and those that have taken place in scientific revolutions. The main support for hypotheses drawn from the analogy comes from research that describes the initial states of learners and compares these with the desired final states. These end-state comparisons, such as provided in the 'motion' and 'force' example, do give a sense that the kinds of conceptual changes students need to undergo to learn may be akin to those that take place in what philosophers and historians of science have characterized as "scientific revolutions." However, even if the *kinds* of changes are strikingly similar, this does not mean that the *processes* of change need in any way be alike. The focus of this research has been on providing analyses of differences between the content, structure, and characteristics of the knowledge on which students and scientists draw, with scant attention being directed to the methods for constructing conceptual structures. The problem of how change is created or the nature of what psychologists call the "mechanisms" of change is just beginning to be addressed in a rigorous way.

Likening the changes and processes of learning and development to those of scientific revolutions does not, of course, solve the problem; it just displaces it. Those who study scientific change have not solved the problem either. In earlier work, I proposed that a promising way of addressing the problem is through extending the analogy to the mechanisms of conceptual change (Nersessian 1992a, 1995c). This move is warranted on the basis that the cognitive tasks in the learning process and in the initial constructive process are similar in salient ways. In both cases, what is needed is to construct new concepts, form new conceptual structures, and integrate the new representation for coherent, systematic use. This is so despite the fact that, in the case of learning, teachers possess the extant knowledge students need to learn, and in the case of first constructing the concepts no one had the answer. The proposal that the cognitive processing required to build a conceptual structure is similar in the two cases is in line with research investigating the hypothesis that cognitive development and learning involve processes of theory change and conceptual change that are similar to those of scientific theorizing and conceptual change (Carey 1985, 1991; Chi 1992; Gopnik and Meltzoff 1997). The point is that the high degree of similarity in the nature of the kinds of changes indicates a relationship in the cognitive tasks. It follows from the proposal that pedagogy and practice would need to be brought more into line. The cognitive procedures employed in the actual construction of concepts should be effective in pedagogical situations. There is precedent for this approach in scientific practice itself. Often when a scientist who has constructed a new conceptualization attempts to communicate it to his peers, the same constructive procedures are employed, effectively leading colleagues through the process of learning the new framework.

Although he did not apply it to his theory of science learning, Kuhn clearly saw what is wrong with the textbook approach. The "concept of science drawn from them is no more likely to fit the enterprise that produced them than an image of a national culture drawn from a tourist brochure or a language text" (Kuhn 1970, p. 1). So, how to determine what the constructive practices are?

7.3.2 A Role for History? Mining the History of Science

The proposal made in the previous section differs significantly from "recapitulation" theories in science education with which it might be compared. Although there are interesting parallels between historical prescientific conceptions in some domains and untutored conceptions, "recapitulating" the historical process is neither possible nor feasible nor desirable. Rather, the suggestion is that the cognitive practices of scientists provide a model for cognitive aspects of the learning activity itself, and with respect to the problem of conceptual change, the history of science is a source for discerning these. For the purposes of developing new pedagogical approaches, the history of science can be viewed as a repository of strategic knowledge of how to go about constructing, changing, and communicating scientific representations. The recommendation, then, is that researchers "mine" the historical data for this knowledge, develop analyses of how the practices are generative, and use what they learn in developing instructional procedures.

Possibly the most widely quoted sentence drawn from philosophy and history of science is that with which Kuhn opened *Structure*: "History, if viewed as a repository for more than anecdote or chronology, could produce a decisive transformation in the image of science by which we are now possessed" (p. 1). In that work Kuhn saw himself as shifting the focus of philosophical analysis from a static view of science to the dynamical perspective opened by examining the history of scientific practices. However, his later shift to language analysis ultimately led him to abandon history as a source for building a theory of scientific change. As he stated in the Rothschild Lecture at Harvard in 1992:

> Given what I shall call the historical perspective, one may reach many of the central conclusions we drew with scarcely a glance at the historical record itself. That historical perspective was, of course, initially foreign to all of us. The questions which led us to examine the historical records were products of a philosophical tradition that took science as a static body of knowledge and asked what rational warrant there was for taking one or another of its component beliefs to be true. Only gradually, as a by-product of our study of historical "facts," did we learn to replace that static image with a dynamical one, an image that made science an ever-developing enterprise or practice. And it is taking longer still to realize that, with that perspective achieved, many of the most central conclusions we drew from the historical record can be derived instead from first principles. Approaching them in that way reduces their apparent contingency, making them harder to dismiss as a product of muckraking investigations by those hostile to science. (Kuhn 1992, p. 10; see also Kuhn 1990, p. 6)

I agree with the dynamical image of science and share Kuhn's concerns about contingency, but the question remains: where do the "first principles" arise? In shifting from examining practices, Kuhn sought these through thinking about languages and how they are learned. In this he reverted to the strategy employed by the static approach of placing the analytical focus on the linguistic dimension of scientific conceptual structures and transferring to science what might be said of languages generally. Clearly scientific conceptual structures can be represented linguistically. But this does not mean that we can learn about the nature of conceptual change in science simply – or even mainly – by investigating the nature of languages and language learning. One important difference between an ordinary language and the language of a science is that the former does not change as drastically as the latter can within a short span of time. Kuhn is right that the history of science has shown us that science is dynamic, continually undergoing processes of construction and refinement. But considering how a language is acquired and transmitted within a community does not address the dynamics of how languages are constructed and change, which is what is required in attacking significant aspects of the problems of conceptual change and incommensurability.

Clearly also, a way needs to be devised to handle the problem of the "apparent contingency" and particulars of case studies within a more general account of the nature of concept formation and change in science. By placing the historical practices within the broader framework of human cognitive activities, cognitive-historical analysis goes beyond the specific case study to more general conclusions about the nature and function of the scientific practices. Such placement aids in establishing that the fragments of scientific research and discovery are representative of scientific practices more generally. As Hutchins has said of studies of situated cognitive practices generally:

> There are powerful regularities to be described at a level of analysis that transcends the details of the specific domain. It is not possible to discover these regularities without understanding the details of the domain, but the regularities are not about the domain specific details, they are about the nature of cognition in human activity. (Woods 1995, p. 15)

I believe Kuhn's earlier insight that a theory of conceptual change would have to be grounded in an examination of the history of scientific practices has not yet been fully exploited. As noted earlier, Kuhn did not address the problem of creating conceptual structures, but from a cognitive-historical perspective the resolution of the problem has implications for the problems of representation and learning. The problem of creation requires grounding in history. Cognitive-historical research shows the constructive practices of scientists in creating new conceptual structures to involve, centrally, model-based reasoning. In the following sections I will provide brief indications of how they function.

7.4 CONCEPTUAL CHANGE: THE ROLE OF MODEL-BASED REASONING

On the Kuhnian model, conceptual change arises from a pattern that consists of an accumulation of anomalies, then a crisis, and then a new conceptual structure that forms as part of a new paradigm. However, the processes through which the new conceptual structure arises are left mysterious. The radical discontinuity view many interpreters have read into Kuhn's work is decidedly unhistorical, and Kuhn, having carried out many historical analyses, could not subscribe to it. Instead, he maintained from the outset that "[n]ew theories . . . in the mature sciences are not born *de novo*. On the contrary, they emerge from old theories. . . ." (Kuhn 1977, p. 229); thus "since the new paradigms are born from old ones, they ordinarily incorporate much of the vocabulary and apparatus, both conceptual and manipulative" of the old paradigms (Kuhn 1970, p. 149). A central contention of the cognitive-historical approach is that the answer to the question of how they are "born from new ones" lies in examining the representational and reasoning practices employed by scientists in constructing new conceptual structures. Through understanding these, an account can be developed of (1) the nature of the commensurability relations that Kuhn intimated to exist between successive representations of a domain and (2) whether and, if so, what kinds of domain-independent constructive practices exist in science. In determining the practices, historical analysis continues to play a central role. But there is also a need to move beyond a historical analysis that describes those practices to an explanatory account that utilizes them in addressing the generative problem of how the reasoning creates new conceptual structures from existing ones.

Although, again, it is not possible to go into the details in depth within the confines of this essay, my account of how model-based reasoning practices are generative of conceptual change derives from extensive historical and cognitive research. The scientific practices are determined by historical research and investigations of contemporary practices by cognitive scientists. These provide the focal points for examining cognitive science research in search of findings that help to explain the cognitive underpinnings of the scientific practices, to formulate hypotheses about why these practices are effective, and to discern ways in which the cognitive research might be challenged by the findings from examining scientific cognition. The cognitive science research pertinent to model-based reasoning is drawn primarily from the literatures on analogy, mental modeling, mental simulation, mental imagery, imagistic and diagrammatic reasoning, expert/novice problem solving, and conceptual change.

The nature of the specific conceptual, analytical, and material resources and constraints provided by the sociocultural environments within and external to the scientific communities in which conceptual changes have taken place have been examined for many episodes and sciences. What stands out from this research is that, in numerous instances of "revolutionary" conceptual change across the sciences, the practices of analogy, visual representation, and thought experimenting are employed. My own historical investigations center on practices employed in physics (Nersessian 1984a, 1984b, 1985, 1988, 1992b, 1992c, 1995b, in press-a, in press-b), but those of other sciences by philosophers, historians, and cognitive scientists establish that these practices are employed across the sciences (see, e.g. Rudwick 1976; Darden 1980, 1991; Holmes 1981, 1985; Latour 1986; Latour and Woolgar 1986; Tweney 1987, 1992; Giere 1988, 1992, 1994; Griesemer and Wimsatt 1989; Gooding 1990; Lynch and Woolgar 1990; Griesemer 1991a, 1991b; Thagard 1991; Shelley 1996; Gentner and Markman 1997; Trumpler 1997). In these practices reasoning is model-based, that is, inferences are made from and through constructing and manipulating models.[3] What the historical and contemporary cases show is that constructing new representations in science often starts with modeling, and this is followed by the quantitative formulations found in the laws and axioms of theories. Model-based reasoning practices are used in communicating novel results and instructing peers within the community in the new representations. Although these practices are ubiquitous and significant, they are, of course, not exhaustive of the practices that generate new representational structures.

7.4.1 Mental Modeling

Within contemporary cognitive science, the hypothesis of reasoning via "mental modeling" serves as a framework for a vast body of research that examines understanding and reasoning in various domains including reasoning about causality in physical systems (see, e.g., DeKleer and Brown 1983), the role of representations of domain knowledge in reasoning (see, e.g., Gentner and Stevens 1983), logical reasoning (see, e.g., Johnson-Laird 1983), discourse and narrative comprehension (see, e.g., Johnson-Laird 1983; Perrig and Kintsch 1985), and induction (see, e.g., Holland, Holyoak, Nisbett, and Thagard 1986). Additionally, there is considerable experimental protocol evidence collected by cognitive researchers that supports claims of mental modeling as significant in the problem-solving practices of contemporary scientists (see, e.g., Chi, Feltovich, and Glaser 1981; Clement 1989; Dunbar 1995, 1999).

Mental modeling, a semantic process thought to utilize perceptual mechanisms in inference, is hypothesized by many cognitive scientists to be a fundamental form of human reasoning. They speculate that the ability evolved as an efficient means of navigating the environment and solving problems in matters of significance to existence in the world. Thus the ability is hypothesized to exist in many creatures, with humans having the ability to create models from both perception and language and having extended its use to esoteric situations such as scientific reasoning. The interpretation of the evidence amassed in the investigations noted previously and numerous others is consistent with the contention that mental modeling is applied across a spectrum of problem-solving situations and in numerous domains, ranging from solving the problem of how to get a chair through a doorway to problems related to narrative and discourse comprehension to problems traditionally classified as falling within the province of deductive and inductive logic. The modeling process is hypothesized to be generative in reasoning because specific inferences can be traced directly to a model.

In the process of mental modeling, a structural or functional analog of a real-world or imaginary situation, event, or process is constructed. The mental model embodies a representation of the salient spatial and temporal relations among and the causal structures connecting the events and entities depicted and other information that is relevant to the problem-solving task. A mental model is not a mental image, although in some instances an image might be employed. It is an analog in that it preserves constraints inherent in what is represented. The representation is intended to be isomorphic to dimensions of the real-world system salient to the reasoning process. Thus, for example, in reasoning about a spring, the mental model need not capture the three-dimensionality of a spring if that is not taken to be relevant to the specific problem-solving task. The nature of the representation is such as to enable simulative behavior in which the models behave in accord with constraints that need not be stated explicitly. For example, for those tasks that are dynamic in nature, if the model captures the causal coherence of a system, it should, in principle, be possible to simulate the behaviors of the system. Thus, the inferential process is one of direct manipulation of the model. Cognitive science claims about the specific nature of the model-manipulation process are linked to the nature of the format of the representation. I will not go through numerous format issues here. It is sufficient to say that mental models are schematic in that they contain selective representations of aspects of the objects, situations, and processes and are thus flexible in reasoning and comprehension tasks.

Only a "minimalist" mental modeling hypothesis is needed in support of the contention that it provides a cognitive basis for taking seriously the modeling practices of scientists as generative in creating conceptual structures: in certain problem-solving tasks, humans reason by constructing an internal model of the situations, events, and processes that in dynamic cases can be manipulated through simulation. Information in various formats, including linguistic, formulaic, visual, auditory, and kinesthetic, can be used in its construction. In mundane cases, the reasoning performed is usually successful. One figures out how to get the chair through the door by means of mental simulation because the models and manipulative processes embody largely correct assumptions about everyday real-world events. In the case of science, where the situations are more removed from human sensory experience and the assumptions are more imbued with theory, there is less assurance that a reasoning process, even if carried out correctly, will yield success. In the evaluation process, a major criterion of success remains the goodness of the fit to the phenomena. The hypothesis is minimalist because it bypasses several issues about the nature of the format of the model and the processes of simulation that are in contention in cognitive science. The cognitive notion of reasoning via mental modeling fits well with the contemporary philosophical claims that scientists apply theories by reasoning with models (Cartwright 1983; Giere 1988; Magnani, Nersessian, and Thagard 1999; Morgan and Morrison 1999). The basic idea is that no matter how scientific theories may *in principle* be represented, models are the mental representations with which a scientist carries out much reasoning and by means of which she thinks and understands through the lens of a conceptual structure. The claim advanced in my research is that modeling, too, plays a central role in how new representations are constructed by scientists.

7.4.2 Model-Based Reasoning

Although in a modeling episode analogy, imagistic reasoning, and thought experimenting are often employed together, I will first discuss how they function separately and then consider what features they share. As with the preceding discussions, only a sketch of an analysis will be presented.

As employed in model-based reasoning, analogies serve as sources of constraints for constructing models. To engage in analogical modeling, one calls on knowledge of the generative principles and constraints for physical models in a source domain. These constraints and principles may be represented mentally and externally in different informational formats and knowledge structures that act as tacit assumptions employed in constructing and transforming models during problem solving. The cognitive literature agrees with the position that analogies employed in conceptual change are not merely guides to reasoning but are generative in the reasoning processes in which they are employed. For example, in investigations of analogies used as mental models of a domain, it has been demonstrated that inferences made in problem solving depend significantly on the specific analogy in terms of which the domain has been represented. One example is a study in which subjects constructed a mental model of electricity in terms of an analogy with either flowing water or teeming objects. Specific inferences, sometimes erroneous, in problem solutions could be traced directly to the specific analogy employed in representing the domain (Gentner and Gentner 1983). Here the inferential work in generating the problem solution clearly was done by using the analogical models.

A reasoning process I have called "generic abstraction" is key in analogical modeling in conceptual change. Conceptual innovation often requires recognition of potential similarities across, and integration of information from, disparate domains. In viewing a model generically, one takes it as representing features common to a class of phenomena. This way of viewing the model can, of course, take place only in the mind. In reasoning, for example, about a triangle, one often draws or imagines a concrete representation. However, to consider what it has in common with all triangles, one needs to imagine it as lacking specificity in the angles and the sides. That is, the reasoning context demands that the interpretation of the concrete polygon be as generic. It was through generic abstraction, for example, that Newton could reason about the commonalities among the motions of planets and of projectiles, which enabled him to formulate a unified mathematical representation of their motions. The analogical model, understood generically, represents what is common among the members of specific classes of physical systems viewed with respect to a problem context. Newton's inverse square law of gravitation abstracts what a projectile and a planet have in common in the context of determining motion. After Newton, the inverse square law model served as a generic model of action-at-a-distance forces for those who tried to bring all forces into the scope of Newtonian mechanics.

A variety of perceptual resources can be employed in modeling. Here I focus on the visual modality since it figures prominently in cases of conceptual change across the sciences. There is a vast cognitive science literature on mental imagery that provides evidence that humans can perform simulative imaginative combinations and transformations that mimic perceptual spatial transformation (Kosslyn 1980; Shepard and Cooper 1982). These simulations are hypothesized to take place using internalized constraints assimilated during perception and motor activity (Kosslyn 1994). Other research indicates that people use various kinds of knowledge of physical situations in imaginary simulations. For example, when objects are imagined as separated by a wall, the spatial transformations exhibit latency times consistent with having simulated moving around the wall rather than through it. There are significant differences between spatial transformations and transformations requiring causal and other knowledge contained in scientific theories. Although the research on imagery in problem solving is scant, recently cognitive scientists have undertaken several investigations examining the role of causal knowledge in mental simulation involving imagery; for example, experiments with problems employing gear rotation provide evidence of knowledge of causal constraints being utilized in imaginative reasoning (Hegarty 1992; Hegarty and Sims 1994; Hegarty and Steinhoff 1994; Schwartz and Black 1996).

The hypothesis that internal representations can be imagistic does not mean that they need to be picturelike. They can be highly schematic in nature. The claim is only that they are modal representations that employ perceptual and possibly motor mechanisms in processing. Thus the fact that some scientists such as Bohr claim not to experience mental pictures in reasoning is not pertinent to the issue of whether this kind of perceptual modeling is playing a role in the reasoning. External visual representations (including those made by gesturing and sketching) employed during a reasoning process are a significant dimension of cognitive activity in science and should be analyzed as part of the cognitive system. These representations can be interpreted as providing support for the processes of constructing and reasoning with a mental model. In model-based reasoning processes, they function as much more than the external memory aids they are customarily considered to be in cognitive science. They aid significantly in organizing cognitive activity during reasoning, such as fixing attention on the salient aspects of a model, enabling retrieval and storage of salient information, and exhibiting salient constraints, such as structural and causal constraints, in appropriate colocation. Further, they facilitate construction of shared mental models within a community and transportation of scientific models out of the local milieu of their construction.

Imagistic representations in physics participate in modeling phenomena in several ways, including providing abstracted and idealized representations of aspects of phenomena and embodying aspects of theoretical models. For example, early in Faraday's construction of an electromagnetic field concept, the visual model he constructed of the lines of force provided an idealized representation of the patterns of iron filings surrounding a magnet. However, cognitive-historical research substantiates the interpretation that later in his development of the field concept, the imagistic model functioned as the embodiment of a dynamical theoretical model of the transmission and interconversion of forces generally through stresses and strains in, and various motions of, the lines (Gooding 1981; Nersessian 1984b, 1985; Tweney 1985, 1992). But, as I have argued (Nersessian 1984b, 1992, in press-a, in press-b), the visual representation Maxwell presented of the idle wheel-vortex model of the electromagnetic aether was intended as an embodiment of an imaginary system. Its function was to capture a generic dynamical relational structure, not to provide a representation of the theoretical model of electromagnetic field actions in the aether.

As a form of model-based reasoning, thought experimenting can be construed as a specific form of simulative reasoning in mental modeling. In simulative reasoning, inferences are drawn by employing knowledge embedded in the constraints of a mental model to produce new states. Constructing a thought-experimental model requires understanding the salient constraints governing the kinds of entities or processes in the model and the possible causal, structural, and functional relations among them. Conducting a simulation can employ either tacit or explicit understanding of the constraints governing how those kinds of things behave and interact and how the relations can change. A simulation creates new states of a system being modeled, which in turn creates or makes evident new constraints. Changing the conditions of a model enables inferences about differences in the way that a system can behave. Various kinds of knowledge of physical situations are employed in imaginary simulations. Because the simulation complies with the same constraints of the physical system it represents, performing a simulation with a mental model enables inferences about real-world phenomena to be drawn. Note that understanding of the mathematical constraints governing a situation is one kind of knowledge that can be used in simulative reasoning by scientists.

In the case of scientific thought experiments implicated in conceptual change, the main historical traces are in the form of narrative reports, constructed after the problem has been solved. These reports have often provided a significant means of effecting conceptual change within a scientific community. Accounting for the generative role of this form of model-based reasoning begins with examining how these thought-experimental narratives support modeling processes and then making the hypothesis that the original experiment involves a similar form of model-based reasoning.

From a mental modeling perspective, the function of the narrative form of presentation of a thought experiment would be to guide the reader in constructing a mental model of the situation described by it and to make inferences through simulating the events and processes depicted in it. A thought-experimental model can be construed as a form of "discourse" model studied by cognitive scientists, for which they argue that the operations and inferences are performed not on propositions but on the constructed model (see, e.g., Johnson-Laird 1983, 1989; Perrig and Kintsch 1985; Morrow, Bower, and Greenspan 1989). Simulation is assisted in that the narrative delimits the specific transitions that govern what takes place. The thought-experimental simulation links the conceptual and experiential dimensions of human cognitive processing (see also Gooding 1992). Thus, the constructed situation inherits empirical force by being abstracted both from experiences and activities in the world and from knowledge, conceptualizations, and assumptions of it. In this way, the data that derive from thought experimenting have empirical consequences and at the same time pinpoint the locus of the needed conceptual reform.

Unlike a fictional narrative, however, the context of the scientific thought experiment makes it clear to the reader that the inferences made pertain to potential real-world situations. The narrative has already made significant abstractions, which aid in focusing attention on the salient dimensions of the model and in recognizing the situation as prototypical (generic). Thus, the experimental consequences are seen to go beyond the specific situation of the thought experiment. The thought-experimental narrative is presented in a polished form that works, which should make it an effective means of generating comparable mental models among the members of a community of scientists.

The processes of constructing the thought-experimental model in the original experiment would be the same as those involved in constructing any mental model in a reasoning process. In conducting the original thought experiment, a scientist would make use of inferencing mechanisms, existing representations, and scientific and general world knowledge to make constrained transformations from one possible physical state to the next. Thus, competence in constructing models and simulations should be a function of expertise. As with real-world experiments, some experimental revision and tweaking undoubtedly goes on in conducting the original and in the narrative construction, although accounts of this process are rarely presented by scientists.

Finally, in mundane cases, the reasoning performed via simulative mental modeling is usually successful because the models and manipulative processes embody largely correct constraints governing everyday real-world events. Think, for example, of how people often reason about how to get an awkward piece of furniture through a door. The problem is usually solved by mentally simulating turning over a geometrical structure approximating the configuration of the piece of furniture through various rotations. The task employs often implicit knowledge of constraints of such rotations and is often easier when the physical chair is in front of the reasoner, acting to support the structure in imagination. As was said earlier, in the case of science there is less assurance that a simulative reasoning process, even if carried out correctly, will lead to a successful outcome – or any outcome at all.

Having considered the model-based reasoning practices separately, we can now extract several key common ingredients. The problem-solving processes in which they are employed involve constructing models that are of the *same kind* with respect to salient dimensions of target phenomena. The models are intended as interpretations of target physical systems, processes, phenomena, or situations. The modeling practices make use of both highly specific domain knowledge and knowledge of abstract general principles. Further, they employ knowledge of how to make appropriate abstractions. Initial models are retrieved or constructed on the basis of potentially satisfying salient constraints of the target domain. Where the initial model does not produce a problem solution, modifications or new models are created to satisfy constraints drawn from an enhanced understanding of the target domain and from one or more source domains (the same as the target domain or different). These constraints can be supplied by means of linguistic, formulaic, and imagistic (all perceptual modalities) informational formats, including equations, texts, diagrams, pictures, maps, and physical models. In the modeling process, various forms of abstraction, such as limiting case, idealization, generalization, and generic modeling, are utilized, with generic modeling playing a highly significant role in the generation, abstraction, and integration of constraints. Evaluation and adaptation take place in light of structural, causal, and/or functional constraint satisfaction and enhanced understanding of the target problem that has been obtained through the modeling process. Simulation can be used to produce new states and to enable evaluation of behaviors, constraint satisfaction, and other factors. Clearly, scientists create erroneous models, so revision and evaluation are crucial components of model-based reasoning. In the evaluation process, a major criterion is goodness of fit to the constraints of the target phenomena, but success can also include such factors as enabling the generation of a viable mathematical representation that can push the science along while other details of representing the phenomena are still to be worked out, as

Newton did with the concept of gravitation and Maxwell with the concept of the electromagnetic field.

To explain why modeling practices figure centrally in conceptual change in science requires a fundamental revision of the understandings of concepts, conceptual structures, conceptual change, and reasoning customarily employed explicitly in philosophy and at least tacitly in the science studies fields more generally. The basic ingredients of that revision are to view a concept as providing a set of constraints for generating members of a class of models and a conceptual structure as an agglomeration of constraints. Concept formation and change is a process of generating new and changing existing constraints. Model-based reasoning promotes conceptual change because it is an effective means of abstracting, generating, integrating, and changing constraints. The domain-independent reasoning practices of analogy, visual modeling, and thought experimenting are prevalent in periods of radical conceptual change because they are highly effective means of making evident and abstracting constraints of existing representational systems and, in light of constraints provided by the target problem, effective means of integrating constraints from multiple representations such that truly novel representational structures result.

Finally, with respect to the role of model-based reasoning in facilitating conceptual change in learning, cognitive research shows that novice students do not have knowledge of the scientific constraints of physical domains and do not know how to view problem exemplars generically (how to abstract constraints). However, they do possess the basic cognitive capacities employed in model-based reasoning: to make analogies, to create mental simulations, and to perform idealization and generic abstraction. Potential developmental factors relating to the ability to employ these kinds of procedural knowledge explicitly are currently not well understood and are in need of investigation. It is clear that students do need explicit instruction in how to employ this procedural knowledge in scientific problem solving. Cognitive-historical research is playing a role in the development of successful model-based learning environments in K-12 physics education (Smith, Snir, and Grosslight 1992; Carey and Smith 1993; Wiser 1995; Jiminez Gomez and Fernendaz Duran 1998).

7.5 CONCLUSION

Problems relating to conceptual change were the focus of Thomas Kuhn's intellectual life. These are difficult but – I believe – not intractable problems.

What makes them especially difficult is that they lie at the interface of history, philosophy, and psychology, and thus the resources of multiple disciplines are required to address them. *Structure* showed the potential fruitfulness of conducting such multidisciplinary research on these problems, and the cognitive-historical method is one attempt to do so. Cognitive-historical analysis produces accounts of science that offer theories of the nature of the reasoning and representational practices employed by scientists, and of why they are effective, that can be subjected to empirical scrutiny. The outline presented here provides an indication of how specific cognitive-historical analyses both further and challenge Kuhn's insights into concept representation, learning, and concept formation.

Notes

I thank Susan Carey for allowing me to interview her about the discussions she had with Thomas Kuhn about cognitive development and Hanne Andersen for providing me with copies of her interviews with him. I appreciate the hospitality and support of the Dibner Institute for the History of Science and Technology, where I was a Senior Fellow in 1999–2000, during which time I conducted research at the Kuhn archives at MIT. Research in this essay was supported by Grant SBE9810913 from the National Science Foundation.

1. I emphasize "published" because in conversation with me and in transcripts of interviews conducted by Hanne Andersen, in March 1994 and October 1995, Kuhn did mention that cognitive psychological research into child development was figuring into the account he was writing in the follow-on book to *Structure* that he was still working on at the time of his death. He gave permission for the free use of the interviews after his death. Although his comments are sketchy, they do provide some pertinent remarks that will be discussed later in this essay.

2. Just what literature in cognitive science Kuhn was aware of and how deeply he had studied any of it is unknown. He did read the review of some of this literature presented in the extended Tech Report (Nersessian 1995a) and commented that he was "altogether sympathetic to [my] viewpoint" (personal correspondence, March 23, 1993). Further, he requested from me specific references in neuroscience, and we discussed his interest in the child development research of Susan Carey at MIT and others investigating the problem of whether one can determine what is innate ("hard-wired") through research into such developmental phenomena as when babies exhibit recognition of object permanence. The only recorded discussions I am aware of are the taped interviews with Hanne Andersen (see note 1). In these he mentions the neural net literature and the developmental literature as pertinent to his "perceptual space" notion and the need for a clear distinction between similar and dissimilar. He states his conviction that the Roschian "graded category structure" will fall out of the neurological case, if it can be made. He also mentions that at least a chapter of the follow-on book

would discuss the child developmental investigations. The book was incomplete at the time of his death and currently is being edited by John Haugeland and James Conant of the University of Chicago.

3. Nickles discusses the relations between the cognitive science notion of case-based reasoning and Kuhn's notion of problem exemplars (Nickles 1998). From a cognitive science perspective, the problem-solving success in case-based reasoning is linked to the *authentic* nature of the exemplary cases employed. A major problem with case-based reasoning is that cases are too specific and problems need to be very close to transfer. As a problem-solving method, it is inflexible in adaptation. In model-based reasoning, more is left unspecified, providing greater adaptability in creative problem solving.

References

Andersen, H., X. Chen, and P. Barker. 1996. "Kuhn's Mature Philosophy of Science and Cognitive Psychology." *Philosophical Psychology* 9: 347–63.

Andersen, H., and N. J. Nersessian. 2000. "Nomic Concepts, Frames, and Conceptual Change." *Philosophy of Science* 67 (special Proceedings issue) S224–41.

Armstrong, S. L., L. Gleitman, and H. Gleitman. 1983. "What Some Concepts Might Not Be." *Cognition* 13: 263–308.

Barsalou, L. 1987. "The Instability of Graded Structure: Implications for the Nature of Concepts." In: U. Neisser, ed. *Concepts and Conceptual Development: Ecological and Intellectual Factors in Categorization.* Cambridge: Cambridge University Press, pp. 101–40.

1992. "Frames, Concepts, and Conceptual Fields." In: A. Lehrer and E. Kittay, eds. *Frames, Fields, and Contrasts: New Essays in Semantical and Lexical Organization.* Hillsdale, NJ: Lawrence Erlbaum, pp. 325–40.

Brown, J. S., A. Collins, and P. Duguid. 1989. "Situated Cognition and the Culture of Learning." *Educational Researcher* 18: 32–42.

Carey, S. 1985. *Conceptual Change in Childhood.* Cambridge, MA: MIT Press.

1991. "Knowledge Acquisition: Enrichment or Conceptual Change?" In: S. Carey and R. Gelman, eds. *The Epigenesis of Mind: Essays on Biology and Cognition.* Hillsdale, NJ: Lawrence Erlbaum, pp. 257–91.

Carey, S., and Xu Fei. 2001. "Infants' Knowledge of Objects: Beyond Files and Object Tracking." *Cognition* 80: 179–213.

Carey, S., and C. Smith. 1993. "On Understanding the Nature of Scientific Knowledge." *Educational Psychologist* 28: 235–51.

Cartwright, N. 1983. *How the Laws of Physics Lie.* Oxford: Clarendon Press.

Champagne, A. B., L. E. Klopfer, and R. F. Gunstone. 1982. "Cognitive Research and the Design of Science Instruction." *Educational Psychologist* 17: 31–53.

Chen, X., H. Andersen, and P. Barker. 1998. "Kuhn's Theory of Scientific Revolutions and Cognitive Psychology." *Philosophical Psychology* 11: 5–28.

Chi, M. T. H. 1992. "Conceptual Change Within and Across Ontological Categories; Examples from Learning and Discovery in Science." In: R. Giere, ed. *Cognitive Models of Science*. Minneapolis: University of Minnesota Press, pp. 129–86.

Chi, M. T. H., P. J. Feltovich, and R. Glaser. 1981. "Categorization and Representation of Physics Problems by Experts and Novices." *Cognitive Science* 5: 121–52.

Clement, J. 1982. "Students' Preconceptions in Elementary Mechanics." *AJP* 50: 66–71.

1983. "A Conceptual Model Discussed by Galileo and Used Intuitively by Physics Students." In: D. Gentner and A. Stevens, ed. In *Mental Models*, Hillsdale, NJ: Lawrence Erlbaum, pp. 325–40.

1989. "Learning Via Model Construction and Criticism." In: G. Glover, R. Ronning and C. Reynolds, eds. *Handbook of Creativity: Assessment, Theory, and Research*. New York: Plenum, pp. 341–81.

Collins, A., J. S. Brown, and P. Duguid. 1989. "Cognitive Apprenticeship: Teaching the Crafts of Reading, Writing, and Mathematics." In: L. B. Resnick, ed. *Knowing, Learning, and Instruction*. Hillsdale: NJ: Lawrence Erlbaum, pp. 453–94.

Conant, James, and John Haugeland, eds. 2000. *The Road Since Structure: Thomas S. Kuhn*. Chicago: University of Chicago Press.

Darden, L. 1980. "Theory Construction in Genetics." In: T. Nickles, ed. *Scientific Discovery: Case Studies*. Dordrecht: Reidel, pp. 151–70.

1991. *Theory Change in Science: Strategies from Mendelian Genetics*. New York: Oxford University.

DeKleer, J., and J. S. Brown. 1983. "Assumptions and Ambiguities in Mechanistic Mental Models." In: D. G. A. Stevens, ed. *Mental Models*. Hillsdale, NJ: Lawrence Erlbaum, pp. 155–90.

Driver, R., and J. Easley. 1978. "Pupils and Paradigms: A Review of Literature Related to Concept Development in Adolescent Science Students." *Studies in Science Education* 5: 61–84.

Dunbar, K. 1995. "How Scientists Really Reason: Scientific Reasoning in Real-World Laboratories." In: R. J. Sternberg and J. E. Davidson, eds. *The Nature of Insight*. Cambridge, MA: MIT Press, pp. 365–95.

1999. "How Scientists Build Models: In Vivo Science as a Window on the Scientific Mind." In: L. Magnani, N. J. Nersessian and P. Thagard, eds. *Model-Based Reasoning in Scientific Discovery*. New York: Kluwer Academic/Plenum, pp. 85–99.

Gentner, D., and D. Gentner. 1983. "Flowing Waters and Teeming Crowds: Mental Models of Electricity." In Gentner and Stevens, eds. (1983), pp. 99–129.

Gentner, D., and A. B. Markman. 1997. "Structure Mapping in Analogy and Similarity." *American Psychologist* 52(1): 45–56.

Gentner, D., and A. L. Stevens. 1983. *Mental Models*. Hillsdale, NJ: Lawrence Erlbaum.

Giere, R. N. 1988. *Explaining Science: A Cognitive Approach*. Chicago: University of Chicago Press.

———. ed., 1992. *Cognitive Models of Science. Minnesota Studies in the Philosophy of Science*, vol. *15*. Minneapolis: University of Minnesota Press.

———. 1994. "The Cognitive Structure of Scientific Theories." *Philosophy of Science* 61: 276–96.

Gooding, D. 1981. "Final Steps to the Field Theory: Faraday's Study of Electromagnetic Phenomena, 1845–1850." *Historical Studies in the Physical Sciences* 11: 231–75.

———. 1990. *Experiment and the Making of Meaning: Human Agency in Scientific Observation and Experiment*. Dordrecht: Kluwer.

Gooding, D. 1992. "The Procedural Turn: Or Why Did Faraday's Thought Experiments Work?" In Giere (1992), pp. 45–76.

Gopnik, Alison, and Andrew N. Meltzoff. 1997. *Words, Thought, and Theories*. Cambridge, MA: MIT Press.

Griesemer, J. R. 1991a. "Material Models in Biology." In: *PSA 1990*. East Lansing, MI: PSA.

———. 1991b. "Must Scientific Diagrams Be Eliminable? The Case of Path Analysis." *Biology and Philosophy* 6: 177–202.

Griesemer, J. R., and W. Wimsatt. 1989. "Picturing Weismannism: A Case Study of Conceptual Evolution." In: M. Ruse, ed. *What the Philosophy of Biology Is: Essays for David Hull*. Dordrecht: Kluwer, pp. 75–137.

Halloun, I. A., and D. Hestenes. 1985. "The Initial Knowledge State of College Physics Students." *AJP* 53: 1043–55.

Hegarty, M. 1992. "Mental Animation: Inferring Motion from Static Diagrams of Mechanical Systems." *Journal of Experimental Psychology: Learning, Memory, and Cognition* 18(5): 1084–1102.

Hegarty, M., and V. K. Sims. 1994. "Individual Differences in Mental Animation from Text and Diagrams." *Journal of Memory and Language* 32: 411–30.

Hegarty, M., and K. Steinhoff. 1994. "Use of Diagrams as External Memory in a Mechanical Reasoning Task." Paper presented at the annual meeting of the American Educational Research Association, New Orleans.

Heider, E. Rosch. 1972. "Universals in Color Naming and Memory." *Journal of Experimental Psychology* 93: 10–20. (See also Rosch, E.)

Holland, J. H., K. J. Holyoak, R. E. Nisbett, and P. R. Thagard. 1986. *Induction: Processes of Inference, Learning, and Discovery*. Cambridge, MA: MIT Press.

Holmes, F. L. 1981. "The Fine Structure of Scientific Creativity." *History of Science* 19: 60–70.

———. 1985. *Lavoisier and the Chemistry of Life: An Exploration of Scientific Creativity*. Madison: University of Wisconsin Press.

Hoyningen-Huene, P. 1993. *Reconstructing Scientific Revolutions: Thomas S. Kuhn's Philosophy of Science*. Chicago: University of Chicago Press.

Jiminez Gomez, E., and E. Fernendaz Duran. 1998. "Didactic Problems in the

Concept of Electrical Potential Difference and an Analysis of Philogenesis." *Science and Education* 7: 129–41.

Johnson-Laird, P. N. 1983. *Mental Models*. Cambridge, MA: MIT Press.

1989. "Mental Models." In: M. Posner, ed. *Foundations of Cognitive Science*. Cambridge, MA: MIT Press, pp. 469–500.

Keil, F. C. 1991. "The Emergence of Theoretical Beliefs as Constraints on Concepts." In: S. Carey and R. Gelman, eds. *The Epigenesis of Mind: Essays on Biology and Cognition*. Hillsdale, NJ: Lawrence Erlbaum, pp. 237–56.

Kosslyn, S. M. 1980. *Image and Mind*. Cambridge, MA: Harvard University Press.

1994. *Image and Brain*. Cambridge MA: MIT Press.

Kuhn, T. S. 1970. *The Structure of Scientific Revolutions*, 2nd ed. Chicago: University of Chicago Press.

Kuhn, T. S. 1977. *The Essential Tension: Selected Studies in Scientific Tradition and Change*. Chicago: University of Chicago Press.

1979. "Metaphor in Science." In: A. Ortony, ed. *Metaphor and Thought*. Cambridge: Cambridge University Press, pp. 409–19.

1990. "The Road Since *Structure*. *PSA 1990* 2: 3–13.

1992. "The Trouble with the Historical Philosophy of Science." Robert and Maurine Rothschild Lecture, Harvard University.

1993. "Afterwords." In: P. Horwich, ed. *World Changes: Thomas Kuhn and the Nature of Science*. Cambridge, MA: MIT Press, pp. 311–41.

Latour, B. 1986. "Visualisation and Cognition: Thinking with Eyes and Hands." *Knowledge and Society* 6: 1–40.

Latour, B., and S. Woolgar. 1986. *Laboratory Life: The Construction of Scientific Facts*. Princeton: Princeton University Press.

Lynch, M., and S. Woolgar, eds. 1990. *Representation in Scientific Practice*. Cambridge, MA: MIT Press.

Magnani, L., N. J. Nersessian, and P. Thagard, eds. 1999. *Model-Based Reasoning in Scientific Discovery*. New York: Kluwer Academic/Plenum.

McCloskey, M. 1983. "Naive Theories of Motion." In: D. Gentner and A. L. Stevens, eds. *Mental Models*. Hillsdale, NJ: Lawrence Erlbaum, pp. 229–33.

McDermott, L. C. 1984. "Research on Conceptual Understanding in Mechanics." *Physics Today* July: 24.

Medin, D. L. 1989. "Concepts and Conceptual Structure." *American Psychologist* 44: 1469–81.

Morgan, M. S., and M. Morrison, eds. 1999. *Models as Mediators*. Cambridge: Cambridge University Press.

Morrow, D. G., G. H. Bower, and S. L. Greenspan. 1989. "Updating Situation Models During Narrative Comprehension." *Journal of Memory and Language* 28: 292–312.

Nersessian, N. J. 1984a. "Aether/Or: The Creation of Scientific Concepts." *Studies in the History and Philosophy of Science* 15: 175–212.

1984b. *Faraday to Einstein: Constructing Meaning in Scientific Theories.* Dordrecht: Martinus Nijhoff/Kluwer Academic.

1985. "Faraday's Field Concept." In: D. C. Gooding and F. A. J. L. James, eds. *Faraday Rediscovered: Essays on the Life and Work of Michael Faraday.* London: Macmillan, pp. 377–406.

1988. "Reasoning from Imagery and Analogy in Scientific Concept Formation." In: A. Fine and J. Leplin, eds. *PSA 1988.* East Lansing, MI: Philosophy of Science Association, pp. 41–8.

1989. "Conceptual Change in Science and in Science Education." *Synthese* 80 (Special Issue: Philosophy of Science and Science Education): 163–84.

1992a. "Constructing and Instructing: The Role of 'Abstraction Techniques' in Developing and Teaching Scientific Theories." In: R. Duschl and R. Hamilton, eds. *Philosophy of Science, Cognitive Science, and Educational Theory and Practice.* Albany: SUNY Press, pp. 48–68.

1992b. "How Do Scientists Think? Capturing the Dynamics of Conceptual Change in Science." In: Giere (1992), pp. 3–44.

1992c. "In the Theoretician's Laboratory: Thought Experimenting as Mental Modeling." In: D. Hull, M. Forbes, and K. Okruhlik, eds. PSA 1992. East Lansing, MI: PSA, pp. 291–301.

1995a. "The Cognitive Sciences and the History of Science." Paper presented at the Conference on Critical Problems and Research Frontiers in History of Science and Technology, Madison, WI.

1995b. "Opening the Black Box: Cognitive Science and the History of Science. *Osiris* 10 (*Constructing Knowledge in the History of Science*, A. Thackray, ed.): 194–211.

1995c. Should Physicists Preach What They Practice? Constructive Modeling in Doing and Learning Physics. "*Science & Education* 4: 203–26.

in press-a. "Abstraction Via Generic Modeling in Concept Formation in Science." *Mind and Society.* In: M. R. Jones and N. Cartwright, eds.

in press-b. "Maxwell and the 'Method of Physical Analogy.'" In: D. Malament, ed. *Essays in the History and Philosophy of Science and Mathematics to Honor Howard Stein on his 70th Birthday.* LaSalle, IL: Open Court.

Nersessian, N. J., and L. B. Resnick. 1989. "Comparing Historical and Intuitive Explanations of Motion: Does 'Naive Physics' Have a Structure?" Paper presented at the annual meeting of the Cognitive Science Society, Ann Arbor, MI.

Nickles, T. 1998. "Kuhn, Historical Philosophy of Science, and Case-Based Reasoning." *Configurations* 6: 51–86.

Perrig, W., and W. Kintsch. 1985. "Propositional and Situational Representations of Text." *Journal of Memory and Language* 24: 503–18.

Pylyshyn, Z. 2001. Visual indexes, preconceptual objects and situated vision. *Cognition* 80: 127–58.

Rosch, E. 1987. "Wittgenstein and Categorization Research in Cognitive Psychology." In: M. Chapman and R. A. Dixon, eds. *Meaning and the Growth of Understanding: Wittgenstein's Significance for Developmental Psychology.* Berlin: Springer, pp. 151–66. (See also Heider, E.)

Rosch, E., and C. B. Mervis. 1975. "Family Resemblance Studies in the Internal Structure of Categories." *Cognitive Psychology* 7: 573–605.

Rudwick, M. J. S. 1976. "The Emergence of a Visual Language for Geological Science." *History of Science* 14: 149–95.

Schwartz, D. L., and J. B. Black. 1996. "Analog Imagery in Mental Model Reasoning: Depictive Models." *Cognitive Psychology* 30: 154–219.

Shelley, C. 1996. "Visual Abductive Reasoning in Archeology." *Philosophy of Science* 63: 278–301.

Shepard, R. N., and L. A. Cooper. 1982. *Mental Images and Their Transformations.* Cambridge, MA: MIT Press.

Smith, C., J. Snir, and L. Grosslight. 1992. "Using Conceptual Models to Facilitate Conceptual Change: The Case of Weight–Density Differentiation." *Cognition and Instruction* 9: 221–83.

Smith, E. E., and D. L. Medin. 1981. *Concepts and Categories.* Cambridge, MA: Harvard University Press.

Spelke, E. S., A. Phillips, and A. L. Woodward. 1995. "Spatio-Temporal Continuity, Smoothness of Motion and Object Identity in Infancy." *British Journal of Developmental Psychology* 13: 113–42.

Thagard, P. 1991. *"Conceptual Revolutions.* Princeton: Princeton University Press.

Trumpler, M. 1997. Converging Images: Techniques of Intervention and Forms of Representation of Sodium-Channel Proteins in Nerve Cell Membranes. *Journal of the History of Biology* 20: 55–89.

Tweney, R. D. 1985. "Faraday's Discovery of Induction: A Cognitive Approach." In: D. Gooding and F. A. J. L. James, eds. *Faraday Rediscovered.* New York: Stockton Press, pp. 189–201.

———. 1987. "What Is Scientific Thinking?" Unpublished manuscript.

———. 1992. "Stopping Time: Faraday and the Scientific Creation of Perceptual Order." *Physis* 29: 149–64.

Viennot, L. 1979. "Spontaneous Reasoning in Elementary Dynamics." *European Journal of Science Education* 1: 205–21.

Wiggins, D. 1980. *Sameness and Substance.* Cambridge, MA: Harvard University Press.

Wiser, M. 1995. "Use of History of Science to Understand and Remedy Students' Misconceptions about Time and Temperature." In: D. Perkins, ed. *Software Goes to School.* New York: Oxford University Press, pp. 23–38.

Wittgenstein, L. 1968. *Philosophical Investigations.* Translated by G. E. M. Anscombe. New York: Macmillan.

Woods, D. D. 1995. "Towards a Theoretical Base for Representation Design in the Computer Medium: Ecological Perception and Aiding Human Cognition." In: J. Flach, P. Hanosok, J. Caird, and K. Vicente, eds., *Global Perspectives on the Ecology of Human–Machine Systems.* Hillsdale, NJ: Lawrence Erlbaum, pp. 157–88.

Kuhn on Concepts and Categorization

PETER BARKER, XIANG CHEN,
AND HANNE ANDERSEN

8.1 INTRODUCTION

In Kuhn's account of the history of science, the nature of concepts and conceptual change looms large. Kuhn found little to admire in contemporary philosophical accounts of science, and he also found himself at odds with the philosophical community on the theory of concepts. Consequently, in the course of developing his philosophical account of science, he was also obliged to articulate a theory of concepts. One of the central ideas of his account, incommensurability, originated as a thesis about concepts. As his account matured, Kuhn came to formulate incommensurability as a thesis about taxonomies. The issue of categorization therefore emerges immediately from his account, with his theory of concepts providing the basis for the conceptual structures that he calls "kind hierarchies."

Kuhn's theory is not without precedent. It builds on the work of Wittgenstein and also reflects Kuhn's early and profound exposure to Kant.[1] In a revealing interview near the end of his life Kuhn said simply, "I am a Kantian with movable categories" (Baltas, Gavroglu, and Kindi 2000, p. 264). Provided that the categories are understood as Wittgensteinean family resemblance concepts, this is a valuable summary. As his philosophy of science developed, Kuhn focused increasingly on the nature of scientific concepts, and his account of concepts gradually became the foundation from which he sought to vindicate his earlier claims on the development and change of scientific knowledge.

Another source for Kuhn's theory of concepts was his early reflection on science teaching, which he came to believe created and sustained the consensus within the scientific community (Kuhn 1959, 1961; Andersen 2000a). Kuhn decided that science teaching is built almost exclusively on exemplary problems and concrete solutions rather than on abstract descriptions and definitions. The term "paradigm" entered Kuhn's work to denote these standard scientific problems.[2]

Within a given discipline, what the research problems "have in common is not that they satisfy some explicit or even some fully discoverable set of rules and assumptions that gives the tradition its character and hold upon the scientific mind. Instead, they may relate by resemblance and by modelling to one or another part of the scientific corpus which the community in question already recognized as among its established achievements" (Kuhn 1962/1970a, pp. 45ff). The central point of Kuhn's argument was therefore that the kind of teaching found within the natural sciences confers the ability to recognize *resemblances* between novel problems and problems that have been solved before. But on Kuhn's view, the recognition of resemblances was not limited to learning science. Soon he began to argue that language acquisition in general was based on learning to recognize resemblances. In his work after *Structure* Kuhn advanced an account of concepts based on similarity rather than rules (Kuhn 1970c, 1974, 1979), an account that developed gradually over the last three decades of his life (Andersen 2001a).

In this essay, we describe the development of Kuhn's theory of concepts and categorization. We also consider the extent to which Kuhn's work on concepts, and related issues in his philosophy of science, received independent support from recent research in psychology and cognitive science. In Section 8.2 we describe how Kuhn developed his theory by building on Wittgenstein's idea of family resemblance but extending his account, especially in offering a solution to the problem of the "open texture." Next, we describe the way in which the accounts of Wittgenstein and Kuhn were independently supported by the work of psychologist Eleanor Rosch and her successors beginning in the 1970s. We then turn to two outstanding problems: first, whether incommensurability is a real phenomenon and, second, whether incommensurable conceptual structures are rationally comparable. In Section 8.3 we propose preliminary answers to these questions based on the theory of prototypes developed in cognitive psychology during the 1980s, although some limitations of the account are noted. In Section 8.4 we consider the frame model of concepts developed during the 1990s, which not only embodies all the features of Kuhn's original theory, but also solves the outstanding problems of the prototype account and naturally accommodates Kuhn's mature work on categorization and incommensurability. We present a detailed example from the history of taxonomy. Finally, in Section 8.5, we review Kuhn's original model of scientific change in the light of our results from contemporary theories of concepts and indicate various new directions.

8.2 KUHN'S THEORY OF CONCEPTS

Modern English-language philosophy continues a long tradition in accepting the view that concepts can be defined by a set of characteristics that
are individually necessary and jointly sufficient for an object to be an instance of the defined concept. This view was attacked by Wittgenstein in
his *Philosophical Investigations*, published posthumously in 1953. Examining
the concept "game," Wittgenstein showed that it might be impossible to
find such a definition. Instead of a single common feature or features shared
by all instances, there were only features common to subsets of instances,
with many different features forming a network that ultimately linked them
all, like the eyes, nose, and hair color linking different members of a single
human family. Wittgenstein pointed out that instances of a concept might
bear no more than a family resemblance to each other, with a complicated
network of overlapping and crisscrossing relations linking them to other
instances (Wittgenstein 1953, §66; cf. Kuhn 1962/1996, p. 45).

Kuhn first adopted Wittgenstein's notion of family resemblance in *The
Structure of Scientific Revolutions* to argue that research problems are related
by resemblance. But gradually Kuhn extended his argument to cover concepts in general, and in developing his account of concepts, he gradually
refined the treatment of family resemblance beyond the notion he had
adopted from Wittgenstein.[3]

8.2.1 Concepts and Family Resemblance

According to Kuhn, teaching and learning depend on examining similar or
dissimilar features of some range of objects (Kuhn 1974, 1979). However,
for the concepts involved in scientific research, this process of concept
acquisition is "excessively complex" (Kuhn 1974, p. 309). To present the
main features of his account, Kuhn developed an example of the transmission of a set of simpler concepts: a child learning to distinguish waterfowl
(Kuhn 1974).[4]

In this example, an adult familiar with the classification of waterfowl
guides a child ("Johnny") through a series of ostensive acts until he learns to
distinguish ducks, geese, and swans. Johnny is shown various instances of all
three concepts, being told for each instance whether it is a duck, a goose, or a
swan. He is also encouraged to try to point out instances of the concepts. At
the beginning of this process he will make mistakes – for example, mistaking
a goose for a swan. In such cases, Johnny will be told the correct concept to
apply to the instance pointed out. In other cases, he ascribes the instance

pointed out to the correct concept and receives praise. After a number of these encounters Johnny has, in principle, acquired the ability to identify ducks, geese, and swans as competently as the person instructing him.

During the ostensive teaching, Johnny has encountered a series of instances of the various waterfowl, and these instances have been examined in order to find features with respect to which they are similar or dissimilar. In this learning process, "the primary pedagogic tool is ostension. Phrases like 'all swans are white' may play a role, but they need not" (Kuhn 1974, p. 309). In this way, a conceptual structure is established by grouping objects into similarity classes corresponding to the extension of concepts. An important feature of Kuhn's account is that this grouping can be achieved solely by learning to identify similarities between objects within a particular similarity class and dissimilarities to objects ascribed to other similarity classes. Hence, for simple categories like "duck," "goose," and "swan," categories may be transmitted from one generation to the next solely by extracting similarity relations from the exemplars on exhibit.

Although everyday experience tells us that ostensive teaching is effective, it is important to understand its limits. At the end of the learning process, Johnny and his teacher agree on the classification of available instances of waterfowl. This does not require that they possess identical conceptual structures. Each kind of waterfowl exhibits a range of features that may be used to judge it similar or dissimilar to other types. Obvious features are beak shape, leg length, neck length, color, and body size. For ostensive teaching to succeed, it is not necessary that Johnny be taught to recognize exactly the same features that his teacher uses to distinguish ducks, geese, and swans. All that is needed is that Johnny arrive at some set of features that permits him to group the waterfowl to the satisfaction of his teacher. Following a family resemblance account of concepts, it is easy to show that Johnny and his teacher may actually employ disjoint sets of features to classify waterfowl, yet agree in the classification of every instance they meet (Andersen, Barker, and Chen 1996, Figure 3, p. 356). Ostensive teaching does not guarantee that all members of a community share the same conceptual structure. It only guarantees that they agree within the limits of the instances examined up to the present.

Kuhn claimed that, in principle, advanced scientific concepts are acquired by the same similarity-based process as everyday concepts; "[T]he same technique, if in a less pure form, is essential to the more abstract sciences as well" (Kuhn 1974, p. 313).[5] Where Johnny was presented with various waterfowl and told whether they were ducks, geese, or swans, science students are presented with a problem situation after first being shown the appropriate expression of a law sketch through which the problem can be solved. Next, the students are presented with further problem situations and must try to assign the appropriate expression for themselves. In this process, the students examine the problems in order to find features with respect to which they are similar or dissimilar. For example, the law sketch $F = m\mathbf{a}$, Newton's second law of motion, applies to the problem of free fall in the form $mg = md^2s/dt^2$, to the problem of the simple pendulum in the form $mg \cdot sin\theta = -md^2s/dt^2$, and to more complex situations in still other forms. In learning scientific concepts, the student is presented with a variety of problems that can be described by various forms of a law sketch. In this process, the student discovers a way to see each problem as *like* a previously encountered problem. Recognizing the resemblance, the student "can interrelate symbols and attach them to nature in the ways that have proved effective before. The law sketch, say $f = ma$, has functioned as a tool, informing the student what similarities to look for, signalling the gestalt in which the situation is to be seen" (Kuhn 1970a, p. 189). A conceptual structure is established by grouping problem situations into similarity classes corresponding to the various expressions of the law sketch. As Kuhn put it: "The resultant ability to see a variety of situations as like each other . . . is, I think, the main thing a student acquires by doing exemplary problems. . . ." (Kuhn 1970a, p. 189).

8.2.2 The Importance of Dissimilarity

Since we can always find *some* resemblance between instances of one concept and those of another, the objection is often raised that a family resemblance account does not suffice to limit the extension of concepts (Andersen 2000b, 2001b). Kuhn recognized this problem (Kuhn 1974, p. 307; similarly Kuhn 1970a, p. 200) but suggested that it could be solved by including among a concept's constitutive relations not only similarities between members of the same class, but also dissimilarities to members of other classes: "[N]ote that what I have here been calling a similarity relation depends not only on likeness to other members of the same class but also on difference from the members of other classes. . . . Failure to notice that the similarity relation appropriate to determination of membership in natural families must be triadic rather than diadic has, I believe, created some unnecessary philosophical problems. . . ." (Kuhn 1976, p. 199).

The dissimilarity relation that Kuhn introduced here is not a relation between the instances of arbitrary pairs of concepts but a relation between instances of concepts in a *contrast set*, that is, a set of concepts that are all subordinates to the same superordinate concept (cf. Kuhn 1983a, p. 682; 1991, p. 4; 1993, pp. 317ff). For example, the concepts "duck," "goose," and "swan" are all subordinates to the superordinate concept "waterfowl."[6] Since they are all subordinates to the same superordinate concept, such contrasting concepts together form a family resemblance concept at the superordinate level, and their instances may therefore be assumed to be more similar to each other than to instances of concepts outside the contrast set. For example, ducks, geese, and swans together form a family resemblance category of waterfowl whose members resemble each other more than they resemble members of contrasting categories such as songbirds and game birds. Kuhn's emphasis on the importance of dissimilarity relations therefore serves to avoid the problem that instances of different but highly similar categories might be mistaken for each other and leads to the view that contrasting concepts must always be learned together: "Establishing the referent of a natural-kind term requires exposure not only to varied members of that kind but also to members of others – to individuals, that is, to which the term might otherwise have been mistakenly applied" (Kuhn 1979, p. 413).

Obviously, this analysis can be extended to new superordinate and subordinate levels. Just as the superordinate concept "waterfowl" can be divided into the contrasting subordinates "duck," "goose" and "swan," each of the subordinate concepts can be further subdivided into the particular species of ducks or geese or swans. The hierarchical conceptual structure that arises is one in which a general category decomposes into more specific categories that may again decompose into yet more specific categories – in other words, a taxonomy. Drawing on the dissimilarity between members of contrasting concepts, family resemblance therefore becomes tied to taxonomies. Kuhn never stated this argument explicitly, but only noted that "[A] fuller discussion of resemblance between members of a natural family would have to allow for hierarchies of natural families with resemblance relations between families at the higher level" (Kuhn 1970b, p. 17, fn. 1).

However, Kuhn also realized that the in-principle problem that anything is similar to anything else in some respect would be solved by the use of contrast sets only if the dissimilarity relations between objects were of a specific kind. Kuhn admitted that if the chains of similarity relations developed gradually and continuously, it would indeed be necessary to define where the extension of one concept ended and the extension of the contrasting concept began: "Only if the families we named overlapped and merged gradually into one another – only, that is, if there were no *natural* families – would our success in identifying and naming provide evidence for a set of common characteristics corresponding to each of the class names we employ" (Kuhn 1962/1996, p. 45). He therefore argued that the possibility of classifying objects into family resemblance classes depends on an "empty perceptual space between the families to be discriminated" (Kuhn 1970a, p. 197, fn. 14; similarly Kuhn et al. 1974, pp. 508ff.).[7]

By the early 1970s, Kuhn had established the foundations of an account of concepts that shared many features of Wittgenstein's family resemblance view, and extended it into new areas with the explicit discussion of dissimilarity relations and empty perceptual space. These ideas might well have languished in the obscurity to which Wittgenstein's proposals had been consigned by analytic philosophers, but for the unexpected appearance of new support for family resemblance theories among psychologists.

8.2.3 The Empirical Vindication of the Family Resemblance Account

During the 1970s, psychologists almost universally rejected the traditional view that concepts can be defined by necessary and sufficient conditions on the basis of research begun by Eleanor Rosch and her collaborators (Rosch 1973a, 1973b; Rosch and Mervis 1975). The single strongest piece of evidence against the traditional view is the demonstration of graded structure as a universal feature of human concepts.

A consequence of the traditional view is that it makes all instances of a concept equal. All objects falling under a concept do so in virtue of sharing the same list of features, and therefore all are equal as instances of the concept. Consequently, it makes no sense to suggest that a particular object is a better example of the concept than another. However, empirical research shows quite the opposite. Human beings actually grade instances as good or bad examples of the concept. This variation in the instances' "goodness of example" is called the concept's "graded structure."

In experiments using human subjects as diverse as Stone Age New Guinea tribespeople and North American university students, Rosch and her collaborators demonstrated that all concepts show graded structures (Rosch 1972 [writing as E. R. Heider], 1973a, 1973b; Rosch and Mervis 1975). Her initial data demonstrated graded structure in everyday perceptual categories for colors and geometrical shapes, and semantic categories for natural objects like birds, animals, trees and fish, and artifacts like furniture, clothing, and tools. Psychologists all over the world replicated these results for natural categories, including facial expressions (Ekman, Friesen, and Ellsworth 1972), locatives (Erreich and Valian 1979), psychiatric classifications (Cantor, Smith, French, and Mezzich 1980), polygons

(Williams, Freyer, and Aiken 1977), and numbers (Armstrong, Gleitman, and Gleitman 1983) and artificial categories consisting of dot patterns (Homa and Vosburgh 1976) or imaginary objects (Mervis and Pani 1980), ad hoc categories (Barsalou 1982), and goal-derived categories (Barsalou 1991). The existence of these graded structures showed the untenability of the earlier view that all objects falling under a concept are equally good instances of the concept, and hence the untenability of the traditional view that concepts can be defined through necessary and sufficient conditions. As these results became known, the psychological community accepted graded structure as a universal feature of real human concepts, an event sometimes referred to as the "Roschian revolution."

Rosch herself recognized the connection between the new results in psychology and Wittgenstein's family resemblance account of concepts. At the same time, Kuhn was developing his own version of the account specifically to understand science. As the new work on concepts by Rosch's successors developed during the next two decades, Kuhn was also developing his own account. The two theories converged, and their mutual support was recognized in the 1990s (Andersen et al. 1996; Chen, Andersen, and Barker 1998). Although psychologists have developed a number of different models of human concepts consistent with Rosch's empirical findings, it would be premature to insist on the total adequacy of any one model (including those discussed later). However, it is clear that any adequate model of human concepts must accommodate the phenomenon of graded structure and acknowledge its universality. Hence, at this moment in history, any account of human concepts consistent with empirical findings in psychology must provide conceptual resources equivalent to those available in the family resemblance account developed by Kuhn, and these resources will lead to the same results: necessary-and-sufficient condition definitions of concepts will be impossible; there will be no single common feature or list of features linking all instances of a concept; and, as Kuhn pointed out, it remains permanently possible that individuals within a single community will employ disjoint features to successfully classify instances into existing categories.

8.3 KUHN'S THEORY OF CATEGORIZATION

8.3.1 Taxonomic Change and Local Incommensurability

As Kuhn's theory of concepts developed, it influenced other aspects of his account of historical change in science, especially the account of incommensurability, perhaps the most important and controversial concept in his account of science (Hoyningen-Huene 1993; Sankey 1994; Hoyningen-Huene, Oberheim, and Andersen 1996; Chen 1997). Incommensurability is a key feature of the conceptual changes that occur during revolutions. In *Structure* Kuhn used gestalt shifts as an analogy to illustrate incommensurability: scientists see things in an entirely different way after a revolution, as if shifting between views of an ambiguous figure (for example, Wittgenstein's duck-rabbit) or suddenly wearing glasses with inverting lenses (Kuhn 1962/1996, pp. 122–6). From the metaphorical description of gestalt shifts, many readers of Kuhn concluded that he believed that paradigms were not comparable, and they consequently charged Kuhn with relativism. However, Kuhn has repeatedly claimed that these charges represent misunderstandings and that incommensurability allows rational comparisons of successive paradigms (Kuhn 1983a, p. 670; 1989, p. 23; 1991, p. 3; Hoyningen-Huene 1993, pp. 206–22).

To show the possibility of rational comparison, Kuhn made several revisions in his later explications of incommensurability. He dropped the gestalt analogy, abandoning the perceptual interpretation as well as the implication that revolutionary changes are instantaneous. Instead he developed a metaphor based on language: during scientific revolutions, scientists experience translation difficulties when they discuss concepts from a different paradigm, as if they were dealing with a foreign language. Incommensurability was confined to changes in the meaning of concepts and became a sort of untranslatability (Kuhn 1970a, p. 198; Hoyningen-Huene 1993, pp. 64–130).

In a dozen articles written during the late 1980s and early 1990s, Kuhn offered a new account of incommensurability, which localized meaning change to a restricted class of kind terms.[8] These kind terms, together with their interconnections, form the taxonomy that classifies the entities studied in a particular scientific field. During a taxonomic change, some kind terms from the old taxonomy are preserved. But at the same time some new kind terms are added, some old ones are deleted, and many others are rearranged in different ways. To make sure that no two kind terms "may overlap in their referents unless they are related as species to genus," systematic regrouping of the referents to which the kind terms refer becomes necessary (Kuhn 1991, p. 4).[9] Sometimes referents previously regarded as quite unlike need to be grouped together, while referents of some single term in the old taxonomy have to be divided between different ones. These changes "affect not just the referents of an individual term but of an interrelated set of terms between which the preexisting population is redistributed" (Kuhn 1989, p. 31). Since such redistribution always involves more than one kind term and since kind terms are always interdefined, taxonomic change cannot be purely local.

On the other hand, because meaning change happens only in a very restricted class of terms, there always exist unchanged concepts that may be used as a basis for rational comparison between rival paradigms. Through the localization of incommensurability, Kuhn hoped to deflect the charge of relativism. If we consider these ideas from the viewpoint of cognitive science, extending the approach taken in the previous section, we find again that research on the nature of concepts in psychology and in cognitive science clarifies the cognitive phenomenon of incommensurability and lends additional support to Kuhn's position.

8.3.2 A Prototype Model of Local Incommensurability

According to Kuhn, incommensurability is directly caused by changes of conceptual structure, in particular, by changes of similarity relations (Kuhn 1970a, p. 200). For example, the incommensurability between Ptolemaic and Copernican astronomy, characterized by the meaning change of some key categories, was a direct result of conflicting classifications of the same objects into different similarity sets. Ptolemaic astronomers grouped the sun, moon, and Mars into one similarity set, "planet," while Copernicans classified them into three different categories.

But how are changes of conceptual structure brought about? Any answer will depend on adopting an account of human concepts. A popular account of concepts available in both contemporary philosophy and cognitive sciences is the so-called feature-list model, which characterizes people's knowledge of a concept as a list of independent features. In the previous section, we examined the problems of a particular version of the feature-list model – the classical account that concepts are defined by a set of necessary and sufficient conditions. Rather than specifying concepts by definitions, more recent feature-list accounts represent concepts by prototypes (Smith and Medin 1981; Homa 1984; Barsalou 1985, 1987, 1990). A prototype is a typical concept representation, which includes a list of features most likely to occur across the exemplars of the concept. In the process of categorization, we regard those referents with features that are highly similar to this list as typical, those less similar as moderately typical, and those with dissimilar features as atypical. The prototype of the concept "chair," for example, includes such features as the number of legs, the type of back, and the construction materials, yielding (for U.S. or European informants) a representation very similar to the four-legged, straight-backed kind often seen in a dining room. Other kinds of chairs, such as modernistic single-pedestal armchairs, are less typical, and barstools are atypical. These different degrees in typicality constitute the graded structure of the concept.

Representing concepts by prototypes can provide a dynamic account of concept formation. According to Barsalou, for example, prototypes are constructed in working memory, but the information contained in prototypes comes from a knowledge base in long-term memory (Barsalou and Sewell 1984, pp. 36–46; Barsalou 1987). The knowledge base for a concept may contain a tremendous amount of information, but only a small fraction of the information in the knowledge base is used to formulate a prototype in a specific situation. The cultural or theoretical stereotype that people have adopted influences which pieces of information in the knowledge base are activated and incorporated into the prototype in a given situation. Consequently, even people using similar knowledge bases may construct different prototypes for the same concept due to different stereotypes. In this way, the prototype account illustrates the critical role of established knowledge, a central point of Kuhn's theory of scientific revolutions.

The impact of stereotypes on individual concepts has been demonstrated empirically. In a psychological experiment conducted by Barsalou and Sewell in 1984, for example, subjects were asked to generate the prototype of a specific concept according to the cultural perspective assigned to them. The results show that those who took an American cultural perspective constructed a prototype of "bird" similar to robins, and regarded swans as only moderately typical, while those who took a Chinese cultural perspective developed a prototype of "bird" similar to swans and regarded robins as less typical (Barsalou and Sewell 1984, pp. 15–26).

Although the impact of stereotypes is localized in individual concepts, the consequences of these local changes are holistic. First, a different prototype will produce a different graded structure for the concept, which includes different good examples, different moderately good examples, and perhaps different atypical examples. The similarity and dissimilarity relations will now attach to a totally different pattern of features. Moreover, as indicated in the previous section, similarity and dissimilarity relations also define the connections between a concept and the others in the same contrast set. The effects of changing a prototype thus can reach the whole contrast set. For example, if the prototype of "bird" is altered from robins to bats, the prototype of "mammal," which belongs to the same contrast set, also needs to be changed. If not, many examples of "mammal" would become notably similar to the prototype of "bird," and the overlap between "bird" and "mammal" could jeopardize the category scheme. In this way, changing the prototype of an individual concept can generate a whole new set of similarity and dissimilarity relations for several related concepts, in particular those from the same contrast set, and lead to translation difficulties and incommensurability between the communities involved. Thus, the prototype account of concept representation supports Kuhn's insight that incommensurability is a regular accompaniment of conceptual change and that incommensurability can be caused by conceptual changes of a small number of concepts.

The prototype account can also lend support to Kuhn's idea that incommensurable paradigms can still be rationally compared. According to Barsalou, the generation of prototypes and graded structures involves interactions between two factors: the stereotype and the knowledge base. The knowledge base for a given concept is an aggregation of various pieces of information about the referents, which may or may not be articulated. For example, the knowledge base for the concept "bird" includes average values on dimensions such as size and shape, as well as correlated properties such as having feathers and laying eggs. The content of a knowledge base is relatively independent of the particular stereotype that people accept. The function of the stereotype is to activate a small fraction of information in the knowledge base and to incorporate this information into the prototype of the concept. Hence, although two persons endorse different stereotypes, it is theoretically possible that their knowledge bases for a given concept overlap and that the information to be incorporated into the prototype is activated (at least partly) within the overlapping section. The possible overlap between knowledge bases and the possible similarities between prototypes generated by different stereotypes thus provide common ground for rational comparison between rival paradigms, quite apart from the common factors already suggested by Kuhn as basis for such comparisons (Chen 1990).

8.3.3 Limits of The Prototype Account

A difficulty for the prototype account may also be raised against accounts that assume that concepts are definable by necessary and sufficient conditions. Such accounts unacceptably limit the allowed patterns of scientific change. The revision of a conceptual structure represented by concepts analyzed in terms of prototypes or necessary and sufficient conditions is an event that must take place at a single moment in time. At one moment, the necessary and sufficient conditions accepted as defining a scientific concept are one particular list or are centered on one particular prototype; at a later moment, the scientific community adopts some new and incompatible list or a new prototype, changing the concept and hence the conceptual structure. As the replacement of any defining condition or the substitution of a new prototype changes the concept completely, it appears that the process of conceptual revision cannot be historically extended. At best the process could last as long as the active debate for the new list of necessary and sufficient conditions or the new prototype structure. This unacceptably restricts the episodes of scientific change that can be accommodated. In particular, recent historical studies show that many episodes of change in science including the one that has been used as a prototype – the Copernican revolution – did not show abrupt change but exhibited strong historical continuity and change by small increments (Barker and Goldstein 1988; Barker 1993, 1996). Neither the necessary-and-sufficient condition account nor the prototype account seems capable of accommodating incremental change as a possible pattern for scientific revolutions.

8.4 CONCEPTS, TAXONOMIES, AND FRAMES

In this section we introduce the dynamic frame representation of concepts developed by cognitive psychologists to capture additional complexities of conceptual systems revealed by experimental studies and prefigured in Kuhn's theory of concepts. In Kuhn's mature work the most important conceptual systems are kind hierarchies or taxonomies. Taxonomies are easily represented by means of frames, but other types of conceptual systems may also be represented. In this section, we use frames to examine a realistic example of taxonomic change from the history of ornithology during the Darwinian revolution. We show both that Kuhn's expectations for the dynamics of taxonomic change are confirmed in detail by this historical case and that the changes may be rationally appraised. In the next section, we apply the same techniques to extend Kuhn's original account of anomalies and to understand several aspects of the Copernican revolution.

8.4.1 Representing Concepts and Taxonomies by Frames

A frame is a set of multivalued attributes integrated by structural connections. (Barsalou 1992; Barsalou and Hale 1993).[10] Figure 8.1 is a partial frame representation of the concept "bird." The frame divides features into two groups, attributes and values. All exemplars of "bird" share the properties in the attribute list such as "beak," "neck," "body," "leg," and "foot."

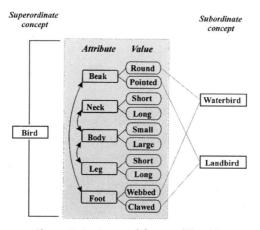

Figure 8.1   A partial frame of "bird."

Properties in the value list and the nodes representing superordinate concepts that lead to them are said to be "activated" (by analogy with the selective activation of nodes in a neural network) when a particular subset is chosen to represent a specific subordinate concept. For convenience and clarity, particular subordinate concepts ("water bird" and "land bird") are indicated in Figure 8.1 by the lines connecting the activated value nodes to additional nodes at the extreme right; however, each subordinate concept can also be understood as a unique pattern of activation for the attribute and value nodes. Each pattern of selection constitutes the prototype of a subordinate concept; for example, a typical waterfowl is a fowl whose values for "beak," "leg," and "foot" are restricted to "round," "short," and "webbed."

The frame representation embodies two important kinds of intraconceptual relation. First, the frame captures hierarchical relations between features. Contrary to the conventional assumption that all features within a concept are structurally equal, the frame representation divides features into two different levels. Some are attributes, such as "beak" and "foot," and the rest are values. A value is always attached to a particular attribute and functions as an instance of the attribute. Consequently, not all features within the superordinate concept are functionally equal: only attributes can be used as classification standards.

The second kind of intraconceptual relation represented in frames appears as what might be called a "horizontal relation" between nodes in the frame diagram. Kuhn sometimes calls this kind of connection the "legislative content" of a concept (1977, pp. 258–60). Elaborating Kuhn's discussion, Hoyningen-Huene calls it "knowledge of regularities" (1993, pp. 13–117). There are connections between nodes at the level of attributes (structural invariants): an instance of "neck" is always physically attached to an instance of "body," and an instance of "leg" is always physically attached to an instance of "body," but an instance of "leg" is never physically attached to an instance of "neck." The suggestion, made about a real, nondefective bird, that "Here is a bird with legs that attach to its neck" would usually be treated as evidence that the speaker did not understand the concept "bird." The claim is not false but nonsensical. The unusual status of claims like "There are no birds with legs that attach to their necks" is the equivalent, in Kuhn's theory of concepts, to Kant's synthetic a priori (Kuhn 1974/1977, p. 312; Kuhn 1991, p. 12). Learning a concept like "bird" involves learning that this kind of constraint exists between its attributes.

There are also constraints that produce systematic variability in values: if the value of "foot" is "webbed," then the value of "beak" is more likely to be "round," or if the value of "foot" is "unwebbed," then the value of "beak" is more likely to be "pointed." These patterns may be understood as physical constraints imposed by nature; webbed feet and round beaks are adapted to the environment in which water birds live, but they would be a hindrance on land. Because of these constraint relations, the attributes "beak" and "foot" must be used together as a cluster in classification.

A frame like Figure 8.1 may be used to represent the taxonomy of birds. It indicates that there is an inclusive relation between the superordinate concept "bird" and the subordinate concepts "water bird" and "land bird," and it also indicates the contrastive relations among concepts within the same subordinate group, because "water bird" and "land bird" should never be applied to the same object. It is acceptable to call a water bird a bird because the concept of the former is subordinated to the concept of the latter in the frame, but it is not acceptable to call it a land bird. In other words, concepts belonging to the same subordinate group cannot overlap in their referents, and so no object is both a water bird and a land bird. This is Kuhn's no-overlap principle for kind terms (Kuhn 1991, p. 4). In the frame representation, both inclusive and contrastive relations are embedded in the internal structure of the superordinate concept. The inclusive relation derives from the attribute list: All subordinate concepts belong to the superordinate one because they all share the properties of the attributes. The contrastive relations derive from the pattern of the activated values: two subordinate concepts contrast if they have different values in the same attribute.

The frame representation also displays the cognitive mechanisms behind the classification process. The frame of a superordinate concept directly determines the possible concepts at the subordinate level. For example, since the frame of "bird" in Figure 8.1 has five attributes and each of them has two possible values, there are 32 possible property combinations ($2 \times 2 \times 2 \times 2 \times 2$) and thereby 32 possible concepts at the subordinate level. But due to the constraints between the value sets, some of these property combinations are conceptually impossible. If this frame is adopted, then there are no instances of "bird" with "round beak" and "clawed foot" or with "pointed beak" and "webbed foot." Some other combinations are not found in nature. The results are only two property combinations ("round beak" with "webbed foot" and "pointed beak" with "clawed foot"), which form two subordinate concepts – "water bird" and "land bird." In this way, the frame specifies classification standards: birds are classified according to their beak and foot.

Originally, our use of the concept "bird" as an example was motivated by Kuhn's story about a child learning the differences between swans, geese, and ducks to introduce this theory of concepts (Section 8.2). While investigating the connections between Kuhn's theory and work in cognitive science, the present authors devised some examples of taxonomic changes that fitted the cognitive analysis (Chen et al. 1998). Later we were surprised to find that the hypothetical examples mirrored the development of ornithological taxonomy during the Darwinian revolution. In other words, our cognitive analysis successfully "predicted" the historical facts. A detailed examination of the sequence of historical changes that occurred in ornithology during the nineteenth century both confirms Kuhn's expectations about the mechanism of conceptual change when one taxonomy replaces another and allows us to refute the charge that such changes are not amenable to rational comparison.[11]

8.4.2 A Frame-Based Interpretation of Taxonomic Change

In the seventeenth century, when the first ornithological taxonomy was developed, birds were simply divided into two classes, "water bird" and "land bird," according to their beak shape and foot structure (Ray 1678). Typical examples of "water bird" were those with a round beak and webbed feet, like ducks or geese, and typical examples of "land bird" were those with a pointed beak and clawed feet, like chickens or quail. By the early nineteenth century, however, many newly found birds could not be fitted into the dichotomous system. For example, a noisy South American bird called a screamer was found to have webbed feet like a duck but a pointed beak like a chicken.

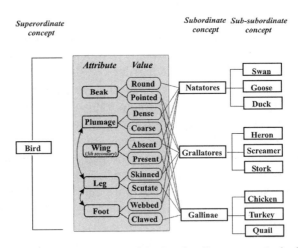

Figure 8.2   A frame representation of the Sundevall taxonomy (only three related subordinate concepts are listed).

To accommodate such anomalies, a popular taxonomy proposed by Sundevall in the 1830s (Figure 8.2) adopted more attributes, including "beak shape," "plumage pattern," "wing-feather arrangement," "leg form," and "foot structure," as classification standards (Sundevall 1889). The five attributes generate more possible property combinations and thereby more possible concepts. The Sundevall taxonomy was more flexible than the old dichotomous system, and was able to accommodate birds like the screamer that were anomalies in the old system. Because "beak" and "foot" are no longer related in the Sundevall system, it becomes possible to have a property combination that includes both "pointed beak" and "webbed feet," the key features of screamers. In this way, Sundevall eliminated the anomaly by putting "screamer" under a new category, "grallatores," independent of "water bird" and "land bird."

The Darwinian revolution caused radical changes in bird classification. Influenced by Darwin's beliefs that species change over time and therefore that affinity among species must be founded on their common origin, ornithologists realized that many features used as classification standards in pre-Darwinian taxonomies were irrelevant, and they began to search for features that could display the evolutionary origin of birds. In a popular post-Darwinian taxonomy proposed by Gadow in 1893 (Figure 8.3), a different set of attributes were adopted, which included "palatal structure," "pelvic musculature form," "tendon type," "intestinal convolution type," and "wing-feather arrangement" (Gadow 1892, pp. 230–56).

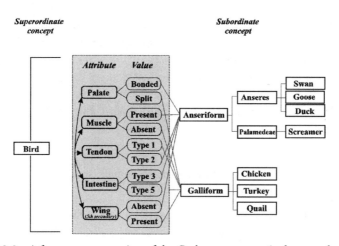

Figure 8.3   A frame representation of the Gadow taxonomy (only two related subordinate concepts are listed).

Embedded in the Gadow taxonomy is a whole new concept of "bird." The strong intraconceptual relations among all attributes reflect the assumption that similarities in these anatomical features reveal a common origin and therefore that the values of these attributes ought to be correlated. The strong constraints among the attributes significantly reduce the number of possible property combinations. For example, the combination "bonded palate" and "presented fifth secondary in the wings" exemplified by screamers becomes impossible, and Sundevall's category "grallatores" with its subconcept "screamer" cannot be included in the contrast set at the subordinate level. At the same time, the similarities between waterfowl and screamers in skull character, skeleton, wing pattern, and feather structure suggested that they should be put under the same covering concept. Consequently, Gadow introduced a new subordinate concept, "anseriform," to denote both waterfowl and screamers.

The frame representation shows why the pre- and post-Darwinian taxonomies were incommensurable and confirms Kuhn's account of how incommensurability arises. Due to addition, deletion, and rearrangement of kind terms, a holistic redistribution of referents occurred. Because of the referent redistribution, many terms in the new taxonomy could not be translated into the old ones, or the other way around. Consequently, it becomes possible but not inevitable that communication between followers of the two systems will be impeded. For example, the followers of the Sundevall taxonomy might regard Gadow's category "anseriform" as confusing because they could not find an equivalent term without violating the no-overlap principle. The referents of Gadow's "anseriform" overlap those of Sundevall's "natatores"; the former includes the latter as a subset, but they are not in species–genus relations. The followers of the Gadow taxonomy, on the other hand, might regard Sundevall's "grallatores" as incomprehensible because of its overlap with "anseriform." But do these difficulties prevent rational comparison of the two taxonomies?

8.4.3 Cognitive Platforms for Rational Comparison of Incommensurable Taxonomies

The pre- and post-Darwinian taxonomies made different predictions of similarity relations. The former put "screamer" and the equivalent of "water bird" under two contrastive covering terms and emphasized their dissimilarity, while the latter put them under the same covering term and emphasized their similarity. But observations of similarity or dissimilarity could not be used directly to test these two rival taxonomies. In a frame representation, similarity between two concepts is described in terms of the matches in the values of relevant attributes. But what should be counted as relevant attributes? Given that the taxonomic change occurred during the Darwinian revolution, ornithologists from either side shared very little in their understanding of their common objects of study. If they selected different attribute lists, would they also make incompatible judgments regarding whether an observation of similarity was relevant?

At first glance, the attribute list in the post-Darwinian taxonomy is considerably different from the one in the pre-Darwinian taxonomy. But it is important to note that these two lists of attributes are compatible: None of the attributes listed in one taxonomy overlap those in the other. A closer examination further shows that the two lists of attributes are similar – all of them are anatomical parts of birds.[12]

The different but compatible lists of attributes embedded in the pre- and post-Darwinian taxonomies of birds provided a common platform for rational comparison. Because the attribute lists were compatible, people from both sides could agree with each other on what attributes should be counted as relevant in judgments of similarity. When observations showed more and more similarities between screamers and waterfowl in skull character, skeleton, wing pattern, muscular system, and digestive system, supporters of the pre-Darwinian taxonomy had to agree that all these similarities were relevant and accept them as legitimate evidence for testing their taxonomy. When observations of the similarities between screamers and water birds became overwhelming, they had no choice but to admit that their taxonomy was in trouble.

Historical evidence indicates that the two rival taxonomies were indeed compared and evaluated in a rational manner. Although there were debates regarding the merits of the two rival systems, criticisms from either side were mainly based on observations of similarity and dissimilarity relations between birds. The main objection to the pre-Darwinian taxonomy was, for example, that it grouped many dissimilar birds together (Newton 1893). Due to the compelling evidence regarding similarity and dissimilarity relations, the community quickly formed a consensus. Before the end of the nineteenth century, the Gadow taxonomy was accepted by the ornithological community (Sibley and Ahlquist 1990).

By providing a representation of the internal structure of concepts, a frame analysis shows that attribute lists embedded in two incommensurable taxonomies can remain compatible. This compatibility provides a cognitive platform for rational comparison between rival taxonomies. In this way, cognitive studies once again support Kuhn's claim that incommensurability does not necessarily entail relativism.

8.5 THE COGNITIVE STRUCTURE OF SCIENTIFIC REVOLUTIONS

8.5.1 Anomalies and the Cognitive Structure of Revolutions

In *Structure* Kuhn claimed to have described, in a preliminary way, a pattern of development that could be found throughout science and throughout science's history. He used historical examples ranging from ancient astronomy and optics to physics in the twentieth century. But from the viewpoint of the historian, it is dramatically implausible to suggest that the usual factors considered in a historical explanation were sufficiently constant over all the periods considered by Kuhn to yield similar structures in each one. Between the ancient period and the twentieth century, the institutional structure of science, its relations to the wider culture, and the education, social class, and career paths of scientists themselves had changed not once but several times. Despite his insistence that the scientific community is the main actor in his account, Kuhn was adamant that such factors played little role in the intellectual changes that were his primary concern.

Rejecting the usual historical factors, a second possibility to justify the appearance of similar structures in different disciplines and different periods might be a logical reconstruction of the kind popular in the twentieth-century philosophy of science. Practitioners of this view, believing that logic stood outside history, imagined that it furnished a basis for universal claims about the structure of all scientific explanations, for example. However, Kuhn criticized logic-based philosophy of science as historically inadequate and largely avoided using its tools or categories (Kuhn 1977, p. 285, and esp. Kuhn 1991).

Should Kuhn's work be seen as no more than a historical generalization based on a large range of sources? Kuhn himself would probably have defended the generality of his results as a consequence of his theory of concepts, although this only pushes the question back one step. For Kuhn, the theory of concepts is conditioned by his examination of a wide range of historical cases but is strongly influenced by the philosophical ideas of Kant and Wittgenstein. In the end, Kuhn would probably have said that his theory of concepts was a priori (Kuhn 1979, p. 418f., Kuhn 2000, p. 264).

The results we have reviewed in psychology and cognitive science place us in a position to offer a different answer. We wish to suggest that a more plausible explanation for both the adequacy and the generality of Kuhn's account is that it builds on cognitive structures that have now been demonstrated by psychologists and cognitive scientists to be universal features of human intellectual activity.

A central contrast in Kuhn's original work is the division between normal and revolutionary science. We may now understand this division as the distinction between research conducted in terms of an existing conceptual structure, without changing that structure, and research proceeding by modifying an existing conceptual structure (Kuhn 1983a, p. 683; 1983b, p. 713). In principle, we should not see this division as corresponding to a linear sequence of historical changes, with normal science succeeded by revolutionary science succeeded by normal science, indefinitely. Both patterns of research may coexist. However, Kuhn's later work suggests reasons for the conservative nature of normal science and for the relative infrequency of the changes in conceptual structure that we recognize as major revolutions.

As emphasized in our initial discussion of family resemblance concepts, the success of a community in classifying available instances of the objects that interest it is no guarantee that all members of the community employ the same features of those objects in arriving a classification (Andersen et al. 1996, p. 356). Expressing this point in terms of a frame representation, it is always possible that different members of the same community select differing attributes, and values of those attributes, in classifying objects. This divergence may become apparent only when an anomalous object appears – a classical Kuhnian anomaly. Such an object, falling between the categories in a single contrast set, may polarize a community into those who believe it can and those who believe it cannot be accommodated within the existing taxonomy. The nineteenth-century discovery of the South American bird called a screamer, discussed in the previous section, may be a good historical example of this phenomenon. Similar dynamics appear in the discovery of nuclear fission (Andersen 1996). However, as our earlier discussion noted, we should not attribute taxonomic changes like those in ornithology during the nineteenth century to single anomalies or expect them to occur at a single moment. In this case, accommodating new discoveries like the screamer led to the abandonment of an established taxonomy and the introduction of a new and incommensurable one. This episode embodies almost all the features called for in Kuhn's original account of scientific change: the old paradigm (taxonomy) generates an anomaly that can only be resolved by replacing it. One of the main assets of the new taxonomy is that it can resolve the problems that led its predecessor to crisis – it can answer the question "Is the screamer a land bird or a water bird?" The theory of concepts we have described provides the resources for understanding both the breakdown of consensus in the scientific community created by an anomaly of this type and the means by which it is resolved.

8.5.2 Revolution without Empirical Anomalies

A second and more problematic case of scientific change may be understood using the same resources. Copernicus's innovations in astronomy were not stimulated by an anomaly that violated the contrast classes for astronomical objects available in the sixteenth century. Rather, his main announced objection to Ptolemaic astronomy was its use of the mathematical device called the "equant point." The Western astronomical tradition had long accepted that all celestial motions were combinations of circles traversed at constant speed. In principle, any celestial motion should therefore have three attributes: "center," "radius," and "speed of rotation" (Figure 8.4a).[13] In the simplest case, we assume that a single point serves both as the geometrical center and as the center of rotation; the geometrical center of a celestial circle serves both as the initial point of its radius and as the point from which the angular motion of an object moving around the circle is measured. Probably because he was unable to accommodate both the direction and the duration of retrogressions using this simple conceptual structure, Claudius Ptolemy, in his main astronomical work, both separated the observer from the geometrical center of the major celestial circle carrying a

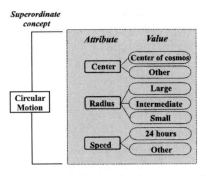

Figure 8.4a Partial frame for "circular motion."

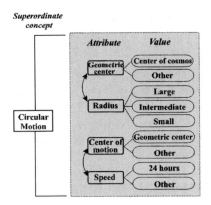

Figure 8.4b Partial frame for "circular motion" modified to accommodate Ptolemy's equant device.

planet and, more radically, separated the center of rotation from the geometrical center (Evans 1998). The removal of the observer (that is, the Earth) from the geometrical center made the circle eccentric. Ptolemy located the center of rotation at the same distance from the geometrical center as the observer but diametrically opposite and called this the equant point. In all his models except those for the sun and moon, Ptolemy employed this unusual conceptual structure.

Although astronomers in the Ptolemaic tradition employed the equant device when making calculations, it was a long-standing source of dissatisfaction with Ptolemy's models. By means of frame diagrams, the problem may be posed as follows: how are we to modify Figure 8.4a to accommodate the equant, and are we obliged to make similar modifications in the frames for other rotating circles? The simplest modification would seem to be to add a new attribute at the same level as the three already included. However,

in the same sense that we cannot specify a radius without specifying a geometrical center, it now appears that we cannot specify the rotation of a circle
without introducing a center of rotation that may differ from the geometrical center. So we also need to introduce constraints showing that these
pairs of nodes can only be activated together or not at all (Figure 8.4b). The
discrepancy in nodes and constraints between Figure 8.4a and Figure 8.4b is
of exactly the same kind as the discrepancy between nodes in incommensurable taxonomies. Historically, astronomers expressed a strong preference
for conceptual structure 8.4a despite the use of the equant as a calculating
device. Copernicus's success in constructing planetary models that avoided
this device – at least overtly – was greeted with acclaim by his contemporaries. What this case teaches us is that conceptual structures may be
objectionable – and hence motivate change – for reasons other than their
adequacy in coping with empirical anomalies. This analysis also shows that
although Kuhn's original exposition of the Copernican revolution could not
be assimilated to his general model of scientific change, if we examine the
conceptual structures represented by the different positions in astronomy
during the Copernican revolution, the same cognitively based theories that
supported Kuhn's original account of anomaly-induced change can also be
used to understand the mechanisms at work here.

The theory of concepts and taxonomic structures developed by Kuhn
and here presented through the frame account also provides a means for
locating incommensurability at particular points within a conceptual structure and appraising its severity (Figure 8.5). Consider a partial frame representation of the main positions in astronomy before and after Copernicus,
ignoring for the moment the complications introduced by the equant and
considering only the major motion of a planet, its so-called proper motion
against the background of fixed stars (Barker 2001). The differences between the two main schools in astronomy before Copernicus come down
to different choices for the values of a single attribute of the celestial circle
corresponding to this motion. Averroists insisted that all celestial circles
must take the Earth as their center (Figure 8.5a). Ptolemaic astronomers
allowed the circle for the proper motion to have a different center, which for
some planets was quite distant from the center of the Earth (Figure 8.5b).

It is surprising to discover that Copernicus's planetary models can be
accommodated by the same conceptual structure as Ptolemaic astronomy
(Figure 8.5c). Although there are minor differences in numerical values for
the attributes "radius" and "speed" (Copernicus generally uses Ptolemy's
distances for example), these differences can be accommodated without
introducing new attributes or new ranges of values. The topography of

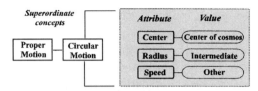

Figure 8.5a   Partial frame for Averroist theory of proper motion.

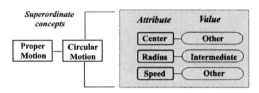

Figure 8.5b   Partial frame for Ptolemaic theory of proper motion.

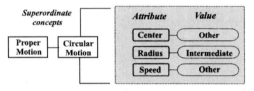

Figure 8.5c   Partial frame for Copernican 1609 theory of proper motion.

Copernicus's frame is identical to the Ptolemiac one. It has the same branch structure and the same nodes linked in the same clusters. From the viewpoint of sixteenth-century astronomers, Copernicus's location of the center of a planet's proper motion at the mean sun was just the choice of a new eccentric center for the circle representing proper motion. But Ptolemaic astronomers were already using such points, and consequently saw Copernicus not as a threat to Ptolemy but as a potential ally in the dispute with the Averroists (Lattis 1994; Barker 1999, 2001).

If we compare these three conceptual structures with the corresponding portions of the frame for Kepler's astronomical theory, a major incommensurability is immediately apparent. Not only have new sets of attributes and values been introduced, but the superordinate node corresponding to "circular motion" in the earlier frame diagrams has now been replaced with the node for a new concept – "orbit" (Barker 2001). It is interesting to note that this revision of nodes occurred in a conservative way: the innovations Kepler introduces fit into the existing conceptual structure and replace existing nodes, conserving the original branch pattern (Barker and Goldstein 2001). However, it is clear that Kepler's work introduced a radical revision in

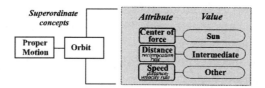

Figure 8.5d Partial frame for Kepler's 1609 theory of proper motion.

concepts. Superimposing the frame diagrams for Kepler's system and any of the earlier ones shows that, reading from the left, we immediately encounter conflicting choices for a series of nodes. The extent to which these changes reach into the superordinate nodes may be used as an estimate of the severity of the incommensurability introduced here (Barker 2001). Using this criterion to compare Figures 8.5c and 8.5d, we see that Kepler's theory of proper motion is incommensurable with Copernicus's to the same degree that it is with Ptolemy's. This is surprising until we recall that it was Kepler's version of Copernican astronomy, not the model proposed by Copernicus himself, that ultimately displaced the Ptolemaic system.

The examples we have considered show that conceptual change may be an incremental process that is historically extended. Given enough incremental change, the revised conceptual structure may be so different from an earlier historical example that a historian of science looking at two periods fifty years or a century apart may mistakenly conclude that the transition from one structure to another was discontinuous (Chen and Barker 2000). Using a tool like the frame model not only provides a means of identifying the small incremental changes that actually linked the two structures, but by locating the positions of the changes it also directs our attention to the historical arguments used to justify them. For example, Galileo's discovery of the moons of Jupiter was important to both Ptolemaic and Copernican astronomers because it showed that four newly discovered objects moved in circles around a center that was clearly not the center of the Earth. In conceptual terms, it showed that the Averroists' insistence on their preferred value for the "center" attribute, and hence the frame in Figure 8.5a, was flatly untenable.

8.6 CONCLUSION

According to the received view of Kuhn's work, incommensurability between rival conceptual systems is either total or risks being total; it prevents meaningful communication between supporters of different systems, and it prevents rational comparison of competing incommensurable systems. Although Kuhn himself repeatedly rejected these interpretations of his work, they continue to dominate the philosophical literature (Curd and Cover 1998). At the same time, philosophy of science has largely turned away from historical studies. One reason for this was the intractability of systems that attempted to do the same historical work as Kuhn without the same imagined philosophical liabilities (Lakatos 1977; Laudan et al. 1986). But a second and more important reason may have been an aggressive campaign mounted by sociologists of science to coopt historical studies of science (Bloor 1976; Shapin 1982). Although many of the methodological criticisms leveled at the historical-orientation philosophy of science by sociologists were accurate, their own program had two major drawbacks: it denied the centrality of the cognitive content of science in explaining scientific change, and it generally included a parallel attack on scientific realism. During the last two decades of Kuhn's life, philosophers of science withdrew from historical work and devoted a disproportionate amount of intellectual effort to defenses of realism.

Perhaps the cognitive rereading of Kuhn will finally deflate some of the myths about his work. On the basis of the cognitive reconstruction of Kuhn we have offered, it is apparent that total failure of communication between opposing groups with incommensurable conceptual structures is not to be expected. Quite the reverse; the analysis shows a wide range of factors that support mutual intelligibility and rational appraisal of competing positions. But the work presented here has a far more important outcome than correcting misreadings of Kuhn. Kuhn's later work, as augmented by results from cognitive theories of concepts, constitutes a complete answer to the sociological critique of philosophy of science.

The analysis we have presented by means of the frame model satisfies all the desiderata that motivated the Strong Programme in the sociology of knowledge. But it does this while restoring the centrality of cognitive content in our philosophical picture of science, and providing empirically licensed access to the conceptual structures employed by scientists today and in history. To review briefly, the Strong Programme required that any account of science be first, causal, that is, empirical; second, reflexive; third, symmetrical, and fourth, impartial. When represented by means of dynamic frames, Kuhn's theory of concepts ceases to be a priori and becomes empirical. It is evidently reflexive: one of the simplest ways to delineate the differences between the prototype model of concepts and the frame model would be to construct frames for the concepts "prototype" and "frame."[14] As for symmetry and impartiality, frame analysis applies equally to accepted and rejected, successful and unsuccessful theories, and its application is independent of the truth or falsity of the theory under examination. The frame model provides a method of representing conceptual structures; using it corresponds to the analysis of meaning, not the evaluation of truth-bearing structures, which is what philosophers of science have generally taken theories to be.

Establishing the positive links we have described between Kuhn's later philosophy of science and empirical investigations of concepts therefore opens a whole new avenue of inquiry into issues in the philosophy of science first examined by Kuhn. This inquiry may well achieve results that are unexpected and that Kuhn himself did not envisage. Nor would we wish to give the impression that the frame model is the last word in the theory of concepts. Like any empirical theory, it is susceptible to improvement or replacement. It remains true, however, that any empirical account of concepts capable of accommodating experimental data gathered from the time of Rosch's original work to the present will also support the account of concepts developed by Kuhn in his mature work and, we maintain, will lead by equivalent reasoning to the results we have documented based on Kuhn's ideas and the frame model. Kuhn's lasting contribution to the philosophy of science may well be his least popular: the concept of incommensurability. But ironically, the theory of concepts developed as he refined this idea now provides a means to restore the central importance of cognitive content in philosophy of science and a means to approach the history of scientific change that places the subject on a secure empirical footing.

Notes

Peter Barker gratefully acknowledges the support of the University of Oklahoma sabbatical leave program, the Danish Institute for Advanced Studies in the Humanities, and Denmark's Nationalbank, for portions of this work. Parts of section 4 were previously published in Chen (2001), copyright 2001 by the Philosophy of Science Association.

1. Kuhn himself describes the profound effect of reading Kant while a student at Harvard (Baltas et al. 2000, p. 264). His debt to Wittgenstein is apparent in *Structure*, the final stages of which were begun only five years after the appearance of the *Philosophical Investigations* (1953) and at the height of interest in Wittgenstein's later work. Kuhn's knowledge of that book and its author may have been mediated by Stanley Cavell when they were both at Berkeley (Kuhn 1962/1996, p. xiii). At the same time, he was in contact with Paul K. Feyerabend, who wrote one of the first and most influential reviews of the

Investigations. However, while Feyerabend remained an outside observer, Cavell was one of only a handful of philosophers who adopted and actively employed the methods of Wittgenstein's later work, as Kuhn would go on to do.

2. The procedure by which science students are supposed to model novel problems on the exemplary problems is analogous to the procedure by which Latin students learn to recite *amo, amas, . . .* , and then conjugate similar verbs by matching the same endings to new stems. Kuhn adopted the term for such standard examples in language teaching, "paradigm," and simply extended it to cover standard examples in science teaching.

3. See Andersen et al. (1996), Barker (1986), and Andersen (2000b) for accounts of the relation between Kuhn's and Wittgenstein's accounts of family resemblance.

4. In his published work, Kuhn never referred to the literature on concept acquisition but drew on everyday experience. For the similarity between Kuhn's account and the account developed by cognitive psychologists on the basis of extensive experiments on concept learning and categorization, see, e.g., Andersen et al. (1996) and Nersessian (1998).

5. The only example of the acquisition of scientific concepts that Kuhn spelled out in some detail is his analysis of how students learn the concepts "force," "mass," and "weight"; see Kuhn (1989, pp. 15–21) and Kuhn (1990, pp. 301–8).

6. Kuhn's restriction of dissimilarity to instances of concepts forming contrast sets can also be found in other fields, such as cognitive psychology (e.g., Rosch 1987, p. 157) or ethnographic semantics and cognitive anthropology (e.g., Conklin 1969 and Kay 1971).

7. On this point, Kuhn explicitly claimed to have moved beyond Wittgenstein: "Wittgenstein . . . says almost nothing about the sort of world necessary to support the naming procedure he outlines" (Kuhn 1970a, p. 197, fn. 14).

8. Kuhn's concept of kind went beyond the one defined by the traditional theory of natural kinds, and Kuhn also disagreed with Hacking, who advocated a notion of "scientific kind" (Hacking 1993, p. 290). Kuhn suggested that kinds are "substances" that "trace a lifeline through space and time" so that they can be reidentified by our "categorizing module" (Kuhn 1993, p. 315; 1990, p. 5).

9. This is the so-called nonoverlap principle for kind terms, which plays a very important role in Kuhn's new incommensurability thesis. For more analysis of the nonoverlap principle and its relations to Kuhn's latest incommensurability thesis, see Chen (1997).

10. Frames were introduced by Minsky in the 1970s to represent knowledge as part of an unsuccessful program to develop artificial intelligence Minsky (1975). Minsky's frames originated from Bartlett's notion of a schema. See Brewer (2000).

11. Recent cognitive studies offer further evidence to justify the use of frames to represent concepts by revealing the connections between concepts and neural structures; see Barsalou (1999), Barsalou, Solomon, and Wu (1999), and Chen (2001).

12. In the light of cognitive studies, there is reason to believe that such a preference was not accidental, but reflects a general feature of human cognition (Rosch, Mervis, Gray, Johnson, and Boyes-Braem 1976; Tversky and Hemenway 1984).

13. For an explanation of the values displayed in the frame, see Barker (2001). For a detailed discussion of the equant problem, see Barker (unpublished).

14. We leave this as an exercise for the reader.

References

Andersen, H. 1996. "Categorization, Anomalies and the Discovery of Nuclear Fission." *Studies in the History and Philosophy of Modern Physics* 27: 463–92.

——— 2000a. "Learning by Ostension: Thomas Kuhn on Science Education." *Science and Education* 9: 91–106.

——— 2000b. "Kuhn's Account of Family Resemblance: A Solution to the Problem of Wide-Open Texture." *Erkenntnis* 52: 313–37.

——— 2001a. *On Kuhn*. Belmont, CA: Wadsworth.

——— 2001b. "Reference and Resemblance." *Philosophy of Science* 69 (Proceedings).

Andersen, H., P. Barker, and X. Chen. 1996. "Kuhn's Mature Philosophy of Science and Cognitive Psychology." *Philosophical Psychology* 9: 347–63.

Armstrong, S., L. Gleitman, and H. Gleitman. 1983. "On What Some Concepts Might Not Be." *Cognition* 13: 263–308.

Baltas, A., K. Gavroglu, and V. Kindi. 2000. "A Discussion with Thomas S. Kuhn." In Kuhn (2000), pp. 255–323. Based on a discussion in Athens, Greece, October 19–21, 1995.

Barker, P. 1986. "Wittgenstein and the Authority of Science." In: W. Leinfellner and F. Wuketits, eds. *The Tasks of Contemporary Philosophy: Proceedings of the Xth International Wittgenstein Symposium*. Vienna: Verlag Holdner-Pichler-Tempsky, pp. 265–7.

——— 1993. "The Optical Theory of Comets from Apian to Kepler." *Physis* 30: 1–25.

——— 1996. "Understanding Change and Continuity." In: F. Ragep and S. Ragep, eds. *Tradition, Transmission, Transformation*. Leiden: Brill, pp. 527–50.

——— 1999. "Copernicus and the Critics of Ptolemy." *Journal for the History of Astronomy* 30: 343–58.

——— 2001. "Incommensurability and Conceptual Change during the Copernican Revolution." In: H. Sankey and P. Hoyningen-Huene, eds. *Incommensurability and Related Matters*. Boston Studies in the Philosophy of Science. Boston: Kluwer, pp. 241–73.

——— Unpublished. "Kuhn, Incommensurability and Cognitive Science." Paper presented at the conference "Kuhn Reconsidered," Virginia Tech, Blacksburg, VA, March 2000.

Barker, P., and B. R. Goldstein. 1988. "The Role of Comets in the Copernican Revolution." *Studies in the History and Philosophy of Science* 19: 299–319.

2001. "Theological Foundations of Kepler's Astronomy." In: J. H. Brooke, M. J. Osler, and J. van der Meer, eds. *Osiris* 16: 88–113.

Barsalou, L. W. 1982. "Ad Hoc Categories." *Memory and Cognition* 11: 211–27.

1985. "Ideals, Central Tendency, and Frequency of Instantiation as Determinants of Graded Structure in Categories." *Journal of Experimental Psychology: Learning, Memory, and Cognition* 11: 629–54.

1987. "The Instability of Graded Structure: Implications for the Nature of Concepts." In: U. Neisser, ed. *Concepts and Conceptual Development: Ecological and Intellectual Factors in Categorization.* Cambridge: Cambridge University Press, pp. 101–40.

1990. "On the Indistinguishability of Exemplar Memory and Abstraction in Category Representation." In: T. Srull and R. Wyer, eds. *Advances in Social Cognition*, Vol. 3. Hillsdale, NJ: Erlbaum, pp. 61–88.

1991. "Deriving Categories to Achieve Goals." In: G. H. Bower, ed. *The Psychology of Learning and Motivation: Advances in Research and Theory*, Vol. 27. New York: Academic Press, pp. 1–64.

1992. "Frames, Concepts, and Conceptual Fields." In: A. Lehrer and E. Kittay, eds. *Frames, Fields and Contrasts: New Essays in Semantical and Lexical Organization.* Hillsdale, NJ: Erlbaum, pp. 21–74.

1999. "Perceptual Symbol Systems." *Behavioral and Brain Sciences* 22: 577–609.

Barsalou, L. W., and C. Hale. 1993. "Components of Conceptual Representation: From Feature-Lists to Recursive Frames." In: I. Mechelen, J. Hampton, R. Michalski, and P. Theuns, eds. *Categories and Concepts: Theoretical Views and Inductive Data Analysis.* New York: Academic Press, pp. 97–144.

Barsalou, L. W., and D. Sewell. 1984. *Constructing Representations of Categories from Different Points of View. Emory Cognition Project Report No. 2.* Atlanta: Emory University.

Barsalou, L. W., K. Solomon, and L. Wu. 1999. "Perceptual Simulation in Conceptual Tasks." In: M. Hiraga, C. Sinha, and S. Wilcox, eds. *Cultural, Typological, and Psychological Perspectives in Cognitive Linguistics: The Proceedings of the 4th Conference of the International Cognitive Linguistics Association*, Vol. 3. Amsterdam: John Benjamins, pp. 209–28.

Bloor, D. 1976. *Knowledge and Social Imagery.* London: Routledge & Kegan Paul.

Brewer, W. 2000. "Bartlett's Concept of the Schema and Its Impact on Theories of Knowledge Representation in Contemporary Cognitive Psychology." In: A. Saito, ed. *Bartlett, Culture and Cognition.* Hove, UK: Psychology Press, pp. 69–89.

Cantor, N., E. E. Smith, R. D. French, and J. Mezzich. 1980. "Psychiatric Diagnosis as Prototype Organization." *Journal of Abnormal Psychology* 89: 181–93.

Chen, X. 1990. "Local Incommensurability and Communicability." In: A. Fine, M. Forbes, and L. Wessels, eds. *PSA 1990*, Vol. 1. East Lansing, MI: Philosophy of Science Association, pp. 67–76.

1997. "Thomas Kuhn's Latest Notion of Incommensurability." *Journal for General Philosophy of Science* 28: 257–73.

2001. "Perceptual Symbols and Taxonomy Comparison." *Philosophy of Science* 69: 68 (special Proceedings issue): 200–12.

Chen, X., H. Andersen, and P. Barker. 1998. "Kuhn's Theory of Scientific Revolutions and Cognitive Psychology." *Philosophical Psychology* 11: 5–28.

Chen, X., and P. Barker. 2000. "Continuity Through Revolutions: A Frame-Based Account of Conceptual Change During Scientific Revolutions." *Philosophy of Science* 67 (Proceedings): S208–S223.

Conklin, H. C. 1969. "Lexicographical Treatment of Folk Taxonomies." In: S. A. Tyler, ed. *Cognitive Anthropology*. New York: Holt, Rinehart & Winston, pp. 41–59.

Curd, M., and J. A. Cover. 1998. *Philosophy of Science: The Central Issues*. New York: W. W. Norton.

Ekman, P., W. V. Friesen, and P. Ellsworth. 1972. *Emotion in the Human Face*. Elmsford, NY: Pergamon.

Erreich, A., and V. Valian. 1979. "Children's Internal Organization of Locative Categories." *Child Development* 50: 1070–77.

Evans, J. 1998. *The History and Practice of Ancient Astronomy*. Oxford: Oxford University Press.

Gadow, H. 1892. "On the Classification of Birds." *Proceedings of the Zoological Society of London*: 229–56.

Hacking, I. 1993. "Working in a New World: The Taxonomic Solution." In: P. Horwich, ed. *World Changes*. Cambridge, MA: MIT Press, pp. 275–310.

Heider, E. R. 1972. "Universals in Color Naming and Memory." *Journal of Experimental Psychology* 93: 10–20. (E. Heider later published under the name E. Rosch.)

Homa, D. 1984. "On the Nature of Categories." In: G. Bower, ed. *The Psychology of Learning and Motivation: Advances in Research and Theory*, Vol. 18. New York: Academic Press, pp. 49–94.

Homa, D., and R. Vosburgh. 1976. "Category Breadth and the Abstraction of Prototypical Information." *Journal of Experimental Psychology – Human Learning and Memory* 2: 322–30.

Hoyningen-Huene, P. 1993. *Reconstructing Scientific Revolutions: Thomas S. Kuhn's Philosophy of Science*. Chicago: University of Chicago Press.

Hoyningen-Huene, P., E. Oberheim, and H. Andersen. 1996. "On Incommensurability." *Studies in History and Philosophy of Science* 27: 131–41.

Kay, P. 1971. "Taxonomy and Semantic Contrast." *Language* 47: 866–87.

Kuhn, T. S. 1959. "The Essential Tension: Tradition and Innovation in Scientific Research." In Kuhn (1977), pp. 225–39.

1961. "The Function of Measurement in Modern Physical Science." *Isis* 52: 161–93; reprinted in Kuhn (1977), pp. 178–224.

1962. *The Structure of Scientific Revolutions*. Chicago: University of Chicago Press.

1970a. "Postscript – 1969" in *The Structure of Scientific Revolutions*, 2nd. ed. Chicago: University of Chicago Press, pp. 174–210.

1970b. "Logic of Discovery or Psychology of Research." In: I. Lakatos and A. Musgrave, eds. *Criticism and the Growth of Knowledge*. Cambridge: Cambridge University Press, pp. 1–24; reprinted in Kuhn (1977), pp. 266–92.

1970c. "Reflections on My Critics." In: I. Lakatos and A. Musgrave, eds. *Criticism and the Growth of Knowledge*. Cambridge: Cambridge University Press, pp. 231–78.

1974. "Second Thoughts on Paradigms." In: F. Suppe, ed. *The Structure of Scientific Theories*. Urbana: University of Illinois Press, pp. 459–82 plus discussion, pp. 500–17. Kuhn's essay is reprinted in Kuhn (1977), pp. 293–319.

1976. "Theory-Change as Structure-Change: Comments on the Sneed Formalism." *Erkenntnis* 10: 179–99.

1977. *The Essential Tension: Selected Studies in Scientific Tradition and Change*. Chicago: University of Chicago Press.

1979. "Metaphor in Science." In: A. Ortony, ed. *Metaphor in Science*. Cambridge: Cambridge University Press, pp. 410–19.

1983a. "Commensurability, Comparability, and Communicability." In: P. Asquith and T. Nickles, eds. *PSA 1982*, Vol. 2. East Lansing, MI: Philosophy of Science Association, pp. 669–88.

1983b. "Response to Commentaries [on Commensurablity, Comparability, Communicability.]" In: P. D. Asquith and T. Nickles, eds. *PSA 1982*, Vol. 2. East Lansing, MI: Philosophy of Science Association, pp. 712–16.

1989. "Possible Worlds in History of Science." In: S. Allen, ed. *Possible Worlds in Humanities, Arts and Sciences*. New York: Walter de Gruyter, pp. 9–32.

Kuhn, T. S. 1990. "Dubbing and Redubbing: The Vulnerability of Rigid Designation." In: C. Savage, ed. *Scientific Theory*. Minneapolis: University of Minnesota Press, pp. 298–301.

1991. "The Road Since *Structure*." In: A. Fine, M. Forbes, and L. Wessels, eds. *PSA 1990*, Vol. 2. East Lansing, MI: Philosophy of Science Association, pp. 3–13.

1993. "Afterwords." In: P. Horwich, ed. *World Changes*. Cambridge, MA: MIT Press, pp. 311–41.

1996. *The Structure of Scientific Revolutions*, 3rd ed. Chicago: University of Chicago Press.

2000. *The Road since Structure*. J. Conant and J. Haugeland, eds. Chicago: University of Chicago Press.

Lakatos, I. 1977. *The Methodology of Scientific Research Programmes*. Cambridge: Cambridge University Press.

Lattis, J. 1994. *Between Copernicus and Galileo: Christopher Clavius and the Collapse of Ptolemaic Astronomy*. Chicago: University of Chicago Press.

Laudan, L., A. Donovan, R. Laudan, P. Barker, H. Brown, J. Leplin, P. Thagard, and S. Wykstra. 1986. "Testing Theories of Scientific Change." *Synthese* 69: 141–223.

Mervis, C. B., and J. R. Pani. 1980. "Acquisition of Basic Object Categories." *Cognitive Psychology* 12: 496–522.

Minsky, M. 1975. "A Framework for Representing Knowledge." In: P. Winston, ed. *The Psychology of Computer Vision*. New York: McGraw-Hill, pp. 211–77.

Nersessian, N. 1998. "Kuhn and the Cognitive Revolution." *Configurations* 6: 87–120.

Newton, A. 1893. *A Dictionary of Birds*. London: Adam and Charles Black.

Ray, J. 1678. *The Ornithology of Francis Willughby*. London: John Martyn.

Rosch, E. 1973a. "Natural Categories." *Cognitive Psychology* 4: 328–50.

———. 1973b. "On the Internal Structure of Perceptual and Semantic Categories." In: T. E. Moore, ed. *Cognitive Development and the Acquisition of Language*. New York: Academic Press, pp. 111–44.

———. 1987. "Wittgenstein and Categorization Research in Cognitive Psychology." In: M. Chapman and R. A. Dixon, eds. *Meaning and the Growth of Understanding: Wittgenstein's Significance for Developmental Psychology*. Berlin: Springer, pp. 151–66.

Rosch, E., and C. B. Mervis. 1975. "Family Resemblances: Studies in the Internal Structures of Categories." *Cognitive Psychology* 7: 573–605.

Rosch, E., C. Mervis, W. Gray, D. Johnson, and P. Boyes-Braem. 1976. "Basic Objects in Natural Categories." *Cognitive Psychology* 8: 382–439.

Sankey, H. 1994. *The Incommensurability Thesis*. Aldershot: Avebury

Shapin, S. 1982. "History of Science and Its Sociological Reconstruction." *History of Science* 20: 157–211.

Sibley, C., and J. Ahlquist. 1990. *Phylogeny and Classification of Birds: A Study in Molecular Evolution*. New Haven: Yale University Press.

Smith, E., and D. Medin. 1981. *Categories and Concepts*. Cambridge, MA: Harvard University Press.

Sundevall, C. 1889. *Sundevall's Tentamen*. London: Porter.

Tversky, B., and K. Hemenway. 1984. "Objects, Parts, and Categories." *Journal of Experimental Psychology: General* 113: 169–93.

Williams, T. M., M. L. Freyer, and L. S. Aiken. 1977. "Development of Visual Pattern Classification in Preschool Children: Prototypes and Distinctive Features." *Developmental Psychology* 13: 577–84.

Wittgenstein, L. 1953. *Philosophical Investigations*. New York: Macmillan.

9 | Kuhn's World Changes
RICHARD E. GRANDY

Of all the controversial elements of *The Structure of Scientific Revolutions* (1962/1970), the most controversial and problematic for the majority of readers are Kuhn's claims about the changes in the world that accompany scientific revolutions. Kuhn's own ambivalence about his doctrine is exemplified by the contrast between the title of Chapter X, "Revolutions as Changes of World View," which places the changes in the minds and theories of the scientists, and the first sentence of that section, which shows the temptation to locate the change in the worlds themselves:

> Examining the record of past research from the vantage of contemporary historiography, the historian of science may be tempted to exclaim that when paradigms change, the world itself changes with it. (1970 ed., p. 111)

Kuhn describes himself as "acutely aware" of the difficulties posed by his locutions:

> The same difficulties are presented in an even more fundamental form by the opening sentences of this section: though the world does not change with a change of paradigm, the scientist afterward works in a different world. (p. 121)

One example he discusses at some length (pun intended) is the pendulum. Heavy objects suspended by ropes or chains had existed for a long time, and certainly their occasional motions had been observed. However, for an Aristotelian this is an example of unnatural motion: The heavy body is moved by its nature toward the center of the Earth and the universe, but it is constrained by the suspension. Rest at the lowest point is the natural outcome. But for an adherent of Galileo's mechanics, we have harmonic motion, motion that is repeated because of the central-tending force of gravity when the body ascends above the lowest point. Perpetual oscillating motion would result were it not for the intervention of frictional forces in the suspending medium and surrounding air. Kuhn culminates this discussion

246

by claiming that "Pendulums were brought into existence by something very like a paradigm-induced gestalt switch" (p. 120). Another example comes from the chemical revolution:

Lavoisier . . . saw oxygen where Priestley had seen dephlogisticated air and where others had seen nothing at all. . . . At the least, as a result of discovering oxygen, Lavoisier saw nature differently. And in the absence of some recourse to that hypothetical fixed nature that he "saw differently," the principle of economy will urge us to say that after discovering oxygen Lavoisier worked in a different world. (p. 118)

IMPLICATIONS FOR OTHER ISSUES

In the vocabulary of the first edition of *Structure*, world changes occur when a scientific revolution occurs because of a paradigm change. Thus world changes are directly connected with the most innovative and controversial part of Kuhn's view, the existence and nature of scientific revolutions. Because world changes are an essential part of this view, an understanding of them will promote understanding of the related issues of rationality and commensurability.

The crucial difference between a change in worldview and a change in worlds is that the former leaves open the possibility of relatively full communication between adherents of different worldviews, whereas the latter seems to imply an impossibility of communication. Two scientists who are inhabiting and describing the same world are still talking about the same things, though they have different perspectives on those things. By contrast, two scientists who live in different worlds are talking about different objects and appear to have no common frame of reference. This latter possibility is famously called "incommensurability" by Kuhn and is one of the most widely discussed concepts in his work.

In choosing the word "incommensurability," Kuhn was well aware of the original mathematical meaning of the term, which is quite distinct from the notion of complete incomparability that critics often impute to Kuhn. For the Greeks, "incommensurable" meant having no common measure. This was the technical term for the demonstrable fact that the side and diagonal of a square have no common measure. If we have a square whose side is one unit long, then the length of the diagonal cannot be expressed as the ratio of two integers, which is equivalent to saying that it cannot be represented by any finite or repeating decimal. Note, though, that although there is no common measure that expresses the *exact* relation, the relation can be expressed to within any required finite accuracy. For example, with the unit square the diagonal has the length square root of 2, which can be expressed to four digits as 1.4142.

It is important to distinguish incommensurability of meaning claims from incommensurability of reference claims. If two scientific communities attach different meanings to the same syntactic objects, then it is still possible that the referents of those terms are the same, or at least are overlapping for the two communities. However, neither sameness of meaning nor exact coextensivess of reference is necessary for two communities to disagree with one another, but neither does such disagreement rule out potential points of testability to compare their claims (Grandy 1983). An extensive discussion of incommensurability (and many other issues) can be found in Hoyningen-Huene (1993) and Hoyningen-Huene and Sankey (2001).

BIOGRAPHICAL OBSERVATIONS

Kuhn was trained as a physicist, receiving the B.S. in 1943, the M.A. in 1946, and the Ph.D. in 1949 from Harvard in that discipline. While he was still a graduate student, James Conant, a chemist who was then president of Harvard, asked him to assist in preparing a historically oriented physics course for nonscience majors. In the process of preparing for this course, Kuhn, who had read little or no history of science previously, spent an extensive period of time reading Aristotle.

He describes how as he read Aristotle he discovered that Aristotle had known almost no mechanics, if we understand mechanics as the system discovered by Galileo, Newton, and others. This baffled Kuhn because Aristotle's contribution to logic remained of central importance at least until the twentieth century, and his observations in biology provided models that were instrumental to the emergence of the modern biological tradition. If Aristotle had been both a keen observer and the epitome of reasoning, how could he be so mistaken (Kuhn 2000, p. 16)?

His difficulty led Kuhn to the reflection that perhaps Aristotle's (translated) words did not mean quite the same thing to the modern reader as they had to Aristotle. This thought, together with continued concentrated immersion in the texts, led to an abrupt revelation:

> Suddenly the fragments in my head sorted themselves out in a new way, and fell into place together. My jaw dropped, for all at once Aristotle seemed a very good physicist indeed, but of a sort I'd never dreamed possible. Now

I could understand why he had said what he'd said, and what his authority had been. Statements that had previously seemed egregious mistakes now seemed at worst near misses within a powerful and generally successful tradition. (Kuhn 2000, p. 16)

This experience initiated the intellectual development that led to *Structure* and his position on revolutionary change of worlds and worldviews, a position that raised problems that he would continue to struggle with until his death in 1996. The careful reader can detect this theme of sudden revision already in Kuhn's first book, *The Copernican Revolution* (1957), although it is probably only with hindsight that one can see the importance of the idea. Writing that book helped to cement many of the major themes of Kuhn's later work in its detailed description of the complex transformation from the world as described by Ptolemaic astronomy and Aristotelian physics (or perhaps medieval neo-Aristotelian physics) to the worldview that developed through Copernicus, Kepler, and Galileo to culminate in Newton.

In assessing this sudden transformation and the extended writing of the book on Kuhn's views, it is essential to recall the unique character of this revolution. Indeed, for many authors it is called *the* Scientific Revolution. Before this revolution, humans saw themselves as situated on a motionless Earth in the center of a relatively small, finite universe. Terrestrial substances were divided into four kinds, and the motions of objects depended on their substances; each kind had a natural motion defined in terms of the center of the universe, located at the center of the Earth. Celestial substances were a different matter, or rather were not matter, and followed paths of circular motion.

By the end of the Scientific Revolution, humans were on an Earth that was not only rotating at 1,000 miles per hour but also was traversing an orbital path around the sun at an even greater velocity. They were not at the center of the solar system, but on the third planet from the sun. Nor is the sun at the center of the universe, for the universe is infinite and there is no center at which to be located. Terrestrial and celestial objects were now subject to the same governing laws, and those laws were abstract, quantitative, and mathematical rather than qualitative and teleological.

Of the subsequent scientific revolutions, the only one that comes anywhere close in scope is the Darwinian revolution. That revolution undermined the one remaining anthropocentric comfort by providing evidence that humans were not created by a higher being who might have had some purpose in putting them on this obscure planet in a solar system that has no privileged location in the universe.

Because the revolution that first concerned Kuhn, and the one to which his first book was dedicated, was the largest and most inclusive revolution, it seems likely that his claims about incommensurability and world change may be somewhat overstated when applied to smaller-scale revolutions. For example, the quantum revolution drastically changed fundamental ideas about causation and the nature of the physical processes underlying our everyday experience. But it did not change our interpretation of those everyday experiences in the way that the Copernican–Newtonian revolution did.

PHILOSOPHICAL CONTEXT

At the time Kuhn wrote *Structure*, the dominant view of scientific theories, which is often called the "Standard View," was that for philosophical purposes they were best thought of as a set of sentences in a formal logical language. "Formally, a scientific theory may be considered as a set of sentences expressed in terms of a specific vocabulary" (Hempel, 1958, p. 46).

One aspect of the Standard View emphasizes the formalization of science in first order logic, but another important aspect concerns the division of the vocabulary into observational and theoretical terms. It was assumed that the observational vocabulary was well understood and unproblematic, and that observational reports were the cumulative basis on which theories, were evaluated. The problematic aspects of the Standard View were thought to lie in the relation between the observational basis and theories, and various quantitative (Carnap 1950) and qualitative (Hempel 1945) approaches were attempted.

Given a clear distinction between theoretical and observational vocabulary, we can divide the sentences of the language into disjoint groups:

1. Observational sentences: sentences containing only observation terms and expressions of sentential logic.

2. Observational generalizations: sentences containing no theoretical terms but including quantificational operators.

3. Sentences including both observational and theoretical terms: sometimes called "bridge principles" or "correspondence rules" or the "dictionary" and understood as providing the connection between the observational and theoretical expressions.

4. Theoretical principles: statements expressed entirely in theoretical and logical terms and articulating the relations among the theoretical terms.

Kuhn, along with Norwood Russell Hanson (1958), Paul Feyerabend (1965), and others (Grandy 1973), questioned the common assumption that scientific inquiry rested on the secure foundation of an observational vocabulary. The observational vocabulary was thought to consist of terms that were intersubjective and whose application was independent of any theoretical considerations, and thus were *theory-neutral*.

Carnap (1956) devoted a long article to "The Methodological Character of Theoretical Concepts," because he recognized that the character of the theoretical language and its relation to the observation language are problematic. However, he moved very quickly over the description of the observation language. He first gave a brief introductory remark that "The observation language uses terms designating observable properties and relations for the description of observable things and events" (p. 38). After a more extensive discussion of some possible constraints on the observational language he settled on two criteria, among others:

1. Requirement of *observability* for the primitive descriptive terms.

   . . .

3. Requirement of nominalism: the values of the variables must be concrete, observable entities (e.g., observable events, things, or thing-moments) (p. 41).

Note that the characterization of the observation language uses the term "observation" and its cognates throughout.

Writing two years later, Hempel (1958) devoted his famous article to "The Theoretician's Dilemma," which derives from the fact that, given a completed axiomatic theory T1, there are technical means to produce a theory T2 in a language that does not have the theoretical terms of the first theory but that has all of the observational consequences of T1. This seems, Hempel worries, to show that theoretical terms are dispensable. Of course, the worry arises only if there is a philosophically significant distinction between the observational and theoretical vocabularies, and that is just what Kuhn questioned. In the next section, I will turn to three examples to illustrate some of the points.

As indicated earlier, Kuhn's was not the only voice criticizing the Standard View. And the attack on the theoretical-observational approach was not the only front in this philosophical skirmish. The opposing views of theories that were proposed by Patrick Suppes (1967, 1969) Evert Beth (1961), Mary Hesse (1966), Bas van Fraassen (1980, 1987), Joseph Sneed (1971, 1977), Wolfgang Stegmüller (1976, 1979), Frederick Suppe (1977), Ronald Giere (1988, 1999), and others varied greatly in details and nomenclature, but all shared the rejection of the syntactic rule-governed notion of theory.

It is important to note that while the labels ("semantic view," "structuralist view," "set theoretic view," "model theoretic view," "model-based view") for these alternatives all emphasize that they are not primarily syntactic, the differences are not as simple as the authors often suggest. While the Standard View treats theories as sets of sentences, each set of sentences is naturally associated with a set of models, a set of structures, and a collection of set theoretic predicates. Moreover, each of the alternative views must resort to some syntactic way of representing its preferred objects. The more important difference is that the new views emphasize that the application of the theory to reality is not given by the syntax but by other elements. The Standard View arguably grew out of the work of Campbell (1920) by a particular route of interpretation. I have argued elsewhere that the alternative views can also be traced back to Campbell but that Suppes presented an alternative way of developing the ideas; thus the most accurate historical name for the cluster of views is the "Campbell–Suppes view" (Grandy 1992).

OBSERVATION AND DATA

One way of expressing part of Kuhn's point about observation sentences is that the relation between everyday vocabulary and data is not simple and straightforward; rather, it requires steps of conceptualization, generalization, and theorizing. One example of how complicated the process of identifying data can be, even very close to home with macroscopic objects, is the Mpemba effect.

The Mpemba Effect

Among the terms that one assumes would be observational by most of the Carnap/Hempel criteria are 'is milk', 'is hot', 'is room temperature', 'is liquid', 'is frozen', and references to time. Thus sentences like "The milk in the brown bucket is frozen" and "The milk in the green bucket is hot" would be observation sentences. However, what science is concerned with is generalizations and their explanation. For example, Bacon and Descartes noted that when put outdoors on a cold night, hot milk freezes faster than room-temperature milk. Even earlier, Aristotle observed: "The fact that the water has been previously warmed contributes to its freezing quickly; for so it cools sooner" (Osborne 1979, p. 416).

With the development of thermodynamics in the nineteenth century, it must have seemed obvious that this generalization was wrong. Since hot milk will take some time to reach room-temperature, and then will take as much time to cool from room-temperature to freezing, it *must* be the case that the room-temperature milk freezes first. To the best of my knowledge, no one offered any explanation of the peculiar alleged generalization reported by Bacon and Descartes (Osborne 1979).

Then in 1963 a Tanzanian high school student, E. B. Mpemba, made the same observation while making ice cream in the freezer compartment of a refrigerator. Risking punishment for abusing the refrigerator, he reported his discovery to his physics class and was rewarded by ridicule. However, Mpemba was very persistent, and when a university physics professor, D. G. Osborne, visited his class, he again reported his discovery. His class and teacher were embarrassed and ridiculed him again, but the physicist was sufficiently intrigued to have a lab assistant attempt to reproduce the result when he returned to his university.

The lab assistant reported that the experiment had come out incorrectly because the hotter liquid froze first, but that he would repeat the experiment until it "came out right." Eventually, Osborne became convinced of the accuracy of the generalization and coauthored a paper with the original discoverer (Mpemba and Osborne 1969).

Thermodynamics was not overthrown by this result. Although there is still some disagreement, the generally accepted explanation of the effect is that, while room-temperature milk remains relatively quiescent during cooling, the greater temperature difference between the cooling surface and the interior of the hot milk produces convection currents in the hot milk. Consequently, in the hot milk, both the process of conduction and the more efficient process of convection contribute to cooling. The moral is that an "observational generalization" that was fairly widely known was discarded for theoretical reasons. And the theoretical reasoning proved too simpleminded an application of the theory to the process in question. In the argument given previously to show that the effect is impossible, we assume that the hot milk had to pass through the state in which the room-temperature milk began, but in fact it never reaches a quiescent room-temperature state.

The Risky Shift

I draw my second example from social psychology. It was generally accepted in the early 1960s that people's attitudes are influenced by social pressures and that conformity is a common result of social interactions. An MIT graduate student designed a study to measure one form of this effect. He used a dozen scenarios, each of which involved a choice between two courses of action. In each scenario both courses were plausible, but one involved potentially greater payoffs and risks – for example, taking a job with a start-up computer company versus taking a position with an established consulting firm.

Subjects were asked to read each scenario and then indicate which choice they would make. After all subjects had indicated their choices, a group of subjects then discussed the scenarios and the pros and cons of each choice. After the group discussion, the subjects were again asked to indicate their preferences privately. The point of the study was to measure the extent to which subjects shifted toward the more cautious alternative as a result of the group discussion.

To the experimenter's surprise, the group discussion produced an average shift toward the less cautious alternative. An explanation of this anomaly was ready to hand, though, because the initial group consisted of graduate students in business administration, and it was plausible that in a business administration school the pressure would be to conform to the norm of risk taking. However, when the study was repeated with various more standard populations (male undergraduate students enrolled in psychology courses), the same result was obtained. The same result was even obtained when experiments were done with female subjects. As these results accumulated, the phenomenon became known as the "risky shift," and it became a research area of specialization. The original study (Stoner 1961) was never published and appeared only in a master's thesis, but it generated numerous follow-ups, which were published. The risky shift represented a well-defined phenomenon that presented a puzzle to be solved within the context of the normal psychology of the time.

As is typical of new scientific specialties, this area of research grew exponentially (numbering over 200 publications total) until about 1970, when various researchers did an item-by-item analysis of the scenarios on the instrument that defined the risky shift. They found that most of the individual items consistently produced a shift toward risk taking, but that some produced no shift and a few items produced a shift toward caution. Up to that point, it was assumed that the effect was uniform, regardless of scenario, rather than depending on specifics of the choices in question. The apparent risky shift was a result of the accidental fact that there were more risk-shifting questions than caution-shifting questions in the original instrument. "[F]ixation on total test scores thus diverted attention away from the most critical information contained in the data and thereby delayed the attainment of a proper understanding of the so-called risky shift" (Cartwright 1973, p. 229). The number of publications on the risky shift then declined exponentially, although not reaching zero until the mid-1980s, and the subsequent research in the area that has derived from that work now has the neutral label "choice shift."

The Pendulum

Let us return to Kuhn's example of the pendulum and consider the difference between the Standard View and Kuhn's. On the Standard View, the law of the pendulum is derived from more basic principles of Newtonian mechanics by logical inference. Bridge principles enter in connecting observational terms with the essential variables of this example, the length of the pendulum, the mass of the bob, and so on.

On the alternative conception, the process is one of constructing a model based on the pendulum law, guided by the Newtonian principles and constrained by experimental facts. If we scrutinize the process, we notice that the "derivation" depends on ignoring the mass of the string from which the bob is suspended, assuming that the mass is zero; also ignoring air resistance, that is, treating air resistance as zero; and assuming, finally, that $\sin x = x$, that is, that the sine of the angle of maximum deflection from the pendulum's rest position equals the size of the angle itself. This last assumption is critical to the derivation allegedly showing that the pendulum's period depends only on its length.

For an Aristotelian, fairly simple observations of any pendulum will indicate discrepancies from the pendulum law that can be taken as a refutation of the "law." For a Newtonian, on the other hand, the discrepancies are understood as reflecting the approximate character of the many assumptions that went into the "derivation" of the pendulum law. What is confirmation for the law, given one theory, is a refutation, given the other. And, of course, the kinds of activities one pursues will be motivated by the theory. For the Newtonian, the pendulum is an important kind of system, and construction of and experimentation with pendulums provide significant developments of more complex laws for more complex pendulum, as well as more complex and exact laws for simple pendulums.

THE DEVELOPMENT OF KUHN'S THOUGHTS ON WORLD CHANGES

In assessing Kuhn's work, it is crucial to bear in mind that although it is the dominant focus of discussions his work, almost to the exclusion of all else, *Structure* was not a book he wanted to write. The quotations at the beginning of this essay indicate to some extent the hesitation and qualifications that Kuhn attached to his descriptions of "world changes." The preface to *Structure* indicates in more detail the extent to which he was aware that there are serious gaps and shortcomings in the philosophical development of key concepts. However, he had contracted to produce a monograph within fairly severe size limits, and the editors were pressing him to complete the manuscript. Thus Kuhn wrote a much shorter book than he wanted to, and he did not take time to master the considerable philosophical literature he knew was relevant but that he had mostly not read.

> I have confessed to a good deal of embarrassment about the fact that I didn't know it [Carnap's work]. On the other hand, it is also the case that if I'd known about it I probably would never have written *Structure*.... (Kuhn 2000, p. 306)

Almost a decade later, after *Structure* had been a runaway sensation, when Kuhn was faced with a decision about revising it, he chose to add a Postscript indicating some of the changes he would make, rather than rewriting *Structure*. Although he published, in 1977, *The Essential Tension*, a collection of his essays and, in 1978, *Black-Body Theory and the Quantum Discontinuity, 1894–1912*, the culmination of decades of historical work on the beginnings of the quantum revolution, when he died in 1996 he was still working on the book he had hoped to write in 1956.

In *Structure* Kuhn used as an analogy or metaphor for alternative conceptions of the world the alternate perceptions that are available alternately, but not simultaneously, of the Necker cube the duck/rabbit, and similar phenomena familiar from Gestalt psychology. By the time he wrote the Postscript, he was beginning to phrase the issues in terms of languages, linguistic communities, and translation.

In his later work, Kuhn fixed on the term 'lexicon' for the central idea of what differentiates thinkers whom he would have described, in the first version of *Structure*, as holding different paradigms. One of the defining features of a lexicon is its holistic character. Lexicons can be holistic because they are taxonomic, involving contrast sets of terms. The terms in a contrast set are mutually exclusive and jointly exhaustive of some domain implicitly or explicitly associated with the contrast set.

> To learn the term 'liquid' for example, as it is used in contemporary nontechnical English, one must also master the terms 'solid' and 'gas' ... which is why the terms involved must be learned together and why they collectively constitute a contrast set. (Horwich 1993, p. 315)

The second kind of holism arises when the terms of the lexicon can only be understood together, that is, they must be learned simultaneously, starting with partial understanding of each and working through increments of understanding. Two of Kuhn's favorite examples of lexicons are those of Aristotelian and Newtonian physics.

I have elsewhere argued that one cannot learn 'force' (and thus acquire the corresponding concept) without recourse to Hooke's law and either Newton's three laws of motion or else his first and third laws together with the law of gravity. (Ibid. p. 315)

One objection that has been raised repeatedly against Kuhn's related claims about incommensurability and world changes is that historians and others, including Kuhn, understand Aristotelian physics, even though they also previously understood Newtonian physics. Thus, the objection runs, these systems can be expressed within the same language. Kuhn's response is to argue that someone who speaks English and knows Newtonian physics and then learns Aristotelian physics is essentially becoming bilingual. He or she is attributing new meanings to terms such as 'motion', and although there are bilinguals who speak both Newtonian English and Aristotelian English, there is no single language that incorporates both theoretical perspectives.

It may have been a strategic mistake for Kuhn to turn from the more psychological claims of *Structure* to the more linguistic claims that he makes later. Many of his ideas have been fruitfully explored by psychologists, such as Brewer and Chinn (1994). Certainly the term 'lexicon' suggests something more specifically linguistic than is his intent. Since the Aristotelian physics was initially expressed in Greek and subsequently translated into Arabic and Latin before making its way into English, it must be that the Aristotelian lexicon is more abstract than the vocabulary of any of these languages used to express it. As discussed earlier, Kuhn's work was part of the impetus that moved philosophers of science away from the Standard View of theories to the family of views that give the linguistic formulations a less central role. His later work seems to be retrograde, at least in placing more emphasis on the linguistic aspect.

In the context of the newer views of theories, one of the critical abilities involved in understanding and using a theory is the ability to interpret the relation between the theoretical models and data or laws. Kuhn's point about world change might be better made in terms of the incomparability of the interpretive skills and motivations that are required for mastering alternative scientific theories. In *Structure* Kuhn insisted that part of his point was that there is no access to a nonconceptualized world, so the emphasis on the *process* of interpretation rather than *rules* for interpretation would be very appropriate.

Further, if one wanted to provide another metaphor or analogy as an alternative to the linguistic one, we could consider more physical processes such as locomotion. A horse can either trot or gallop across a pasture; either gait will produce the result of change of position. And for an intermediate range of velocities, the same speed can result from both processes. But the two kinds of motion are incompatible with one another (Stein, Mortin, and Robertson 1986).

Kuhn and others argued that observation is theory laden, partly by arguing that perception involves at least some top-down elements driven by theory and that there is no pure observation language. But perception and language are not the only elements that are theory laden. Attention, memory, motivation, and comprehension are also arguably affected by theory (Brewer and Lambert 1993). Attention to this broader range of theory-laden processes together with the motor metaphor might provide a means to develop Kuhn's idea further, keeping the emphasis on the interaction of the scientist and world while somewhat deemphasizing the more extreme ontological claims.

References

Beth, Evert. 1961. "Semantics of Physical Theories." In: Hans Freudenthal, ed., *The Concept and the Role of the Model in Mathematics and Social Sciences*. Dordrecht: Reidel, pp. 48–51.

Brewer, William F., and Bruce B. Lambert. 1993. "The Theory-Ladenness of Observation: Evidence from Cognitive Psychology." *Proceedings of the Fifteenth Annual Conference of the Cognitive Science Society*. Hillsdale, NJ: Lawrence Erlbaum.

Brewer, William F., & C. A. Chinn. 1994. "Scientists' Responses to Anomalous Data: Evidence from Psychology, History, and Philosophy of Science." In: *PSA*, Vol. 1. East Lansing, MI: Philosophy of Science Association, pp. 304–13.

Campbell, N. R. 1920. *Physics: The Elements*. Reprinted as *Foundations of Science*. New York: Dover, 1957.

Carnap, Rudolf. 1950. *Logical Foundations of Probability*. Chicago: University of Chicago Press.

1956. "The Methodological Character of Theoretical Concepts." In: Herbert Feigl and Michael Scriven, eds. *The Foundations of Science and the Concepts of Psychology and Psychoanalysis* (Minnesota Studies in the Philosophy of Science 1). Minneapolis: University of Minnesota Press, pp. 38–76.

Cartwright, Dorwin. 1973. "Determinants of Scientific Progress: The Case of Research on the Risky Shift." *American Psychologist* 28: 222–31.

Feyerabend, Paul. 1965. "Problems of Empiricism." In: R. Colodny, ed. *Beyond the Edge of Certainty*. Pittsburgh: University of Pittsburgh Press, pp. 145–260.

Giere, Ronald N. 1988. *Explaining Science*. Chicago: University of Chicago Press.

1999. *Science without Laws*. Chicago: University of Chicago Press.

Grandy, Richard, ed. 1973. *Theories and Observation*. Atascadero, CA: Ridgeview Press.

1983. "Incommensurability: Kinds and Causes." *Philosophica* 32: 7–24.

1992. "Theories of Theories: A Perspective from Cognitive Science." In: John Earman, ed. *Inference, Explanation and Other Frustrations: Essays in the Philosophy of Science*. Berkeley: University of California Press, pp. 216–33.

Hanson, Norwood Russell. 1958. *Patterns of Discovery*. Cambridge: Cambridge University Press.

Hempel, C. G. 1945. "Studies in the Logic of Confirmation." *Mind* 54: 1–16, 97–121.

1958. "The Theoretician's Dilemma." In: Herbert Feigl, Michael Scriven, and Grover Maxwell, eds. *Concepts, Theories and the Mind–Body Problem* (Minnesota Studies in the Philosophy of Science 2). Minneapolis: University of Minnesota Press, pp. 37–98.

Hesse, Mary. 1966. *Models and Analogies in Science*. Notre Dame, IN: University of Notre Dame Press.

Horwich, Paul, ed. 1993. *World Changes: Thomas Kuhn and the Nature of Science*. Cambridge, MA: MIT Press.

Hoyningen-Huene, Paul. 1993. *Reconstructing Scientific Revolutions: Thomas S. Kuhn's Philosophy of Science*. Chicago: University of Chicago Press.

Hoyningen-Huene, Paul, and Howard Sankey, eds. 2001. *Incommensurability and Related Matters*. Dordrecht: Kluwer Academic Publishers.

Kuhn, T. S. 1957. *The Copernican Revolution: Planetary Astronomy in the Development of Western Thought*. Cambridge, MA: Harvard University Press.

1962/1970. *The Structure of Scientific Revolutions*. Chicago: University of Chicago Press.

1977. *The Essential Tension: Selected Essays in Scientific Tradition and Change*. Chicago: University of Chicago Press.

1978. *Black-Body Theory and the Quantum Discontinuity, 1894–1912*. Oxford: Oxford University Press.

2000. *The Road since Structure: Philosophical Essays, 1970–1993 with an Autobiographical Interview*. Edited by James Conant and John Haugeland. Chicago: University of Chicago Press.

Mpemba, E. G., and D. G. Osborne. 1969. "Cool?" *Physics Education* 4: 172–5.

Osborne, D. G. 1979. "Mind on Ice." *Physics Education* 14: 414–17.

Shapere, Dudley. 1984. *Reason and the Search for Knowledge*. Dordrecht: Reidel.

Sneed, Joseph. 1971. *The Logical Structure of Mathematical Physics*. Dordrecht: Reidel.

1977. "Describing Revolutionary Scientific Change: A Formal Approach." In:

R. E. Butts and J. Hintikka, eds. *Historical and Philosophical Dimensions of Logic, Methodology and Philosophy of Science*. Dordrecht: Reidel, pp. 245–68.

Stegmüller, Wolfgang. 1976. *The Structure and Dynamics of Theories*. New York: Springer-Verlag.

1979. *The Structuralist View of Theories*. New York Springer-Verlag.

Stein, Paul S. G., L. I. Mortin, and G. A. Robertson. 1986. "The Forms of a Task and Their Blends." In: S. Griller, P. S. G. Stein, H. Forssberg, and R. M. Herman, eds. *Neurobiology of Vertebrate Locomotion*. Hampshire, U.K.: Macmillan, pp. 201–16.

Stoner, J. A. F. 1961. "A Comparison of Individual and Group Decisions Involving Risk." Unpublished master's thesis, Sloan School of Management, Massachusetts Institute of Technology.

Suppe, Fredrick, ed. 1977. *The Structure of Scientific Theories*, 2nd ed. Urbana: University of Illinois Press.

Suppes, Patrick. 1967. "What Is a Scientific Theory? In: Sidney Morgenbesser, ed. *Philosophy of Science Today*. New York: Basic Books, pp. 55–67.

1969. "Models of Data." In: P. Suppes, ed. *Studies in the Methodology and Foundations of Science*. Dordrecht: Reidel, pp. 24–35.

van Fraassen, Bas. 1980. *The Scientific Image*. Oxford: Oxford University Press.

1987. "The Semantic Approach to Scientific Theories." In: Nancy Nersessian, ed. *The Process of Science*. Dordrecht: Martinus Nijhoff, pp. 105–24.

10 | Does *The Structure of Scientific Revolutions* Permit a Feminist Revolution in Science?

HELEN E. LONGINO

10.1

Kuhn's influence on feminist science studies and feminist theory of knowledge might well be understood as an example of the principle of unintended consequences. Kuhn's notions of theory-laden meaning and observation and of revolutionary science were embraced by feminist thinkers, who applied them in ways that seem their natural and logical extensions. Judging from remarks in later essays such as "The Trouble with the Historical Philosophy of Science," Kuhn would have had serious reservations about these applications, as he had about many of those in science studies who took his views as a mandate to inquire into the social nature of scientific inquiry.[1] Nevertheless, the power of his challenge to logical empiricist philosophy of science provided a philosophical basis for a wide range of critical approaches to the sciences.

When *The Structure of Scientific Revolutions* burst upon the academic scene in the early 1960s, the second wave of feminism was in its earliest stages: identifying the forms of legal discrimination against women, challenging the cultural expectations of femininity, agitating for access to contraception and abortion, and rebelling against the second-class status accorded to women in the civil rights and antiwar movements. By the early 1970s, feminists in the academy had expanded the reach of feminism to analysis and critique of the research and scholarship that supported the discriminatory legal and social treatment of women. They argued that the traditional academic disciplines were guilty not only of professional discrimination in university admissions, hiring, and promotion, but also of scholarly discrimination. History, literary studies, sociology, and anthropology were characterized by an exclusionary focus on men's activities and accomplishments and a minimizing account of women, women's activities, and gender relations. Psychology and biology seemed to rationalize this imbalance by supporting views of male and female nature that coincided with the *Kinder, Kuche, und Kirche* view of women's roles in the social world.

Nowadays we would call the focus on masculine activities "androcentrism" and the minimizing of women's activities "sexist" or "gender-biased"; in the beginning, there was no language with which to identify and diagnose the (mis)representation and neglect that were the lot of women.

Feminist researchers uncovered the activities of women ignored in conventional scholarship and challenged the values that privileged men's contributions to social and cultural life over women's contributions. Feminist historians began to reveal the shifts in consciousness of women's situation, the long but forgotten legacy of feminist activity in the past, and to make clear the shifts in gender ideology and relations over time. Feminist literary scholars analyzed the sexual politics of canonical works of literature. They reclaimed writers such as Sappho, Jane Austen, and Emily Dickinson and reconsidered the literary values that consigned them to the margins of literary history. While disciplines such as history and literary studies were obviously susceptible to charges of bias and more responsive to new directions, those disciplines that cloaked themselves in the garb of scientific objectivity and neutrality posed a quite different problem.[2] If hypotheses prejudicial to women passed the standards of scientific scrutiny, not only the content but the forms of validation of that content required challenge.

Kuhn's *Structure* offered a vocabulary for articulating the complex critique of science and of its ideology that feminist scientists sought to develop, and many feminist biologists and psychologists referred to Kuhn in their work. In spite of Kuhn's animating and legitimating role in the initial stages, however, a number of his ideas are in considerable tension with the aspirations of feminist scientists and philosophers of science. This essay will describe the landscape opened to feminists by Kuhn's work, showing how Kuhn's ideas made possible an increasingly sophisticated and far-reaching understanding of gender ideology in science. I will then discuss the limitations of those ideas from a feminist perspective and indicate how feminists have modified them to support a more transformative agenda.

10.2

It is difficult in 2002 to credit the kinds of ideas about women and gender relations that commanded scientific respectability in the 1950s and 1960s. As though the suffrage movement had never happened, these exhibited a remarkable continuity with ideas current in the nineteenth century. In keeping with a legal system that subordinated married women to their husbands and a culture that saw motherhood as the ultimate female accomplishment, psychologists attributed docility, dependence, and nurturance to women and assertiveness, independence, and competitiveness to men. Women who exhibited the latter rather than the former were deemed unhealthy, but the masculine traits were the signs of human psychological well-being.[3] Psychological sexism began to give way under assault from empirical researchers who rejected the stereotypes and sought to establish unbiased standards for mental health.[4] These challenges were developed in the name of science and objectivity.

The biological sciences, although harboring just as much sexism, however, seemed impervious to feminist critique. This was due in part to their more secure position in the scientific hierarchy and in part to the embeddedness of biological sexism in more extensive theoretical structures. Sociobiologists held that several biological factors accounted for most social behavior. For example, the different patterns of courting and sexual behavior were explained by differential parental investment on the part of males and females – males having a minor investment in each offspring and females, whose eggs represented a greater investment of resources, having a major investment. Males found reproductive advantage in frequent mating; females found reproductive advantage in careful selection of mates. To make a long story short, the patterns of male dominance and female subordination observed in just about every human society had their basis in biological differences. Ethologists obligingly found male dominance everywhere, not just in human societies, but also in other primates, in birds, in mountain sheep. And for each instance there was a biological basis. Sociobiology was a solution to the problem of self-sacrificing behavior in a variety of species. Evolutionary theory held that variations that conferred survival advantages were inherited, but how could a behavior that conferred disadvantage be inherited? The sociobiological answer to that question was known as "kin selection." The genes of relatives of the self-sacrificing individual were passed on to offspring, and because relatives share genes, the self-sacrificing individual's genes, some of them, too, found their way into successive generations. The account of sex differences was just part of a much bigger theoretical picture. Views about human evolution located the selection pressures favoring distinctively human anatomical adaptations in male behavior: Not only were men dominant by nature in contemporary societies, but it was male variability in the past that provoked evolutionary change.

Biologist Ruth Hubbard, writing about evolutionary theory, ethology, and sociobiology, took an approach whose broad outlines she attributes to Kuhn. "Every theory is a self-fulfilling prophecy that orders experience into the framework it provides.... There is no such thing as objective value-free science,"[5] she says before documenting the multitude of ways in which students of animal behavior ascribed stereotypical feminine characteristics to female organisms (or organisms identified as female) from algae to apes. What they claim to observe in nature are the very codes of behavior prescribed for human societies by Victorian mores. Scientists are constrained by the language available to them to describe behavior; their vocabulary as well as their gender ideology produce androcentric and sexist accounts of social behavior. Even when their descriptions indicate female activity rather than passivity, they read them as conforming to gender stereotypes. Hubbard quotes passages from Darwin such as the following from *The Descent of Man*: "Man is more courageous, pugnacious and energetic than woman, and has more inventive genius."[6] She summarizes his view as follows:

> So here it is in a nutshell: men's mental and physical qualities were constantly improved through competition for women and hunting, while women's minds would have become vestigial if it were not for the fortunate circumstance that in each generation daughters inherit brains from their fathers.[7]

Darwin's ideas about male and female roles in evolution are not restricted to the 1870s but, as Hubbard shows, are repeated in the work of ethologists and physical anthropologists in the 1970s.

The approach that focused on the vocabulary of a theory could also work for neuroendocrinological approaches to behavior. The language used to describe the behavior of girls and boys was saturated with gender theory masquerading as common knowledge. For example, girls who engaged in activities stereotypically associated with boys were referred to colloquially as "tomboys," while boys who engaged in the less strenuous activities stereotypically associated with girls were described as afflicted with the "sissy syndrome." Research on children who had been exposed to anomalous levels of gonadal hormones in utero purported to show an increased incidence of tomboyism in girls exposed to excess levels of androgenic hormones in utero and an increased incidence of sissy syndrome in boys exposed to insufficient levels of androgenic hormones in utero. The gender loading extended from the labels for behavior to the very identification of the gonadal hormones themselves. Male and female gonads secrete a set of chemically very similar steroidal hormones. The gonads differ in the relative proportion of these steroids that they produce, but some quantity of all these hormones is necessary for proper physiological function in male and female mammalian organisms. A number of feminist scholars have examined the discussions in the 1930s concerning appropriate nomenclature for the gonadal hormones. In spite of their chemical similarity and their physiological roles in both male and female organisms, the researchers who wished to identify them by gender prevailed over those who preferred a more neutral form of identification. Even more striking was the asymmetry in labeling. Those hormones secreted in greater quantities by male gonads were called "androgenic" (male-producing), while those secreted in greater quantities by female gonads were called "estrogenic" (frenzy-producing). This labeling had consequences for subsequent research: the multiple functions of the hormones were not recognized for decades.[8]

The story of gonadal hormone research thus provided an excellent case for application of Kuhn's notions of theory-laden observation and theory-laden meaning. Theory operated at several levels. In the first instance, theory about gender difference informed the ways in which the hormones were identified and labeled. In the second, that identification and labeling determined what physiological effects of hormone secretion were observed and recorded. Kuhn's ideas of theory-ladenness gave feminist scientists and scholars a language in which to express their perception that even methodologically impeccable science could nevertheless incorporate social biases. Its very impeccability, in turn, gave those biases intellectual respectability. Other critics have argued that plain old empiricism has the resources to support critical examination of scientific sexism,[9] but Kuhn's way of putting things was preferred by those feminists who thought that the problems for women posed by the sciences ran deeper than sloppy observation practices. There was a connection between the content of theories in sociobiology and neuroendocrinology with the institutional exclusion of women from scientific education and careers. Kuhn's larger picture of scientific change, which emphasized the sociological factors in scientific revolutions, offered a means of articulating and examining that connection.

Kuhn's notions of theory-ladenness could explain how two researchers could look at a pride of wild horses, one seeing a male with his harem of attendant females and the other seeing a group of females tolerating the presence of their stallion in exchange for his services. They seemed to offer ways to make sense of the perpetuation of gender stereotypes in an area allegedly characterized by objective empirical methods. This is why even scholars who seemed only to be calling into question the empirical adequacy of biological descriptions of females and female-identified behavior invoked Kuhn, or Kuhnian ideas, in elaborating their critiques. The problem wasn't individual biased scientists but a shared gender ideology. The difficulty, however, is that feminists also wanted to say that one description of the horses is right.

Although Hubbard cites Kuhn at the beginning of the essay, she makes clear that the observations reported in support of views about the centrality of males are just wrong. The philosophical views that launch the essay are left behind. She concludes her essay by stating that the gender-biased "paradigm of evolution" requires that women "rethink our evolutionary history."[10] Part of this rethinking requires getting close to the "raw data." Donna Haraway took Hubbard and other feminists arguing as she had to task for employing the analytic framework of Kuhn for critique and the empiricist framework he had criticized in putting forward a positive program for research.[11] Surely the problem was not Hubbard's but the poverty of the philosophical frameworks she was given to work with. Kuhn gave feminists a platform from which to reject the idea that reports from the field of submissive females and dominant males were just the facts. While he gave feminist scientists a way to talk about the ways in which a socially shared gender ideology had colored observation of males and females of all biological species, his analysis of scientific revolutions did not give them a language or rubric for describing the kinds of changes they wished to recommend. This point becomes clearer in thinking about the work of feminist philosophers of science.

10.3

Feminist philosophers of science, too, made use of Kuhn's ideas. They focused on different themes in Kuhn's work, extending and modifying his claims about the character of scientific knowledge and about scientific change to address a series of epistemological concerns.

Kathryn Addelson invoked Kuhn both in ethical and in epistemological contexts. The women's movements of the nineteenth and twentieth centuries, Addelson argued, were simultaneously enactments of and calls for moral revolution.[12] Women participating in those movements were stepping out of the prescribed behavior for women by speaking in public in assembly halls and in the streets, thus forcing themselves into public affairs, and the content of their message was a demand for change in those prescriptions that they violated. In the nineteenth century the demands were for the right to vote, to higher education, to property, to divorce, to participation in the civic life of society. In the twentieth century the demands included reproductive rights, an equal rights amendment, equal opportunity, and comparable worth. A moral revolution does not consist in bringing a society's behavior or lower-level commitments into conformity with its higher-level principles, but rather in a deeper change in those constitutive principles, indeed in the very concept of morality. In this way, said Addelson, a moral revolution was similar to a Kuhnian scientific revolution, which involved a change not only in descriptions and explanations of nature, but in the very criteria by which descriptions and explanations were evaluated.

Where Hubbard had been concerned to show the seepage of stereotypes of social life into scientific ideas, Addelson elaborated the connection between the content of ideas and forms of social life. She also appealed to a Kuhnian framework to raise issues about scientific knowledge. Here, she was interested in Kuhn's notion of a paradigm. This enabled him to understand scientific knowledge as consisting not just in "theories and laws, but also metaphysical commitments, exemplars, puzzles, anomalies, and various other features."[13] Paradigms guided practice, and it was practice that was central to scientific inquiry, not the doctrinal results of practice.

From Addelson's point of view, Kuhn's construal of science as activity, as practice, and his documentation of the rise and fall of theories in the course of scientific change helped to focus attention on the social dynamics among scientists, those that contributed to the persistence of a theory and those that contributed to its replacement by a new one. Kuhn's remarks concerning the adherents of old paradigms and the champions of the new are well known: long-time adherents of paradigms are not converted to the new but retire, leaving the field for others, while champions of new ones tend to be young, uninvested in the success of the old ideas and likely to benefit from the adoption of new ones. Addelson saw Kuhn's work as opening up questions of cognitive authority. Debates during paradigm shifts were contests for cognitive authority, and because of the conceptually pervasive character of paradigms, the outcome of such contests included shifts in the authority to define the fundamental structures of our common world. The victory of an atomistic physical theory in early modern Europe was the triumph of a metaphysical view that extended beyond physics into social life (as individualism).

Kuhn's acknowledgment of the multiple factors influencing individuals' theoretical, experimental, or practical preferences during paradigm shifts suggested that the boundaries between scientific and extrascientific considerations were fuzzy and/or porous. What made intuitive sense to an individual was an important factor in the judgments of plausibility that cumulatively tipped the balance to one or another of the contestants. But what made intuitive sense, argued Addelson, was largely influenced by one's social experience. To the extent that the metaphysical outlook of those who participated in and gained authority in the resolution of scientific controversy reflected their social experience, to that extent the metaphysical outlook thus legitimated for the culture at large reflected and thus reinforced a particular social reality.

Addelson focused on sociology, showing how a functionalist metaphysics was expressed in the research agenda and results of 1950s American sociology. She cited anthropological research from the 1970s documenting the different social realities of women and men and of members of different socioeconomic classes. These claims were then integrated in her claim that a system in which only some kinds of people were absorbed into the locus of cognitive authority, the scientific professions and leadership positions in that profession, was a system in which the metaphysical outlook of that class shaped that of the rest of society.

> The leading physicists, biologists, and philosophers of science ... live in societies marked by dominance of group over group. As specialists, they compete for positions at the top of their professional hierarchies that allow them to exercise cognitive authority more widely. Out of such cultural understandings, it is no wonder ... that our specialists present us with metaphysical descriptions of the world in terms of hierarchy, dominance, and competition.[14]

Addelson recognized the power of scientific inquiry not only to shape a society's worldview, but also to represent the world in ways that worked. Her point was that by paying attention to its social structure and correcting the disproportionate privileging of one social group, we could eliminate continuing irrationalities. Of course, with this claim, she lays herself open to the same kind of challenge Haraway raised for Hubbard's vision of a feminist approach to evolution. From within what paradigm are these alleged irrationalities identified as such? Why not call for a completely different science or for the social conditions that might result in such?

Sandra Harding discussed both *The Structure of Scientific Revolutions* and *The Copernican Revolution* in her book *The Science Question in Feminism*.[15] She hailed the former for its demonstration that the rational reconstructions of scientific judgment offered by logical empiricists were misrepresentations of the historical situations whose logic they sought to elucidate. Like Addelson, she saw this volume as legitimating a naturalized approach in science studies, one that looked particularly at the role of social relations to provide explanations of scientific outcomes. This should, in principle, extend to the study of the role of gender relations in the production of science. Harding writes that the Kuhnians and post-Kuhnians, by persisting in treating gender as a biological rather than as a social relation, failed to take the

Kuhnian program to its logical extension. That is, they felt free to ignore the effects of gender relations and hence missed an important aspect of the development of modern science.

In a discussion of the historiography of the Scientific Revolution, however, Harding is more critical of Kuhn. *The Copernican Revolution*, in her reading, participates in the treatment of the Scientific Revolution as an instance of the triumph of intellect over superstition. Harding draws especially on passages likening the medieval mind, the mind committed to an Aristotelian worldview, to the minds of children and primitives, and reads Kuhn as celebrating the release of science from morality and politics effected in the sixteenth and seventeenth centuries. This strikes me as not quite fair. *The Copernican Revolution* contributed to the power of the later *Structure* by demonstrating the coherence, plausibility, and empirical adequacy of the Aristotelian physics and worldview. That Kuhn was less able to see into the worldview that promoted and was promoted by the intellectual and technical accomplishments of Copernicus, Galileo, Newton, and their fellow natural scientists does not diminish the implication that modern science, too, is in a similar relation of mutual support with a larger worldview that includes moral and political views as well as metaphysical ones.

This mutual support is precisely what Harding wishes to demonstrate. Rejecting the standard picture of the Scientific Revolution as an origin myth, she fills in the framework provided by *Structure* with work by Marxist historians of science to show the social and political dimensions of the Scientific Revolution. The Scientific Revolution was associated with the end of the feudal order and the emergence of a new middle class, with antiauthoritarianism, with belief in progress, with humanitarian ideals, and with a division of labor that separates the methodical investigation of nature (science) from the maintenance of the institutions that support that investigation (politics). These social and political developments coemerge with a cosmology characterized by atomism (the view that nature is constituted of ultimately uniform and least bits of inert matter), value neutrality (the impersonal universe that replaces the teleological universe of the medievals), and faith in method (as guarantor of impartiality and independence from political and religious authority). However insightful the Marxist and post-Kuhnian social and historical studies of science were, they neglected the gender relations that were part of the new European world order. Harding cites the work of feminist scholars Ludmilla Jordanova, Carolyn Merchant, and Evelyn Keller to suggest the gendered dimensions of the new world order – its restriction of property rights to male members of the new middle class and the reconstruction of masculinity to harmonize with the new values of early modernism.

Harding's treatment of the possibility of feminist science shows her deepest debt to Kuhn. Feminists are like the seventeenth-century radicals in challenging contemporary structures of authority, in believing in progress insofar as that includes overcoming gender, race, and class hierarchies, stressing educational reform and humanitarianism. And Harding claims that feminists seek knowledge that unifies empirical with moral and political understanding. Harding's view is that this "successor" would be unrecognizable from within the categories of current mainstream science. Thus she treated the relationship between current science and science acceptable to feminists as, like that between Aristotelian science and cosmology and the New Science of the seventeenth century, one of incommensurability. The new science of the twenty-first century would be a unified science but not, as envisioned by the Vienna Circle, a unified science that took physics as its foundation. The new science would be directed by moral and political beliefs, and thus, according to Harding, would take social science, not physics, as its foundation. "Science and theorizing itself" must be reinvented.[16]

Another feminist scholar took a somewhat different but no less radical lesson from Kuhn. Evelyn Fox Keller has been the most visible of feminists concerned with the sciences. She has consistently urged the viability of models of complex interaction in contrast with the reductionist and linear analysis she sees as characterizing contemporary science. Her concern has not been the description of females and gender relations, but the ways in which gender ideologies have been expressed in areas of science having nothing to do with gender or social behavior. Keller writes as a scientist as much as a historian and philosopher, and reports being struck by the resistance or indifference of scientists themselves to Kuhn's claims.[17] Keller noted that while Kuhn's views of scientific change had laid the groundwork for research that investigated the social dimensions of scientific practice and judgment, he had not himself pursued such investigations, thus leaving open the exact nature and role of social and cultural factors in scientific practice. But she noted, "the direct implication of [Kuhn's claims] is that not only different collections of facts, different focal points of scientific attention, but also different organizations of knowledge, different interpretations of the world, are both possible and consistent with what we call science."[18] Where Harding had linked Kuhnian with Marxist historiography, Keller proposed instead to employ the tools of psychoanalysis to explain simultaneously the scientific community's resistance to Kuhnian ideas, the gendering of past and contemporary science, and the way out of what she saw as a scientific dead end.

Keller relied primarily on what is known as "object relations theory." According to this theory, one of the maturational tasks of infants and children is the development of individual identity. The relations the child has with its closest adults profoundly affect this process and have lasting effects in its overall outlook on and behavior in the world. Male and female infants in typical Western families faced distinctive challenges the psychic resolution of which shaped their orientation to social and physical reality, an orientation that expressed itself cognitively, affectively, and practically. Boys had to achieve their individual identities in a context in which their primary adult figure was their mother and from which their father was largely absent. In a sex-differentiated social and domestic world, their task was then to become something about which they knew very little. Their developmental energies were therefore directed to not becoming that which they knew – their mother. As a consequence, the identity of boys and the men they became was fragile and needed constant reinforcement. One psychic strategy for coping with this need was to develop exaggerated psychic detachment from others. Little girls, on the other hand, because their task was to become female, tended to be overattached.

Keller applied this analysis of psychological development to explain features of the sciences. The strategy of distancing and disidentification expressed itself affectively in what Keller called a "stance of static autonomy." Because the conditions of masculine individuation induced deep anxieties, it required continual confirmation, provided most vividly and reassuringly by domination of that which one needed not to be. To this point, the analysis is in keeping with that pursued by other object relations feminists.[19] Keller's innovation was to extend it to conceptions of knowledge and of science. In parallel with static autonomy, a cognitive attitude dubbed by Keller "static objectivity" emerged as an aspect of personal development. Static objectivity was characterized by its equation of knowledge with emotional detachment from and control over the objects of knowledge and by its treatment of the pursuit of knowledge, scientific inquiry, as an adversarial process. Static objectivity was contrasted with dynamic objectivity, which aimed at a reliable understanding of the world that granted to its elements their independent integrity and affirmed the connectivity of subjects and objects of knowledge. Knowledge is understood neither as detachment and control nor as loss of identity, but as flexible connection and relationship that acknowledges the autonomy of objects. The normal developmental processes of boys and girls led them to identify the behaviors associated with static autonomy and static objectivity with masculinity. Femininity, by contrast, was characterized by overidentification and the submergence of individuality. Dynamic autonomy and objectivity were (by implication) orientations that could be achieved only through struggle against the prevailing social, including gender, norms.

Keller supported her thesis that modern science was constituted by static objectivity by quoting from writers from Bacon to Simmel to contemporary scientists, and by showing how certain research programs in the sciences were driven by a goal of dominating nature. She supported the feasibility of her alternative – dynamic objectivity – by citing researchers such as Michel Polanyi and Barbara McClintock, who advocated and practiced approaches to science characterized by that attitude. Feminists, including Ruth Hubbard and Sandra Harding, had deplored the reductionism that seemed to characterize modern science. Harding attributed this to the social and economic conditions that permitted the development of modern science. Keller argued that that reductionism was part of a worldview whose tenacity was due to its psychic roots.

Keller could then explain the resistance to Kuhn in the scientific community as a reaction to the threat to cognitive autonomy posed by Kuhn's in-principle acceptance of the role that extrascientific social or subjective factors could play in determining scientific judgment. Where she differed from Harding was not only in stressing the psychological dimensions of scientific cognition, but in affirming that static objectivity was primarily a feature of the ideology of science rather than of its actual practice. Where the ideology of science stressed a unity of purpose in emotional detachment from and practical domination of nature, study of the practices of science revealed a greater variety and richness of ideas. Keller is famous, of course, for her exposition and advocacy of the work of geneticist Barbara McClintock, but other scientists, too, exemplified the ideal of dynamic objectivity, the ability to move in and out of intimate closeness with the objects of knowledge, to employ empathy rather than distance in seeking understanding. These cognitive capacities were associated for Keller with representation of the natural world as complex and heterogeneous, as contrasted with its representation as reducible to one basic level and ultimately explicable by simple one-way causal models. The ideology of science and its emotional connection to an ideology of masculinity explained why interactionist approaches such as McClintock's were consistently marginalized in favor of approaches that pursued forms of knowledge congruent with domination of rather than coexistence with the known. An alternative form of science suitable to feminist purposes did not need to be reinvented. We needed only to look more closely at forms of practice currently relegated to the margins of science for our models.

By stressing the availability throughout science's history of models of natural processes that employed representational or explanatory principles out of step with the mainstream, Keller departed from Kuhn's picture of scientific growth and change. Kuhn held that normal science in a field was characterized by a single explanatory approach and that the presence of multiple approaches signaled its immaturity. In addition, as noted in the discussion of Harding, Kuhn argued that successive (or contesting) theories of the same subject area were incommensurable. Keller does not treat McClintock's views about the mutability of the genome as involving theory-laden observations that researchers committed to different theories could not share. She understands the mainstream rejection of McClintock's views as a function of the mainstream's attachment to a conception of scientific knowledge and an associated metaphysics of nature to which McClintock's views simply did not conform. And while Harding seems to embrace incommensurability in her description of the relation between mainstream science and the science that will replace it, in other ways her conception, too, is at odds with the Kuhnian prescription. The feminist scientific revolution advocated by Harding will come about not because empirical anomalies accumulate and throw the current paradigm into crisis, but because changes in social values and relationships require a different way of knowing the natural world. Kuhn's conceptions of scientific knowledge and scientific change are of value to both of these thinkers because of the challenge he articulates to the then regnant logical empiricist philosophy of science. Science was either a battle between contesting paradigms (revolutionary science) or puzzle solving within a paradigm (normal science). But this characterization of science offered no tools for thinking about how to effect change. These feminists, however, were interested not just in understanding science but also in changing it.

10.4

It is telling that feminists appealed to Kuhn to legitimate their rejection of positivism (whether its philosophical expression in logical empiricism or its popular expression as scientism) but left Kuhn entirely or partially behind when talking about alternative forms of scientific knowledge. Kuhn's views are a hindrance to that project. There is, however, a way of thinking about scientific inquiry and scientific knowledge that, while indebted to Kuhn and reasonably seen as a product of the Kuhnian revolution in philosophy of science, does not impose the same constraints on the feminist project. Epistemological pluralism, that is, pluralism about knowledge, is grounded in broadly speaking Kuhnian insights about the history of science, but it employs some different philosophical principles. These enable explanation of androcentric or sexist science as something more than just empirically inadequate science, without undermining the case for an alternative. To see this, I recapitulate the relevant basic philosophical ideas of *The Structure of Scientific Revolutions*.

Kuhn claimed that successive theories about the same subject matter, say bodies in motion, were both in contradiction with one another and incommensurable, by which he meant that such theories could not be empirically tested vis-à-vis one another in the mode envisaged by empiricists. That is, their relationship was not such that they could be comparatively evaluated against a common set of data or facts. Kuhn's explanation for this incommensurability is the theory dependence of meaning and of observation. Logical empiricists held that observation was independent of theory and that the meaning of observation terms and statements was independent of theory. Meaningfulness and confirmation (evidential support) flowed from observation to theory. Kuhn, by contrast, argued that the meaning of observation terms was determined by theory and that the meaning of theoretical terms, too, shifted when their theoretical context changed. For example, "mass" in classical physics refers to a quantity that is conserved, while "mass" in relativity physics refers to a quantity that is (under some conditions) convertible to energy. So what might seem to be common observation terms affording a shared point of contact with the observable world turned out to be, on this theory of meaning, no more than homonyms.[20] Kuhn also held that observation itself was theory-determined, and he supported this contention by citing a variety of psychological experiments that demonstrated the dependence of perception on expectation. One consequence of these views about meaning and observation is that genuine communication between scientists holding different theories, in the grip of different paradigms, is impossible. They may use language that sounds similar, they may point to the same phenomena in their sensory range, but the terms they use are different in meaning, and what they observe when looking at the same phenomena is also different.

Kuhn's views about meaning and observation were most unsettling to philosophers of science. Combined with the view that evidence for scientific hypotheses and theories lies in what can be observed, which Kuhn did not deny, evidential reasoning seemed to be circular: a theory was supported by observations whose content and description were determined by the theory. To counter the charge that this made theory choice entirely subjective (a charge made plausible by Kuhn's analogies with religious conversion), Kuhn claimed that theory choice in science was guided by a set of values.[21] These included accuracy, internal and external consistency, simplicity, breadth of scope, and fruitfulness. While the precise interpretation and relative priority or weight assigned to these values might differ in practice, they nevertheless provided a constant, a touchstone, by reference to which scientific judgment, theory choice, could be understood to be objective.[22] It is clear from Kuhn's discussion of these values, however, that they do not offer an independent yardstick, or as he put it, an algorithm, for the comparison of theories, nor could there be such a yardstick, given his interpretation of incommensurability. Kuhn sometimes elaborated the theory-ladenness of meaning and observation by implying that scientists who held different theories inhabited different worlds. There are different ways of understanding such a claim, but as an articulation of incommensurability, it does not serve feminist science scholars well.

Feminist science scholars want to affirm the (gender) value-ladenness of much contemporary science, the success of that science by conventional measures of success, and the need for (or desirability of) an alternative to the mainstream trends in science. They do not dispute all of the science to which they object merely on the grounds of empirical adequacy, but also on the grounds that it encodes and thus reinforces noxious (sexist, racist, capitalist) social values. They inhabit the same world as do the scientists to whose theories they object – they want to see different scientific accounts of that world. They are not content to ascribe differences to the inhabitation of different worlds or to semantic or cognitive incommensurabilities. They don't just want to do science in their other world; they want to change the way mainstream science is done in our common world. It is not that feminists are committed to a worldview from which it is impossible to understand the science they oppose. They would say they understand it only too well.

I would locate the source of the ultimate unsuitability of Kuhn's views to feminist projects in his notions of the theory dependence and theory-ladenness of meaning and observation. Since these doctrines are problematic on other grounds (both conceptual and empirical) as well, we should look elsewhere for philosophical support. The pluralism of contextual empiricism is based in Kuhnian insights about the nature of scientific change, but it relinquishes the theory-ladenness of meaning and observation as explanations of incommensurability.

Contextual empiricism treats the apparently equivalent empirical adequacy of different theories not as a matter of theory ladenness, but as a function of differences in background assumptions facilitating inferences between data and hypotheses.[23] The language used to articulate or describe them is independently meaningful. Contextual empiricism sees the logical problem that gives rise to multiple theories as underdetermination (the gap between our evidential resources, whatever we can observe or measure, and our explanatory aspirations, the discovery of principles, capacities, or causal regularities underlying what we experience). This gap is bridged by background assumptions that constitute the context in which empirical, that is, observational, data acquire evidential relevance. A change in assumptions brings a change in evidential relevance. One of the advantages of contextual empiricism is that it offers an account of the historical phenomena that Kuhn sought to explain, that is, that two scientists could look at the same thing – a sealed jar with a dead mouse or a sunset or a pride of lions – but explain what they saw quite differently. Contextual empiricism is, therefore, compatible with pluralism: incompatible theories of the same phenomena can both offer adequate accounts. While pluralism holds that such theories can offer correct accounts, their correctness is judged from the perspective of different background assumptions and cognitive goals. Pluralism also holds that in such cases theories are partial or incomplete, unable to encompass all the aspects of a complex phenomenon in their range. Of course, contextual empiricism has its own philosophical difficulties, which I have addressed elsewhere.[24] Here I want to stress the advantage to feminist science studies of giving up theory-ladenness for contextualism. There are three points of contact.

10.4.1 Regarding Incommensurability

The Kuhnian appeal, as we have seen, is to theory-ladenness, which as a general theory of meaning holds that the meanings of all terms in a theory are determined by the theory. Terms have no independent meaning outside of the theory. This approach to meaning, and its corollary concerning observation, while promising to explain how one researcher can see submission where another sees craftiness or how one sees dominance where another sees dependence or stress, is in the end not helpful to feminists because it leaves them unable to criticize the misrepresentations of gender as incorrect for anyone, regardless of their gender ideology. It disables empirical critique of sexist science.

Contextual empiricism permits a different approach to incommensurability. It does not take either theory or experience as a foundation of meaning. It thus departs from both Kuhnian semantic holism and logical empiricist semantic reductionism. While maintaining that the contents of meaning and observation are not theory-determined, it does agree that the categories of observation and measurement are theory- or context-relative. Apparent incommensurability arises when measurements are not separable from their context of measurement. That context provides the questions, the goals, and the standards of measurement. What counts as an observation in one context may not in another. Two theoretical approaches to a phenomenon might be incommensurable to the extent that they take different aspects of the phenomenon to be evidentially relevant or employ different measurement scales relevant to contrasting questions and cognitive goals. These are not incommunicable, as the semantic approach to incommensurability implies, and while neither of the theories provides a common standard, researchers employing different theoretical approaches may still share enough outside of their theories to engage critically with each other's ideas and observations. Treating incommensurability as a function of context avoids the undermining of the feminist empirical critique of sexist science deplored by Haraway.

10.4.2 Regarding Paradigms and Normal Science

Kuhn stated that a main characteristic, almost a defining condition, of normal science is the organizing of research under a single paradigm. Contextual empiricism is compatible with the form of pluralism that holds that, in many cases, the phenomena to be explained are so complex that multiple approaches are necessary to provide a comprehensive account. Any single account, while correct, is in such cases incomplete. A clear example is organismic development. Both a gene-centered account and an environmental account of the development of some trait may be correct but partial. Their theoretical structures are such that they cannot, however, be combined into a single account. The existence of multiple approaches is not the sign of scientific immaturity or of preparadigmatic revolutionary science, but if required by the phenomena, it may be an unavoidable feature of normal science. While Keller herself might not endorse this pluralism, pluralism seems to offer a better account of the existence of multiple research traditions in the sciences such as she documents than do Kuhnian paradigms.

10.4.3 Regarding Values and Scientific Judgment

Kuhn held that the values determinant of (objective) scientific judgment were variably interpreted and variably weighed or prioritized, and even that individual scientists might interpret them in ways influenced by personal, subjective factors. Nevertheless, he also held that they were internal to the scientific community and that the ones he cited were in some way constitutive of scientificity. A contextualist holds that there can be no such in-principle circumscribing of scientific values. The values Kuhn listed are those conventionally recited by philosophers, but they reflect a particular intellectual tradition. There are other values that can be advocated that stand in complicated relations with the conventional ones. And, contra those who saw comfort for social studies of science in Kuhn's ideas, paradigm-governed science suggests that once a paradigm shift has occurred, a single set of values (with an implied prioritizing and interpretation) becomes normative, so that scientific judgment is once again fully internal.

Contextual empiricism, then, follows the Kuhnian approach in taking fidelity to the actual practice of science as a criterion of adequacy for a theory of scientific knowledge. It also stresses the complexity of scientific judgment, its dependence on factors not given in the immediate experimental or observational situation. The differences I have just cataloged, however, make it more amenable to the concerns of feminist science studies.

10.5

There is one point, however, where Kuhn offers a potentially significant jumping-off point. The last of the scientific values he discusses is fruitfulness. Now this could be understood as comparable to having empirical content, since one way a theory or paradigm can be fruitful is by generating empirical consequences. But Kuhn glosses this value in an interesting way. For him fruitfulness is a theory's or paradigm's capacity to generate interesting puzzles or problems to work on, that is, its capacity to direct research, to provide intellectual challenges. This introduces a note of pragmatism into an otherwise representational account of inquiry. Feminists have been concerned not only with the representation of gender and the use of gender in the representation of nature, but with the ways in which scientific ideas are deployed in the social world. Feminists are concerned to support forms of science that will distribute power throughout society rather than concentrating it in experts. Feminists have become concerned to support forms of inquiry that will preserve rather than consume natural resources. Feminists are concerned to encourage noninvasive and nondominating models of inquiry. Now it may well be that Kuhn's understanding of fruitfulness is entirely inward-looking, restricted to the puzzle-generating capacity. But there seems no in-principle reason not to extend the value of fruitfulness pragmatically understood to include these outward-looking ways in which a theory might be fruitful. If this licenses the evaluation of a theory by reference to the particular kinds of interventions it permits in the world outside the laboratory or seminar room, then we count ourselves indebted to a thinker who included pragmatic as well as representational concerns among the values that ought to guide scientific judgment. And if feminist values come to prevail in that evaluation, then *The Structure of Scientific Revolutions* will turn out, in spite of my earlier reservations, to have abetted a feminist revolution in science.

Notes

1. Thomas Kuhn, "The Trouble with the Historical Philosophy of Science," Robert and Maurine Rothschild Distinguished Lecture, November 19, 1991, Cambridge, MA: An Occasional Publication of the Department of History of Science, Harvard University.

2. I don't mean to minimize the resistance that feminist historians and literary scholars encountered in their efforts to correct scholarly bias, but rather to point to a qualitatively different problem facing feminist thinking about the sciences: a conception of science that to a large extent they themselves shared.

3. A study by Inge Broverman and her colleagues demonstrated the pervasiveness of this double bind for women in the thinking of clinical psychologists. See Inge Broverman, D. M. Broverman, F. E. Clarkson, P. S. Rosenkranz, and S. R. Vogel, "Sex Role Stereotypes and Clinical Judgments of Mental Health," *Journal of Consulting and Clinical Psychology* (1970) 34: 1–7.

4. See, for example, Naomi Weisstein, "Psychology Constructs the Female," in Vivian Gornick and Barbara Moran, eds., *Woman in Sexist Society* (New York: Basic Books, 1971), pp. 133–46; Eleanor Maccoby and Carol Jacklin, *The Psychology of Sex Differences* (Stanford, CA: Stanford University Press, 1974); Paula Caplan, Gael MacPherson, and Patricia Tobin, "Do Sex Differences in Spatial Ability Really Exist?" *American Psychologist* (1985) 40(7): 786–98. In many ways, this work recapitulates the critique of sex differences that research and ideology performed decades earlier by psychologists such as Leta Hollingworth. The collective amnesia regarding such critique is part of the atmosphere that made a deep analysis such as Kuhn offered so attractive.

5. Ruth Hubbard, "Have Only Men Evolved?" in Ruth Hubbard, Mary Henifin, and Barbara Fried, eds., *Women Look at Biology Looking at Women* (Cambridge, MA; Schenkman, 1979), p. 9.

6. Charles Darwin, *The Origin of Species and the Descent of Man* (New York: Random House, Modern Library Edition, n. d.), as quoted in Hubbard, "Have Only Men Evolved?", p. 19.

7. Hubbard, "Have Only Men Evolved?", p. 20.

8. This story is told in a number of recent histories of reproductive endocrinology. See Nellie Oudshorn, *The Making of the Hormonal Body* (New York: Routledge, 1997), and Anne Fausto Sterling, *Sexing the Body: Gender Politics and the Construction of Sexuality* (New York: Basic Books, 2000). One ironic aspect of the ideological construction of hormonal identity is the labeling of equine estrogen, "premarin," suggesting that it is derived from mares, when it is actually derived from the urine of stallions.

9. See, for example, Noretta Koertge, "Methodology, Idealogy, and Feminist Critiques of Science," in Peter Asquith and Ronald Giere, eds., *PSA 1980*, vol. 2 (East Lansing, MI: Philosophy of Science Association, 1981), pp. 346–59.

10. Hubbard, "Have Only Men Evolved?", p. 31.

11. Donna Haraway, "In the Beginning Was the Word: The Genesis of Biological Theory" *Signs: Journal of Women in Culture and Society* (1981) 6(3): 469–82.

12. Kathryn Addelson, "Moral Revolution," in Julia A. Sherman and Evelyn Torton Beck, eds., *The Prism of Sex* (Madison: University of Wisconsin Press, 1979), pp. 189–227; reprinted in Addelson, *Impure Thoughts* (Philadelphia: Temple University Press, 1991), pp. 35–61.

13. Kathryn Addelson, "The Man of Professional Wisdom," in Sandra Harding and Merrill Hintikka, eds., *Discovering Reality* (Dordrecht: Reidel, 1983), p. 166.

14. Ibid., p. 184.

15. Sandra Harding, *The Science Question in Feminism* (Ithaca, NY: Cornell University Press, 1986), pp. 197–210.

16. Ibid., p. 251.

17. Evelyn Fox Keller, *Reflections on Gender and Science* (New Haven, CT: Yale University Press, 1985).

18. Ibid., p. 5.

19. One of the best-known applications of object relations theory to gender relations is Nancy Chodorow, *The Reproduction of Mothering* (Berkeley: University of California Press, 1978).

20. This theory can't be right, since "mass" refers to the same feature of bodies in the two theories. One problem with Kuhn's view of meaning is that he seems to have made no distinction between defining properties and contingent features. This is in some ways consonant with Quine's views about meaning, but to treat all contingent features as defining properties as Kuhn seems to have done leaves one no longer able to say of a statement that it is false (and uncertain of what it means to say that it is true). Kuhn expended considerable effort over the years trying to make his notion of meaning incommensurability plausible, but he did not, to my knowledge, address this aspect of the view. Cf. his Presidential Address to the Philosophy of Science Association: The Road since Structure," in Arthur Fine, Micky Forbes, and Linda Wessels, eds., *PSA 1990*, vol. 2 (East Lansing, MI: Philosophy of Science Association, 1991), pp. 3–13. Reprinted in Thomas Kuhn, *The Road since Structure*, edited by James Conant and John Haugeland. (Chicago: University of Chicago Press, 2001), pp. 91–104.

21. Thomas Kuhn, "Objectivity, Value Judgment, and Theory Choice," in *The Essential Tension* (Chicago: University of Chicago Press, 1977), pp. 320–39.

22. This aspect of Kuhn's views has been recently taken up by some feminist philosophers of science, but as part of a discussion in general of the notion of epistemic
of cognitive values in science. Feminists emphasize either the role of contextual values in determining the weight or application of epistemic values or the
variety of possible cognitive values the choice among which can be seen to
have social and/or cultural dimensions. See Alison Wylie and Lynn Nelson,
"Coming to Terms with Value(s) of Science: Insights from Feminist Science
Studies Scholarship," Workshop on Science and Values, Center for Philosophy
of Science, University of Pittsburgh, October 9–11, 1998, on the first strategy,
and Helen Longino, "Cognitive and Non-Cognitive Values in Science: Rethinking the Dichotomy," in Lynn Hankinson Nelson and Jack Nelson, eds.,
Feminism, Science and Philosophy of Science (Boston: Kluwer, 1996), pp. 39–58, on
the second.

23. Equivalent empirical adequacy is not the same as empirical equivalence. The
latter requires that two theories have the same empirical consequences; the
former requires only that two theories be equally successful in predicting observations, but the set of observations relevant to the theories may not be the
same.

24. Helen E. Longino, "Toward an Epistemology for Biological Pluralism,"
in Richard Creath and Jane Maienschein, eds., *Biology and Epistemology*
(Cambridge: Cambridge University Press, 2000), pp. 262–86; *The Fate of Knowledge* (Princeton: Princeton University Press, 2002).

Selected References in English

At this time, the most complete published listing of Thomas Kuhn's publications can be found in Kuhn's posthumous *The Road since Structure*, cited subsequently. That volume and *The Essential Tension* contain most of Kuhn's principal philosophical and historical-methodological articles. See also the extensive listing of references to work by and about Kuhn in *Reconstructing Scientific Revolutions*, by Paul Hoyningen-Huene, the most thorough treatment of Kuhn's work to about 1990. I also include two examples of business applications of Kuhn's ideas (Barker and Christensen). Various journals have hosted special issues on Kuhn (e.g., *Configurations* and *Science and Education*), and several universities have sponsored conferences on Kuhn's work and influence.

Books by Thomas Kuhn

Kuhn, Thomas. 1957. *The Copernican Revolution*. Cambridge, MA: Harvard University Press.

— 1962. *The Structure of Scientific Revolutions*. 2nd edition, enlarged, 1970; 3rd edition, 1996. Chicago: University of Chicago Press.

— 1977. *The Essential Tension: Selected Essays in Scientific Tradition and Change*. Chicago: University of Chicago Press.

— 1978. *Black-Body Theory and the Quantum Discontinuity, 1894–1912*. New York: Oxford University Press. Reprinted with an afterward, "Revisiting Planck" (a response to critics), in 1987.

— 2000. *The Road Since Structure: Philosophical Essays, 1970–1993*. Edited by James Conant and John Haugeland. Chicago: University of Chicago Press.

Kuhn, Thomas, John Heilbron, Paul Forman, and Lini Allen. 1967. *Sources for the History of Quantum Physics: An Inventory and Report*. Philadelphia: American Philosophical Society.

Selected Publications about Thomas Kuhn and/or His Influence

Andersen, Hanne. 2000. *On Kuhn*. Belmont, CA: Wadsworth.

Andersen, Gunnar. 1994. *Criticism and the History of Science: Kuhn's, Lakatos's, and Feyerabend's Criticism of Critical Rationalism*. Leiden: Brill.

Andresen, Jensine. 1999. "Crisis and Kuhn." *Isis* (supplement) 90: S43–S67.

Barker, Joel. 1992. *Paradigms: The Business of Discovering the Future.* New York: HarperCollins.

Barnes, Barry. 1982. *T. S. Kuhn and Social Science.* New York: Columbia University Press.

Bird, Alexander. 2000. *Thomas Kuhn.* Princeton: Princeton University Press.

Buchwald, Jed Z., and George Smith. 1997. "Thomas S. Kuhn, 1922–1996." *Philosophy of Science* 64: 361–76.

Caneva, Kenneth. 2000. "Possible Kuhns in the History of Science: Anomalies of Incommensurable Paradigms." *Studies in History and Philosophy of Science* 31: 87–124.

Cedarbaum, Daniel. 1983. "Paradigms." *Studies in History and Philosophy of Science* 14: 173–213.

Christensen, Clayton. 1997. *The Innovator's Dilemma.* Boston: Harvard Business School Press.

De Mey, Marc. 1982. *The Cognitive Paradigm.* Dordrecht: Reidel.

Donovan, Arthur, Larry Laudan, and Rachel Laudan, eds. 1988. *Scrutinizing Science: Empirical Studies of Scientific Change.* Dordrecht: Kluwer.

Fuller, Steve. 2000. *Thomas Kuhn: A Philosophical History for Our Times.* Chicago: University of Chicago Press.

Gross, Paul, and Norman Levitt. 1994. *Higher Superstition: The Academic Left and Its Quarrels with Science.* Baltimore: Johns Hopkins University Press.

Gross, Paul, Norman Levitt, and Martin Lewis, eds. 1996. *The Flight from Science and Reason.* New York: New York Academy of Sciences.

Gutting, Gary, ed. 1980. *Paradigms and Revolutions.* Notre Dame, IN: University of Notre Dame Press.

Heilbron, John. 1998. "Thomas Samuel Kuhn, 18 July 1922–17 June 1996." *Isis* 89: 505–15.

Horwich, Paul, ed. 1993. *World Changes: Thomas Kuhn and the Nature of Science.* Cambridge, MA: MIT Press.

Hoyningen-Huene, Paul. 1993. *Reconstructing Scientific Revolutions: Thomas Kuhn's Philosophy of Science.* Chicago: University of Chicago Press.

　　1997. "Thomas S. Kuhn." *Journal for General Philosophy of Science* 28: 235–56.

Hoyningen-Huene, Paul, and Howard Sankey, eds. 2001. *Incommensurability and Related Matters.* Dordrecht and Boston: Kluwer.

Koertge, Noretta, ed. 1998. *A House Built on Sand: Exposing Postmodernist Myths about Science.* New York: Oxford University Press.

Lakatos, Imre, and Alan Musgrave, eds. 1970. *Criticism and the Growth of Knowledge.* Cambridge: Cambridge University Press.

Laudan, Larry. 1979. *Progress and Its Problems.* Berkeley: University of California Press.

　　1996. *Beyond Positivism and Relativism.* Boulder, CO: Westview Press.

Margolis, Howard. 1987. *Patterns, Thinking, and Cognition.* Chicago: University of Chicago Press.

1993. *Paradigms and Barriers: How Habits of Mind Govern Scientific Beliefs.* Chicago: University of Chicago Press.

Merton, Robert. 1977. *Sociology of Science: An Episodic Memoir.* Carbondale: Southern Illinois University Press.

Sankey, Howard. 1994. *The Incommensurability Thesis.* Aldershot: Avebury.

Sankey, Howard. 1997. *Rationality, Relativism, and Incommensurability.* Aldershot: Ashgate.

Sardar, Ziauddin. 2000. *Thomas Kuhn and the Science Wars.* New York: Totem.

Scheffler, Israel. 1967. *Science and Subjectivity.* Indianapolis: Bobbs-Merrill.

Shapere, Dudley. 1984. *Reason and the Search for Knowledge.* Dordrecht: Reidel.

Sharrock, Wes, and Rupert Read. 2002. *Kuhn.* Oxford: Blackwell.

Sokal, Alan, and Jean Bricmont. 1998. *Fashionable Nonsense: Postmodern Intellectuals' Abuse of Science.* New York: Picador.

Stegmüller, Wolfgang. 1976. *The Structure and Dynamics of Theories.* New York and Berlin: Springer-Verlag.

Suppe, Frederick. 1974. "The Search for Philosophic Understanding of Scientific Theories." In: Frederick Suppe, ed. *The Structure of Scientific Theories*, 2nd ed. Urbana: University of Illinois Press, 1977, pp. 3–232.

Verronen, Veli. 1986. *The Growth of Knowledge: An Inquiry into the Kuhnian Theory.* Jyväskylä: Jyväskylän University Library.

Von Dietze, Erich. 2001. *Paradigms Explained: Rethinking Thomas Kuhn's Philosophy of Science.* New York: Praeger.

Index